An Introduction to Social and Political Philosophy

Elements of Philosophy

The Elements of Philosophy series aims to produce core introductory texts in the major areas of philosophy, among them metaphysics, epistemology, ethics and moral theory, philosophy of religion, philosophy of mind, aesthetics and the philosophy of art, feminist philosophy, and social and political philosophy. Books in the series are written for an undergraduate audience of second- through fourth-year students and serve as the perfect cornerstone for understanding the various elements of philosophy.

Moral Theory: An Introduction by Mark Timmons

Epistemology: Classic Problems and Contemporary Responses by Laurence BonJour

Aesthetics and the Philosophy of Art: An Introduction by Robert Stecker

An Introduction to Social and Political Philosophy

A Question-Based Approach

Richard Schmitt

ROWMAN & LITTLEFIELD PUBLISHERS, INC.
Lanham • Boulder • New York • Toronto • Plymouth, UK

ROWMAN & LITTLEFIELD PUBLISHERS, INC.

Published in the United States of America
by Rowman & Littlefield Publishers, Inc.
A wholly owned subsidiary of The Rowman & Littlefield Publishing Group, Inc.
4501 Forbes Boulevard, Suite 200, Lanham, Maryland 20706
www.rowmanlittlefield.com

Estover Road
Plymouth PL6 7PY
United Kingdom

British Library Cataloguing in Publication Information Available

Library of Congress Cataloging-in-Publication Data

Schmitt, Richard, 1927-
  An introduction to social and political philosophy : a question-based approach /
Richard Schmitt.
     p. cm. — (Elements of philosophy)
  Includes bibliographical references and index.
  ISBN 978-0-7425-6412-1 (hardcover : alk. paper) — ISBN 978-0-7425-6413-8 (pbk. ;
alk. paper) — ISBN 978-0-7425-6526-5 (electronic : alk. paper)
  1. Political science—Philosophy. I. Title.
JA71.S287 2009
320.01—dc22   2008053645

Printed in the United States of America

∞™ The paper used in this publication meets the minimum requirements of American
National Standard for Information Sciences—Permanence of Paper for Printed Library
Materials, ANSI/NISO Z39.48-1992.

Contents

Preface

> Put it how you will, philosophy is only the art of discrimination. The country bumpkin makes use of all the principles of philosophy, though indirectly, latently . . . the philosopher gives them to us pure.
>
> *The Reflections of Lichtenberg*, trans. Norman Alliston, p. 78.

Plato's Socrates not only stands at the beginning of Western philosophy, but he also set debates in motion, which have not yet come to an end, about the best method for teaching philosophy. In the *Meno*, Plato offers us the picture of Socrates demonstrating how one can teach an uneducated slave boy geometry by asking him a series of questions. In the course of this conversation, the slave boy discovers certain properties of squares. He "remembers," Socrates seems to suggest, what he has always known from previous lives. Learning does not consist of listening to grandiose discourses of Sophists; knowledge is not inculcated by the teacher in the student, but it is recovered by the student in the course of questioning by the teacher. The student is not passive in learning, but rather is actively trying to retrieve knowledge already possessed by him or her without his or her being conscious of having it. Learning is "anamnesis" not only in geometry, but also in all knowledge, including the knowledge of right and wrong, of "virtue."[1]

This controversy about pedagogy begun by Socrates continues to this day. Paolo Freire's *Pedagogy of the Oppressed* uses language quite close to that of Socrates when he contrasts the "banking method" of teaching—in which the teacher supposedly fills the students' heads with knowledge—with "conscientization," in which the students actively discover what, in some sense, they know already but have not, so far, been aware of knowing. In the course of learning, they become conscious of what they know already.[2] Once we look beyond the similarity in the language used by Socrates and Freire, of course, we see that their projects are quite different. Socrates reflects about how to make men virtuous; Freire's goals are modern: the liberation of the downtrodden, particularly in countries suffering from massive poverty.

In the *Meno*, Socrates drew a general contrast between learning as a process in which the teacher, who possesses knowledge, conveys it to or *instills* it in the students, and learning as the discovery of knowledge by the students with the *help* of the teacher. In the former process, the teacher does most of the talking; the students listen and take in what they hear and try to remember it. In the latter, the students are active and the teacher's role is, to use a modern term, to *facilitate* the students' enterprise. In the former conception of teaching, the teacher is the knower and the students try to emulate him or her; in the latter case, knowledge is not transmitted from teacher to student but rediscovered by the students themselves.

This general distinction has burgeoned in our day into a large range of different pedagogical projects. They seem united at first in their opposition to "lecturing" as the proper method for teaching almost anything, but as we look at the different pedagogies in more detail, it soon emerges that behind this opposition to lecturing and behind the advocacy of "active learning" hide a number of fairly different educational projects. The advocates of active learning, for instance, contrast a classroom in which the teacher stands in front and talks while the students write down what he or she says, with a classroom in which students work in small groups, talk to the student next to them for a while, write brief essays in class, hold formal debates in front of the class, or engage in cooperative investigations—all of which are instances of active learning. In all of this, the teacher does not transmit knowledge but facilitates it.[3]

The contrast between lecture and the active student takes a different form in what is known as Socratic teaching, in which the teacher is at pains not to tell the students anything but elicits knowledge from them through patiently and carefully framed questions. Here any kind of transmission of knowledge from teacher to student is proscribed, although it is clearly permitted in what is called active learning. The teacher's efforts at facilitating learning are limited to asking questions, whereas in active learning, the teachers have a much wider repertoire of activities at their disposal.[4]

The contrast between lecturing and students discovering knowledge for themselves takes a different form in the pedagogical project called "Problem-based Learning." Here students are given carefully developed sets of problems that they need to discuss among each other to formulate a set of questions. Next they need to marshall the relevant knowledge they possess already to discover where they need to find additional information. Once the questions are clear and the students have discovered what information is still missing, they proceed to acquire that knowledge with whatever are the appropriate methods. Problem-based learning is widely used today in medical education both in the United States and abroad[5]; it is supported by a number of foundations and in general use in many U.S. colleges and universities.[6]

The general contrast, drawn first by Socrates, is used to describe an interesting range of different methods of teaching, not only in philosophy, but also in almost all subjects; these methods are today used at all levels of education from the early grades of primary school to advanced professional education. Each different pedagogical enterprise makes somewhat different justificatory claims. Problem-based learning is often recommended as a way of teaching students to learn. With new medical knowledge being discovered daily, the advocates reason, there is more knowledge available than can be taught in four years of medical education. Schools must not limit themselves to transmitting existing knowledge because that is a task that cannot be finished in four years. Instead medical students must be made into lifelong learners. The Socratic method and active learning method are often recommended for different reasons, namely because they make learning more interesting for students; students therefore pay more attention in class; and they are more likely to remember what they learn because they were active in the acquisition of that knowledge. Moreover, learning with the use of either method is more fun.

But the general contrast between "passive" and "active" learning, between lectures to instill knowledge or some alternative in which students participate more actively in the class, is often overdrawn. Philosophers, with the exception of Socrates, have all committed their thoughts to writing, which other philosophers read and interpret. Reading and writing are quite similar to giving lectures; they all give systematic and lengthy expositions of a set of ideas. It is of minor importance whether these lengthy expositions are spoken or written. Certainly in the transmission of philosophy, lecturing or writing is not always to be condemned, but it is, on the contrary, a useful technique. In a range of contexts, lecturing is a useful procedure. At professional meetings, for instance, an investigator reports on his or her work; there is nothing the matter with talking at some length about problems, methodologies, and results, as well as about further questions that arise in the course of this research and the controversies stirred up by it. Also in advanced seminars someone, teacher or student, may summarize a body of information for the benefit of the members. Such a presentation, if well done, may prove extremely useful. Political leaders are briefed by experts about the history of a foreign country, about the antecedents of a current problem, or about the details of a new legislative initiative. Here lecturing seems the most efficient method for providing a survey of a large body of information possessed only by experts and specialists. It would be ludicrous to suggest that the specialists use the Socratic method to convey their information or that the politicians be sent out to discover the contents of the briefing for themselves.

Nevertheless the controversy set in motion by Plato's *Meno* is an important one. We need to question the usefulness of lecturing in teaching at all levels. Too many teachers think that their job is to begin talking when they enter the classroom and to continue for fifty minutes until it is time to end the class. But in a variety of different teaching situations, lecturing as the *main* educational method is not the best method of pedagogy. It is not the most useful way of proceeding with the audience to which this book is addressed: college undergraduates who are taking their first course in philosophy. For them, I am firmly convinced, lecturing should be subsidiary to class discussions in which students are invited to take on one philosophical problem after another to learn how one thinks philosophically. For students new to philosophy, classes should convey a feel for the philosophical project. Why do philosophers do what they habitually do? That, I believe, is not best conveyed to students in lectures—for instance, when we quote Aristotle as saying that "philosophy begins in wonder"—but in reflecting about the many different problems that all of us encounter more or less daily that launch our thinking about the more abstract principles that are the bread and butter of philosophers.

Philosophers raise questions and frame answers; they construct and criticize arguments to support those answers. They tell stories, often real, more often made up, and draw philosophical lessons from them. They engage in lengthy controversies with one another. They disagree with each other about the precise nature of their enterprise and the standards for philosophical competence. Questioning, arguing, criticizing, telling stories, philosophers produce the content of philosophy that has grown to an impressive body of work over the span of more than twenty-five hundred years. Their activities produce the content; content and activities are distinct but also, of course, intricately connected with each other.

Teachers of philosophy tend to focus their classes on the content of philosophy. We explain to our students the problems philosophers have raised, the solutions proposed, and their weaknesses. In the course of these presentations, we try to explain to our students the structure of arguments and the importance of constructing tight ones. If we prefer to avoid the history of philosophy, we display the content of philosophy by discussing standard problems—the problem of free will, the problem of the existence of god, the problems of sovereignty or of justice.

I myself have taught philosophy in this manner for many years. It seemed to work reasonably well with students who were especially well prepared, who were articulate, good readers and writers. They could write good papers about the texts they had read or the standard problems that had been explained to them in lectures. It was much more obviously less successful in classrooms in which many students had no more than an average preparation, where many were the first members of their families to go to college. These students frequently had difficulties reading the eighteenth-century English of Hobbes and Locke. Unaccustomed to questioning their own opinions or those of others and lacking adequate skills in constructing systematic and well-argued expository prose essays, they had difficulties appreciating the efforts philosophers make to support their insights with arguments. Introductions to the history or to some of the standard problems of philosophy left them more often confused instead of enlightened. For them, introductions to philosophy focusing on the content of philosophy were not successful.

With an emphasis on the content of philosophy—that is, on the theses defended by philosophers—a few better-prepared students came away with a good knowledge of what philosophers had said and argued for. But even they remained more often than not bewildered about the reasons for taking on all these arguments. Philosophy remained for most of them—well-prepared students and others—an enterprise that was perhaps intellectually challenging but that remained pretty useless—in the category of crossword puzzles or Sudoku. Well-prepared or not, the majority of students remained uncertain why anyone would bother thinking about these issues. The sources of philosophical perplexity and the reasons for its urgency tend to remain hidden when we focus on content in our teaching. Few students in either group acquired a lively sense of what moved anyone to raise philosophical questions in the first place. Primary attention paid to philosophical results does not bring out the origins of philosophical questioning in everyday life as clearly as one would wish. It leaves students with the impression that philosophy is at best an intriguing, but quite esoteric undertaking that one may enjoy while a student but must then jettison once one enters the "real" world of one's own family and career.

Students acquainted mostly with some of the content of philosophy rarely gain a good sense that philosophy begins when ordinary persons confront common moral dilemmas or disagreements about moral issues or issues in politics. Sooner or later, everyone confronts serious quandaries about telling lies or being truthful, about keeping promises, and similar moral questions. When others disagree with us about the morality of a course of action, we need to explain ourselves by explaining how we see this matter and why. We need to support our moral views with arguments, stories, or perhaps appeals to authority. As citizens, we must decide questions that concern specific freedoms: questions about banning books considered racist or about pornography considered a form of violence against women. We need to confront questions concerning property such as taking by eminent domain or blocking development of land that is home to a rare species of animal or plant. Ordinary citizens, if they are thoughtful, will do the best they can with those questions. If their introductory philosophy course gives them some practice in thinking about issues of this sort, they may well do a little better in their deliberations.

Discussions of these everyday issues sooner or later will lead back to the discussion of general moral or political principles. If we reflect long enough about free speech or the freedom to own private property, we will have to ask ourselves how those freedoms are to be justified—whether, for instance, by an appeal to utilitarian principles or in some other way. After extended discussions of specific freedoms, questions about the nature of freedom, in general, become unavoidable. Sooner or later, one needs to ask what justice is, what rights are, and how one can bolster one's claims to specific ones. Everyday philosophical questions lead inevitably into more abstract and more technical discussions.

But philosophy did not start out as a discussion of such general principles. Plato's Socratic dialogues begin with everyday problems: the treatment of slaves, one's duties to one's parents, courage. Only after extended reflection on fairly concrete problems do abstract general moral and political principles move to the center of the discussion. These discussions of principles and their epistemology are of great interest to us as philosophers. But they are much more abstract than everyday moral dilemmas, and for many of the students that I have known, the connections between the day-to-day moral questions they encounter, and sometimes wrestle with, and these more abstract discussions of moral principles are often quite obscure. They may read Mill, Kant, Aristotle, or McIntyre and even find that reading interesting. But they have a hard time bringing those discussions to bear on what they worry about when their own lives force moral deliberation on them: What to do when, for instance, they feel the obligation to divulge a secret they are sworn to keep, when there is an unexpected pregnancy, or when questions arise about academic cheating. As a consequence, what they learn about philosophy in talking about the great philosophers does not, for them, have a clear bearing on the moral problems they face. What they learn in philosophy courses may be interesting to them, but its use is limited.

With this in mind, I have shifted my teaching more and more to beginning with fairly concrete dilemmas in recent years. I have shifted from concentrating on conveying the content of philosophy to encouraging students to participate in the activity of philosophy by paying serious and systematic attention to the philosophical problems everyday existence raises for everyone. In this way, some students begin to see how philosophical questions arise in our ordinary life. After a while they feel the push to connect these everyday quandaries to the more abstract and technical questions discussed in canonical texts or contemporary work.

In addition, having found that the approach centered on the content of philosophy did poorly with students with only average preparation for college, I tried to enter into philosophy through its activity, by raising somewhat familiar ethical dilemmas and having the students learn to think methodically about them. Engaged in activities that seemed at least moderately familiar, it was easier for students to participate actively and many engaged with some enthusiasm in arguing philosophical questions that were, at first, fairly concrete but came to be more general and abstract as the semester progressed.

This book, accordingly, will approach philosophy, in the first place, as activity, as raising questions, trying to formulate answers, and providing argued support for those. The text therefore concentrates, at the outset, on concrete debates. In the Socratic contrast between teaching as instilling knowledge in students or as helping students to discover it for themselves, this books sides firmly with Socrates—without committing itself to any thesis about the immortality of the soul, of course. It will give students practice in reflecting about actual moral and political difficulties they encounter in everyday life. It will allow them to practice getting together relevant facts and examining how opposing views on any given issue may be presented as strongly and persuasively as possible. For that purpose many questions for the students are scattered widely throughout the text. Instructors should pick some of these questions—whichever they believe to be pedagogically or philosophically most useful or interesting. There are too many questions in the text to be discussed carefully in one semester. Further, this text does not just raise questions but invites the students to consider them carefully. It invites them to think philosophically, first in situations that are familiar and comfortable and then, gradually, in settings that are more abstract, and perhaps, less familiar. In the process, students encounter the more general principles needed to give reasonable accounts of their answers to concrete moral or political questions.

Thus, for instance, in the first chapter, students will have engaged in philosophical discussions for about sixty pages before I raise the question of what philosophy is. Students are then encouraged to reflect about what they have been doing for a while now—considering moral and political questions. Instead of telling them what philosophy is, the book points out the general features of what they have been engaged in. In this way the connection emerges between relatively familiar issues and more abstract, less familiar philosophical reflections—in this case, questions about philosophical activity itself. The discussion of the nature of philosophy merely articulates an already familiar exercise and ways of questioning and thinking. Teaching philosophy becomes an exercise in Socratic "anamnesis."

For this reason, the first chapter begins with debates about property rights, the conflicts of free speech rights, the right to be secure from racist slurs, and the right to publicly criticize government war efforts. In the course of these specific discussions, concepts like freedom and rights come up repeatedly so that by the end of that chapter we are able to begin to discuss liberal theory for the first time. That discussion is continued and deepened by going into more detail about the nature of rights and how we justify claims to possess specific rights in chapter 3, in the context of questions about property rights. The discussion of liberalism continues in the final chapter when the republican principles of the founders of our country confront contemporary liberal conceptions of liberty. The historical roots of liberalism come to the fore in lengthy excerpts from John Locke and Thomas Hobbes in chapter 2 that elaborate quite different attitudes of Americans to the conflict between liberty and the security of individuals, as well as of the entire nation.

Clearly philosophers disagree about how their subject is best taught. The present book is on the side of active philosophizing by the students and less supportive of the pedagogical efficacy of lectures—however brilliant. But there is no question that both methods have their advantages and disadvantages. Classes centered on discussion have more difficulty in presenting a certain body of material systematically. Students using this book learn a good deal about standard philosophical problems and different solutions offered to those problems. At the end of the course they should be familiar with different elements of liberal political theory. But that information is not presented in a systematic way. There is no presentation, say, of liberal political theory that moves from its historical antecedents to contemporary incarnations and the debates among liberals to, finally, some major critiques of liberalism. Instead, different aspects of liberal theory are conveyed at different junctures of the continuing arguments about living free lives.

Some instructors—those sufficiently troubled by this absence of a systematic exposition of liberal theory—may want to present some final lectures that summarize the philosophical results examined in the course of the semester. For their use I am appending a list of standard elements in a comprehensive presentation of liberalism paired with the sections of this book in which these elements are discussed. This will make it easier for the lecturer to refer students back to the different portions of the book they have studied in the course of the semester.

Liberal Theory

History

Republican Freedom: Chapter 5, B. What Is Freedom? Republican and Liberal Conceptions of Freedom

Hobbes and Locke: Chapter 2, A. Social Contract Theories, C. Philosophy of Mutual Trust and D. The Power of the Government

What Is Liberalism? Chapter 1, F. Liberalism

The Public and Private: Chapter 3, E. Liberalism and Paternalism; Chapter 5, A. The Good Citizen and Chapter 5, B. What Is Freedom?

Political Power Derives from the People: Civil Disobedience, Chapter 2, G. Citizen and Government

Problems of Liberalism: Chapter 1, D. When Citizens' Rights Conflict and Chapter 1, E. When Rights Conflict

Negative and Positive Freedom: Chapter 1, G. Different Freedoms: Freedom From and Freedom To.

Economic and Political Freedom: Chapter 1, F. Liberalism, subsection on What Do Liberal Principles Mean? Rawls and Nozick on Equality; Chapter 3, D. Philosophy of the Free Market

Rights

Chapter 3, H. Rights

Justice

Chapter 3, G. Distributive Justice

Equality

Equality of Opportunity. Chapter 1, C. The Many Faces of Equal Opportunity; Chapter 3, I. Equality

Democracy

Chapter 4

Critiques of Liberalism

Marxist

Chapter 3, C. Socialism

Feminist

Chapter 3, K. Feminist Critique of Rights

Communitarian

Chapter 1, F. Liberalism, subsection on Communitarianism

Anarchist

Chapter 2, Section E

NOTES

1. Plato, *The Dialogues of Plato*, vol. 1 (New York: Random House, 1920), 361–66.

2. Paolo Freire, *The Pedagogy of the Oppressed*.

3. Retrieved August 26, 2008, from University of California, Davis website: trc.ucdavis.edu/TRC/ta/tatips/activelearning.pdf.

4. Retrieved August 26, 2008, from Critical Thinking Web site: www.critical-thinking.org/articles/the-role-socratic-questioning-ttl.cfm.

5. A 1993 article mentions Harvard, Mercer, McMaster, and Bowman Gray as U.S. medical schools using problem-based learning. See Robert S. Donner, MD, and Harmon Bickley, MD, "Problem-based learning in American medical education: An overview," *Bull Med Libr Assoc* 81(3) July 1993.

6. Retrieved from Rapid Intellect website: www.rapidintellect.com/AEQweb/mop4spr01.htm.

How to Use This Book

This book is designed to introduce students not only to the content of philosophy, but also to the activity of thinking philosophically. It aims to provide practice in formulating philosophical questions, as well as in proposing answers supported by good reasoning. For this purpose the text is liberally interspersed with questions that should stimulate philosophical reflection.

The text contains more questions than could usefully be discussed in the course of a semester. Students and instructors must therefore choose those questions for discussion that strike them as most interesting.

Choosing too many questions, one incurs the danger of being able to provide merely a superficial discussion of each. Choosing no questions, students will miss the opportunity to develop their skills in philosophical thinking.

Chapter One

Freedom: Possession or Process?

INTRODUCTORY QUESTIONS

What Is Freedom?

The walls of my local post office are adorned with the legend "Land of the Free, Home of the Brave." Below that a sign reads "No Loitering, Police Take Notice." Are those two signs at odds with each other? You might think that in a free country a public building would allow citizens to take shelter from inclement weather, but not our post office. Here you need to have post office business; you need to come in and do what you need to do and then leave. *No loitering.* Although some people are offended by this sign, many would defend it. You do not want people living in the post office lobby because the rent on their apartment is overdue. You do not want the place to be overrun by the homeless, drunks, or addicts. You cannot do whatever you choose in the post office just because it is a public building.

Discussion Question

Is there an inconsistency between saying that ours is the land of the free and the "No Loitering" sign in the post office? Give reasons for your answer.

In our national anthem, we describe our country as "the land of the free." We are accustomed to describing ours as "a free country" and to hearing this country referred to as "the leader of the free world." We say that "we have freedom" and think not only that we are fortunate but also that, having freedom, we are better than those who do not. Nothing symbolizes our sense of being securely in possession of freedom as clearly as the monumental Statue of Liberty in New York harbor. Emma Lazarus's poem inscribed in its base refers to immigrants as "huddled masses yearning to breathe free." It conveys the image of immigrants passing the Statue of Liberty and coming through Ellis Island to the United States where, henceforth, they will be free. Using these images we think of freedom as firmly in our possession, freedom as something we do not need to worry about, and as something we have come what may. Just as we rely on the love of our parents and the loyalty of our friends, we count on the permanence and solidity of freedom. Parents and friends will be with us through thick and thin. They will forgive us when we falter and give us a helping hand to rise again. Our freedom, we believe similarly, will always protect us when we are in need. It will always stand as a wall between us and overly ambitious government functionaries or fellow citizens who are bullies. Our freedom, we believe, is secure.

The national anthem, a Fourth of July speech, or comments made when we unveil yet another memorial to soldiers who died in a foreign war, are not the places to develop a complex understanding of freedom. In those contexts it is all right for us to say that we are free and dispense with all the qualifications. But we must not allow these patriotic occasions and the rhetoric appropriate to them to mislead us into thinking that our freedoms are immune to controversy, that we can always count on them protecting us, and that we all agree with each other on what they are. Distracted by pious patriotic phrases, we fail to see that we do not clearly understand or agree with one another what freedom is or even less where it is threatened by our immediate neighbors, the community, or the government.

Americans are proud to live in the land of the free but they do not always reflect carefully about their freedom. The idea of freedom is not as simple and clear as we often assume. In this chapter we will examine some aspects of freedom and the many interesting questions they raise for us. Here is a commonplace example of the problems freedoms raise for us.

Conflicts over the Limits of Freedoms

A few years ago, a Texas dentist invested his savings in a large piece of land at some distance from downtown. As the town grew in the direction of his land, the dentist was getting ready to develop that acreage, but then scientists at the local university discovered that his property was home to a rare insect, which, just an eighth of an inch long, had never been found anywhere else. With this discovery, the federal Endangered Species Act of 1973 came into play. For the sake of preserving this rare and endangered species of small insect, the government prohibited any further site preparation and construction. The development came to an abrupt halt. The fact that the endangered animal was barely visible to the naked eye made no difference. The dentist, prevented from cashing in on his investment, went to court and the case began winding its way up to the Supreme Court where the entire Endangered Species Act will be challenged by the plaintiffs.

Discussion Questions

Did the Endangered Species Act limit the prospective developer's freedom? If so, does he still live in the "land of the free"?

How can the government justify its interference with the developer's freedom?

Give reasons for your answer.

This is an ordinary example of the conflicts that freedom brings with it. We say that freedoms are never unlimited: my freedom ends where its exercise harms my neighbors as a group or individually. Although that is easily said, as our story illustrates, in real cases the limits between the freedom of one person and that of another is difficult to fix and is rarely fixed without serious controversy.

"The sole end for which mankind are warranted, individually or collectively, in interfering with the liberty of action of any of their number, is self-protection. . . . the only purpose for which power can rightfully be exercised over any member of a civilized community, against his will, is to prevent harm to others." Thus wrote John Stuart Mill, the great English philosopher and defender of individual liberty in his essay *On Liberty* in 1859. I am free to use my property as I please unless my sound system keeps my neighbors awake at night, my septic system pollutes a neighboring stream, or my dogs terrify children passing on the sidewalk in front of my house. It ends where, as in the dentist's case, my use of my property conflicts with the requirements, as determined by Congress, of conserving rare species.

None of these limits are so obvious that no one would quarrel with them. None of them are immutably set in stone. They are all open to negotiation and may be changed. Today, there is pretty widespread agreement that no one should be allowed to make excessive noise, especially at night, but in neighborhoods adjacent to college campuses conflicts over loud parties often go on for many years. The precise limits of the freedom of the neighbors to sleep peacefully and the students' freedom to party remain to be negotiated in each place, over and over again. There is agreement that no one should be allowed to discharge raw sewage into streams, but the owners of antiquated septic systems struggle against state mandated improvements that cost them thousands of dollars. The details of how to clean up our waterways and, especially, who will bear the financial burden remain to be negotiated. There is less agreement whether my neighbor may have his lawn treated with pesticides and chemical fertilizers, even when those chemicals will run off into the nearby pond. There the fertilizer encourages the growth of weeds harmful to fish. I live close to that pond by choice because I am an avid fisherman. But now there are fewer fish in the pond; my neighbor indirectly interferes with my interests as a fisherman. Nevertheless, his use of chemical fertilizer on his lawn is, so far, widely regarded as a legitimate exercise of his freedom, but I do not agree with that.

All of these limits change over time, as the consequence of study and negotiation between conflicting interests. Regulations of septic tanks have become much more stringent in recent years as have been concerns about the preservation of endangered species. Federal legislation—the Endangered Species Act—has empowered the Secretary of the Interior and the Secretary of Commerce to prohibit development of the habitats of endangered species of plants and animals for housing or for growing crops. But the extent of this sort of government regulation is not yet settled. Court cases are still being filed as a means of negotiating the precise limits of governmental regulation to protect the environment and the limits of the rights of private property. On the other hand, there is so far limited regulation of chemical lawn treatments.[1]

The examples show us that, contrary to what we often think, freedom is not a settled possession. The citizens of a free country cannot quietly enjoy the blessings of liberty but are, precisely because they are free, embroiled in fairly steady streams of controversy, disagreement, debate, and judicial and political conflicts. The life of a free society involves endless disagreements of different sorts. Being free is work that involves disagreements, reflection, and political action. Imagine, by contrast, an authoritarian country where police are always ready to admonish citizens with their batons. Their job is to keep the peace, and they take that seriously. Disagreements are not tolerated; missing is precisely the freedom to make claims for yourself against others. Harmony prevails at the expense of freedom.

The Texas dentist whom the government prevented from developing his property did not lose his freedom, not even his freedom to own property, and to use it in all legal ways as he pleases. He encountered a specific controversy about the limitations of his freedom of property imposed by a particular law, the Endangered Species Act, and the specific conditions of his property. It is not useful to say that "we have freedom"; it is better to say that we have many different freedoms and where they impinge on the freedoms of others is often a source of disagreement and conflict. *Freedom* is no more than a collective name for many different kinds of freedoms.

This chapter is devoted to explaining these basic features of a free society. It will discuss such questions as

- Is freedom a secure possession of U.S. citizens?
- Who shall be free?
- Do the freedoms of different groups conflict?
- What is equal opportunity?
- What are legitimate limits on free speech?
- Is the freedom of some citizens ever a threat to the freedom of others?
- How do we argue for liberal principles?
- What is the role of government in a free society?
- What is philosophy?

FREEDOM AND EQUALITY

Is everyone free in the land of the free or only some? For most of our history, some citizens had a good deal of freedom and others little. One of the most profound struggles in our history has been the attempt to assure equal freedom for all, and that struggle is not yet over.

Who Shall Be Free? A Brief History of the United States

The land of the free came into existence by usurping the land of other peoples. The early English settlers came to Massachusetts to escape religious repression, but they were not prepared to extend religious tolerance to anyone else. Not even fellow immigrants were allowed to deviate from the official orthodoxy. Roger Williams and Anne Hutchinson were expelled from the Massachusetts Bay Colony for advocating religious tolerance. Mary Dwyer was hung by the Puritans in 1660 for being a Quaker. The American Indians were considered "savages" and "heathens." Converting them to the one true faith was one of the official justifications of settling in the New World.[2]

American Indians

Seventeenth-century Europeans thought of the Indians as primitive people— that is, nomads who did not practice agriculture and had no governmental institutions. They believed that the Indians roamed the land, never settling anywhere for long, unfamiliar with the institution of private property. The immigrants from England brought those beliefs with them to the New World. The indigenous people they encountered there were, however, quite different. The Mayflower arrived in Massachusetts in November of 1620. The people who had survived the voyage were not prepared to grow crops for themselves, and anyway, it was not the season for planting. Those who survived owed their life to the corn and other staples they either stole from or were given by the Indians. It must have been quite clear that their preconceptions about the nomadic native inhabitants were mistaken. The people whose land they invaded were by no means nomads. Their agriculture flourished and yielded enough of a surplus to sustain themselves and the newcomers through the harsh New England winter.

Self-interest may have encouraged the settlers to maintain their European preconceptions about the American Indians. If land was not owned or improved by anyone, it was there for the taking. The new settlers need have no scruples about taking the land they found, as long as they could maintain their preconceived belief that no one was working the ground and growing crops on it. Although their experience contradicted them, they had a strong interest in holding on to their ideas of the Indians as primitive nomads who had not settled, let alone improved, the land by their own work.

The new immigrants from England were rigid in their religious beliefs. Notwithstanding their own suffering from religious intolerance back home, they were inflexibly narrow-minded. In the background of that intolerance stood the five-hundred-year struggle European Christians had won against the Muslims with the expulsion of Muslims and Jews from Spain—a process completed just before Columbus left on his voyage to America. For centuries in the crusades to take back Jerusalem from the Muslims, in the persecution of the Jews in Europe, in the Inquisition that rooted out heresy with torture and public burnings of its victims, and the wars and upheavals occasioned by the Protestant reformations, Europeans had murdered, raped, and pillaged in the defense of the one true God—theirs. Religious intolerance anchored in a sense of divinely ordained superiority to other nations was deeply ingrained in the European view of the world. The American Indians bore the brunt of that.[3]

To a considerable extent, the collapse of Indian cultures was the result of the terrible accident that American Indians had no autoimmune defenses against the diseases that traveled with the Europeans, such as hepatitis A, the plague, and measles—diseases which had not previously existed on the American continent. As a consequence of early contacts with European fishermen around Newfoundland, or with Dutch and French fur traders, whom they supplied with the coveted pelts, Indians experienced a series of epidemics in the early years of the seventeenth century. Populations shrunk by up to 95 percent in some estimates. It was more difficult, therefore, for the new immigrants to understand that the American Indians had a complex culture that included their own methods of agriculture, as well as hunting and fishing, because that culture was, at the time, quite precarious. The Europeans' lack of curiosity about the native inhabitants was encouraged by the enormous devastation wrought by the epidemics in the Indian population. Most of the English settlers never discovered that the American Indians had developed forms of democracy unknown to the English immigrants. Each band of families had its own leader, but that leader's decisions needed to be ratified by the members of the band. England was to take important steps on the road to democracy in the seventeenth century. But the American Indians were clearly ahead of the European immigrants with respect to democratic political institutions.

Arguably, American Indian civilization was ahead of the Europeans in other respects. Indians were clean; some of the English and French immigrants had not taken a single bath in their entire life. They plainly smelled bad. Indian children were treated less harshly than European children. Indian children were free to roam the countryside and explore their world until marriage.[4] Europeans put their children to work at age seven. Other differences between the Indians and the English settlers caused serious debates between settlers and native inhabitants. Indians were willing to go hungry for short periods in the depth of winter when food was scarce. Snug in their tepees with the snow piled up high on the outside they went without food for a few days when hunting was poor and their supplies of corn had run out. They were willing to put up with that for the sake of not working quite as hard as the Europeans during the rest of the year and for the sake of being able to have mobile dwellings that could be pitched near their corn and squash fields in the summer and then be moved to winter quarters when the days got cold. Europeans settled, as they had in England, in houses. They stored food for the winter. They were more susceptible to starvation.[5] For that, they needed to work dawn to dusk in the spring, the summer, and the fall.

Greed for land, the religious intolerance bred in Europeans by centuries of religious warfare, the collapse of the Indian cultures due to disease, all conspired to leave American Indians as outcasts from the new nation that arose in the seventeenth and eighteenth centuries on this continent. The majority of Europeans never surrendered their image of the "savage"—noble in the eyes of some Europeans, but regarded as inferior by others. American Indians needed to be civilized or exterminated.[6] The same majority was not prepared to share the land they had invaded. To justify that, the American Indian needed to be excluded from the U.S. culture that was developing in the seventeenth and eighteenth centuries. To this day, American Indians have to struggle for the freedoms of other Americans. If ours is the land of the free, its original inhabitants are not included in our free institutions.

African Slaves

The first Africans were imported into the continental United States in 1619, to the Virginia colony of Jamestown (although their status as slaves only developed over a period of years after their first arrival in Virginia). In the South and in other parts of the United States, the bulk of the hard labor to produce food and staples was done by slaves for 250 years or more of our history. These slaves, too, aspired to freedom but their petitions went unheard; their uprisings were suppressed ruthléssly. There were major slave revolts in 1712, 1739, 1741, 1800, 1811, 1815, 1816, 1822, 1836, and 1839, and many more minor skirmishes in the war between the slaves and their masters. If they could not rise up, they damaged farm equipment, tore down fences, and made other kinds of mischief, such as stealing sheep and chickens. Many slaves ran away. In portions of the slave south, the flight of slaves was enough of a problem for plantation owners that they patrolled the roads nightly to watch for slaves attempting escape. Their first emancipation was incidental to the issues between North and South during the Civil War. But ten years after the end of the Civil War, a new regime of racial oppression was imposed by state laws, and enforced by the power of the various states and the terrorism of lynchings. A second emancipation needed to be fought for bitterly and is still not complete. The freedom of white America came at the expense of the freedom of the enslaved African Americans and of American Indians.

Women

Until the twentieth century, women were not just second-class citizens. They were not citizens at all. They were not voters, and until the middle of the nineteenth century they could not own property—whatever they may have earned was the property of their fathers or husbands; they were excluded from the public and political sphere because they were confined to their homes, by law as well as custom. They had fewer educational opportunities and could with few exceptions not live as independent adults as men could. (For more details, see chapter 4).

Only a minority of the inhabitants of the land of the free enjoyed freedom, and those who did could not have enjoyed their freedom had it not been for the work and the deprivations of the unfree. The freedom of citizens existed at the expense of the lack of freedom of the majority of the people.

Discussion Question

Considering our history of depriving the majority of Americans of elementary freedoms, what do you think now about our description of our country as "the land of the free"? Give reasons for your answer.

Other Debates about Who Shall Be Free

Now new debates about who shall enjoy our freedoms are rising up with respect to persons whose sexual choices are not those of the majority. Should all couples be free to marry and have their unions officially recognized and legitimated by the state, or should that freedom be restricted to heterosexual couples? Freedom is not a secure possession; it is instead the source of endless controversy, conflict, and unrest. A different debate is coming up about immigration. Are the freedoms Americans claim for themselves, but withheld from many of their fellow citizens, *American* freedoms that only we are entitled to, or are they *human freedoms* that should be open to everyone? I believe, as I shall discuss in chapter 3, that everyone is entitled to a minimal decent level of life. Are Americans the only ones entitled to that, or should the same right be extended to Mexicans and other Latin Americans, to people in Africa and Asia? Our answer to that question will have obvious implications for the policy we advocate with respect to legal immigration and the treatment of illegal immigrants.

Discussion Questions

1. *List arguments for and against allowing gay couples to get married.*
2. *Assemble different views about immigration from the Internet. What do you think is the most just immigration policy for the United States? Give reasons for your answer.*

THE MANY FACES OF EQUAL OPPORTUNITY

We agree that ours is a free country to the extent that all citizens have equal freedoms. We regret the past in which freedoms were restricted to limited groups such as white male property owners, or all white men, and we deplore the present where equal freedoms still are not accessible to all. But what are equal freedoms?

"That's simple" you say. "We have equal freedoms when all of us are able to participate in government or all are able to enjoy their property securely." In the past, slavery was protected by law and the law took the side of the slave owners against the slaves' legitimate strivings for freedom. The disenfranchisement of women was enshrined in the law and enforced by the police and the courts. So were the laws against working people organizing themselves to improve their working conditions. Equal freedoms exist only when the laws apply equally to all and when they allow the same range of activities to all persons. All are equally free when laws protect everyone's right to political participation and protect everyone's right to own property, to speak their mind, and to fashion good lives for themselves as long as they allow equal freedoms to others.

Legal equality, however, is not sufficient for equal freedom. The law may treat you no better or no worse than your neighbor, but she has help with her house and her children and thus the free time to take classes and become a docent at the museum or develop a career as a therapist or educational consultant. You have a job and do most of the housework and have no time to develop your exceptional voice or the promise you showed in college as a writer of short stories. Your neighbor is free to make something of herself, to develop some of her talents and you are not. She has more freedom than you. Equality before the law is necessary but not sufficient for equal freedom. If we just consider the law, many of us have the same freedom. If we look at the real conditions under which people live, we see that some people have a much better opportunity to avail themselves of the freedoms allowed by law than others. To many people that seems unfair. Equal opportunity, we tend to think today, is an important element of freedom. Everyone must have comparable opportunities. We therefore tend to say that equal freedom does not just mean "equal legal rights" but "equal opportunity."

Discussion Questions

1. *Do all Americans have equal freedom as long as they are subject to the same legal restrictions?*
2. *Or must we say that not all Americans are equally free as long as some have a much better chance to use the freedoms allowed by the law than others?*
3. *What opportunities do you believe everyone ought to have available in life? Give reasons for your answer.*

It would be easy to get into a number of difficult, complex debates about what sorts of equal opportunities everyone might be entitled to. The phrase *equal opportunity* could easily mislead us into the belief that all should have the same or similar opportunities. Because persons differ widely in their conceptions of the best life, clearly they need different opportunities to fulfill their dreams. If all had literally the same opportunities, few would be able to live the life they prefer. In addition, people are different; some are frugal, whereas others prefer champagne and caviar on private yachts in exotic locations. Is everyone entitled to the opportunities for what they consider a good life? In response to those sorts of difficulties, some philosophers have drawn up lists of fundamental capabilities that all humans need to satisfy to live a fulfilled life. Not surprisingly, it is difficult to get widespread agreement on what opportunities every human being is entitled to.

To avoid these complex debates, it must suffice, for the present, to observe that the phrase *equal opportunity* has primarily a negative intent: we have come to believe that certain specific kinds of unequal opportunity are unacceptable. We no longer believe, for instance, that a person has no right to education or only to an inferior one if his skin is dark or she is female. Poverty, as we noted previously, should not prevent anyone from becoming as competent a person as their native abilities will allow them to be.

Equal Economic Opportunity: The Continuing Debate over Affirmative Action

In 1954, the Supreme Court declared that segregated education was not in keeping with U.S. freedoms. Henceforth schools had to be integrated. In 1964, during the administration of President Lyndon Johnson, after powerful agitation by black Americans and some white allies, the nation faced up to the fact that blacks still were not allowed to vote, that black education was not equal to that of whites, and that public facilities from transportation to public restrooms and water fountains were still segregated. Would-be black voters were kept from the polls by discriminatory applications of literacy tests for voting or by charging a special poll tax. If that failed to keep blacks from the ballot box, brutal intimidation was often used. A new Voting Rights Act was passed in 1964; segregation was made illegal.

But it now became clear that racist sentiments and practices are not easily eradicated merely by passing laws. Often, in the past, federal legislation aiming to extend the same freedoms to all had been ignored or countermanded by the actions of state legislatures. Racial and gender discrimination had been maintained by landlords or employers who refused to allow blacks and white women equal access to economic opportunities. Schools refused to consider applications by women or blacks. Passing laws had been shown to be insufficient for creating greater equality in the nation. After all, the situation of black Americans had not improved significantly in the one hundred years since the end of the Civil War and the passage of the Thirteenth, Fourteenth, and Fifteenth Amendments to the Constitution guaranteeing everyone—on paper—equal rights and opportunities. In the South, existing law still decreed that blacks had to go to separate and inferior schools and colleges; they were still excluded from the political process and only had access to low-paying jobs. In the North, housing was strictly segregated and so were, for the most part, educational opportunities, and economic prospects for blacks were inferior to those for whites. Equal freedom for all was not going to be assured by legislation alone; it became clear that a major effort of government supervision and enforcement would have to be mounted to assure that all Americans had the same freedoms whatever their color, and we added somewhat later, their gender.

This insight gave rise to a variety of Affirmative Action programs. The Civil Rights Act of 1964 made racial discrimination in public places, such as theaters, restaurants, and hotels, illegal. It also required employers to provide equal employment opportunities. Federal funding for projects could now be cut off if there was evidence of discrimination based on color, race, or national origin. This law was followed in 1965 by the Executive Order 11246 establishing the President's Commission on Equal Employment Opportunity whose role it was to enforce the equal employment opportunity provisions of the 1964 law. These enforcement activities began by scrutinizing hiring practices: did employers make good faith efforts to hire persons of color by advertising their jobs in places where blacks might see the job opening? Did they recruit in places where they had not recruited before, say, in predominantly black high schools or colleges? But these early affirmative action efforts that attempted to recruit persons previously excluded had little effect on equalizing opportunities. The targeted recruitment efforts yielded few hires of persons of color.

These failures of more extended recruitment efforts were thought to have several distinct causes. On the one hand, it was thought that the injuries of centuries of abuse held black people back from making full use of the opportunities that were opening up. On the other, it was thought that many blacks lacked the education for jobs now open to them. Affirmative action required that everyone be given access to the best education they could use.

In a commencement speech at Howard University in Washington, D.C., the leading black institution of higher learning, President Johnson described that problem as follows: "You do not take a person who, for years, has been hobbled by chains and liberate him, bring him up to the starting line of a race and then say 'you are free to compete with all the others,' and still justly believe that you have been completely fair."[7] Simply recruiting in places where whites had not recruited before would not create equal opportunities because, President Johnson and many others believed, black Americans had been oppressed, given second-rate educations, and forced to live under excessively difficult and often degrading conditions. They had been deprived of the vote, and therefore, of political power. The effects of such harsh treatment meted out to many generations of black Americans would not fade away overnight. Special efforts were needed to rectify the damages done to generations of blacks by their mistreatment.

But, on the other hand, the civil rights legislation of the 1950s and 1960s did not change whites overnight, either. After centuries of deeply rooted prejudice against blacks and women, those attitudes faded slowly and have still not disappeared. Although genuine efforts were being made to improve educational and economic opportunities for blacks, the efforts were hindered by another obstacle to truly equal opportunity for all. Discrimination against blacks, racism, had been integral to U.S. life for centuries. The passage of the Civil Rights Act did little to eliminate the large emotional reservoirs of racial prejudice among Americans. The government could make businesses and schools interview applicants of color who, before, would not even have been considered for a job or admission to school, but when it came to the final decision it was much harder to make sure that racial prejudice did not disadvantage black applicants as it had for so long. The only way to deal with this deeply entrenched racial prejudice was to look at actual hires or at school admissions. Did the numbers of black hires increase? What percentage of the black persons interviewed actually were hired or admitted to educational programs? If those numbers remained low, it seemed that one needed to set goals that, over a period, would assure that all Americans had the same opportunities.

The reformers of the 1960s and 1970s were not satisfied to pass one more law that declared that racial prejudice, discrimination, and segregation were illegal. They wanted that legislation to have results, to change the face of the United States, to make our nation truly a nation that provided equal opportunity for all. We had claimed to be such a nation for a long time while at the same time making sure that equal opportunity would never become a reality. Now the time had come to do what we had claimed for many years to be doing: to construct a social system that guaranteed real equality of opportunity to everyone.

With that, affirmative action programs were extended beyond energetic recruitment efforts to assure that blacks and women would not only be recruited but would also actually be hired for jobs or actually admitted to colleges, universities, and professional schools. The term *affirmative action* came to have several meanings: (1) affirmative action programs attempted to extend recruitment efforts to all qualified applicants, regardless of race or gender. (2) affirmative action programs strove to achieve certain predetermined results — (a) That could be done by setting what came to be called "quotas" as was the case in the program of the medical school of the University of San Diego, which we will discuss in a moment. Here a determinate number of places were set aside for minority candidates who would be admitted even if their scores were lower than those of whites. (b) Other schemes had all applicants compete with one another, but minority applicants would receive a certain number of points just for being black, Hispanic, or American Indian.

These different affirmative action projects have not only occasioned a great deal of controversy but also raise serious moral issues.

Is Discrimination Morally Wrong?

Your first inclination may be to answer this question with a resounding *yes*. But before you do that consider this:

What *is* discrimination? I treat someone differently from all others in view of a characteristic that is not relevant to the transaction between us. I do not rent an apartment to you because you are black, do not hire you for a job because you are a woman, or do not treat you respectfully because you are an immigrant with poor English. That is discrimination and many people today agree that it is morally wrong. I can try to defend myself against the accusation that I am discriminating by arguing that the characteristic I take into account when refusing to rent my apartment to you is relevant to this transaction. Charging higher auto insurance rates to persons under twenty-five, for instance, is not discriminatory because drivers in that age range have a larger number of accidents. It is not age that determines the differential rates but the larger numbers of automobile accidents that involve persons under twenty-five.

But if I refuse to rent an apartment to you or to give you a job because you are pigeon-toed or knock-kneed, is that immoral? That is not quite easy to say. It depends on whether in so doing I make you feel bad, insult you, or expose you to ridicule. Those things are frequently regarded as immoral because they are failures to respect others. There is no defense for being gratuitously insulting or causing pain by sheer indifference to the feelings of others. Not letting you have an apartment or a job because I do not like something about you is immoral only insofar as it has those results. No one has a moral obligation to be fully rational at all times. I may act on my prejudices, and as long as I am not injuring anyone else, I am not open to moral criticism. I am free to avoid the company of people against whom I have what I know to be an irrational aversion. I may refuse to do business with them as long as I take care of their feelings and their sense of themselves. As an example, I have big ears, and some people do not like that. If some student does not register for my class because she does not like my big ears, I will not feel unduly upset. No great harm is done by the occasional person who dislikes my big ears. It is not important. We should allow each other our small irrationalities.

Discussion Questions

I run a video store. I refuse a job to a sixteen-year-old neighborhood kid unless he promises to remove all rings, studs, and other piercings from his face. Is that immoral? Is it wrong in some other way?

Suppose I let him work in the store as he is but subject him to a constant barrage of derogatory remarks and bad jokes about his looks, whether there is anyone in the store or not. Is that immoral?

Give reasons for your answer.

But if I do not let you have an apartment or a job because you are black or female, all of a sudden everything is different. What I am doing here is not giving in to some odd idiosyncrasy of mine. I am doing serious harm because my act is part of a society-wide pattern of conduct, shared by almost all, which makes you an outcast, and less of a person, and allows you less freedom and fewer opportunities than others. Discrimination is immoral when, in discriminating, I participate in a social project of excluding certain groups from full citizenship and full participation in other aspects of our social life. But it is not immoral in itself, but because of the devastating effects it has on your life and on the lives of the vast majority of your group.

It is often said that it is immoral to judge strangers on the basis of generalizations about their appearance such as their skin color, their clothes, or their speech. But in a society where one has as much mobility as in ours, one encounters persons daily one does not know and one needs to make snap judgments about them: Are they safe to sit next to at a lunch counter? Is it all right to ask this person for directions? Will this driver let me enter a main road ahead of her? Can I leave my house while this stranger is painting the walls? It seems morally permissible to answer such questions on the basis of ideas about how this person looks, how they talk, whether they are black or white, skinny or fat, tall or short, smiley or dour. But on the other hand, condemning others on the basis of broad generalizations—usually false—about the honesty or intelligence of large groups of persons does untold damage to the lives of its victims. We need to lean on generalizations, but many are utterly unacceptable.

Discussion Questions

Is discrimination always morally wrong, or only when it is directed against groups that the entire society regards as inferior?

When are we justified in relying on a generalization about the appearance of strangers and when must it be condemned?

Give reasons for your answer.

The Remedy: Affirmative Action

In the 1960s it became clear, if it had not been clear long before that, that laws demanding equal opportunity for all needed to be enforced energetically if they were to have their intended effect. Affirmative action programs were introduced to enforce them.

Many of these programs were voluntary. Thus, for instance, the faculty of the University of California at Davis decided to institute a special affirmative action program in 1969 that set aside sixteen places in each new medical school class of one hundred students. These places were reserved for black and other minority applicants and the test scores and grade point averages for these places could be lower than those required of white applicants to the medical school.

In the early 1970s one white applicant, Allan Bakke, failed to gain admission to the medical school although his grades and test scores were higher than those required of black applicants. After being rejected twice, Bakke sued and his case ended up before the Supreme Court. Bakke pointed out that by reserving sixteen places for persons of color from whom lower scores were accepted than from the white students, his chances of admission were reduced in favor of less qualified students. Whereas before his chance was 1 in a 100, after affirmative action programs came in, his chance had been reduced to 1 in 84. That, he claimed, violated the Fourteenth Amendment to the Constitution.

The case went through the courts and ended up in the Supreme Court. Its opinion was divided in complex ways so that subsequent court decisions about affirmative action often disagreed with one another about the precise import of the *Bakke* decision. But this much is clear—that the Supreme Court agreed with Bakke that the affirmative action program at the University of San Diego violated the equal protection clause of the Fourteenth Amendment. The Fourteenth Amendment states that "No State shall make or enforce any law which shall abridge the privileges and immunities of citizens of the United States; nor shall any State deprive any person of life, liberty, or property, without due process of law; nor deny to any person within its jurisdiction the equal protection of the laws." Because different admission standards were applied to different applicants by the University of San Diego medical school, the Court decided, this program was not in conformity with the Fourteenth Amendment. At the same time, the Supreme Court also decided that affirmative action programs, structured differently, would be admissible. The majority opinion asserted that it was legitimate for the admissions office of any school to seek to increase the diversity of its student body. Schools could therefore take account of the racial or gender characteristics of applicants if some races or genders were underrepresented in the student body. But although race and gender could count in applications, the court also insisted that all students had to compete against one another for admission; all had to be judged by the same criteria. There could not be separate competitions for whites and for blacks or for men and for women.

This position was upheld by the Supreme Court when, in 2003, the majority decided in *Grutter v. Bollinger* that the University of Michigan Law School could count race as one of the factors relevant to admission to the law school. However, in the same year, the Supreme Court rejected the system used by the University of Michigan undergraduate admissions office. Applicants were assigned points for grades, test scores, and so on. Everyone with one hundred points or more would be invited to attend the university. Points were given not merely for academic achievement but also for being the children of alumni, for being athletes, for living in the upper peninsula of Michigan, a remote and less developed part of the state. Extra points were also allowed for students who were black, Hispanic, or American Indian.

The position of the Supreme Court on affirmative action is thereby left in disarray. Quota systems are clearly held to be unacceptable, but some affirmative action programs were considered legitimate, whereas others that seem to be similar have been declared unconstitutional.

Did Bakke Suffer an Injustice?

Here is the most frequently cited reason for siding with Bakke: discrimination against entire groups is wrong whether those groups are black or white, female or male. The United States is committed to equal opportunity for all, or as we also say, to a "colorblind society" or "a level playing field." Everyone should be judged by the same criteria.

What follows are some of the arguments against those offered to support affirmative action programs.

The Variety of Affirmative Action Programs

Affirmative action—arrangements that give special treatment to certain groups in access to jobs or to schools—were not invented in the 1960s. Colleges have, for many years, made admission easier for the children of alumni. In the hope that alumni would show their gratitude by being especially generous, many colleges have applied less stringent standards to alumni children who were applying for admission. The same applies to athletes whose promise of bringing glory (and financial gain) to the college's team was a reason for setting academic standards somewhat lower for them than they were for non-athlete applicants. The most impressive example of affirmative action programs, of course, was the special treatment of veterans who, on account of their service in the armed forces receive preferences for all sorts of government jobs on the federal, state, and municipal levels. These veterans' preferences are not limited to front-line soldiers but to anyone who has served honorably in the armed forces. Before anyone replies that, after all, these veterans had made a great contribution to their country, they need to remember that slavery began in earnest in the American colonies around 1660. The contributions made to the

United States by slaves are inestimable, as are the contributions by countless generations of women. By the time Bakke complained that he was displaced in the medical school by a black applicant, the black student's ancestors had labored for three hundred years to build our current wealth and had labored not only with little or no compensation but had earned only contempt for their efforts. No one sued to overturn veterans' preferences or the preferences given to athletes and to alumni children. But once preference was given to persons of color or, later, to white women, an enormous uproar was raised that has still not died down.

Discussion Questions

In school admissions, we have always allowed schools to give preference to some groups over others: athletes, children of alumni, and children of the very rich. Ivy League schools have traditionally tried to achieve geographical balance in their student body. It was easier for an Alaskan student to get into Harvard than for someone who grew up in the shadow of Harvard Yard. Governments have legislated preferences for veterans.

Do affirmative action programs for blacks or for women violate principles not violated by these other preferences?

What shall we say about the fact that some people who are fully qualified cannot go to school because they cannot afford it. Does that violate the principle of equal opportunity?

Was Bakke an innocent victim?

If special benefits are to be extended to blacks or to women, it would seem unjust to place the burden for those efforts on individuals such as Bakke whom no one had accused of being racially prejudiced or to have taken unfair advantage of prevailing prejudices against blacks or women. Not only had Bakke not owned slaves but no one accused him of treating blacks ill simply for their color. If we are going to distribute job and education opportunities unevenly, the price for that political decision should not have to be paid by people who bear no responsibility for the current disadvantages of blacks and white women.

The defenders of affirmative action reply that Bakke's private opinions about race and gender are not at issue. But we may ask whether Bakke was the beneficiary of previous racial and gender exclusions. Prevailing racial and gender exclusions have the effect of limiting the pool of people allowed to apply, for instance, to the medical school at the University of California at Davis. Suppose we had not had a two-hundred-year history of excluding black men and women from higher education. Then Bakke would have had to compete with a much larger pool of applicants that would have included all the women and all the black men then, in fact, excluded by prejudice and its consequences. Women and black men, until the late 1960s virtually barred from many educational opportunities, were more than half the U.S. population. If all racial and gender exclusions had disappeared a long time ago, the pool of applicants to the University of California Davis medical school might well have been double its size in the early 1970s when Bakke applied. He would have had to compete against twice as many applicants. Because his scores were toward the bottom of one hundred mostly male, white applicants, the odds of his having been admitted to medical school would be slim. With a larger pool of applicants for the same one hundred places, the required grades and test scores would most certainly have been higher than Bakke's. If Bakke did get admitted, he owed that not only to his own merit, as shown by his grades and test scores, but also to the fact that racism and sexism had artificially restricted the pool of applicants to the medical school. Even if he, personally, had not encouraged or supported racist exclusions of blacks, Bakke profited from racial and gender prejudice because it worked to limit access to higher education. He cannot plead innocence in racial and gender matters.

Critics of affirmative action keep pleading, in one form or another, that in a fair society everyone should have access to resources depending on their own merit, their abilities, and their hard work. Nothing else should matter. But when we think about people getting ahead on the basis of their own talent and effort alone, we are thinking about a system in which rewards are handed out to winners in competitions. In a fair society, as we think about it, the jobs go to those who win the competitions for good schools, for good grades in school, and for the good jobs they apply for. Ideally we think the best person should win the competition and get the best job. But who wins the competition surely depends on who is allowed to compete. In a society like ours where many people are not able to compete fairly for the really good jobs because they are too poor to get a good education or because they are the targets of prejudices against women or against black men, the people who are admitted to the competition are lucky but not necessarily the best. If the competition is fair, they are the best of a limited group of people who get a chance to compete because their families have some money, have good connections, or are not the targets of race or gender prejudices. There was nothing particularly fair about admitting Bakke to the medical school because the competition was not truly open to all. The game that Bakke won, after the Supreme Court decided that he should be admitted to the medical school, was fixed.

Discussion Question

Was Bakke an innocent victim of the University of California's affirmative action program, or was he implicated in the racial and gender discrimination widespread in our society and therefore legitimately denied admission in favor of a minority candidate? Give reasons for your answer.

Equal Opportunity: Safety

Equality before the law, we saw previously, does not guarantee equal freedom for all because not everyone is equally able to avail themselves of the freedoms guaranteed by the law. Hence we concluded that for all to be equally free, everyone must have equal opportunities.

So far we have examined equal opportunity only with respect to education and employment. Equal opportunity in those areas has attracted an enormous amount of attention that has tended to overshadow unequal opportunities in other areas. For many members of our society, unequal opportunity does not exclude them from work or education, but excludes them, for instance, from equal use of public spaces. Notoriously, women feel and are much less safe in our society and thus their opportunities to be out and about are much more limited than those of men. Statistics about the relative safety of men and women are contested, but it seems clear that men are much more widely victimized by violent assault in the street, or in bars.[8] Women, on the other hand, are the almost exclusive victims of sexual violence.[9]

"Twenty-five percent of women do not walk alone in their own neighborhoods after dark, and 3 percent of men do not.

Sixty-eight percent of women do not go to bars or clubs alone after dark, and 5 percent of men do not.

Forty-nine percent of women do not use public transportation alone after dark, and 23 percent of men do not.

Fifty-two percent of women do not go to parks alone after dark, 10 percent of men do not.

Forty-eight percent of women say they do not go downtown alone after dark, and 7 percent of men do not.

Are women being unnecessarily cautious compared to men? Consider the statistics:

One in three women is hit or raped by a husband in her lifetime.

One in five women between the ages of fifteen and twenty-one years old is hit or raped by a dating partner.

The leading cause of women's visits to hospital emergency rooms is domestic violence—causing more visits than rapes, muggings, and car accidents combined.

Eighty-five percent of girls (under eighteen) report some form of sexual harassment in school.

Seventy-eight percent of women (college age or older) are sexually harassed in the workplace or classroom.

More than one in ten women is stalked during her lifetime, with approximately six million women stalked every year." [10]

Discussion Question

Being subject to more sexual violence and intimidation than men in our society, do women have equal opportunities for moving freely through the society? Give reasons for your answer.

Equal Opportunity: Social Mobility

Many Americans believe that in the United States it is entirely up to you where you end up in social and economic standing. If you are bright and willing to work hard, you can be born poor and end up wealthy. Their place in society of Americans depends, many believe, primarily on the ability and hard work of the individual. "You can be president," we tell young children, even if they had to skip breakfast at home because there was no money to buy milk and cereal.

What are the facts? A recent study by the Pew Charitable Trusts about social mobility shows that although most Americans have a higher income than their parents this "does not necessarily mean that they are moving up the economic ladder compared to their parents or other families. Only one third are . . . upwardly mobile. Another third are downwardly mobile." [11] If we group Americans by their income, we get a pyramid: at the very top are a few billionaires; at the bottom are a significant number of persons who are below the federal poverty line and a larger number of the so-called "working poor" — families whose members work a minimum wage job, or often more than one, and still do not quite have enough money for a decent standard of living. *Social mobility* refers to the likelihood that children move up (or down) in this pyramid compared to the other families. If you grow up poor and end up in a middle-class professional job, you are upwardly mobile. If you grow up in a middle-class, professional family and end up working minimum wage jobs, you are downwardly mobile. The report by the Pew Charitable Trusts shows that one-third of Americans remain in the same level of the income pyramid as their parents; one-third advances and ends up on a higher level of the income pyramid; one-third moves down and ends up on a lower level of the income pyramid than their parents.

These facts are familiar. What they mean for equal opportunity is, however, a matter of debate. The numbers of upwardly and downwardly mobile persons do not show *why* some people manage to move up and others move down. Do some people move up because they are clever and hardworking, because they are just luckier, because they are slightly corrupt, or because they are better looking with whiter teeth? The explanation that people move up or down depending on their talent and diligence is not proven or disproved by the existing numbers about mobility.

This controversy shows that it is by no means clear what equal *economic* opportunity consists of. But we do know that education is important for success in our society. Yes, Bill Gates dropped out of college before graduating, but it was Harvard he dropped out of, not a neighborhood public, two-year college in his native Seattle. Does everyone have equal educational opportunities in our society? If some people have a substantial discretionary income to spend on the best education for their children so they can attend the best (and most expensive) schools and get the best training, all the while meeting others who are similarly advantaged, and most Americans have little if any income free to spend on the education of their children, do all children have equal opportunities? Do they all start the race at the same starting line?

Discussion Questions

Do all U.S. children have the same educational opportunities? If not how do you suggest we make opportunities more equal? Give reasons for your answer.

WHEN CITIZENS' FREEDOMS CONFLICT

Freedom, we said at the beginning of this chapter, is not a secure possession. Instead it allows claims for freedoms, and often these claims lead to extensive controversies. The debate about affirmative action originated with the claims for equal freedoms made by citizens who had previously been seriously deprived. At other times, debates erupt when freedoms of one person or group run into opposing claims for freedoms of a different person or group. Free institutions give rise to disagreements when the freedoms claimed by one group appear to limit the freedoms of another.

Limits on Free Speech

Imagine this scenario: an English teacher assigns *The Adventures of Huckleberry Finn* to her high school class. Some black students and their parents object to the book because of its excessive use of the word *nigger* and the negative portrayal of black American slaves. They demand that the book not only *not* be assigned as required reading, but also be taken off the library shelves.

Defenders of free speech are outraged; white opponents of racial discrimination support the demands of the black parents.[12]

This story is not purely imaginary. Ever since its publication, Mark Twain's *The Adventures of Huckleberry Finn* has been a controversial book and has been banned in a number of local schools and libraries. The first objection to Twain's book is that the language used and attitudes displayed are racist. These, black students and parents say, cause intense pain to children and adults who are already subject to racial exclusions and harassment in their daily life. Parents, wanting to shield their children from pain, object to the book being assigned. Opponents of banning reject that argument. Although we can all sympathize with parents' desires to shield their children from pain, that desire cannot prevail against First Amendment protections of speech. The First Amendment, they say, protects speech even though it is offensive to some. The First Amendment clearly tells us that we need to bear the pain of being offended by speech for the sake of our own and everyone else's freedom to speak our mind. The fact that certain utterances make other people unhappy is not a sufficient reason for censoring those utterances.

The First Amendment is terse; it does not overwhelm with definitions or fine details. It states: "Congress shall make no law respecting an establishment of religion, or prohibiting the free exercise thereof; or abridging the freedom of speech, or of the press; or the right of the people peaceably to assemble, and to petition the Government for a redress of grievances." It leaves it to later generations to decide what "abridging the freedom of speech" consists of. Obviously we are still struggling with problems of interpretation of this brief phrase.

But the matter does not end there, of course. Speech often provokes action and the parents who object to *The Adventures of Huckleberry Finn* allege that the frequent use of racial epithets and the misrepresentation of black American slaves as unintelligent and superstitious fuels the tendency toward racist action that is always close to the surface in our society. The effect of prevailing racist attitudes is to limit the freedom of blacks, Hispanics, and others. In trying to limit the free speech rights of those who want *The Adventures of Huckleberry Finn* to remain in school libraries and continue to be assigned in courses, the objectors try to protect their own freedoms. In a free society, the freedoms of different groups or individuals tend to conflict and thus create controversy. That clearly adds a whole new dimension to the question of whether this particular book should be assigned to students or be withdrawn from the library. But that added dimension only introduces new uncertainty into this debate. Causal claims that certain sorts of speech are the cause of certain sorts of actions are not always easy to prove. Many students have read *The Adventures of Huckleberry Finn* in school; few have been convicted of attacks on black Americans. But what influence has the book had on the continued prejudice against black Americans? That question seems impossible to answer. It is difficult to provide the facts needed to support banning a book on the grounds that it may inspire racist actions. This line of thinking therefore does not easily yield an entirely convincing conclusion. It does not resolve the controversy.

In recent years, some school districts have removed novels by Maya Angelou, a black American author, and her fellow black American writer, Toni Morrison, from the curriculum because white parents felt that these books portrayed whites in an unfavorable light. But are these complaints comparable to the complaints of black American students and parents? Black Americans have been the constant targets of racial denigration and exclusion for centuries. Speech—name calling, insults, talking patronizingly, telling persons that they were not wanted in this place or that—was always a part of this denigration and exclusion. Against that background we can be sympathetic to the claim that *The Adventures of Huckleberry Finn* cannot be considered merely a literary work, but also, on the part of white society, a component of the continued effort to deny the freedoms of black citizens. The situation of white parents who want to exclude novels from the school curriculum because they present unflattering portraits of whites is quite different. Whites do not have the same history of exclusion and denigration. It is impossible for them to claim that the novels they object to are parts of a more comprehensive action by black Americans of excluding whites from the society. Whites are not an oppressed and excluded minority; they still have most of the money and the power in the society. They object to speech, which should be free—even if it offends.

Discussion Questions

1. *Freedom of speech protects against censorship of speech that offends some listeners. But free speech, like other freedoms, is not unlimited. What sorts of limits on speech do you consider legitimate? Consider cases of speech considered pornographic, unpatriotic, or a threat to national security. Be as specific as you can in your answer.*

2. *If we decide to ban racist speech directed against black Americans, must we ban derogatory speech against whites, Irish, Jews, or Catholics? Give reasons for your answer.*

Freedom of speech and our other liberties are not best thought of as a possession, something we have and we can take pride in owning. Liberty is better thought of as a *process* of negotiation between different groups, groups that are themselves changing over the years, about the precise outlines of the freedoms we allow ourselves and others. Often the claims to freedom of different groups conflict without the hope of a settlement satisfactory to everyone. Controversies die down rather than being resolved only to flare up again at a later time.

Controversies about free speech also arise often between citizens and the government. The Constitution guarantees rights to free speech. It states that "Congress shall make no law . . . abridging the freedom of speech, or of the press." It left it to later generations to decide what "free speech" consists of. What sort of speech is to be protected? Not surprisingly, this question has occasioned many complex debates. Freedom of speech is not a secure possession but a complex process of disagreements and the adjudication of those disagreements. Here is just one episode in the long process of working out what, for different generations, should count as protected speech.

Free Speech and National Security: The Case of Charles Schenck

In 1917, after the United States entered World War I, Congress passed the Espionage Act, which forbade, among many other things, anyone to "willfully obstruct . . . the recruiting or enlistment service of the United States, and . . . [to] willfully utter, print, write, or publish any disloyal, profane, scurrilous, or abusive language about the form of government of the United States, or the Constitution of the United States, or the military or naval forces of the United States, or the flag . . . or the uniform of the Army or Navy of the United States, or any language intended to bring the form of government . . . or the Constitution . . . or the military or naval forces . . . or the flag . . . of the United States into contempt, scorn, contumely, or disrepute"[13]

Discussion Question

Read the wording of the Espionage Act carefully. Do you think that it is a legitimate restriction on freedom of speech? Give reasons for your answer.

In 1917, the Socialist party instructed its secretary, Charles Schenck, to prepare and distribute a sizable number of leaflets urging young men to refuse to be drafted, but to resist only peacefully. Schenck was arrested for violating the Espionage Act. Schenck's defense was that the Espionage Act violated his freedom of speech. The leaflets he distributed objected to the draft on constitutional grounds. It said that drafting men was denying them fundamental freedoms guaranteed by the Thirteenth Amendment of the Constitution.

The Supreme Court rejected Schenck's defense and let his conviction stand. The majority opinion was written by Justice Oliver Wendell Holmes who argued that, of course, freedom of speech was never unlimited. It did not protect the action of someone "falsely shouting fire in a theater and causing a panic." Free speech must be limited to cases where there is no "clear and present danger," that the speech would produce "substantive evils." Whether or not speech was to be free depended in part on the situation. Speech exhorting young men not to allow themselves to be drafted might be protected in peace time but would, in time of war, be a grave threat to the nation and could therefore be prohibited.[14]

The phrases *falsely shouting fire in a theater* and *clear and present danger* have become so much part of our ordinary U.S. vocabulary that we rarely stop and think about their meaning.

Discussion Questions

1. *A clear and present danger suggests a truck bearing down on you as you cross the street, or a bridge collapsing just as you approach it. But were Schenck's 16,000 leaflets threatening to fatally undermine the United States' war effort in 1917? At the height of the war, four million men were in the U.S. Army; half of them stationed in Europe. So 16,000 were not many leaflets considering the size of the military. The leaflets were only distributed locally in New York; they never reached most of the draftees.*

2 *Do you believe that the clear and present danger doctrine presents a threat to our liberties? Give reasons for your answer.*

The First Amendment does not protect "shouting fire falsely in a crowded theater"—using speech to create panic and possible injuries. Your speech is not protected by the First Amendment if you shout racist epithets at me. If you utter falsehoods to misrepresent an automobile you are trying to sell to me, you are guilty of fraud. Fraudulent utterances are not protected free speech; neither are falsehoods uttered deliberately to damage someone's reputation. If you spread lies about someone, you may find that you are liable for libel or slander.

Discussion Question

Lying is, in many cases, not regarded as speech protected by the First Amendment. It is illegal for car salesmen or real estate agents to defraud customers by misrepresenting their product. It is illegal to lie under oath in a court of law. We accept those limitations on free speech. Should we also make it illegal for politicians to mislead voters by misrepresenting their record or making promises they do not keep? Give reasons for your answer.

On the other hand, free speech imposes on every speaker the obligation to speak responsibly, to refrain from claiming to speak the truth where one does not have the relevant evidence, to avoid hurting others by one's speech unless one has good reasons to believe that speaking out is, in this case, in the long run, more important than avoiding harm to others. Free speech rights may be abused not only by those trying to censor speech, but also by those who are invoking their own rights to free speech. In recent years, a number of countries experienced serious riots protesting a series of cartoons derogatory of the prophet Muhammad, published first in a Danish newspaper and then in a number of other European publications. The editor of the Danish newspaper defended his actions by appealing to his rights of free speech. But does that right allow me to insult others just because I think that the insult is funny? What purpose was served that was more important than the well-being of millions of followers of Islam? Further doubt on the validity of the newspaper's free speech defense is cast by the fact, reported by a British newspaper, that "*Jyllands-Posten*, the Danish newspaper that first published the cartoons of the prophet Muhammad that have caused a storm of protest throughout the Islamic world, [previously had] refused to run drawings lampooning Jesus Christ." The newspaper well understood how sensitive many people are to ridicule of their religion. They were unwilling to incur the wrath of their Christian readers but did not care about the pain they would cause readers who are Muslims.[15]

Why is Free Speech Important?

One of the tasks of philosophy is to question what everybody takes for granted. Americans, however they may disagree on other topics, believe fervently that speech should be free and that everyone ought to be allowed to say what they think even though that may at times offend their fellow citizens or put fear in the hearts of government bureaucrats. It is time therefore to ask ourselves whether that shared dogma is defensible. What do we gain by speech being (more or less) free? Is it worth fighting over? Why do we just not let the government set limits on what we can say or what may be written in the press? Doing that would save us a lot of disagreements and a lot of aggravation.

There are obvious objections to free speech. Free speech often offends; it creates or aggravates social conflict. If my speech deeply offends others, they may well bear me a grudge or seek revenge by injuring me. Free speech occasions long-term divisions and conflicts. It allows the spread of opinions destructive of social harmony that undermine morality and other established values in the society. It allows people to question religious beliefs accepted for two thousand years or more and to cast doubt on equally established rules of conduct in sexual and other matters. Its shared beliefs and values give a society strength that allows it to last through difficult times. When those beliefs and values are weakened, so is the entire society. Free speech allows every Tom, Dick, and Harry who know nothing about government to attack those who are running our country and keeping it safe in perilous times or to cast aspersion on our leaders. It allows the ignorant to sow confusion among the citizens, to undermine patriotic devotion and civic dedication. Everyone, however ignorant or irrational, is allowed to slander the economic system that has made our standard of living the highest ever known by human beings. Free speech makes us forget that speaking must depend on thorough study of what one is speaking about and that one must speak responsibly and thoughtfully at all times. It seems to imply, quite erroneously, that everyone's opinion is valuable and worth listening to. It is not self-evident that freedom of speech is as precious as we often proclaim.

The episode about striking *The Adventures of Huckleberry Finn* from the reading list in high school and banning it from the school library shows how much time is spent arguing questions about the precise limits of free speech. Think of the time and energy we could save if we limited speech and avoided these endless controversies. How much paper and ink are wasted on heated debates about free speech! Free speech makes trouble. Imagine how much more calm and peaceful our country would be if not every malcontent were allowed to make a big noise about whatever he or she wants to complain about. If people kept their criticisms to themselves, there would be fewer divisions in the population; we would be more unified and be able to work together to make life better for everyone.

Discussion Question

List as many arguments as you can for and against free speech.

What can we say in behalf of free speech? In the final chapter we will have to reflect about the more general question of why we consider freedom important. Clearly, freedom of speech will prove to be important because freedom, in general, is valuable for reasons to be presented herein.

But freedom of speech is essential, in its own right, as a precondition for democratic government. A people cannot govern themselves—if only indirectly—unless they are able to utter criticisms of the government and discuss alternative policies openly among each other. In chapter 4, we will discuss democracy in more detail and also the critiques of democracy that philosophers have formulated in the last two thousand years. A second defense of free speech depends on our being able to defend democracy as a desirable form of government. But as we shall see, defending democracy requires some effort.

A third argument for protecting speech was first offered by the German philosopher, Immanuel Kant, in a pamphlet first published in 1784, with the title *What Is Enlightenment?* We want adults to think for themselves instead of accepting prejudices and superstitions unthinkingly. In denying free speech to grown men and women or censoring their opinions and limiting what they may read or see on the stage, in the cinema, or on television, governments or churches treat mature adults as if they were children. But if one is never given the opportunity to think for oneself one will not learn to do so. Free speech is necessary for us all to become as level headed, independent, and reasonable in our opinions as we can be.

A further argument for valuing freedom of speech is due to John Stuart Mill, the nineteenth-century English philosopher and advocate of equal freedom for all. Suppose, he said, that an opinion that is prohibited is actually true. The most famous example of that is the case of Galileo, who was forced by a Catholic Church, which maintained that our earth is the center of the universe, to recant his theory that the sun was the center of the solar system. The progress of science was thereby retarded by the church limiting free speech and arrogating to itself the authority to decide matters of truth and error.

Truth and error, Mill argued, come to light only as a result of extended discussion; without it we will never know whether our beliefs are reliable. These discussions must be free in the sense that no opinion is to be excluded from the beginning; all views must be open to discussion and which are most reliable will emerge from the extended conversation. Even if an opinion is not completely correct, that too, Mill points out, will emerge only if opposing ideas may be freely discussed. Free discussion is the school in which we learn the truth. It is indispensable if we are to acquire knowledge about the world in which we live and about ourselves.[16]

Discussion Questions

The case of Galileo shows that religious authorities should stay clear of scientific controversies, such as the debates over astronomy or, today, evolutionary theory. But should ordinary citizens like you and I—neither theologians nor evolutionary biologists—be allowed to participate in the debates about evolution? Does Mill's argument establish that everybody regardless of their technical competence should be allowed free speech? Give reasons for your answer.

LIBERALISM: DEFENDING EQUAL FREEDOMS FOR ALL

What Is Liberalism?

It is time for us to look back over this chapter. We need to notice that there is a shared belief in equal freedom for all human beings underlying the sharp disagreements we have examined. Imagine the conflict over *The Adventures of Huckleberry Finn* a hundred or even fifty years ago, when most white Americans regarded blacks as a lesser breed. The common complaints of black parents over assigning Twain's book in classes would have been ridiculed and ignored. There might well have been threats or actual violence. Not so today. The debate over high school reading lists is conducted against the background of equal freedom for all. However inconvenient and irritating, the complaints of black parents are taken seriously and debated. The same applies to the discussions of affirmative action. They could only become as heated and as complicated as they are today because the claims of blacks and women are now being heard.

This commitment to equal freedom for all is the center of liberal political philosophy. Liberal political institutions "do justice to the equal importance of all persons."[17] Because all are equal in importance as persons, all are entitled to equal freedoms. This belief has a long history. Everyone is familiar with the opening sentences of Thomas Jefferson's Declaration of Independence stating that "all men are created equal." "Liberty, equality and solidarity" were the famous watchwords of the French Revolution at the beginning of the nineteenth century. Today our children recite the Pledge of Allegiance, which promises "liberty and justice for all," in school.

This may be to us, in Jefferson's language, a "self-evident truth" but it has not always been so. The great Greek philosopher Aristotle begins his discussion of politics by distinguishing three grades of human beings: men, women, and slaves. Slaves are equipped to do menial work on the farm or to produce tools, clothing, bread, and wine in different workshops. Masters are suited to occupy themselves with "philosophy or with politics," and, of course, to give orders to slaves and to women. "[T]he male is by nature superior, and the female inferior; and the one rules and the other is ruled."[18] Aristotle's teacher, Plato, was equally convinced that human inequality is a fact. Some men were better, more talented and more deserving of freedom and the goods of this world than others. Throughout the middle ages up to the sixteenth century in Great Britain, human inequality was taken for granted. Human beings were unequal; they were entitled to different degrees of freedom and to different lives. A familiar image in ancient and medieval times likened society to a human body. The persons who rule the state and all their subjects were like the brain; the persons who did the dirty work were comparable, perhaps, to the intestines. All were part of an organic whole; all depended on the cooperation of all the other parts of the body or the other layers of society. But at the same time, all had to do their proper work. For some, that work was ruling and commanding others; for others, their proper work demanded that they obey. For some that meant living a rich and leisurely life and engaging in literature and the arts, as well as the noble arts of warfare. For others, it meant a poor life of drudgery under the command of others.

Liberal political principles, which state all human beings are entitled to equal freedom, have been slowly gaining dominance in the Western world since the sixteenth century. Obviously they have more often been honored in the breach, more often neglected or violated than obeyed, but they have had a powerful hold on the imagination. Those who were excluded, who were denied freedom and treated unequally, appealed to those principles and thereby gained the high moral ground. In the world of the Greeks, slavery was a given. It did not need any justification. In the modern world, at least, arguments were needed to justify the institution and to justify depriving human beings of freedom. The belief in equal freedom stood in the background, and its demands needed to be shown not to apply to slaves or to women. Liberalism, the advocacy of maximum freedom for all, is deeply embedded in U.S. political life. Liberal political principles are central to our culture.

Before we can enter into a discussion of that tradition, we need to note that, in recent years, in the United States the word *liberal* has become a term of criticism among people vying for elected office. Calling someone a liberal is frequently meant and received as an insult. Conservative political candidates who condemn their competitors as liberal accuse these other candidates of committing a large number of political and policy errors, such as spending public moneys irresponsibly and of being excessively permissive, for instance, of homosexuals, or of criminals. Liberals, in the critical sense, are portrayed as indifferent to traditional moral and religious values and inclined to underestimate the importance of the two-person, heterosexual marriage to the well-being of the nation. Conservatives accuse the persons they call liberals of ever expanding government powers and of being contemptuous of individual freedom because they want to regulate everything. In particular, so-called liberals are thought to be hostile to private enterprise and to the inventiveness of privately run companies.

In political theory, the word *liberalism* is used quite differently. It stands for these principles: liberals believe in the importance of individual freedom; they believe that all citizens (and perhaps all human beings) are not only entitled to freedom but are entitled to *equal* freedoms. With this starting point, liberals tend to divide into two different kinds. In the nineteenth century, liberals were mainly interested in economic freedom. They believed in free trade and opposed tariffs and other restraints on trade between countries. Similarly they thought that it was important and beneficial within any country to give free rein to the acquisitive activities of individuals.

This kind of liberalism that pins its hope on unrestrained capitalist economic activity suffered a serious setback in the worldwide depression in the 1930s. The incredible suffering produced by widespread unemployment during those years moved liberals to think of freedom not only as economic freedom for enterprises, but also as a minimal security for individuals and their families. At that point, President Franklin Delano Roosevelt proclaimed his "four freedoms" (to be discussed fully later), of which "freedom from want" was one of the four. Liberalism was transformed into a doctrine that not only insisted on the central importance of freedom, but also insisted that we must be equally free, to the extent that no one must suffer poverty, disease, and social dislocation to a much greater extent than anyone else. The implication of that has been that the government has an important role in assuring that the capitalist economy would be adequately supervised to avoid another world-wide depression on the scale of the 1930s.

In modern times, liberalism begins with the English philosopher, John Locke, who argued in his *Second Treatise on Civil Government* (1689) for a democratic form of government. His exposition begins with the assertion that "by nature" all humans are free and equal, an opinion echoed in Jefferson's Declaration of Independence, with its claim that all human beings received from God the rights to "life, liberty and the pursuit of happiness." These liberal ideas return in the writings of French philosopher, Jean-Jacques Rousseau, whose *Social Contract,* published in 1762, begins with the words "Man is born free and everywhere we see him in chains." Rousseau thought that freedom, although indubitably a right of every human being, was suppressed in many societies. He, too, argues for a form of democratic government to allow everyone the freedom to which they are entitled by nature. The next century saw the development of liberal political philosophy in the book *On Liberty* (1859) by Mill. Here we encounter the same idea that all adults are entitled to equal freedom and that the freedom of each may be limited only where it interferes with the same freedoms of others.

Discussion Questions

What is meant by "equal freedom for all?" Sometimes we mean that no one's concerns should be ridiculed or ignored because of their race or gender. But should the opinions of all count in a public debate regardless of the level of education, intelligence, or expertise of the speaker? Should the stupid, the ignorant, the superstitious, or irrational have the same freedoms to participate in political debates as the intelligent, rational, and well educated? Give reasons for your answer.

Today liberalism is the dominant system in political philosophy. Ever since John Rawls published his *Theory of Justice* in 1971, a large body of work has been produced by philosophers trying to persuade us that a good society will grant far-reaching freedoms to all citizens. Included in their list of freedoms are all the ones with which we are familiar from the Constitution and the Bill of Rights. But one kind of freedom plays a larger role in most liberal political theories than it does in the U.S. Constitution and that is the freedom to shape one's own life as one chooses. The center of contemporary political liberalism is the claim that every person should be able to choose his or her way of life and be allowed to follow that.

When Locke discussed democracy he asked himself how we can make sure that elected representatives faithfully represent the interest of the people who elected them. Locke's answer points out that the representatives, once they return to private life, will be subject to the laws they themselves passed when they were in the government. It is in the representatives' interest to avoid passing laws that will be onerous to them once they return to private life. Representatives that consult their own self-interest in their legislating will represent their voters faithfully.[19]

Obviously that argument would only be persuasive if the representatives were similar sorts of persons and lived similar sorts of lives to those of their fellow citizens who elected them. Locke's argument makes sense in a rather homogeneous society where most citizens live lives similar to those of all other citizens, under the same conditions, with similar goals for their lives, and according to similar values in their daily existence. That may have been true in seventeenth-century England where the right to vote was given only to a small group of large landowners. But it is not true today. People today lead different lives, have different goals, have different conceptions of what is most important in the world and how one should live from one day to the next. The insistence of contemporary liberals that the central freedom for all of us is the liberty to live life as we choose it, reflects the tremendous diversity of forms of life in our world. Pluralism is a central fact of our world and liberals insist that it must be honored in the different lives of all of us.

Discussion Questions

Interpreting "equal freedom for all" as respecting different ways of life, does not, of course, mean that the murderers or rapists should be respected for their life choices. But some people work hard to raise their families, are helpful to their friends and neighbors, and take an active interest in the affairs of their community. Shall we give equal respect to them and to those who spend their time drunk, who neglect their children, throw garbage in the street, and are usually rude to their neighbors? Shall we respect parents who, for religious reasons, refuse to have their children inoculated or to allow them to receive lifesaving blood transfusions? What differences in ways of life deserve our respect? Give reasons for your answer.

Communitarianism

Central to liberalism is the idea that each of us is capable of choosing how best to live—that is, how to shape lives for ourselves so as to make the most of them. Given that capacity, liberalism insists, we ought to be able to exercise it freely and none should be prevented from choosing the best lives for themselves. Everyone should have equal freedom to make those choices. The normative claim of liberalism that we ought to be able to choose how to live, presupposes some factual claims about human nature: that all of us are, in fact, able to make those choices. But not all philosophers are convinced that these factual claims are correct.

Communitarians insist that liberalism exaggerates the extent of individual autonomy; that is, that the values by which we live are not chosen by each of us individually but are, on the contrary, derived by us from the shared values of our communities. This criticism states a commonly known fact that one's values are deeply affected by one's upbringing and the values held by those around one, by family members, friends, teachers, ministers, politicians, and others. The children of Republicans are more likely to vote Republican when they grow up; the children of Catholics are most likely to follow the Catholic faith themselves when they become adults. Few sons of generals become pacifists; not many young people raised in urban landscapes end their lives raising vegetables or milking cows. It is misleading to speak of values, moral and otherwise, as freely chosen when, in fact, we acquire many of our most dearly held values as children from the adults who help us grow into adults. To a considerable extent one's values are not chosen at all but are given to us by our families and larger social environment in the course of our upbringing and education.

Autonomy is, as a matter of fact, limited, the Communitarians insist, and it is not a desirable trait. What I choose, I can later reject. I can change my life and surrender a life I adopted previously. I can say that I made a mistake when I chose a certain way of life or certain values. Chosen values or ways of life lack seriousness and the weight of deeply held values. Moral values or values about what really matters in human life are not so easily jettisoned. I share those values with my community; they have impersonal force; I cannot alter them at will. The liberal's doctrine of individual autonomy does not do justice to the power of one's values, to the weight they carry for each of us, manifest, for instance, in the burden of guilt we experience when violating accepted moral values. Values I choose autonomously need not make me feel guilty when I ignore them. I can simply change my mind. The values of the community are not that easily surrendered.[20, 21] Liberals reject these criticisms.[22]

Discussion Question

Many people hold contradictory opinions about their values. They say, on the one hand, that everyone more or less chooses his or her values. But they also believe that one's values are determined to a significant extent by one's family and social environment. Which of these two inconsistent beliefs is more likely to be true? Give reasons for your answer.

Is Liberalism Valid?

Liberal theory faces two major challenges: the first is to support the claim that all human beings are entitled to equal freedom. After all, most of humanity in the last ten thousand years has agreed that men are superior to women and that slavery is a perfectly justified institution. In the West, superior men were white; elsewhere they were Greek men, Chinese, or Kikuyu rather than Ibo. Male supremacy conjoined with xenophobia has held sway and still does in most parts of the world. Xenophobia is, for sure, not unknown in the United States. The number of groups in the United States advocating an end to all immigration has risen sharply in the last few years.[23] If we, on the contrary, continue to assert that all adult human beings have a legitimate claim to equal liberty, we need to support that opinion in some way. We need to show that ours is more than an irrational prejudice.

Liberal theorists have not done well with that challenge. In the eighteenth century, liberals simply claimed that God has endowed all of us with equal rights to liberty. But how did Locke or Jefferson know that? There is no place in the Bible where equal liberty is decreed by God, the prophets, or Jesus. Jesus talked a lot about treating the poor well and about loving and aiding one's neighbor. He treated some women with great respect, but nowhere does he tell us that all human beings should be equally free. It is not clear where the eighteenth-century belief in divine backing for liberal principles comes from.

In our day, liberal theorists tell us that if we consulted everyone under proper conditions, they would all agree to liberal principles. Thus, Rawls imagines a situation where all humans are ignorant of their personal interests and are therefore able to think about the world from an objective and impartial point of view. In that situation, he asserts, all would agree to a version of liberal political principles. All would agree that everyone is entitled to equal freedom.[24] Martha Nussbaum finds a corresponding agreement among actual humans with respect to her particular formulation of liberal principles.[25] Both justifications of liberalism assume what they should prove. If you consult the opinion of all and are prepared to give equal weight to everyone's opinion, you have already assumed that human beings are, in some fundamental respect, equal. But this equality was supposed to be proved, not assumed, for the sake of argument. Liberal theorists today are in no better position with respect to the validity of liberal principles than were their forebears in the seventeenth and eighteenth centuries.

Discussion Questions

Not everyone in our world agrees that men and women are entitled to equal freedom. Consider the following statement:

> *What does it mean to be one flesh? Several times in the New Testament, this term is mentioned in reference to a husband and wife, and each time, it speaks of two becoming one . . . two individuals . . . man and woman . . .becoming one. When the two become one, there is now only one head . . . the husband. Ephesians 5:23—'**For the husband is the head of the wife, even as Christ is the head of the church: . . .** ' So, we are not talking about some two-headed monster. Because the husband is to be the head of the home, the wife's role in the home is to be in submission to her husband. Ephesians 5:22—'Wives, **submit yourselves unto your own husbands, as unto the Lord.**' To be in submission means 'to yield, resign or surrender to the power, will or authority of another.' Let me add right here, this is not just an outward act. True submission comes from within the heart. It is quite easy to submit on the outside and all the time be rebelling on the inside. If you are trying to live like that, I guarantee that you are having constant turmoil within. Real peace only comes when we acknowledge the God-given role of our husband as the head and we in submission to them.[26]*

Defend equal freedom for women against that statement.

What Do Liberal Principles Mean? Rawls and Nozick on Equality

Liberalism defends equal freedom for all adult human beings, but that, of course, is a terribly vague statement. The second challenge liberalism faces is to specify what this equality consists of. Jefferson owned slaves, and Locke profited from the slave trade. Once you look at the details of the *Second Treatise on Government*, the democracy Locke argued for turned out to exclude slaves, women, and wage workers from political participation. His conception of God-given equality is clearly quite different from ours today.

But even contemporary theorists think about equality in different terms. Some Liberal theorists defend a version of New Deal equality in which the government not only has an obligation to exclude no one through legislation from participating in politics and the economic life of the nation, but also has a positive obligation to see to it that everyone has a minimum standard of a good life. Other theorists, who also believe that all adult human being have equal rights, conclude from that premise that enormous differences in wealth are legitimate to the extent that they benefit those in the society who are worst off. Others believe that government efforts to alleviate the suffering of the poor not only violate equal human freedoms of all, but are also, in practice, counterproductive. The same premise apparently yields opposite conclusions.

Rawls argues that liberalism commits us to the following two principles of justice:

(a) each person has the same indefeasible claim to a fully adequate scheme of equal basic liberties, which scheme is compatible with the same scheme of liberties for all; and

(b) social and economic inequalities are to satisfy two conditions: first, they are to be attached to offices and positions open to all under conditions of fair equality of opportunity; and second, they are to be to the greatest benefit of the least advantaged members of society (the difference principle).[27]

The first of these principles asserts that all are entitled to equal liberty. The second part of the second principle is of particular interest here. It states that existing economic inequalities in a society need to be justified and envisages this sort of justification: if we are going to have highly skilled heart transplant surgeons, we need to pay them more than people who clean floors or flip burgers to the extent that it is in the interest of the people who do menial jobs and earn minimum wage that heart transplants be available when someone needs one. Paying the heart surgeon more than the fast-food cook is justified if it serves the interest of the least advantaged. To the extent that the rich spend their money on solid gold bathroom faucets or buying mink coats for call girls, the income differences are not justified and should be ameliorated by governmental action. Implicit in this second clause of Rawls's second principle of justice is a whole program of governmental action to even out all those economic inequalities among citizens that do not benefit the bottom layers of the social pyramid.

The same liberal principles that Rawls appeals to—that all adult humans have equal rights—can lead a theorist to different conclusions. Starting out with traditional liberal principles, Robert Nozick argues that economic inequality—however large—is legitimate and that government actions to reduce these inequalities are coercive and therefore threats to human freedom. His book *Anarchy, State and* Utopia,[28] begins with the words, "Individuals have rights, and there are things no person or group may do to them without violating their rights" (ix). The first part of the sentence is uncontroversial; the second asserts, in effect, that rights are absolute and that it would be wrong to limit these rights under any conditions.

We need to stop and think about that for a moment. The freedoms we have spoken of so far—freedom to speak one's mind and to publish material, the right to life, to being secure, and the right to equal access to the opportunities offered by one's society—are all conditional; they may be limited under specific conditions. Free speech is not protected when it endangers others or the nation as a whole: it is illegal to distribute classified military information. It is also illegal to libel others by spreading hurtful lies about them. Our right to life is curtailed when the country's defense compels us to risk that life or, perhaps, when we unlawfully take the life of another. We commonly think of rights and freedoms as powerful but as limited. But as Nozick sees it, there are some rights that are never limited by circumstances, and to infringe on these rights is always wrong.

From this beginning, Nozick goes on to raise the question of when, if ever, is it legitimate for the government to take property from individuals—for instance, through taxation— to redistribute goods from those who have very much to those who have very little. To answer that question, Nozick determines under what conditions property is legitimately acquired or transferred to another. Property is acquired legitimately when someone's acquisition does not "worsen the situation of another"(175). Imagine an early settler family finding its way to North America. The continent is sparsely populated. The family is fortunate to find itself on shore where no one else lives; there are no settlements and no signs of gardens or farms. So they go to work, felling trees, building a dwelling, putting the seeds, which they had the foresight to bring with them, in the ground. They are lucky and manage to catch some wild goats and domesticate them, and before long, they live a frugal but contented life on the new continent. The farm they are building up is their legitimate property; no one is burdened by their efforts of cultivating their small portion of the wilderness. The family thrives; they have children who take over the property when they reach adulthood and so on through the generations. Each generation manages to add a bit to the family wealth through hard work or voluntary trades with others. The family's original wealth was acquired legitimately; it was increased by equally legitimate means. If today, the descendants of the original settler family are among the wealthiest Americans, their ownership credentials are beyond reproach because they acquired every part of it legitimately.

Here we return to the idea that some rights are absolute. Among those Nozick counts property rights. How can that be, you say. Do we not owe the government taxes to pay for schools, roads, or defense? Nozick replies, "Taxation of earnings from labor is on a par with forced labor"(169). If you pay taxes, the hours you work to earn the tax payments is time you do not work for yourself or to meet your own interests and needs. If you are forced to pay taxes—

you do not give a sum of money to the government out of sheer patriotism or your love for those who govern you—you are *forced* to work for those hours or days needed to earn your tax money. What else are you doing then, but doing forced labor? In our society, where we value freedom, and are—according to liberal principles—entitled to equal freedom, forced labor is unacceptable.

Discussion Question

Let us accept for the moment Nozick's idea that we own legitimately whatever we or our ancestors acquired without harming anyone else. On that principle how many Americans who are well off today can claim to own their property legitimately? Give reasons for your answer.

The conclusion seems inescapable that taxing citizens to finance schemes for bettering the condition of those who are not well off violates the freedom of those with money, which they have presumably, earned with their own hard work. Notice that Rawls and Nozick agree that all are entitled to equal freedoms but use that premise to argue for different conclusions. Rawls argues against economic inequalities unless they benefit those who are worse off— as in the case of higher pay for heart transplant surgeons. Nozick argues for the opposite view, that taking money from the better off to improve the lot of the worse off violates the liberal freedoms we believe all are entitled to.

Discussion Questions

Nozick assumes that citizens are unwilling to pay taxes to help the less fortunate. If the government does so, it needs to force citizens to participate in this redistributive project by paying taxes. But is it possible that Nozick is mistaken about this?

Do you think that you have some obligation to help the less fortunate? If your answer is "yes," who do believe deserves help?

Do you believe that the government has a legitimate role in the project of helping the unfortunate? Give reasons for your answer.

Acquiring Property Legitimately

How Can These Two Authors Reach Such Opposite Conclusions?

Some get rich because they are especially talented at making money; some are lucky, and some are less scrupulous than others. Often those different factors interact: It takes a special talent to notice when luck smiles on you, when circumstances present you with an opportunity to make a great deal of money. The rest of us might just stumble right past this great chance because we do not have the same commercial intelligence.

If you are smart enough to take opportunity by the horns, Nozick thinks, you deserve the wealth that comes to you as a result. "Not so" says Rawls because we are not entitled to the wealth we earn due to special talents. A principle widely shared and accepted by both Rawls and Nozick says that we own legitimately what we worked for. Property owned fairly is property we worked for. But our talents are ours from birth: that is, they are encoded in our genes. We do not have them because we worked hard in school or at previous jobs; we get them from nature. If our special intelligence, artistic talent, or athletic prowess belongs to us by nature, the wealth it earns us is not ours due to our hard work and thus is not owned legitimately. Hence the ingenious entrepreneur is not entitled to a larger income than the hardworking plodder. To be sure the entrepreneur, the famous artist, or the star athlete must work hard to develop their talent. But they are successful because they have a talent to develop. The untalented may work equally hard but their results are less spectacular. Both should be rewarded in proportion to their work; not in proportion to their talents. Both Rawls and Nozick agree that we own legitimately what we, or someone else, earned. But they disagree on what we can count as earnings. Nozick is willing to regard the property of the extraordinarily gifted as earned; Rawls is not.

Discussion Question

Are we legitimate owners of the results of special talents we have? Give reasons for your answer.

DIFFERENT FREEDOMS:
FREEDOM FROM AND FREEDOM TO

The debate about affirmative action is a debate about one aspect of freedom—that is, the freedom to compete with everyone else for the rewards the society has to offer. But what is that freedom? As long as black men and all women were segregated by law, as long as they were forced to go to inferior schools and few good jobs were open to them, they were not free to compete. But once the 1964 Civil Rights Act had been passed, and all segregation, mandated by state law in a number of Southern states, had been declared illegal, did black Americans now not have the same freedoms of whites? No longer could segregationists call on the police to enforce exclusions of black Americans; black Americans now had the same right to attend schools, to apply for good jobs, to move into previously whites-only parts of town, or to vote. To be sure, schools and employers could still refuse to consider applications by women or black men; one can be constrained by the government as well as by private groups. Equal freedom consists in not being prevented from doing what government or fellow citizens allows others. If the laws that limit what we may do are the same for all of us, and private prejudice does not hold some of us back, then all of us are free to the same extent. This kind of freedom is often called "freedom from"; it consists in not being prevented by law, by the police or other arms of the government, or by private groups from doing something. It is, as Isaiah Berlin put it, "an open door." If all have the same doors open for them, then all have equal freedoms.[29]

But consider once more the line from President Johnson's speech at Howard University: "You do not take a person who, for years, has been hobbled by chains and liberate him, bring him up to the starting line of a race and then say "'you are free to compete with all the others,' and still justly believe that you have been completely fair."[30] Sometimes opening a door is not enough. People for whom certain doors have been closed literally for centuries may not be prepared to pass through them once they have been opened by law. Having attended, on the whole, inferior schools compared to those attended by white children, being, in addition, forced to work only the worst paying jobs, young people coming from black families were perhaps legally free to apply to Harvard for their college education, but they had neither the money nor the academic preparation to be able to get admitted, or if admitted, to attend Harvard. They did not know anyone who attended prestigious schools, which until then had been reserved for whites. They were not familiar with what you need to do to get admissions to such schools. If they managed to gain admission they would have had great difficulties functioning in an environment so utterly alien to them. Do we still want to say that they were as free as middle-class white young people to attend any school they chose? It seems heartless to answer that question in the affirmative. Freedoms that are mine by law do not seem fully real if my circumstances prevent me from using them. It would be cruel to overlook that and criticize me for not availing myself of the freedoms that are made available to me. Considering that, many philosophers say that there is a second sense of freedom, sometimes called "freedom to," which requires not only the (legal) permission to do certain things but also the material wherewithal, health, minimal economic resources, educational preparation, or whatever else may be necessary to use the opportunities that have been opened for one. On that conception, freedom requires not only the absence of restraints but also the minimal conditions needed to avail oneself of negative freedom, if one so chooses.

"Freedom to" became an important idea in U.S. public policy when, in the 1930s, President Roosevelt proclaimed the Four Freedoms. It was the aim of his administration, often referred to as the "New Deal," to assure those freedoms for all citizens.

> In the future days, which we seek to make secure, we look forward to a world founded upon four essential human freedoms.
>
> The first is freedom of speech and expression—everywhere in the world.
>
> The second is freedom of every person to worship God in his own way—everywhere in the world.
>
> The third is freedom from want—which, translated into world terms, means economic understandings which will secure to every nation a healthy peacetime life for its inhabitants—everywhere in the world.
>
> The fourth is freedom from fear—which, translated into world terms, means a world-wide reduction of armaments to such a point and in such a thorough fashion that no nation will be in a position to commit an act of physical aggression against any neighbor—anywhere in the world.[31]

The struggle for freedom has been a powerful moving force in our history. But in this history, different ideas of freedom have come to the fore. Different generations of Americans have understood freedom differently. The framers and signers of the Declaration of Independence considered themselves free if they possessed "life, liberty and the pursuit of happiness" or as they put it more succinctly later in the same paragraph, their "safety and happiness." Freedom, in their eyes, was protection against a tyrannical government that threatened to interfere in their lives and the security of their property. It was freedom from. In the 1930s, Roosevelt spoke about a different conception of freedom when he proclaimed freedom from want and freedom from fear as aims of the government. Every citizen was to be guaranteed not only freedom of speech and religion and political participation, but also a decent living to be enjoyed in peace. Instead of being the enemy from which the Constitution was to shield us, the government was now the agency that would guarantee us freedom to in the form of economic security.

Discussion Questions

Consider the difference between freedom from and freedom to as applied to physically handicapped persons. Does the government have an obligation to make public buildings wheelchair accessible, or should we be satisfied that no laws prevent persons in wheelchairs from entering, say, a courthouse or a state capital? Or consider a comparable debate concerning the education to be offered to learning-disabled children. Give reasons for your answers.

What the Government Does to Protect Freedom To

When we think about freedom as requiring economic security, pictures come to mind of the poor, the helpless, and the destitute. Much of the debate between the traditional idea of freedom as a defense against abuses of government power and the more modern idea of freedom, which also includes government providing economic security, tends to develop into a debate about social welfare programs designed to ease the lives of the poor. But that is a one-sided understanding of the idea of freedom as economic security.

We expect our government to assure everyone a minimal range of life options. Prominent among those is providing educational opportunities. The rich can afford to send their children to private schools and private colleges. The government provides public schools, community colleges, and state colleges and universities for the children not only of the poor, but also of the middle classes, who would not be able to afford tuition at private educational institutions. Although many people look askance at welfare programs for the poor, they firmly expect the government to provide some old-age pensions for them when it comes time for them to stop working.

Freedom provides the possibility of running one's own life. For the founders, their large landholdings provided that possibility. All they needed was the assurance that the government would not interfere with them. For the ordinary city dweller in our time, the government needs to provide a floor under the economy, and it needs to provide education and work for all. But, in addition, it needs to provide a wealth of information to enable us to live lives that we have some control over. In our consumer society, a great deal of information is required to make reasonable choices. One more aspect of freedom to is the government's provision of consumer information. Ordinary purchases in the market of consumer goods have become quite complex. It is more and more difficult for the ordinary buyer to find out whether products are safe. That applies to machines like lawn mowers or to furniture like baby cribs, as well as to items designed to make us safer, such as motorcycle helmets. The government now expends considerable funds and energy to test consumer products and to make sure that they are provided with labels warning consumers of dangerous uses. In the background of these efforts stands the idea that freedom requires security—not only economic security but also security in the use of consumer goods, which have become too varied and too complicated for ordinary consumers to be able to select those that are safe and to use them safely.

Our freedom involves citizen participation in government. Representatives are chosen in periodic elections; they are paid by the government and provided with the perquisites of office such as ornate meeting rooms, libraries, secretarial help, and travel funds. The government provides for local, county, state, and federal elections and provides funds for all the representatives elected in those different places. Would you want to say that we are free to vote and to participate in government as long as no armed police or soldiers prevented you from voting, even though the government, as an economy measure, had dissolved the office of voter registration and dismissed the election commissioners? One of the ways we expect the government to provide freedom to for us is by organizing elections and funding the work of the persons elected.

Sudden disasters, such as hurricanes, floods, earthquakes, and droughts, disrupt the free life of anybody who falls victim to such disasters, whether rich or poor. Suddenly deprived of a home, persons are unable to meet their daily needs. They may have considerable financial resources, but those are all of little avail when the town is devastated by a tornado or by a tsunami wave. We expect our government to provide first aid to these victims regardless of the size of their savings accounts or their investments.

Providing economic security, moreover, does not only consist of giving economic support to those who have little or nothing or to those who work hard, but do not manage to earn enough to support their families, but to all. Local governments, as well as states, frequently give tax breaks or sizable cash incentives to locate manufacturing plants or shopping malls in their region rather than somewhere else. Such subsidies are given to private concerns by the government to create jobs for the citizens of the region. Private companies receive money or tax breaks from the government in the expectation that they will increase employment for ordinary citizens. To preserve the jobs of miners, the federal government has given hefty subsidies to coal mines since the early years of the twentieth century. It is generally accepted that job creation is a legitimate concern of the government. For that purpose, it may give money provided by taxpayers to private companies to make some jobs more secure.

Providing economic security also involves helping those who are doing well today but whose economic future is threatened. Notable examples of that are the government subsidies to agriculture, which are defended on the grounds that farmers, without price support, would not be able to stay in business. Farm subsidies support their jobs and their way of life. We believe that the role of the government includes assuring citizens that they can secure decent employment. We look to the government, not only to provide economic security for those who would be destitute without that help, but also to those who would suffer from serious economic losses without government financial assistance. Welfare—that is, government support that is sometimes monetary but often also provides information, education, training or infrastructure—is not only for the poor. Government subsidies go to the steel industry and to oil and coal companies. Truckers are subsidized in the form of a network of federally funded interstate highways. Newspaper and magazine publishers receive government subvention in the form of reduced postage for mailing newspapers and magazines. Many companies commercialize products that result from government financed research in universities and hospitals. Much of the research and development for successful medicines is done at public expense. All citizens look to the government to protect their economic well-being. Depending on whose numbers we use, the government spends as much or more on "corporate welfare" as on welfare programs for the lowest income people in the United States.[32]

We hear a great deal today about the blessings of the free market untrammeled by government regulation. If such a market exists anywhere, it does not exist in the United States. Our government anxiously watches the performance of the economy. It raises the interest rate at the slightest sign of inflationary pressures; it lowers that rate if the economy is sluggish. Few observers complain about this government interference with the goal that everybody work and live under economically beneficial circumstances. (We will return to the free market in Chapter 3.)

Discussion Question

Using the Internet, make a list of twenty or more government programs favoring specific limited groups of citizens. Decide which of these programs are defensible and which are not, giving reasons for your decision in each case. State the criteria you used in making your decision.

The conception of "freedom to' is presupposed by government projects to provide services for those who are not wealthy. Those services range from public education to old age pensions in the form of Social Security, from support for the unemployed or insurance to cover injuries sustained on the job to food stamps, medical, and other housing subsidies, programs to retrain people for new jobs, and many others. These services also involve disaster relief when storms strike, as well as support for agriculture and other businesses that are in danger of failing without help from the government. They include financial support for industries to encourage them to create new jobs. Quite obviously some of these programs are controversial. This controversy only demonstrates that we, in our society, operate with two different conceptions of freedom. When the government seems to us to interfere excessively, we fall back on the eighteenth-century idea of freedom from as the absence of coercion. When our life is threatened by natural disasters, economic crisis, the economic effects of technological change, an excessive demand for information required for making reasonable choices, we are much more inclined to adopt the New Deal conception of freedom to, which expects the government to bolster our freedom by preserving jobs and a stable economy or advise us on consumer choices.

Discussion Question

In practice everyone accepts government assistance. No one refuses help from the National Guard when a flood has forced them to wait for rescue on the roof of their house. The important debate is about individual cases of government assistance programs, which we disagree over passionately. For example, consider flood insurance provided by the government to people who build their houses on the ocean's edge in areas subject to periodic flooding. Do you think that these persons are entitled to government subsidized flood insurance? Give reasons for your answer. Can you think of comparable cases?

Review Question

The burden of this chapter has been to show that freedom is not something we possess securely but a complex process of negotiations over the conflicting freedoms.

Make as long a list as you can of other common conflicts over freedom: for instance, clashes over dress codes, smoking in public, or mandatory use of seat belts.

Classify the examples you find into the different sorts of conflicts they are: where one person's freedom appears to threaten that of another, where people claim different rights or different freedoms, where rights conflict, and where people understand freedom in different ways.

Does a commitment to a liberal political philosophy help us resolve some or all of these conflicts?

WHAT IS PHILOSOPHY?

Philosophers like to begin with the most abstract questions and work their way down to more concrete levels. Those more concrete questions are sometimes treated separately as "applied" philosophy. In this chapter, we have followed the opposite strategy, engaging first in specific and concrete controversies only to proceed slowly to the more abstract issues about liberalism, the different conceptions of what freedom is, and questions about defending one's choice of liberal political principles. In this way we have seen how the abstract questions philosophers discuss, which so often baffle the beginner in philosophy, gain their importance because they underlie the more specific, everyday conflicts and disagreements. The specific debates about free speech, about who should be allowed to say and to read what, as well as debates about the distribution of opportunities, all presupposed the belief that all adults are entitled to equal freedom. The specific disagreements discussed previously in this chapter arise because we all subscribe to liberal political principles that all are entitled to equal freedom. But these liberal political principles bring their own questions and disagreements with them, which philosophers discuss at great length. These discussions gain their importance from providing the foundations for debates about more concrete and familiar disagreements.

It is now time to ask the most abstract philosophical question of all: what is philosophy?

In the course of answering that question I will also explain why this chapter follows the unconventional path it takes.

Western philosophy begins with Plato, who lived in Athens, Greece, in the fifth century BC. There were philosophers before him but only fragments of their work have been preserved. Plato's writings are the first works in Western philosophy to have survived the turmoil of twenty-five hundred years of Western history. Plato presents his philosophy in the form of conversations—dialogues—in which Plato's teacher, Socrates, asks ordinary persons questions about the important issues in human life: about courage and how we learn, about justice and the good society, about love and the human soul, and about death and survival after death. Philosophy treats topics of concern to everyone. *All people will at times ask philosophical questions.*

Socrates, who is the central figure in Plato's *Dialogues*, had been Plato's teacher. He himself never wrote anything. For him, philosophy consisted of conversations between ordinary people in which they try to discover how to live well individually and in groups. By not writing down the conclusions of these conversations, or even the conversations themselves, Socrates may have indicated that what matters in philosophy is, primarily, the conversation. Philosophy is important insofar as it enables us to improve our life. We do not learn from books how to live well but from our own intellectual and moral efforts. Many life situations confront us with difficult decisions that demand of us that we think carefully. No better way of thinking about difficult life questions exists than to talk to others—that is, to persons we know and trust. Philosophical conversation is an ingredient in running one's life thoughtfully. It is an aspect of living well. Hence each person must think for himself or herself about life and how to live it well. The conclusions others draw when thinking may well be relevant to my life also. But as long as I am not willing to think about my life and how I am living it, those philosophical conclusions are of purely academic interest. They do not serve to make mine a good life. By not thinking about my own life, I signify that living a good life is no concern of mine.

This is the Socratic form of philosophy. Plato, who revered Socrates, presented that form of philosophy for us in his dialogues. But he also was the founder of a different kind of philosophy. That sort of philosophy is not done by all human beings when they talk to each other while trying to find their way in life, but it is done by a special group of persons who call themselves philosophers, who spend all their time thinking about the sorts of problems that come up in ordinary daily life. But because they do this all the time, their reflections tend to be much more detailed than what we ordinarily think about in our Socratic conversations. They become fairly technical, and ordinary persons, who have to put food on the table and clothes on their backs, have less time for philosophical conversations and often find them difficult to follow. Philosophy becomes a specialty taught in colleges and universities, fully accessible only to specialists. The technical, professional philosophy has the same starting points as Socratic philosophy, but it is no longer conducted in the context of ordinary people trying to be thoughtful about their life problems. It becomes a conversation between persons—many of whom are indeed quite clever—who try to clarify intellectual problems that fascinate them.

These professional philosophers have a rather different idea of philosophy from Socrates. Their goal is to construct "theories"—of morality, of politics, of knowledge, and so on. They are looking for results that one can write down, read, and debate. Much professional philosophy seeks results in the form of books or articles that are fully accessible only to specialists in the field and which, however persuasively argued, give rise to unending controversies among the specialists. Socratic philosophy seeks results one can see in persons whose thoughtful consideration of their own lives and those of others have led them to grow and to reach greater wisdom and maturity as persons.

This book continues the tradition of Socratic philosophy. It takes up questions about freedom, about property, about democracy, and about morality in the everyday contexts in which we encounter them. We began with the plight of the Texas dentist who buys land to develop it and then finds that he is prevented by environmental legislation from doing so. Are his freedoms violated? Many of us believe that to be free means to be left alone to live our lives as we please without interference by government or church. But, of course, many of us also look to the government to provide security—that is a part of freedom, not only security from violent neighbors, but also in the face of natural or economic disasters, when hurricanes, unemployment, or unexpected grave illness strikes. Many, who are quite comfortable now, expect the government to make sure that their businesses will survive into the future by providing various subsidies. By subscribing to the two different conceptions of freedom we embroil ourselves in difficult questions. How extensive are the services we expect from the government? How much should those who have to pay taxes support those who do not have to? Abortion has provoked bitter controversies. Should we allow it as an exercise of a woman's freedom to use her body as she chooses, or must we limit that freedom because the embryo is a human being with rights to life just like the rest of us?

But these questions, many people think, are really matters of opinion. With respect to the freedoms of different persons and the conflicts between them, different persons have different ideas. We may try to persuade others, whose opinions are different from our own, to change their minds, but we are rarely successful in that. The disagreements we encounter in the debates we have considered in this chapter cannot be resolved by showing that one party to a dispute is right beyond the shadow of a doubt and others wrong. People have different opinions and that is all there is to it. There is not much point in engaging in long, philosophical arguments about freedom, or about specific freedoms, about who has a right to do what.

This view is widely held. It is not false, but it exaggerates the difficulties in reaching agreement about many philosophical issues. It also does not see that conversations about questions in philosophy are important even if the conversation does not end with everyone agreeing. There are many questions that are matters of opinion where one cannot expect to find clearly correct and clearly incorrect answers. But conversations about these matters are nevertheless terribly important, both in close relationships as well as in free societies. Convincing others of the truth of our own beliefs is not the only, or even the most important, goal of human conversations.

Close relationships in which the partners are unwilling to confront their own and the other's moral and political judgments remain on the surface and are always threatened by instability. Intimate relationships involve unity; the two partners are, as we say, "joined together"; they are "one." But to the extent that they never confront each other's deepest moral stances, their unity is shaky. Their unity is strong only when they are willing to think about what moral values they need to transmit to their children and what sorts of relationships between men and women they need to model for them? What will they teach them about the importance of good citizenship. How will the father and the mother react when they discover that their teenage daughter has been sleeping with her boyfriend? As long as their ideas about these and many other questions are left unexplored, the couple's unity is untested and may, when facing a test, crumble.

Imagine two young persons about to finish college who are each beginning to think of settling down and starting their own family. They meet; they like one another; they spend time together; and they discover that they enjoy each other's company. In their conversations they also find that they agree in many important respects: they seem to have a similar sense of what is important in their lives and what less so. They seem to agree to a considerable extent about what it is right to do and what not. They both take their family life seriously; each likes the other's family and is welcomed warmly by them. They become good friends, but it is quite a while before they begin to think to themselves that maybe they love that other person. They are giving themselves time to see how the relationship develops. Their close connection grows and both are thinking to themselves about perhaps sharing their future together, but they have not yet shared those thoughts with each other.

One day the woman discovers that she is pregnant. After being first confused and startled, she finds herself filled with happiness at the prospect of having a child with this man who has become dear to her. She had not planned to get married anytime soon or to have children, but confronted by the fact of her pregnancy, she finds that she would be happy to change her plans. When she shares her happy plans with her boyfriend he begins to talk about her having an abortion. His first reaction is clearly the opposite of hers. She is appalled. Their conversation shows a deep disagreement about abortion; he is ready to consider it, whereas she thinks that it is quite wrong. Equally hurtful to her is his readiness to encourage her to have an abortion. Obviously he does not share her happy anticipation of a shared family life and children. Maybe, she thinks, he really does not love her. He is afraid of being encumbered by her and by a child. He is not ready to settle down with her. Their conversation quickly degenerates into an angry fight. He slams out of the house. She cries herself to sleep.

He returns in the middle of the night, apologetic about having been angry and not really having listened to her and her feelings and thoughts about the pregnancy. But the disagreement remains. If these two are going to continue along their path toward a harmonious lifelong relationship, they need to talk about abortion and about their different feelings about it to come to some compromise on this difficult topic. She says that she could never have an abortion because her church forbids it. He reminds her that her church also forbids the use of birth control and of premarital sex and that neither of those prohibitions has ever troubled her. She needs to think more deeply about her feelings about abortion and what supports them. Is she just repeating what the nuns and the priests have been drumming into her for many years? What is her reason for being so appalled at the idea of having an abortion? He, on his side, needs to ask himself why he did not hesitate for a moment to recommend an abortion. Did he perhaps not take abortion seriously enough? Had he really ever thought about it? He needs to think about children and about long-term commitments, especially to this woman.

Building strong committed relationships requires work. One kind of work is just having extended conversations where values seem to differ. At issue is not only the question of the value of human life, even prenatally, but also questions about sexuality. Does either of them think of sex as slightly sinful and justified only if it results in children? What does each of them think about the role of women? Is it to have children and raise them, while the man goes out and earns a living, or do they agree that working and raising children are the jobs of both in the marriage? In the course of these conversations each comes to understand more clearly his or her own thoughts and feelings about the issue as well as those of the other person. Couples that refuse that work of exploring their disagreements weaken their relationship. It is bound to remain superficial if it leaves the deepest emotions of each partner untouched.

Individuals are not the only persons that need to engage in serious discussions of moral issues. Political communities act; they need to formulate policies to act on. In many situations, the policies adopted are shaped by the people with power. They simply do what they believe to be right or to be in their best interest. Societies where freedom is not valued will be ready to impose the opinions of the powerful on everybody. Fundamentalist societies decree how women will dress, whether they will be allowed to go to school, or whether they will be allowed to have jobs outside the home. The women themselves are usually not consulted; their preferences are ignored. They are denied the freedom to make important decisions about their own lives. Imposing the moral and religious ideas of some portions of a society on everybody else without consulting those others denies them the freedom to run their own lives. To the extent that ours is a free society, disagreements about serious moral issues may not be settled by some groups forcing their opinion on everyone else. Instead we discuss openly such serious moral issues as the questions about abortion, about what sorts of written material should be banned because it is pornographic or racist, about the obligations that we have to each other as fellow citizens, and about the extent to which those of us who have should help take care of those who have not. Freedom is preserved only where conversations over serious disagreements take the place of coercion. Everyone's opinion must be heard. Whatever final compromise is acted on by the government must have emerged from a public discussion in which all could freely say what they thought about a given issue and where everyone's opinion is heard and counts.

In political communities, it is destructive to say "everybody has his or her own opinion" because unless all opinions are consulted and listened to respectfully, the opinions of some override those of others, and freedom is compromised. Refusal to confront disagreements about difficult issues—often issues in morality or in politics—can have only one outcome, namely that the powerful enact their opinions and everyone else is deprived of their full freedom of participation in political decision making. Refusal to engage in these public discussions of morality allows a few to dominate the entire society and to restrict freedoms.

Freedom—the free institutions in which we can confront and try to resolve peacefully the many disagreements we have about our own freedoms and those of others—can exist only in a society that is willing to engage in philosophical conversations. These philosophical conversations are difficult and they are often frustrating. It is quite tempting to want to avoid them. Avoid them we do when we say, "Oh, these are just subjective opinions" or "Everyone has his or her own opinion." Saying that, we avoid the difficult conversations about the fundamental values and issues that are the essence of a free society. We allow those with political power to make choices for all of us regardless of whether their moral convictions coincide with ours. We cannot very well boast of our freedoms, and at the same time avoid engaging with our fellow citizens in conversations about what divides us. Philosophy is an essential part of a free society.

QUESTIONS FOR REFLECTION AND DISCUSSION

1. Look again at this story about the Texas dentist who is prevented from developing his acreage by the Endangered Species Act. Suppose the dentist is quite elderly. He says, "These endangered insects will not be extinct before I die. Why should I care what happens after my death?" Clearly environmental actions aim to maintain a livable natural environment not only for ourselves but also for future generations. But do we have any obligations to future generations? Why should we not feel free to exploit existing natural resources to the fullest and let future generations take care of themselves?

   If you want to say that, yes, we owe something to our children and the children of other people in our generation, and to their children, what precisely do we owe them? Should we set up trust funds for them so that they will never have to work? What sorts of provisions do we have to make for their future?

   If you say, yes, we have some obligation to future generations, do we also have obligations to our ancestors? (Clearly members of other cultures believe that fervently.) Do we have obligations, for instance, to soldiers that died in U.S. wars for the defense of freedom? Should you, for instance, vote and be active in politics to preserve the freedoms that they died for? If you are reasonably comfortably off, do you owe anything to your grandparents who came to the United States poor and worked incredibly hard all their lives to lay the basis for your present economic well-being? Should you perhaps seek out a recent immigrant and help him to get their education or find a decent job?

2. We claim freedom of movement as one of our basic rights, although it is not explicitly mentioned in the U.S. Constitution. It is rather a universal human right.

   How then can the U.S. government restrict the travel of its citizens? Sometimes travel is limited to areas deemed exceptionally unsafe. At other times, travel is restricted for political reasons. Go to the Internet and look up travel restrictions to Cuba.

   Then consider whether the government in restricting the travel of Americans to Cuba is infringing on fundamental rights.

3. We all are familiar with the idea that free speech may be limited when it constitutes a "clear and present danger" to the functioning of the government. But it is not easy to say when speech constitutes a clear and present danger.

   Consider the following statements by famous Americans and try to imagine the situation when they might be considered a clear and present danger. Would you regard any of them as "disloyal"?

   "Liberty has never come from government. Liberty has always come from the subjects of government. The history of liberty is the history of resistance." — Woodrow Wilson

   "Resistance to tyranny is obedience to God." — Thomas Jefferson

   In 1786–1787 farmers in Western Massachusetts suffering because they were indebted to the banks due to poor economic conditions, rose up in an armed rebellion against the state government in Boston that had refused to protect them against foreclosures. Thomas Jefferson reacted to Shay's Rebellion, as this uprising came to be called, by writing in a letter to James Madison: "The late rebellion in Massachusetts has given more alarm than I think it should have done. Calculate that one rebellion in thirteen states in the course of eleven years is but one for each state in a century and a half. *No country should be so long without one*" (italics added).

4. Abraham and Ahmed live in houses across from each other. They have been neighbors for years and are on good neighborly terms. Occasionally they chat with each other and admire the flowers in their front yards and praise each other's children.

Abraham's grandparents died in Nazi concentration camps. His parents were sent to England as children and were then brought to the United States. Ahmed's grandparents fled their olive groves in what is now Israel when the state of Israel was established in 1949.They emigrated to the United States where Ahmed's parents and Ahmed himself were born. Like many Jews, Abraham supports Israel as a safe place for Jews who faced bitter persecution everywhere else. In Ahmed's family the loss of the family olive groves, which generations of ancestors had cared for lovingly, is still the source of great sorrow. Abraham and Ahmed have rather different ideas about Israel and its relationship to the Palestinians but they like being neighbors, they like each other, and so they stay away from a painful and emotional topic.

Then the local state college invites a Palestinian to speak who uses quite harsh language to criticize what he terms the oppression of Palestinians by Israelis. He refers to Jews as neo-Nazis. The Jewish community is outraged and demands the resignation of the college president. The local Palestinian and Arab communities rally around the president. There are public meetings full of angry speeches, outraged letters to the newspaper, and a large number of e-mails to congressional representatives, to the governor, and to the trustees of the state college system.

The conflict escalates when, after a week of meetings, protests, and demonstrations, nothing whatsoever happens. Everyone in power sits tight and waits for this crisis to blow over. The president of the local state college does not resign; elected and appointed officials do nothing. The Jewish community prints up posters showing Israeli children killed by a suicide bomber at a shopping mall with a caption that calls all Palestinians murderers. Abraham posts one of these on his front lawn. Not to be outdone, Ahmed puts a poster on his lawn showing Israeli soldiers mistreating Palestinian youth. The caption compares Israelis to Nazis.

That night, the neighbors hear what they think are shots. They call the police. Both Abraham and Ahmed deny firing shots. Both claim to have been asleep in their beds. The police demand that they take down their posters in the interest of keeping the peace. Both refuse. They are arrested for disturbing the peace.

What do you think about this local state college inviting a person known to be an ardent enemy of the Israelis? Was that within the purview of their rights to free speech?

Do you think that Abraham and Ahmed were within their First Amendment rights when they put up their posters?

Do you think that the police had a right to ask Abraham and Ahmed to take down their posters?

Were they right to arrest the two?

5. Consider the uproar over the cartoons making fun of Muhammad. No one should have been surprised when Muslims were deeply offended by them. Can we demand that newspapers censor themselves to avoid offending anyone's religious or other sensibilities? Does a publication need to justify itself if some members of the public find it offensive? Is it ever permissible for a newspaper or book to offend sections of the public? If so, under what conditions? What are the responsibilities of speakers and writers whose activities are protected by the right of free speech?

   Comparable questions need to be raised about the speech of private persons. What if an anti-Semitic joke you tell at a party offends one of the guests? Can you tell that person to "lighten up" or criticize them for lacking a sense of humor? Do you need to apologize? Should the host of the party show you the door for offending one of the other guests?

6. The military allows homosexuals as long as they are "in the closet." Open, practicing homosexuals are discharged. Get the information on the "don't ask, don't tell" policy of the armed forces, as well as the official justifications for discharging open homosexuals from the armed forces. Do you think this policy is justified or is it an interference with the different moral beliefs and practices of homosexuals?

7. Most states forbid two men or two women to marry. By implication, the government orders men and women to either remain unmarried or to marry a person of the opposite sex. Do you think the government should tell you whom to marry?

   In thinking about this, remember that not too long ago it was illegal for whites and blacks to get married. Is the prohibition of homosexual marriage comparable?

   What would you think if government policy about permitting marriages involves a health issue, if the government forbids persons positive for human immunodeficiency virus (HIV) to get married or prohibits marriages where one or both partners have a sexually transmitted disease? Consider that we have no problem making child marriages illegal, which are acceptable in other cultures.

   What restrictions on marriage are defensible? At what point do they interfere with our personal liberty?

   Get all the information you can about the controversy over homosexual marriage. Compare it to legislation against polygamy. If we allow gay marriage should we reconsider the prohibitions of polygamy? List the reasons for and against allowing homosexuals to marry. Decide which policy is most in keeping with our belief in personal liberty.

8. When confronted with moral questions about what sort of respect we owe our parents or our employers or about telling the truth and not divulging information we have promised to keep secret, many people say "that's a matter of opinion." They mean by that, that it is no more worth having a conversation about questions like these — moral questions — than it is about whether chocolate ice cream is better than vanilla. But these same people will, of course, lay down the law to their children about matters of honesty, of drinking and driving, and of teenage sex. They often justify that by saying that they are, of course, responsible for their children. But does their responsibility for their children imply that they insist that chocolate ice cream is preferable to vanilla? Surely, if moral issues are our personal opinions, I have no obligation to impose my opinions on those for whom I have responsibility.

   If you believe that moral questions are "a matter of opinion" explain how you will raise (or are raising) your children. If they come home drunk at age ten will you say "I don't think that's right but, of course, that's just my opinion?" Or will you read your kid the riot act? How can you justify that? (It is not enough to say that you are responsible for them. Think about that!)

9. Consider the case of the young couple confronted with an unexpected pregnancy. What would you do in such a case? What do you think of the man's behavior? How do you think the two should respond to this unexpected development? What will help to cement their relationship? Will it help to buy a couple of six-packs and watch some football games?

10. Under the heading of "positive freedom" we have mentioned a wide range of government programs. These programs are controversial for different reasons. We therefore need to examine some of them separately. In many cases the criticisms of such programs are based on factual claims that require careful scrutiny.

   A. Welfare Programs. These programs are often criticized because they are said to allow some people to live comfortably without working or making serious efforts to improve their lives while many other people work very hard to support themselves, and incidentally, pay the taxes that finance welfare programs. Go on the Internet and find how much money the government spends annually on welfare, and find as much support as you can for the frequent stories of welfare fraud. What percentage of welfare recipients actually work? What percentage of them are on welfare all their lives? What percentage of people end up on welfare or homeless due to disastrous illness or divorce or due to the off-shoring of their work?

Once that information has been assembled, consider the arguments in favor of or opposed to welfare programs for the poorest members of our society.

B. The GI Bill that sent a large number of World War II veterans to college and graduate school. Do you think that all veterans were good students or were there people who "took advantage" of these programs. How does that affect your estimate of the worth of the GI Bill?

C. Agricultural price support programs. For city dwellers they tend to raise food prices. Why should the urban United States support the lifestyle of farmers? Did U.S. farmers support the lifestyle of steelworkers when their jobs were being sent offshore?

Once again, get the facts about farm price support programs. How much do these programs cost? Who benefits from them and who is harmed by them? Do the arguments used against social welfare for the poor apply also to farm price support programs? Should the government continue to support U.S. farmers?

D. Get information about government tax breaks for large corporations. How are those tax breaks justified? Are those plausible justifications? Should we continue tax breaks for large corporations, and if so, under what conditions?

NOTES

1. *Boston Globe,* April 10, 2005, A4.
2. James Wilson, *The Earth Shall Weep: A History of Native America* (New York: Grove Press, 1998), 63.
3. Wilson, *The Earth Shall Weep,* 30.
4. Charles C. Mann, *1941: New Revelations of the Americas before Columbus* (New York: Alfred C. Knopf, 2005), 41.
5. William Cronon, *Changes in the Land: Indians, Colonists, and the Ecology of New England* (New York: Hill and Wang, 1983), 41.
6. Wilson, *The Earth Shall Weep,* 289.
7. Ira Katznelson, *When Affirmative Action Was White: An Untold History of Racial Inequality in Twentieth-Century America* (New York: W.W. Norton Co., 2005), 175.
8. "Violent crime rates declined for both males and females since 1994," *Bureau of Justice Statistics*, retrieved February 14, 2008, from Office of Justice Programs website: www.ojp.usdoj.gov/bjs/glance/vsx2.htm.

9. "Rape and Sexual Assault: Reporting to Police and Medical Attention, 1992–2000," *Bureau of Justice Statistics*, 1992–2000, retrieved February 14, 2008, from Office of Justice Programs website: www.ojp.usdoj.gov/bjs/pub/ascii/rsarp00.txt.

10. Rus Funk, "Statistics Reflecting Women's Attitudes towards Their Personal Safety," retrieved February 14, 2008, from JIST Publishing website: http://jist.mw.net/shop/web/press-room/media-resources/quick-facts/statistics-reflecting-women2019s-attitudes-toward-their-personal-safety.

11. "Economic Mobility Project," retrieved November 11, 2007, from Pew Trusts website: www.pewtrusts.org/our_work.aspx?category=428.

12. Nat Hentoff, *The Day They Came to Arrest the Book* (New York: Bantam Doubleday Dell Books for Young Readers, 1982).

13. "The Espionage Act, May 16, 1918," retrieved November 11, 2007, from Fordham University website: www.fordham.edu/halsall/mod/1916espionageact.html.

14. "Clear and Present Danger," retrieved September 10, 2007, from Wikipedia webiste: http://en.wikipedia.org/wiki/Clear_and_present_danger.

15. "Danish Paper Rejected Jesus Cartoon," retrieved February 22, 2006, from The Guardian website: www.guardian.co.uk/international/story/0,,1703501,00.html.

16. John Stuart Mill, *On Liberty* (Oxford, Blackwell, 1948): chapter 2.

17. Thomas Nagel, *Equality and Partiality* (New York: Oxford University Press, 1991), 5.

18. Aristotle, *Politics*, Book I, Chapter 6.

19. John Locke, *Second Treatise on Government and A Letter on Toleration* (Oxford: Basil Blackwell, 1948), paragraph 138.

20. Michael Sandel, *Liberalism and the Limits of Justice* (Cambridge: Cambridge University Press, 1982).

21. Alisdair MacIntyre, *After Virtue* (South Bend, IN: Notre Dame University Press, 1981).

22. See for instance, John Rawls, *A Theory of Justice* (Cambridge: Harvard University Press, 1971), 259.

23. Retrieved from National Jewish Democratic Council blog website: http://njdc.typepad.com/njdcs.blog/2007/05/is_xenophobia_o.html.

24. John Rawls, *Justice as Fairness: A Restatement* (Cambridge: Harvard University Press, 2001), 15.

25. Martha C. Nussbaum "Human Capabilities, Female Human Beings," in *Women, Culture and Development,* ed. Martha C. Nussbaum and Jonathan Glover (Oxford: Oxford University Press, 1995), 63–115.

26. "The Woman's Role in the Home," retrieved January 2, 2008, from Learn the Bible website: www.learnthebible.org/woman's_role_in_the_home.htm.

27. Rawls, *Justice as Fairness,* 42.

28. Robert Nozick, *Anarchy, State and Utopia* (New York: Basic Books, 1974).

29. Isaiah Berlin, *Four Essays on Liberty* (Oxford: Oxford University Press, 1969), xlii.

30. Katznelson, *When Affirmative Action,* 175.

31. Franklin Delano Roosevelt, "The Four Freedoms," retrieved May 30, 2006, from www.libertynet.org/edcivic/fdr.html.

32. "Boston Globe Series on Corporate Welfare," retrieved September 5, 2006, from Boston Globe website: www.corporations.org/welfare/#globe.

FURTHER READINGS

Nat Hentoff, *The Day They Came to Arrest the Book* (New York: Dell, 1986). Although a work of fiction, this book is a plausible and instructive examination of the problems confronting advocates of free speech in debates over a book considered racist by some parents.

Ira Katznelson, *When Affirmative Action Was White: An Untold History of Racial Inequality in Twentieth-Century America* (New York: Norton, 2005). Supplies the needed facts to argue usefully about affirmative action programs.

Terence Reynolds, ed., *Ethical Issues: Western Philosophical and Religious Perspectives* (Belmont, CA: Thomson-Wadsworth, 2006). Part 3 provides a variety of perspectives on the debate about abortion.

Catherine MacKinnon, *Women's Lives: Men's Laws* (Cambridge, MA: Harvard University Press, 2004), 297–359. A hard-hitting critique of the pornography industry.

Isaiah Berlin, *Four Essays on Liberty* (Oxford: Oxford University Press, 1969). The classical argument for limiting freedom to freedom from and against government supporting freedom to.

Chapter Two

The Citizen and the Government

When the delegates to the Constitutional Convention meeting in Philadelphia in the summer of 1787 had completed their work and signed their names to the document they had produced on September 17, the proposed constitution still needed to be accepted by the separate states. Each state was due to hold a ratifying convention; the members were to be elected by all eligible voters — that is, white, male property owners. After nine of the original states had ratified the new constitution, it would go into effect and a new government would come into existence.

By the next summer, eight of the required nine states had ratified the new constitution. But there existed serious opposition in the two most populous states of Virginia and New York. The opponents of the proposed constitution had many objections, but one that was heard over and over again was the absence of a bill of rights in the new constitution.

The framers of the Constitution had discussed at some length whether to include a list of rights of individual citizens in the Constitution. They decided that each state could and did, in most cases, list the rights and freedoms of individual citizens and that the newly established federal government was not empowered to interfere, for instance, with freedom of religion or freedom of speech. The federal government they were establishing had carefully limited powers that would not be a threat to individual liberties. Hence, they argued, a bill of rights would be unnecessary.

Not everyone agreed with that. In Virginia and in New York, the absence of a bill of rights seemed so serious to many representatives in the ratifying conventions that they were prepared to vote against the new constitution and against the new government to be established, even though everyone agreed that the existing government was not equipped to lead the new nation toward freedom and prosperity. For awhile, it looked as if the Constitution might not be accepted without a great deal of further debate and the possibility existed that the whole project of establishing a government of the United States of America would fall apart in sharp disagreements and party squabbling.

The Virginia ratifying convention finally accepted the Constitution as proposed in Philadelphia when James Madison and some of the other framers of the original document changed their mind about including a bill of rights. Like the majority in Philadelphia, Madison had originally thought that a bill of rights would be superfluous because the newly established federal government had no powers to threaten individual liberties. In addition, he thought that a bill of rights would have limited usefulness. If the majority of legislators of a state belonged to one church, they would surely not be hindered by a bill of rights in their desire to make their own religion the official religion of that state. He had seen that happen in his own state of Virginia where the majority of the people were quite content to make Episcopalian Christianity the official religion. A bill of rights, Madison concluded, would not protect minorities against the wishes of the majority in matters of religion, of speech, and of political dissent.

Thomas Jefferson, with whom Madison corresponded about this question, replied that Madison had overlooked the role an independent judiciary could play in protecting civil liberties, *if* the Constitution enumerated civil rights that were protected. A bill of rights, Jefferson argued, might not deter a majority from riding roughshod over the rights of a minority, but it would enable that minority to avail itself of the protection by the judiciary by going to court and suing for the preservation of those of its rights that were enumerated in a bill of rights. Jefferson argued, and Madison at last agreed, that a bill of rights would provide a shield for the liberties of minorities who could protect themselves against majorities by appealing to the courts.

This discussion acknowledges clearly that liberty has two enemies in any country: the government and the citizenry. The government can limit freedoms by using its police power against people it does not like. Critics of the government who ask uncomfortable questions about public uses of tax money, for instance, may find themselves incarcerated or worse. But citizens may also lose their freedoms because their fellow citizens do not respect them. In democracies, those who hold unpopular opinions often find their freedoms curtailed by legislation—laws regulating sexual conduct, laws forbidding the sale of birth control devices or the distribution of birth control information, laws that limit free speech or impose religious practices, laws that allow employers to fire employees for holding unpopular opinions. By carefully enumerating and limiting the powers of the government, the Constitution tries to protect the freedoms of citizens. By providing a bill of rights and an independent judiciary, it provides assistance to minorities whose rights are threatened or actually trampled on by the majority.

A free society must pay careful attention to the relations between citizen and government. In relation to freedom, government plays a complicated role. Frequently it is a threat to citizens' freedom, for instance, by restricting free speech or by establishing one religion to the exclusion of all others. But at other times, the government may also protect some groups of citizens against an oppressive majority. At times, police protect unpopular protesters against the anger of the majority of the population. At other times, the police uses its superior weaponry to inflict damage on citizens whose only crime is to have a dark skin or be unable to speak proper English. The consideration of freedom in the preceding chapter leads us inevitably to take a closer look at the relation between citizens and the government.

This chapter will consider these questions:

- What can we learn from previous generations of political philosophers about the legitimate power of the government to limit individual freedom?
- Going beyond the soothing rhetoric of "the land of the free," what has our history been in the United States with respect to freedom?
- What are the basic traits of human beings? Are they motivated primarily by self-interest or are they amenable to moral restraints of their selfish pursuits?
- What about anarchism and the opposition to government of any kind?
- Does freedom require that citizens trust one another?
- How is trust fostered in a society?
- What are the citizens' obligations to the government?

SOCIAL CONTRACT THEORIES

The State of Nature

Seventeenth-century England was torn apart by disagreements about how the country should be governed. Some looked to a monarch to govern; others believed that the people should be able to govern themselves. There were many opinions in between those two extremes. Thomas Hobbes, John Locke, and other political theorists all used the same device to develop and to defend their different views. They imagined a country without any government and asked themselves what life would be like in that condition. From their description of life without government they then deduced the proper role of government. This state without government they called "the state of nature." In their story they imagined that human beings did not always live in societies with an established government but decided to found one to free citizens of certain tasks that each had had to perform where no government existed. Government was a human contrivance instituted deliberately to overcome certain difficulties in the state of nature.

Neither Hobbes nor Locke invented this device of imagining a state of nature to develop from there a conception of a society organized with its own and appropriate form of government. It had been used by many political thinkers before. An early version of it showed up in *The Republic* of Plato, a Greek philosopher who lived in the fourth century BC. But political philosophers never agreed whether the story about the state of nature was just a handy invention, the sort of intellectual construction we might call a "model," which allowed us to state clearly what we thought government should be like, what governments would be expected to do, and what government activities might be legitimate. Some philosophers have always spoken of the state of nature in this way, as a handy fiction, or a thought experiment. But others, Locke and Hobbes among them, insisted that the state of nature actually existed. They considered it a historical condition, which they knew to be real because they could see it still in existence in some parts of the known globe. So, for example, as we saw in the previous chapter, Europeans believed that the original inhabitants of the North American continent lived in a state of nature because they did not have governments, as Europeans understood government. That belief was convenient for the new settlers because it meant that there existed no American Indian government, and therefore no laws governing property. As a consequence, the land in North America was not owned by anyone. It was there for the taking, and take it they did.

The Englishmen who first settled New England in 1620 actually drew up a social contract among themselves that they signed before landing in Plymouth. In it they

> solemnly and mutually in the Presence of God and of one another, covenant and combine ourselves together into a civil Body Politick, for our better Ordering and Preservation, and Furtherance of the Ends aforesaid; And by Virtue hereof to enact, constitute, and frame, such just and equal Laws, Ordinances, Acts, Constitutions and Offices, from time to time, as shall be thought most meet and convenient for the General good of the Colony; unto which we promise all due submission and obedience.[1]

The social contract was not just a philosophical theory for Englishmen in the seventeenth century. It was a method for giving legitimacy to the governments they set up in the New World. The relations between citizens and the government were a major concern; the story of the state of nature that was ended when everyone agreed to establish a government served to define the rights and obligations of citizen as well as the limits of government power.

Thomas Hobbes

Thomas Hobbes lived in England in the seventeenth century. These were perilous times: a period of regicide and civil war that was followed by a republican government. The civil war lasted from 1642 to 1651; Charles I was beheaded in 1649; at the end of the war in 1651, Oliver Cromwell, the victorious general, established a dictatorship that lasted until his death in 1658. The monarchy was restored in 1662 with the ascent of Charles II to the throne. In 1688, the parliament contrived to have James II, the successor to Charles II, replaced by William of Orange. During all these years, the country resounded with wide-ranging debates about religion, political freedom, and democracy, with demands that all property owners, even the smallest and most humble of farmers, should be allowed the vote and to participate in the nation's politics. It was a time of fear, much conflict, and uncertainty, and Hobbes's political philosophy speaks to those who live in similarly confusing and frightening times.

He was born in 1588, the year in which the British navy defeated the large and thus far invincible Spanish Armada near the coast of Southern England where Hobbes was born. His mother, Hobbes claimed, was frightened into early labor by the naval battle near their village. He later said of himself that "fear and I were born twins." Hobbes's family was of modest means and learning, but he proved himself to be bright and was sent to study at Oxford University where he did well. He spent most of his life as a tutor to young aristocrats and as secretary to powerful political figures. He died in 1679 at the age of 91.

The issues in the turmoil in seventeenth-century England were complex; they involved opposition to the king himself and to the king's religion, Catholicism. They involved controversies about the power of the king as opposed to that of the elected parliament. There was a power struggle between the large landowners and an alliance of smaller farmers and a rising class of capitalist businessmen in London. In the course of these upheavals, England became a constitutional monarchy. At the beginning of the century, the king could convoke the parliament or rule without its advice as he pleased. At the end of the century, parliament and the monarchy solidly shared power. England and the world had passed another milestone on the long road toward democratic government.

Hobbes was a royalist, a defender of Charles I and of the monarchy, in general. At the outbreak of the civil war he fled to France where he remained until after the end of the war. Locke, about forty-five years younger than Hobbes, was born in 1632 and lived until 1703. Like Hobbes, the son of a humble family, Locke, too, managed to receive an Oxford education and spent much of his life as the secretary of powerful aristocrats. The formative years of Hobbes's experience were those of the civil war and the unrest that preceded and followed it. More of Locke's life was spent in the years that witnessed the consolidation of parliamentary power in which elected representatives became an essential part of the British political system and individual freedoms flourished. Not surprisingly, therefore, Hobbes defended absolute monarchy—kingly power that was not subject to or limited by law—whereas Locke defended a type of electoral democracy. Hobbes's monarch was to be above the law. The elected government Locke advocated was subject to the laws it passed.

Hobbes's Account of the Social Contract (Excerpts from *Leviathan*)

Here follows Chapter 13 of Book 1 of Hobbes's major work *Leviathan* published in 1651:

> Nature has made men so equal in their physical and mental capacities that, although sometimes we may find one man who is obviously stronger in body or quicker of mind than another, yet taking all in all the difference between one and another is not so great that one man can claim to have any advantage of strength or skill or the like that can't just as well be claimed by some others. As for strength of body: the weakest man is strong enough to kill the strongest, either by a secret plot or by an alliance with others who are in the same danger that he is in.
>
> As for the faculties of the mind: I find that men are even more equal in these than they are in bodily strength. . . . Prudence is simply experience; and men will get an equal amount of that in an equal period of time spent on things that they equally apply themselves to. . .
>
> *Competition*: This equality of ability produces equality of hope for the attaining of our goals. So if any two men want a single thing that they can't both enjoy, they become enemies; and each of them on the way to his goal (which is principally his own survival, though sometimes merely his delight) tries to destroy or subdue the other. And so it comes about that when someone has through farming and building come to possess a pleasant estate, if an invader would have nothing to fear but that one man's individual power, there will probably be an invader—someone who comes with united forces to deprive him not only of the fruit of his labor but also of his life or liberty. And the successful invader will then be in similar danger from someone else.
>
> *Distrust*: Because of this distrust amongst men, the most reasonable way for any man to make himself safe is to strike first, that is, by force or cunning subdue other men—as many of them as he can, until he sees no other power great enough to endanger him. This is no more than what he needs for his own survival, and is generally allowed. . . .

Glory: Every man wants his associates to value him as highly as he values himself; and any sign that he is disregarded or undervalued naturally leads a man to try, as far as he dares, to raise his value in the eyes of others. For those who have disregarded him, he does this by violence; for others, by example. . . .

So that in the nature of man, we find three principal causes of discord. First competition, secondly distrust, thirdly glory. . . .

This makes it obvious that for as long as men live without a common power to keep them all in awe, they are in the condition known as 'war'; and it is a war of every man against every man. For WAR doesn't consist just in battle or the act of fighting, but in a period of time during which it is well enough known that people are willing to join in battle. . . . what constitutes war is not actual fighting but a known disposition to fight during a time when there is no assurance to the contrary. All other time is PEACE.

Discussion Questions

Most Americans are competitive; we have learned to compete while playing sports, competing for college admissions, jobs, and good deals at auctions. Do you think that it is only the threat of punishment that keeps us from running roughshod over the needs of our neighbors or even family members? What do you think of Hobbes's claim that competition for survival puts all of us at war with one another? Give reasons for your answer.

Therefore, whatever results from a time of war, when every man is enemy to every man, also results from a time when men live with no other security but what their own strength and ingenuity provides them with. In such conditions there is no place for hard work, because there is no assurance that it will yield results; and consequently no cultivation of the earth, no navigation or use of materials that can be imported by sea, no construction of large buildings, no machines for moving things that require much force, no knowledge of the face of the earth, no account of time, no practical skills, no literature or scholarship, no society; and—worst of all—continual fear and danger of violent death, and the life of man solitary, poor, nasty, brutish, and short. It may seem strange to you, if you haven't thought hard about these things, that nature should thus separate men from one another and make them apt to invade and destroy one another.

So perhaps you won't trust my derivation of this account from the nature of the passions, and will want to have the account confirmed by experience. Well, then, think about how you behave: when going on a journey, you arm yourself, and try not to go alone; when going to sleep, you lock your doors; even inside your own house you lock your chests; and you do all this when you know that there are laws, and armed public officers of the law, to revenge any harms that are done to you.

Ask yourself: what opinion do you have of your fellow subjects when you ride armed? Of your fellow citizens when you lock your doors? Of your children and servants when you lock your chests? In all this, don't you accuse mankind as much by your actions as I do by my words? . . . .

It may be thought that there has never been such a time, such a condition of war as this; and I believe it was never generally like this all over the world. Still, there are many places where people live like that even now. For the savage people in many parts of America have no government at all except for the government of small families, whose harmony depends on natural lust. Those savages live right now in the brutish manner I have described. Anyway, we can see what way of life there would be if there were no common power to fear, from the degenerate way of life into which civil war has led men who had formerly lived under a peaceful government. Even if there had never been any time at which individual men were in a state of war one against another, this is how kings, and persons of sovereign authority relate to one another at all times. Because of their independence from one another, they are in continual mutual jealousies. Like gladiators, with their weapons pointing and their eyes fixed on one another, sovereigns have forts, garrisons, and guns on the frontiers of their kingdoms, and permanent spies on their neighbors—this is a posture of war, as much as the gladiators' is. But because in this the sovereigns uphold the economy of their nations, their state of war doesn't lead to the sort of misery that occurs when individual men are at liberty from laws and government.

In this war of every man against every man nothing can be unjust. The notions of right and wrong, justice and injustice have no place there. Where there is no common power, there is no law; and where there is no law, there is no injustice. In war the two chief virtues are force and fraud. Justice and injustice are not among the faculties of the body or of the mind. If they were, they could be in a man who was alone in the world, as his senses and passions can. They are qualities that relate to men in society, not in solitude. A further fact about the state of war of every man against every man: in it there is no such thing as ownership, no legal control, no distinction between mine and thine. Rather, anything that a man can get is his for as long as he can keep it. So much for the poor condition that man is actually placed in by mere nature; but as I now go on to explain, he can extricate himself from it, partly through his passions, partly through his reason.[2]

Discussion Question

Do you agree with Hobbes that words like right, wrong, justice, injustice, mine, yours, have meaning only where there is government that promulgates laws? Notice the implication of this that all laws are, by definition, just. Give reasons for your answer.

Hobbes on Human Nature

Chapter 13 is justly famous, if only for its impressive clarity and directness. Hobbes is moving in the direction of an account of the relations of government and citizen by way of a narrative about the state of nature and the social contract that puts an end to it. What we have seen so far is the description of the state of nature—that is, what human beings are basically like and how they relate to each other where no government exists. He then provides us with some evidence that his description of human nature and life in the state of nature are accurate.

According to Hobbes, human beings act to satisfy their desires. Because we live in a world of relative scarcity, we come into conflict with each other when two of us want the same thing and there is not enough of it to satisfy both of us. Human beings are therefore, Hobbes says, forever in competition with each other. This makes us distrustful of one another, on one hand, and desirous of power, on the other. If we are to compete successfully, if we are going to be able to take what we want or need from others, we need to be more powerful than they. Power is needed to survive. But power is not only necessary to win in the competition that is human life under conditions of scarcity; it also gives pleasure to those who possess it. We enjoy being powerful and we take pleasure in having others recognize our power. We want others to defer to us and look up to us. We are always striving for glory, Hobbes says. We might express this by saying that we like being famous, that we want the social status one gets from being recognized by all as a powerful person—that is, someone who can get what he or she wants under conditions where you and I, not being powerful and not being celebrities, might go empty-handed.

In a world in which there is no public authority to keep us in line, any person is a threat to every other person because we are all competing with one another; all of us are seeking to be more powerful than the others and thus are rightly suspicious of each other. Such a condition can only be described as a "war of all against all," not because we are always actively fighting each other but because, in this situation, fights may break out at any moment. Human beings in the state of nature live constantly on the brink of serious conflict and of potential violence; they live in a state of permanent insecurity.

You think that is exaggerated? Hobbes points out that we lock our houses. But we do not think that that is enough; just locking your house does not assure the safety of our possessions. In addition, we lock up our precious possessions in cupboards or safes. When they go out, many persons are armed, even though we do, after all, live under a government and its police force and courts that keep the mutual animosity between human beings under some sort

of control. Governments have weapons and superior military power to subdue the members of the society that are prone to violence. But weapons sales
nevertheless remain brisk, and we are told, most of the guns are sold to law-
abiding citizens who are trying to protect themselves.

Nations are not under an international government. There exist no international institutions that have the same police power to wield against member countries that the government wields in our country to keep the peace
among citizens. In the international arena there exists no higher power to
stop armed conflicts. Without a government to prevent wars, nations are indeed in a constant state of war against each other. There is hardly a moment
in human history when two nations are not at each other's throat, killing each
other's citizens and destroying each other's farmlands and houses. Hobbes's
strongest argument for his description of human life in the state of nature is
this reference to the constant warfare between nations. They are still with respect to each other in a state of nature; no government can subdue their competition, distrust, or desire for glory, and hence war is a permanent fixture in
human existence. Even in our time, when there exists not only the United
Nations (UN), with its occasional peacekeeping missions, and many other
international economic, cultural, and aid organizations, but also regional organizations such as the North Atlantic Treaty Organization (NATO), the
world is pretty constantly at war. The UN and other international organizations are at the beck and call of the most powerful nations. The international
organizations do not serve to limit the power and the power politics of individual nations but are much more often the tools of power politics. Considering that, how can one deny that the state of nature is a sad, and indeed, ter-
rifying reality?

Discussion Questions

*How persuasive are Hobbes's arguments to show that without government we
would all be in a state of war with one another? There is hardly a day that
two nations are not at war. Do you lock your car, your house, and your safe
because you do not trust anyone at all? Give reasons for your answer.*

A PHILOSOPHY FOR THE FEARFUL?

This is the world seen through the eyes of a person thoroughly frightened.
They need to struggle for whatever they want against others who want the
same good. Other persons are competitors, indeed enemies, who want to take
from them what they need. The presence of others is always a potential threat;
one needs to approach others with caution and be wary of their intentions.

One needs to approach them prepared to find them hostile; one needs to cultivate a healthy fear of one's neighbor. In Hobbes's state of nature, no one can trust anybody.

This grim picture of human society before the establishment of government flows from Hobbes's conception of the fundamental traits of human beings. The persons he describes have only one goal in life and that is to satisfy their individual needs. Everyone wants things and because many of the things we want are scarce, we need to compete with others to get them. Giving up on something one wants for the sake of keeping the peace, yielding to another from affection or even a sense of duty is unknown among the creatures Hobbes describes. His human beings are complete egoists; nothing matters to them except their own, individual pleasure and well-being. Hence the ubiquitous competition and distrust that Hobbes sees as the main characteristic of human society without a government to keep order. Humans are selfish; getting what they want is their primary concern.

They are for that reason fundamentally isolated. There is no room in the state of nature for love or friendship. Hobbes, as does Locke, regards the original inhabitants of the North American continent as persons who still live in the state of nature (in the seventeenth century.) They do not know either love or friendship, he thinks, because they are merely trying to meet individual needs, if necessary, at the expense of others. Hobbes writes "the savage people in many parts of America have no government at all except for the government of small families, whose harmony depends on natural lust." If persons in the state of nature have families at all, they are maintained not by mutual trust, let alone by love, but merely by sexual desire. Couples remain together not because they trust or love one another but merely because they need each other's bodies to satisfy their own sexual needs. For us, perhaps, trust, love, friendship, and sharing are possibilities, but we do not live in a state of nature. We live in organized societies where harmony is maintained by the government and its laws, and by a police force to enforce the laws. There is no such superior force in the state of nature; hence everyone is savage and a threat to everyone else.

Discussion Questions

Do you recognize yourself in Hobbes's description of human nature? Are you better than that? Give reasons for your answer.

"Land of the Free, Home of the Brave"

The grim picture that Hobbes paints of human beings and their relations to each other helps us understand the recurrent crises of freedom in our own country. It helps us think more clearly about episodes like the conviction of Charles Schenck for posting leaflets that urged young men to resist the draft peacefully. In times of peace and prosperity, the risk involved in trusting our fellow citizens is fairly small. When citizens enjoy a comfortable prosperity, even the utterly selfish would not be able to do us serious harm. There are no foreign or domestic enemies to whom someone can betray us. In times of prosperity, competition for goods, wealth, and power is moderated because many, if not all, persons have enough and are not terribly anxious about procuring what they want. But when, as in time of war or of serious international conflict, the danger increases, the price we might have to pay for treason and disloyalty in our ranks rises sharply. Citizens become more fearful; their well-being seems under immediate threat—often from rather shadowy adversaries. It becomes harder to trust others and those who try to sow dissension by promoting vague rumors about internal and external enemies have an easier time finding a credulous audience. As mutual trust and harmony in the society ebbs, citizens are more willing to believe the rumor mongers—that is, the persons sowing dissension by uncovering previously unsuspected enemies everywhere. As we become more frightened, we trust our neighbors less and believe those more readily who confirm our worst fears. We find ourselves in a state of mind where it is easy to believe that we are always on the brink of serious conflict with others: that is, that we live in a "war of all against all."

Americans have often agreed with Hobbes that freedom is dangerous and needs to be curtailed to keep the peace within our society. Allowing Japanese-Americans freedom of movement, rather than keeping them under surveillance in detention camps, when the Japanese entered a war against us, seemed to be inviting sabotage from the enemy. Allowing Communists the freedom to speak freely, to teach children, and to hold jobs as script writers in Hollywood seemed to allow enemies open channels for spreading their propaganda in the early years of the Cold War. In times when we feel seriously threatened, it is tempting to give credence to those who agitate against one group or another—against pacifists or anarchists in time of war, or as we shall see, against Japanese-Americans after Pearl Harbor and against Communists in the beginning of the Cold War. The value of freedom, our own and even more that of others, ebbs in times like those. The more frightened we are, the more ready we are to pay a high price in freedom for security promised to us by the enemies of freedom. At times like those, the United States is neither the land of the free nor the home of the brave. It is more like a Hobbesian nightmare of mutual distrust and violence. In times of great fear, the government is allowed more power, and citizens lose freedom. The balance of power between government and citizen shifts in favor of government.

Here are some examples of national panics during which we became intensely distrustful of others and saw freedom primarily as a source of danger—that is, as a threat to our security rather than as a good to be pre-served at all cost.

Fearful Americans Limit Freedom for the Sake of Security

Throughout our history we have experienced periodic crises of confidence in a free society and its institutions. These periods of distrust in freedom have been an element in our life as a nation since the early 1790s when Congress passed the Alien and Sedition Acts. The Sedition Act allowed the government to prosecute anyone for making statements critical of the government. Under the latter provision, a number of newspaper editors went to jail. In the 1960s, the Supreme Court declared the Sedition Act to be unconstitutional. Passed in 1798, the Alien Exclusion Act allowed the government to deport aliens considered dangerous by the government.[3] The Alien Exclusion Act is still in force. However, much of the United States is a "nation of immigrants," those of us who have been here for a while are often afraid of more recent arrivals.

During the Civil War, President Abraham Lincoln limited freedoms of speech and of the press and suspended the writ of habeas corpus, which is one of the most ancient of traditional liberties in Anglo-Saxon jurisprudence. In a habeas corpus petition prisoners challenge the legality of their imprisonment. The government is forced to state the charges laid against a person and defend itself against an accusation of unlawful imprisonment. It is a powerful safeguard individuals have in our legal system against arbitrary arrest and imprisonment. Once those writs can no longer be used, the government can imprison anyone without needing to defend that arrest and prove its legality. The government can lock up anybody and throw away the key.

The Palmer Raids

In 1917, the United States entered World War I on the side of Britain and France against imperial Germany. In the same year, the Bolsheviks made a successful Communist revolution in Russia. The early postwar years in the United States were disturbed by fears of this new Communist nation. At the same time, there was a good deal of labor unrest. A West Coast strike of dock workers was broken by the U.S. Marines; steelworkers struck for the eight-hour day. In addition, several U.S. cities witnessed large-scale race riots. In the midst of all this, the women's suffrage and the prohibition amendments were passed. Anarchists attempted to assassinate several public officials.

The U.S. government responded to the anxieties occasioned by these different events with massive raids on labor unions and Communist party offices—often without warrants. Resident aliens were detained, often under deplorable conditions, and then summarily deported without any due process. They were simply put on a ship bound for Russia. These raids are referred to as the "Palmer Raids," named after the then Attorney General of the United States, Alexander Mitchell Palmer, who himself had been the target of an assassination attempt.

Among the deportees was Emma Goldman, a fiery orator, who had been spreading anarchist doctrine for a number of years as she traveled all over the United States giving speeches. Believing that all governments are the tools of the wealthy and powerful, anarchists believed that ordinary persons would be better off running their own lives without interference by any government. (See more about anarchism later.) Accordingly, they advocated, among other things, what was then called "free love"—a doctrine now commonly shared by many, that a person's sexual life is a purely private matter. Sex was not only to be permitted among marriage partners but under any condition as long as it was not coerced. At the time that was a shocking doctrine.

The case of the anarchists was complicated by the fact that some of them used violence. Alexander Berkman, Goldman's lover, tried but failed to assassinate the steel magnate Henry Clay Frick and spent seventeen years in prison for that. Another anarchist, Leon Czolgosz, assassinated President William McKinley in 1901, and Goldman supported him publicly. Always on the side of the oppressed, the poor, the unemployed, and women, but not always respectful of currently dominant opinion, Goldman was described as one of the most dangerous people in the United States by J. Edgar Hoover, then a young prosecutor.

Discussion Question

Read up on Emma Goldman on the Internet. Was the government justified in arresting her without a warrant and deporting her without a court hearing? Give reasons for your answer.

Was Goldman considered dangerous for her actions or for her opinions? No one had ever accused her of anything more serious than speaking out. Was she inciting violence or was she merely uttering unpopular opinions? There still is no agreement on that. But in the anxious postwar years in 1919 as radicals took over the Russian government, labor was restless in the United States, and women agitated fiercely for the vote, that fine distinction was swept away. The dangerous radicals, read "the people we are afraid of," had to go; they were put aboard a ship and literally sent "back to Russia." Free speech and the United States' other traditional liberties had to yield to fear.

Japanese Internment

For the generation that lived during World War II, the bombing of Pearl Harbor in December of 1941 had much the same effect as the attacks of September 11th had on the present generation of Americans. Shocked and panicked, many Americans expected the worst. They considered a Japanese invasion of the West Coast imminent. Unprepared for Pearl Harbor, as we were for September 11th, they feared that all persons of Japanese origin would prove treacherous and unreliable as many of us today lump together all "Muslims" or all "Arabs" and are deeply distrustful of them. Notwithstanding the fact that 63 percent of the 112,000 Japanese Americans on the West Coast were U.S. citizens and that many families had young men serving in the U.S. military, all Japanese-Americans not in the military were moved into internment camps where they remained until the end of the war. Forced to leave in a great hurry, many sold their property at a mere fraction of its value. Most had been good citizens and had not given anyone any reasons for suspecting their loyalty to their adopted country. But with the country afraid of a Japanese invasion, they were suddenly seen as potential threats to everyone's security. There was a good deal of opposition inside the U.S. government, as well as outside of it, to this internment of Japanese Americans. But the dominant sentiment in the country was that the nation faced unparalleled threats and could not afford, under those conditions, to respect the liberties guaranteed by our Constitution. Liberty had to surrender to panic.

McCarthyism

The Communist Soviet Union and the center of the capitalist world, the United States, were military allies during World War II. The underlying distrust between the two nations may have been put aside for the purpose of winning the war against Nazi Germany, but it remained in the background only to emerge more powerfully than ever when World War II came to an end. U.S. fear of communism was heightened by the actions of the Soviet Union after the war. The Soviets made a concerted attempt to create a ring of Communist nations on their borders from the Baltic to Poland to Czechoslovakia. In Greece they fomented a civil war in which the Communist Party tried to take power. In 1949, the Communists led by Mao Zedong took power in China. The Korean peninsula, which at the end of World War II had been partitioned into a Communist North Korea and a capitalist South Korea linked closely to the United States, erupted into war in 1950 when North Korea, heavily armed by the Soviet Union, overran South Korea. The United States hastily organized a UN force—in effect a U.S. military force—to enter the war against North Korea and when U.S. forces crossed the thirty-eighth parallel—the line that divided South Korea from the North—China entered the war on North Korea's side. After enormous loss of life on all sides, the war ended in 1954. Korea remains divided to this day.

During those years, Americans felt threatened by a worldwide Communist movement, which they saw as unified, large, and powerful. As happened so many times before, there was a tendency to focus all this anxiety on a specific group of persons. At the beginning of World War II it was the Japanese-Americans who bore the brunt of U.S. fears. In the 1950s, attention was drawn to members of the American Communist Party as a focus of U.S. fears of the Soviets, the Chinese, and the North Koreans. The American Communist Party was small, but the anti-Communist anxieties drew a larger circle that included "communist sympathizers" and "communist dupes." All U.S. citizens became, potentially, suspect. Those with left-wing political leanings, or with friends belonging to organizations regarded as left-wing by the Communist hunters, were now fair game for having their loyalty to the United States questioned and investigated. The original vehicle of the persecution was a congressional committee known as the House Un-American Activities Committee (HUAC). It was joined by an ever-widening group of copycat public and private committees charged to ferret out the disloyal. HUAC had been in existence since the late 1930s but only gained importance during the red scare of the 1950s.

In the early years of the Cold War, Communists, suspected Communists, and their sympathizers were hunted up, harassed, and in some cases blacklisted so that no one would give them a job; they were unable to work. After 1940, when the Smith Act was passed by Congress, it was illegal to "knowingly or willfully advocate . . . overthrowing the Government of the United States or of any State by force or violence;" a few members of the Communist Party were tried, convicted, and jailed. (In 1957, the Smith Act was declared unconstitutional by the Supreme Court.) After 1947, government employees were subjected to "security checks" to investigate their political memberships. Similar pressures were brought to bear on professors in many state, as well as private colleges and universities. These efforts were aimed at rooting out people who were considered not "loyal" which meant, in practice, that their political views were not those of the majority and of the Communist hunters.[4]

Trials, like those under the Smith Act, were complex undertakings that consumed a great deal of time, money, and effort. It was easier to interrogate suspect persons in public before the HUAC and in front of a whole host of other congressional, government, and private committees, all of them asking about the membership of the Communist Party and of the more or less loosely affiliated organizations. People called before these committees were asked about their own affiliation with the Communist Party and were then asked to name other members. Those who refused "to name names" were often cited for contempt of Congress, and in some cases, sent to jail.

Government at all levels—federal, state and local—hastened to pass laws requiring loyalty oaths of their employees, including teachers at all levels of the educational system. The oath affirmed loyalty to the various levels of government. The persons taking the oath affirmed that they did not intend to overthrow the government. Refusal to sign the oath carried with it the penalty of losing one's job. Subsequently, the Supreme Court found most of these laws excessively vague and therefore unconstitutional, but not before the lives of many Americans had been seriously disrupted.

In the state of heightened national anxiety, people often lost their jobs or were shunned in their community simply because they were called up before one of these committees. Suspected Communists and other leftists were exposed to serious social pressure and had their freedoms violated. The best known example of that were ten Hollywood screenwriters, accused by HUAC of being "disloyal." Before the committee they pleaded their First Amendment rights to free speech and beliefs and refused to testify. They believed that the First Amendment protected their freedom to have whatever political beliefs they chose as long as no one could prove that they had broken any laws. But the congressional committee took a different view of their refusal. They were held in contempt of Congress, tried, and convicted. They had expected to be vindicated before the Supreme Court but lost there when the Supreme Court refused to reconsider convictions in lower courts. Many of them went to prison. Their crime essentially was to refuse to name names and to draw others into the persecutions of "suspected traitors." They were, after that, blacklisted in the movie industry. Some of them continued to work by writing under a pseudonym. Others went to Europe to work there.

Discussion Questions

Constitutional guarantees protect us against government attempts to regulate political opinions and their expression. But do those constitutional guarantees also protect us against the demand from private employers that we disown certain political views and not express them? Are they allowed to blacklist employees jailed for their political views? Give reasons for your answer.

After the Supreme Court had refused to uphold First Amendment Rights as a defense against the many different investigating committees, many people who were unwilling to name names pleaded the Fifth Amendment that protects persons against self-incrimination. The courts, including the Supreme Court, accepted that, but the anti-Communist crusaders turned it into an admission of guilt. Pleading the Fifth was construed as an admission of guilt of some sort. Many people were fired from their jobs for pleading the Fifth Amendment. Many other persons had to face investigative boards at work.

Discussion Question

Look up the Fifth Amendment. Is it fair to assume the guilt of someone who pleads the Fifth Amendment in Court and to act on that assumption? Give reasons for your answer.

The government and private companies instituted loyalty review boards to ferret out Communists and their sympathizers, and persons found to be "disloyal" to the United States were dismissed from their jobs. In many cases employees were found to be disloyal on the basis of secret Federal Bureau of Investigation (FBI) information that was never shared with them. They had no way of defending themselves adequately or showing that the evidence against them was weak or an outright falsehood. These private loyalty review boards were not subject to the same rules as proceedings in a court of law. The employees found disloyal did not have to be considered innocent until proven guilty, they were not privy to the information used against them, and they had no right to attorneys in defending themselves.

The USA Patriot Act

Soon after the September 11th attacks, Congress passed the USA Patriot Act, which significantly limited citizen protections against previously illegal government surveillance, search, and seizure. The courts still have to rule on that act, but it may well be seen in future years as one more instance of our ambivalence about freedom. Once again unfocused public fears find a concrete anchor in persecutions of Muslims, and more generally, persons of mid-Eastern origins. Additionally, the government has, at present, extended the legal category of persons called "enemy combatants." These are persons captured fighting our troops although they are not soldiers. The favorite examples are spies caught in the act. The government now applies this designation much more widely than previously sanctioned by the courts to persons captured suspected of having given assistance to Al Qaeda or the Taliban.[5] Anyone so designated can be detained indefinitely without access to legal assistance whether that person is a resident alien or a citizen. Many persons have been and are still being detained, and their cases are slowly making their ways through the courts. In a parallel maneuver, the government has used immigration issues to arrest more than a thousand individuals of mid-Eastern origins on the grounds that their immigration papers were not in order. Persons arrested have been held incommunicado for extended periods; immigration hearings are, unlike court proceedings, closed to the public. Persons considered to be a threat by the government, in effect, lose the traditional immunities of citizens, the protection against being held without due process, or the obligation of the government to bring people to speedy trial, and to justify arresting persons in a court of law.

Discussion Questions

Look up summaries of the USA Patriot Act. Which provisions do you think might threaten traditional American freedoms?

What do you think about those provisions? Should they remain in the law or be rescinded? Give reasons for your answers.

We are still too close to September 11th and these government measures against persons who are suspected of being a threat to our security to be perfectly certain whether this is one more example of our surrendering our freedoms in the hope of finding ourselves more secure. In retrospect it seems clear that the serious injuries done to so many Japanese-Americans, and after that war, to many suspected "Communists," did not protect us because whatever the real threats in those periods may have been, the persons persecuted were not part of them. The same may well turn out to be true another time in our day: the people targeted at the beginning of the twenty-first century as threats to our nation's security may well be innocent of that. Harassing and maltreating them may not enhance security because the threats, which seem real to us today, come from elsewhere.

This history of repeated periods of national panic when we are willing to sacrifice our own freedom, and even more, the freedom of others, to our national security suggests that our self-representation as the "land of the free" is incomplete and one-sided. Yes, we value freedom and are willing to defend it at considerable sacrifice at times. But we are also afraid of it and are willing, at other times, to limit it severely to protect ourselves against threats to our national security — threats that later generations often characterize as mostly imaginary.

Hobbes paints a gloomy picture of human beings and their relations to one another. All are out for themselves; no one has any sympathy for others or real love. Cooperation is possible only where individuals pursue the same interests. Under those conditions extreme distrust is the only rational policy; threats are everywhere and vigilance is the preferred policy. Although many readers find Hobbes's presentation of our personal and social life to be exaggerated, a look at our history shows that again and again in times of perceived national crisis, we have adopted a Hobbesian attitude, seeing enemies everywhere and prosecuting them relentlessly. We shall consider the implications of that attitude for government and for individual freedom later.

First, we need to consider a rather more sanguine picture of human beings and of social life. Frequently we have adopted that view in shaping national policy. It too has been developed for our consideration by one of the great seventeenth-century political philosophers, Locke.

PHILOSOPHY OF MUTUAL TRUST

Not all crises or all situations when the nation seems under threat and security is at a premium produce the sort of panic that makes citizens willing to surrender freedom even if its loss is not certain to make us more secure. There are times of national conflict or international threat in which our dedication to freedom is only intensified. At such times Americans rally to increase the freedom of those previously deprived and consolidate the freedom of those already free. Two periods come to mind as examples:

In the 1930s, during the Great Depression, 25 percent of the workforce was unemployed. Homeless men, or entire families, roamed the country riding the freight cars illegally, desperately looking for work. The economic system had clearly broken down and there was a lot of talk in the air about abolishing capitalism, of replacing it by socialism or communism, and of making a revolution. For anyone whose property or political power gave them an investment in the existing system, however ineffective at that time, it was a frightening time. It would have been easy for the nation to lose its nerve and to find scapegoats to persecute. There existed groups that wanted to push the country in that direction, but they were, at the time, in the minority. The majority of Americans reacted to the uncertainties and threats of the times in a much more generous fashion.

Instead, with the so-called "New Deal," Americans embarked on a bold new project to assure a minimum of economic security for everyone in the country. It was the beginning of Social Security, unemployment compensation, insurance to protect people who were hurt at work, and programs to rescue the poorest of the poor. It was, above all, a major effort to find work for everybody, to allow everyone to be a useful citizen, to do work they would get paid for and which would, if at all possible, give them the satisfaction of using their abilities to be useful and productive. On the other hand, government instituted controls over the banking system and over investments to protect the public against unscrupulous and unsound business practices. A new spirit invaded the United States, a spirit of cooperation, of believing that every citizen was valuable and important and deserving of a good life. With that belief came a relatively greater willingness for those who were well off to pay taxes to support programs for those whose life was more difficult.

Here is how a participant in the early years of the Roosevelt administration remembered it years later: "The climate was exciting. You were part of a society that was on the move. You were involved in something that could make a difference. Laws could be changed. So could the conditions of people. . . . The New Dealers were different. I'm not only talking about policy people. I am talking about clerks, who felt what they were doing was important. You did not take time out for lunch because of a job that had to be done."[6]

Our experience was similar during the Vietnam War. The nation had just experienced more than ten years of bitter struggle over civil rights. Animosities within the nation, between races, between regions of the country, and between local government and the government in Washington were intense. Lives were lost; dissent ran high. And then we found ourselves engaged in an unpopular war in Southeast Asia. This war seemed to many a major confrontation with communism, as represented by the two large and threatening nations, the Soviet Union and Communist China. To others it seemed no more than a terrible waste of U.S. and Vietnamese lives for the sake of maintaining preeminent power for the United States and U.S. business around the globe. Embroiled in bitter internal struggles, we were at the same time facing threats abroad. But once again we did not falter. We did not retreat into panic that regarded freedom as a small price to pay for the mere promise of greater security. Instead we, once again, expanded the social measures intended to alleviate suffering of all of those whom this society had left behind. Under the slogan of "The Great Society," new social programs tried to give every child a healthy start through the Head Start program that provided the same preschool classes for the sons and daughters of the poor that many middle-class children received to prepare them for primary education. Medicare extended health insurance to the elderly and Medicaid helped the poor to pay for health care. A variety of programs assisted poor school districts to improve the education their children received and others made it possible for young people with limited income to go to college. Food stamps and school lunch programs addressed the problems of malnutrition. In many different ways the society extended itself to try to give every child a fair start in life. Affirmative action programs (see chapter 1) tried to heal the damages done by three hundred years of racial and gender segregation. With support from a majority of Americans, the nation embarked on concrete programs to enhance "liberty and justice for all." No longer was that a pious wish uttered in patriotic rituals. We decided to be serious and try to realize this great ideal, even during the war we were fighting in Vietnam.

In both of these periods, Americans rejected the Hobbesian view of human nature and of society: they refused to see each other as utterly selfish competitors. However fearful, they did not retreat to the attitude where the freedom of others or even our own was worth little and was seen mostly as a threat because it provided the opportunity for others to do us harm. We continued to believe that everyone is entitled to freedom, that we all have moral worth, and that our actions are motivated not only by self-interest but by a serious regard for morality.

In these periods, our attitudes and conduct exemplified the view of human beings and political society held by Locke.

Discussion Question

The preceding paragraphs presented the social programs of the "New Deal" and the "Great Society" as examples of respect for everyone's equal freedom. What would be an alternative to that reading of our history?

The State of Nature as Locke Saw It (Excerpts from *The Second Treatise on Government*)

Coming to maturity almost fifty years after Hobbes, Locke experienced the coming of peace and the resolution of the bitter conflicts of the English Civil War of the 1640s. The conflict between the supporters of the monarchy and the supporters of a democratic republic was resolved in a constitutional monarchy; extended toleration moderated the discord between the religions. In 1688, in an upheaval, mostly peaceful, that is today known as the "Glorious Revolution," James II, a Catholic, was replaced by William and Mary, both Protestants, and Parliament became one of the centers of power in the English state. In the light of that experience, Locke came to believe that compromise was possible in human societies and important change could be produced peacefully. Unlike Hobbes, he did not think that every conflict threatened to end in violence.

More confident and more trusting in the peaceful possibilities of human association, Locke sketches out a different and much more complex vision of the state of nature. As Hobbes sees human beings, they have desires and act to satisfy those. Thwart a man's desires and he will fight you. Human beings are competitors with the each other in pursuit of the goods that satisfy their needs and wishes. In the state of nature, human beings are governed only by the desire to survive. There are no rules of conduct in that condition. What anyone chooses to do is open to criticism only if it does not produce the intended results.

But in Locke's view of the state of nature, human conduct is subject to moral rules. What a person does may be counterproductive but may nevertheless be morally justified. Or it may be morally wrong even though it accomplishes the intended results. Human beings are free by nature and anything one does to violate another's freedom is wrong. Even in the state of nature we regard each other as moral beings, as creatures with rights to life, to freedom, and to the protection of property. Locke's political philosophy is deeply imbued with liberal values: every human being has its own value and dignity; everyone is entitled to equal freedom. Human beings are more than animals seeking to satisfy their needs; they are beings with moral standing that commands respect from other humans. Even in the state of nature they have the obligation to respect the integrity of other humans. They may not violate the others' freedoms or property.

Here is what Locke tells us about the state of nature in *The Second Treatise on Government* (1690).

Chapter 2: The state of nature

4. To understand political power correctly and derive it from its proper source, we must consider what state all men are *naturally* in. It is a state in which men are perfectly free to order their actions, and dispose of their possessions and themselves, in any way they like, without asking anyone else's permission—all this subject only to limits set by the law of nature.

It is also a state of equality, in which no-one has more power and authority than anyone else; because it is simply obvious that creatures of the same species and status, all born to all the same advantages of nature and to the use of the same abilities, should also be equal in other ways, with no-one being subjected to or subordinate to anyone else, unless God, the lord and master of them all, were to declare clearly and explicitly his wish that some one person be raised above the others and given an undoubted right to dominion and sovereignty . . .

6. But though this is a state of liberty, it isn't a state of license in which there are *no* constraints on how people behave. A man in that state is absolutely free to dispose of himself or his possessions, but he isn't at liberty to *destroy* himself, or even to destroy any created thing in his possession unless something nobler than its mere preservation is at stake. The state of nature is governed by a law that creates obligations for everyone. And reason, which *is* that law, teaches anyone who takes the trouble to consult it, that *because we are all equal and independent, no one ought to harm anyone else in his life, health, liberty, or possessions*. This is because we are all the work of one omnipotent and infinitely wise maker; we are all the servants of one sovereign master, sent into the world by his order to do his business; we are all the property of him who made us, and he made us to last as long as *he* chooses, not as long as *we* choose; we have the same abilities, and share in one common nature, so there can't be any rank ordering that would authorize some of us to destroy others, as if we were made to be *used* by one another, as the lower kinds of creatures *are* made to be used by us.

Everyone is obliged to preserve himself and not opt out of life willfully, so for the same reason everyone ought, when his own survival isn't at stake, to do as much as he can to preserve the rest of mankind; and except when it's a matter of punishing an offender, no-one may take away or damage anything that contributes to the preservation of someone else's life, liberty, health, limb, or goods.[7]

Discussion Question

Locke argues that human beings, even in the state of nature, have certain moral obligations to one another to respects each other's equal freedom. Look at the text carefully and determine what Locke's reasons are for that opinion. How powerful do you think those reasons are?

Human beings have desires—Locke of course agrees on that with Hobbes—and paramount among them is the desire for survival. But our pursuit of the goods that satisfy our desires is limited by our obligations to other persons. We need to avoid harming them. In a world in which compromise is possible, in which other persons are not always enemies and therefore to be distrusted, it is only reasonable that we should avoid making enemies by injuring others. In Locke's more trusting view of the world not every person is automatically an enemy. It is reasonable, therefore, to demand of ourselves that we not make enemies if we can possibly avoid it. Hobbes thought that all human beings are inevitably each other's enemies; each is a mere means to another's ends. But according to Locke, we live in a world in which others are not to be used as means to our own ends, a world in which we can share with the others without fearing that they will take advantage of us, a world in which respecting the freedom of others and caring for their well-being is the most reasonable course of action.

Discussion Question

The belief in the intrinsic importance and dignity of all human beings is an essential part of traditional liberal political principles. Human beings are entitled to equal freedoms because they are all equally valuable. How would Hobbes argue against this principle? How persuasive do you think his arguments are?

THE POWER OF THE GOVERNMENT

Hobbes and Locke on Government

Hobbes (Excerpts from Leviathan)

Having exhibited his ideas about human nature in his story about the state of nature, Hobbes is now ready to develop his theory of government and its relations to citizens. In the state of nature human life is "solitary, poor, nasty, brutish, and short." To save us from this deplorable condition we need a superior force to make rules and to enforce them vigorously so as to suppress the constant and deadly competition that is the state of nature. Government must above all be strong. It must be able to establish laws and to keep order so that we may trust that our neighbors will not harm us at every turn, that they will keep at least some of their promises, that contracts made can be expected to be fulfilled, and that disagreements will be litigated in a court of law rather than being settled by hired thugs. Given his view of human life, Hobbes looks for security from a government that is strong enough and determined enough to preserve us from our neighbors, let alone our enemies, by enforcing the laws against violence, theft, and fraud with the utmost diligence. Government must be able to do whatever is necessary to force everyone to refrain from robbing or murdering their competitors, and instead, to compete only with nonviolent means. It can succeed in keeping the peace only if it is given free rein; freedoms guaranteed to all citizens should not be allowed to restrict the state when upholding law and order. Citizens have no rights against the government; its actions serve the single purpose of suppressing violence. If peace is to be preserved, citizens cannot have constitutionally guaranteed freedoms that might interfere with law enforcement and peacekeeping. Government power may not be restricted by laws; the government must be above the law.

Chapter 17. The causes, creation, and definition of a commonwealth

Men naturally love liberty, and dominion over others; so what is the final cause or end or design they have in mind when they introduce the *restraint upon themselves* under which we see them live in commonwealths? It is the prospect of their own preservation and, through that, of a more contented life; that is to say, of getting themselves out of the miserable condition of war which (as I have shown) necessarily flows from the natural passions of men when there is no visible power to keep them in awe and tie them by fear of punishment to keep their covenants and to obey the laws of nature . . .

For the laws of nature—enjoining justice, fairness, modesty, mercy, and (in short) treating others as we want them to treat us—are in themselves contrary to our natural passions, unless some power frightens us into observing them. In the absence of such a power, our natural passions carry us to partiality, pride, revenge, and the like. And covenants without the sword are merely words, with no strength to secure a man at all. . . .

The only way to establish a common power that can defend them from the invasion of foreigners and the injuries of one another, and thereby make them secure enough to be able to nourish themselves and live contentedly through their own labors and the fruits of the earth, is to confer all their power and strength on one man, or one assembly of men, so as to turn all their wills by a majority vote into a single will. That is to say: to appoint one man or assembly of men to *bear their person*; and everyone to *own* and *acknowledge himself to be the author of* every act that he who bears their person performs or causes to be performed in matters concerning the common peace and safety, and all of them to submit their wills to his will, and their judgments to his judgment.

This is more than mere agreement or harmony; it is a real *unity* of them all. They are unified in that they constitute *one* single person, created through a covenant of every man with every other man, as though *each* man were to say to *each* of the others:

'I authorize and give up my right of governing myself to this man, or to this assembly of men, on condition that you surrender to him your right of governing yourself, and authorize all his actions in the same way.'

When this is done, the multitude so united in one person is called a COMMONWEALTH, in Latin CIVITAS. This is the method of creation of that great LEVIATHAN, or rather (to speak more reverently) of that *mortal god* to which we owe, under the immortal God, our peace and defense. For by this authority that has been given to him by every individual man in the commonwealth, he has conferred on him the use of so much power and strength that people's fear of it enables him to harmonize and control the wills of them all, to the end of peace at home and mutual aid against their enemies abroad. . . .

Chapter 18. The rights of sovereigns by institution

A commonwealth is said to be 'instituted' when a multitude of men agree and covenant—each one with each other—that when some man or assembly of men is chosen by majority vote to present the person of them all (that is, to be their representative), each of them will authorize all the actions and judgments of that man or assembly of men as though they were his own, doing this to the end of living peacefully among themselves and being protected against other men. This binds those who did not vote for this representative, as well as those who did. For unless the votes are all understood to be included in the majority of votes, they have come together in vain, and contrary to the end that each proposed for himself, namely the peace and protection of them all.

From the form of the institution are derived all the power and all the rights of the one having supreme power, as well as the duties of all the citizens. I shall discuss these rights, powers, and duties under *twelve* headings. . . .

Secondly, what gives the sovereign a right to bear the person of all his subjects is a covenant that they make with one another, and not a covenant between him and any of them; there can't be a breach of covenant on *his* part; and consequently none of his subjects can be freed from subjection by a claim that the sovereign has forfeited his right to govern by breaking his covenant with his subject(s). It is obvious that the sovereign makes no covenant with his subjects on the way to becoming sovereign. . . .

Fourthly, because every subject is by this institution of the commonwealth the author of all the actions and judgments of the sovereign, it follows that nothing the sovereign does can *wrong* any of his subjects, nor ought any of them to accuse him of injustice. For someone who acts by the authority of someone else can't in acting wrong the person by whose authority he acts; but according to this institution of a commonwealth, every individual man is an author of everything the sovereign does; so someone who complains of being wronged by *his sovereign* complains about something of which *he himself* is an author; so he oughtn't to accuse anyone but himself. . . .

Fifthly, following from the preceding point: no man who has sovereign power can justly be put to death or punished in any other way by his subjects. . . . And therefore,

Sixthly, it is for the sovereignty to be the judge of what opinions and doctrines are threats to peace and what ones tend to support it; and consequently of which men are to be trusted to speak to multitudes of people, on what occasions, and how far they should be allowed to go; and of who shall examine the doctrines of all books before they are published."[8]

What Hobbes describes in these pages is often called *absolute monarchy* or *dictatorship*—a government that is not subject to the laws it makes. It is absolute precisely because there are no rules to limit its power—it may do whatever it can do. It should do whatever is necessary to keep the peace. Citizens have no claims against the monarch and no freedoms which the monarch must respect at all costs. They have no right to complain about the monarch because they have hired him, as it were, to do whatever is necessary to protect them against one another. Hobbes rejects any claims that citizens have inherent freedoms, merely by virtue of their humanity.

Discussion Questions

1. *Hobbes believes that a government allowed to use whatever violence it deems necessary and which is not restricted by legislatures, citizens rights, and courts defending them can keep order and secure the lives of citizens. Consider the effectiveness or lack thereof of violence in war, in civil strife, as well as in education or child rearing. How plausible is Hobbes's claim?*

2. *Do you believe that governments not subject to law can enhance the security of citizens? Give reasons for your answers.*

Locke (Excerpts from The Second Treatise on Government)

Locke provides a different picture of government because his view of human beings is different. To be sure, human beings have their desires and often get carried away by them; they do what they know to be wrong because it invades the freedom of others. But human beings are not only motivated by desire, they also have a moral sense. However powerful desires, some of them are wrong and should not be satisfied. Morality distinguishes between desires one should resist—such as wanting to murder someone, take their property, or "bear false witness" against them—and those one may yield to. Humans know that they are entitled to freedom and they know that others are owed the same freedoms. We are complex creatures and live in the conflict between the sense of what is morally right and of what we want. Caught in these dilemmas, we need a government to gently move us away from being overcome by our desire and to remind us of our moral obligations. We definitely do not want that government to violate the freedoms that make us genuinely human. A government must respect our freedoms. We have the right to remove a government that fails to do so.

> 95. Men all being naturally free, equal, and independent, no one can be deprived of this freedom, etc. and subjected to the political power of someone else, without his own consent. The only way anyone can strip off his natural liberty and clothe himself in the bonds of civil society is for him to agree with other men to unite into a community, so as to live together comfortably, safely, and peaceably, in a secure enjoyment of their properties and a greater security against outsiders. Any number of men can do this, because it does no harm to the freedom of the rest; *they* are left with the liberty of the state of nature, which they had all along. When any number of men have in this way consented to make one community or government, that immediately incorporates them, turns them into a single *body politic* in which the majority have a right to act on behalf of the rest and to bind them by its decisions. . . .
>
> 97. Thus every man, by agreeing with others to make one body politic under one government, puts himself under an obligation to everyone in that society to submit to the decisions of the majority, and to be bound by it. Otherwise—that is, if he were willing to submit himself only to the majority acts that he approved of—the original compact through which he and others incorporated into one society would be meaningless; it wouldn't be a compact if it left him as free of obligations as he had been in the state of nature. . . .

Chapter 9: The purposes of political society and government

> 123. If man in the state of nature is as free as I have said he is—if he is absolute lord of his own person and possessions, equal to the greatest and subject to nobody—why will he part with his freedom? Why will he give up this lordly status and subject himself to the control of someone else's power? The answer is obvious:
>
> Though in the state of nature he has an unrestricted right to his possessions, he is far from assured that he will be able to get the *use* of them, because they are constantly exposed to invasion by others. All men are kings as much as he is, every man is his equal, and most men are not strict observers of fairness and justice; so his hold on the property he has in this state is very unsafe, very insecure. This makes him willing to leave a state in which he is very free, but which is full of fears and continual dangers; and not unreasonably he looks for others with whom he can

enter into a society for the mutual preservation of their lives, liberties and estates, which I call by the general name 'property.' (The others may be ones who are already united in such a society, or ones who would like to be so united.)

124. So the great and chief purpose of men's uniting into commonwealths and putting themselves under government is *the preservation of their property*. The state of nature lacks many things that are needed for this; I shall discuss three of them. First, the state of nature lacks an established, settled, known law, received and accepted by common consent as the standard of right and wrong and as the common measure to decide all controversies. What about the law of nature? Well, it is plain and intelligible to all reasonable creatures; but men are biased by self-interest, as well as ignorant about the law of nature because they don't study it; and so they aren't apt to accept it as a law that will bind them if it is applied to their particular cases.

125. Secondly, the state of nature lacks a known and impartial judge, with authority to settle all differences according to the established law. In that state everyone is both judge and enforcer of the law of nature, and few men will play either role well. Men are partial to themselves, so that passion and revenge are very apt to carry them too far, and with too much heat, in their own cases; and their negligence and lack of concern will make them remiss in other men's cases.

126. Thirdly, the state of nature often lacks a power to back up and support a correct sentence, and to enforce it properly. People who have committed crimes will usually, if they can, resort to *force* to retain the benefits of their crime; this includes using force to resist punishment; and such resistance often makes the punishment dangerous, even destructive, to those who try to inflict it.

127. Thus mankind are in poor shape while they remain in the state of nature—despite all their privileges there—so that they are quickly driven into society. That is why we seldom find any number of men living together for long in this state. The drawbacks it exposes them to . . . make them take refuge under the established laws of government, and seek there to preserve their property. This is what makes each one of them so willingly give up his power of punishing, a power then to be exercised only by whoever is appointed to that role, this being done by whatever rules are agreed on by the community or by those whom they have authorized to draw up the rules for them. This is the basic cause, as well as the basic justification, for the legislative and executive powers within a government as well as for the governments and societies themselves. . . .

Chapter 11: The extent of the legislative power

134. The great purpose for which men enter into society is to be safe and at peace in their use of their property; and the great instrument by which this is to be achieved is the laws established in that society. So the first and fundamental *positive* law of any commonwealth is the establishing of the legislative power; and the first and fundamental *natural* law—which should govern even the legislature itself—is the preservation of the society and (as far as the public good allows it) the preservation of every person in it.

This legislature is not only the supreme power of the commonwealth, but is sacred and unalterable in the hands in which the community have placed it; and no other person or organization, whatever its form and whatever power it has behind it, can make edicts that have the force of law and create obligations as a law does unless they have been permitted to do this by the legislature that the public has chosen and appointed.

Without this, the law would lack something that it absolutely must have if it is to *be* a law, namely *the consent of the society*. Nobody has power to subject a society to laws except with the society's consent and by their authority; and therefore all the obedience that anyone can owe, even under the most solemn obligations, ultimately terminates in this supreme power—the legislature of the commonwealth—and is governed by the laws it enacts. . . .

135. Though the legislature (whether one person or more, whether functioning intermittently or continuously at work) is the supreme power in every commonwealth, there are four important things to be said about what it may *not* do . . . First, it doesn't and can't possibly have absolutely arbitrary power over the lives and fortunes of the people. For the legislative power is simply the combined power of every member of the society, which has been handed over to the person or persons constituting the legislature; there can't be *more* of this power than those people had in the state of nature before they entered into society and gave their power to the community. Nobody can transfer to someone else more power than he has himself; and nobody has an absolute arbitrary power to destroy his own life, or take away someone else's life or property. . . .

136. Secondly, the legislature or supreme authority cannot give itself a power to rule by sudden, arbitrary decrees. It is bound to dispense justice and decide the rights of the subject by published standing laws, and known authorized judges.[9]

What a difference between these two conceptions of government! Hobbes is only interested in establishing a government forceful enough to keep the peace. Locke's central concern is a government that governs only with the consent of the citizens and preserves their property. As Hobbes sees the political landscape, the main threat comes from citizens trying to meet their needs by violent means. Locke, on the other hand, believes that the main threat comes from governments violating citizens' property rights and governing without the consent of the people. Beginning with two different conceptions of human nature, these two theorists arrive at different conceptions of the relation between government and citizen.

HOBBES, LOCKE, AND THE ANARCHISTS

Anarchists prize individual liberty above all; not surprisingly, therefore, there are many different versions of anarchism. But all are united in their love of liberty. Bakunin, an eloquent nineteenth-century Russian anarchist, put the matter as follows:

> I am a fanatic lover of liberty, considering it as the unique condition under which intelligence, dignity and human happiness can develop and grow; not the purely formal liberty conceded, measured out and regulated by the State, an eternal lie which in reality represents nothing more than the privilege of some founded on the slavery of the rest. . . . No, I mean the only kind of liberty that is worthy of the name, liberty that consists in the full development of all the material, intellectual and moral powers that are latent in each person; liberty that recognizes no restrictions other than those determined by the laws of our own individual nature, which cannot properly be regarded as restrictions, since these laws are not imposed by any outside legislator beside or above us, but are immanent and inherent, forming the very basis of our material, intellectual and moral being — they do not limit us but are the real and immediate conditions of our freedom.[10]

Discussion Question

Bakunin talks about two different kinds of freedom "formal liberty" and "real liberty." Explain the difference between the two.

Anarchists are, as a consequence of their intense love of liberty, extremely suspicious of government. Henry David Thoreau expresses their views about government perfectly when he opens his essay on "Civil Disobedience" with the sentences "I heartily accept the motto—That government is best which governs least and I would like to see it acted up to more rapidly and systematically. Carried out it finally amounts to this, which also I believe: —That government is best which governs not at all."[11] Anarchists provide two reasons for their hostility to governments.

Governments, they point out, are massive purveyors of violence and coercion. They are a constant threat to individual freedom. The symbol of government power is the policeman, armed and ready to coerce citizens into obeying the law. But that is just the beginning of government coercion. There is the taxman to take your taxes from you, the board of health inspector to look behind the stoves for dirt in restaurants but also in private homes, the animal control officer to check whether you have too many pets, or the wrong kind, in your house, the fire department inspector to check your safety provisions, and the building inspector to make sure that you use copper rather than plastic pipes where those are not permitted by local building codes. The board of education determines how your children will be educated, the water department makes sure that your children drink fluoride in the drinking water, regardless of what you may think of that. Officials in city hall give you permission to have a dog or to get married. On numerous occasions when you are trying to live a decent life and be a good citizen, the government suddenly appears on the scene to tell you what to do and to make sure that you do not do what the government forbids. The government gives permission where none ought to be needed. We think of ourselves as free citizens but the anarchists remind us of the ever present interference by the government in what should be our private affairs. In the view of the anarchists, government is not the benign peacekeeper envisaged by Locke but the coercive busybody that Hobbes advocates.

Anarchists point to a second oppressive role of governments. In most societies, our own included, there are significant differentials of power between different citizens. Some citizens get their way more often than others; in a conflict with others, they are more likely to be able to make the other do what they want. Government is not, as Locke thought it should be, an impartial arbiter in the conflicts between citizens. Government is, in fact, on the side of the rich and powerful. It enforces the injustices that the ruling strata of the society perpetrate against the rest of us.

Discussion Question

Make a rough sketch of the different groups of people in our society and indicate which have the most power and which the least. Order the list by how powerful each group is.

Anarchists also believe that most, if not all, differentials of power are unjust. We examined the controversy over the justifications of inequality in the preceding chapter by considering the disagreement between John Rawls and Robert Nozick. The anarchists certainly side with Rawls in this, asserting that existing inequalities are the result of injustice: the people who are rich have become rich at the expense of the poor; they do not deserve their wealth because it is ill-gotten gain.

Anarchists rest their second argument against government on this belief that most, if not all, inequalities in wealth and power are unjust. The government, they say, is usually on the side the rich and powerful. It more often helps the landlord to evict a tenant than it forces the landlord to provide the services a tenant pays for. It more often arrests and imprisons the poor who commit small crimes than it prosecutes and punishes the large business operators who defraud others of millions or even billions of dollars. It enforces environmental legislation against the homeowners saddled with obsolete septic systems and ignores big industries who discharge large amounts of wastes into rivers and the ocean. Government is suspect because it sides with the powerful and adds to the burdens of the poor, of the hardworking men and women who are the backbone of any country.

Discussion Question

Do you agree with the anarchists that governments, most of the time, side with the rich and powerful against common men and women? Give reasons for your answer.

Locke agrees with the anarchists that equal freedom for all is of the essence of a good society but disagrees with them about the nature of government. Unlike the anarchists, he believes that it is possible to establish governments that do not coerce citizens because they are no more than the representatives of the will of the people. When such governments exert compulsion on citizens they are only exerting pressures the citizens want to exert on themselves.

Discussion Question

How can Locke justify the existence of government when he also recognizes that all human beings are entitled to equal freedom?

The anarchists answer that the existence of government cannot be justified. They invite us to consider human history and to mention any occasions where citizens assembled to conclude a social contract. Most likely the social contract entered into by the pilgrims arriving in the New World will be one of a short list of examples. The anarchists will then ask us for examples of governments that originated in wars, which were established by superior powers to rule over those who were less powerful. We will have too many examples of those. The anarchists will conclude from this experiment that governments, in the overwhelming number of cases, were established by force and often by force of arms, that their power derives not from the consent of the ruled but from the capacity of the powerful to coerce everyone else. The story of governments established with the consent of the governed is a myth that the powerful invented to hide their own violence and coercion.

Discussion Questions

1. *What can Locke reply to this anarchist challenge?*
2. *Consider our own history. Is the establishment of our republic an example of Locke's story about social contracts, or does it support the anarchist claim that most governments are coercively imposed by the few on the many?*
3. *What would Hobbes have to say about anarchists?*

WHO IS RIGHT?

Arguments from Human Nature

Both Hobbes and Locke present their pictures of human nature as proven fact, borne out by experience, by our own behavior, or by the experience of the relationships between nations. They therefore each claim that their conception of good government—government that is above the law or government elected by the people and subject to the laws it makes itself—is justified by looking at the facts about human nature. But the factual claims they make are incompatible. The facts claimed by one of them must be mistaken. How can we decide whom to believe? Philosophers have argued back and forth without coming to a conclusion and the arguments still continue.

This is not a problem peculiar to Hobbes or Locke. Central to many disagreements about ethics and politics are divergent opinions about human nature. If one agrees with Aristotle that men are, by nature, superior to women and to slaves (see chapter 1), one is not likely to agree with liberal political philosophers that all human beings are entitled to freedom and equality. That idea, so familiar to us, presupposes a certain view of human nature: namely that all adults are capable of living free lives—something that Aristotle would certainly have denied. The rise of beliefs in equal freedom for all was accompanied by a fundamental change in the conception of human nature. Aristotle and his Greek contemporaries discerned the capacities for a free life only in men; they are now attributed to all human adults with very few exceptions. The conception of human nature has changed.

In the preceding chapter, we looked at one of many debates among liberal political theorist—the disagreement between Rawls and Nozick about redistributive social programs. One of the issues between those two philosophers also concerns what humans are like. Nozick believes that property rights are absolute, that they may not be infringed on for the sake of raising funds from the rich to better the life of the poor. He rests that belief on his picture of humans as being distinct individuals who may not be used for the benefit of others. As human beings, "what matters to us in addition to our experiences? First we want to *do* certain things . . . we want to *be* a certain way."[12] What we want is to live our lives ourselves. Nozick's description of human nature leaves out what Rawls puts almost in first place: that human beings want to *cooperate* with one another, that it is of the essence of our human nature that we are social beings who live with others. Nozick sees human beings as solitary; their life with others does not determine their nature. Everyone has rights which they want to see preserved and are willing, themselves, to work hard to preserve. Their nature is, we might say, asocial. Not so in the view of Rawls who sees us as essentially wanting to live well together. Central to Rawlsian human beings is desire to live in a just society where each is not merely defending individual rights but wants to cooperate, wants to see to it that others have their equal rights met. The central idea for Nozick's men and women are individual rights; for persons, as Rawls sees them, the central demand is for mutuality and reciprocity of rights and freedoms.

The same appeal to different conceptions of human nature is frequent in debates outside of professional philosophy. Men who view women as sexual objects first, and as human beings in their own right second, defend that by appeals to human nature, to the constant urgency of male sexual desire. Defenses of wives subordinating themselves to their husbands (chapter 1) appeal to scripture but also to a definite conception of what women—all women, everywhere—are like and what their purpose is in the world. Defenses of free market institutions, which we will examine in chapter 3, similarly rest on specific claims about the self-regarding and competitive nature of human beings.

Discussion Questions

Many communities when confronted with a significant influx of new immigrants will react negatively. Immigrants are not respected; they are met with suspicion and made to feel unwanted. In many communities, the elderly whose children are grown and have moved away, will balk at paying for education, on the grounds that they do not have children in school. Both of these phenomena are often explained by saying that it's "human nature" to distrust strangers or to be unwilling to pay for the education of other people's children. When people offer that explanation, what are they telling us?

1. *That xenophobia and narrowly self-regarding behavior are a part of every human being's makeup, regardless of where they live or in what historical period.*

2. *That people are often, but not always, xenophobic and narrowly self-regarding and*

   a. *such behavior, being a part of human nature, cannot be changed and humans will always be that way?*

   b. *or such behavior is difficult to change?*

Which of these do you think people mean when they use "human nature" explanations? Which of these, if any, are true? Give reasons for your answers.

Human Nature and Human Society

Philosophers often ask whether Hobbes's or Locke's account of the state of nature is true. But that may not be the best question to ask. Whether the world

is a totally fearful place where all are enemies of all, or whether there are possibilities of peaceful negotiation and of mutual caring is not so much an objective fact independent of ourselves but depends on our own state of fear or of
trust. *Experience shows that our perceptions of the world are often self-fulfilling.* If I am afraid of everyone and approach everyone with distrust, others will
reciprocate and together we create a world as Hobbes describes it. If there is
room in our world for trust, for love, and for respect of the other's moral character, cooperation as well as freedom and democracy become reasonable possibilities. The pictures drawn by Hobbes and Locke of human nature and the
human condition—which they call the state of nature—are, if they are widely
held, self-fulfilling prophecies. As we saw previously in this chapter, at times
in our history, a Hobbesian picture of human nature dominated our thinking
and our emotional life: we saw enemies everywhere and were sure they were
lurking just around the corner even when we did not see them. Where many
people live by that picture of themselves and their fellow citizens, distrust is
rampant and all are trying to save themselves, even if that means betraying
their best friends or libeling the innocent. At other times, most of us held more
sanguine views of our nature and in that more trusting and confident atmos-
phere, many people did extraordinary work to better the lives of many and to
improve the life of our nation as a whole. Different versions of human nature
are not so much givens but creations of humans themselves.

How to Create Trust

The experiences of Father Greg Boyle in his work with gang members in East
Los Angeles are an interesting example of the complex interdependence between the behaviors of human beings and how they are being treated by their
fellow humans. Trust blossoms where people trust one another. Father Boyle
was originally drawn into this work when, in his role as pastor to people living in public housing projects, he had to comfort families whose young men
died in gang wars. Talking to the young people he begins to understand that
many of them have never had a regular job. When his efforts to find work for
them—which many of them want—are unsuccessful, he starts up small industries, such as making T-shirts, or removing graffiti from walls, to be able
to find work for at least some of them. Many come from dysfunctional families ravaged by drugs, unemployment, and the rejection by Angeleno society
at large. Growing up in housing projects and as targets of fierce racial prejudice, these young people find the acceptance they often miss at home, in their
families of origin, in gangs. Poorly educated, largely excluded from the job
market, they end up making money by selling drugs, and many of them die
young as victims of their destructive and dangerous way of life.[13]

With Father Boyle these young men act differently than they do when facing police. With him they have one kind of personality: they are gentle, affectionate, striving for responsibility and dignity. They love Father Boyle. He is their friend; they talk to him and trust him as he trusts them. They take him seriously and try to come up to his expectations for them: that they find regular work, that they try to get an education, that they be respectful of their women friends, and that they take responsibility for their children and be better fathers to them than their own fathers had managed to be for them. Father Boyle respects them as serious human beings and for that reason makes demands on them. Police officers, on the other hand, do not trust them. The common wisdom among the police is that these young people understand and respect only violence. To the dehumanizing distrust of the police, the gang members react with brutality.[14] They justify the police distrust of them by acting as the police expect them to act.

Father Boyle shows them unwavering affection and trust—by no means uncritical, to be sure. He condemns their behavior but he never writes them off as persons. Unlike the police he does not think that these young men and women are worthless human beings; he does not think that he is wasting his time in his efforts on their behalf. Good Christian that he is, he does not forget that they too are children of God. The young people reciprocate. In relation to him they are as caring, responsible, hardworking young men and women as circumstances allow them.

Many of them come to a bad end anyway. However hard they may try to leave the drugs and crime behind, to give up gang warfare and become dependable, diligent citizens, not all of them succeed—for many the task is too difficult. But their failures are not exclusively their own faults. Their position in the society and the treatment they receive in many places wears them down. Yes, they fail; but so does the society.

Discussion Questions

Father Boyle distinguishes sharply between someone's actions and their worth as a person. Many people do bad things, but he thinks no one ever becomes a worthless person. The police disagree. They conclude that the young gang members who sell drugs and commit murders are thoroughly bad persons. Do you agree with Father Boyle or the police? Do human beings ever lose their worth as human beings? How would one argue for or against these views?

Trusting or not trusting, respecting others or not—both involve human relationships. The character of the relationship depends on all the persons involved. Father Boyle's young men and women did not trust police because their encounters with them had been violent and demeaning in the past. If one or another police officer tried to win their confidence by treating them respectfully and attentively, perhaps, after a while, they might have wondered whether this officer was different from all the others and might have tried to establish a less hostile relationship. But it is also possible that they would never overcome their prejudice and continue to be cold and harsh with any police officer and the officers, in their turn, would give up discouraged. However the relationship develops, it is made by all the persons involved. Its degree of trust or mistrust results not from anyone's fixed human nature but from the ways the participants have shaped the relationship they have.

Our generalizations about human nature are not statements of facts, but are self-fulfilling prophecies. Each of us is more or less selfish in relation to some other persons and different in relations to others with whom our relationships are different. That is the lesson to be learned from the story about Father Boyle and the young gang members who have a different relationship to him than they do to the police. In the former, they are honest, affectionate human beings who try hard to do what is right and not to disappoint Father Boyle. In relation to the police they are just as rough and beyond ordinary social standards of decent behavior as many police officers believe them to be. In both relationships everyone contributes to the relations between persons by their own actions and their expectations of the other. The models of political society presented to us by Hobbes and Locke do not describe an independent reality, but rather two different kinds of social conditions that arise depending on the ways we act in relation to each other.

Relationships are shaped by all participants. In many cases we manage to develop mutually trusting relationships to other persons. Sometimes, the trust of one person does not enable the other to act so as to deserve that trust. Every person has relationships to many different persons at the same time. Being trusted by Father Boyle was important to all the young people with whom he worked. But all of them also had many other relations in which they met only distrust and rejection. Father Boyle's trust was not enough to outweigh all the other relations of theirs in which they were more or less openly treated as enemies. They continued to act as the enemies that they were perceived as by so many others, often their families, their teachers, and members of rival gangs. The human nature of each of us is shaped by the many different relationships we have to so many different persons. Because we sustain different relationships to different persons, we are different in these different relationships. We do not have a uniform human nature in all our relationships but are rather an often inconsistent bundle of different personalities within one and the same person.

The Character of an Entire Nation

We have been speaking about individual persons and how they have different personalities in different relationships and in different social contexts. But our discussion about freedom and about the relation between citizens and their government concerns our nation as a whole, the "land of the free." What lessons can we draw about our nation as a whole from our better understanding of human nature as something created by us in our different human and social relationships?

Nations are complex. The bumper stickers that sprouted everywhere after September 11 proclaiming that "United We Stand," desperately denied what we all know to be true: namely that our nation consists of many different groups whose relations are not always harmonious and amicable. Every citizen belongs to groups in which he or she is respected as a human being, with a moral nature, each with rights and freedoms. In the neighborhood, the church, the bowling team at work, or many other groups, the golden rule is in force. Everyone takes pains to treat others civilly and respectfully because they expect the same treatment from others. Everyone expects to be treated, at least, politely by others. They count on being secure in their persons and their property, and therefore, attempt to treat others in the same way.

But for each group whose members command respect from one another, there are other groups whom one regards as different. Members of these other groups are not considered equally deserving of respect and civil treatment. One refers to those other groups as "they" and ascribes negative qualities to every one of them. In some cases these "they," the others, were Communists, including anyone who ever attended a meeting considered in some way tainted by communism, and all them were all considered to be "traitors." In other cases they were Japanese Americans, all equally suspect of treason because of their origins or that of their parents or grandparents. Prochoice groups regard opponents of abortion as wild-eyed religious fanatics or as male chauvinists who want to consign women once again to the home and the kitchen, to keep them "barefoot and pregnant" to be completely controlled by men. Abortion opponents, in their turn, think of the pro-choice groups as consisting of completely amoral, bra-burning feminists who hate men, hate children, and are devoid of any of the traditional nurturing qualities of women. Different ethnic groups regard each other with profound distrust; speakers of different languages consider each other inferior and unreliable. The ancient Greeks regarded other nations as "barbarians"—literally "people who babbled," who spoke unintelligibly because they did not speak Greek. Contemporary opposition to bilingual education, bilingual signs in

public places, or bilingual electoral ballots still act from the same conster-
nation in the face of people whom we cannot understand. Racial animosities
create group enmities. Regional differences breed negative stereotypes of the
"effete" East, of "hillbilly" Appalachia, and the shallow, "beautiful" people
of Southern California. One tends to characterize those others, who are not
part of one's own group in hostile or condescending terms ascribing notably
negative qualities to every single member of the group. Fully aware of the
great diversity of human beings in our group, we tend to hold on to simple
generalizations concerning others.

There are "in groups"—groups to which I belong in which I receive respect and good treatment—and "out groups," groups that we, in my group,
regard with suspicion and to whom we deny the rights and freedoms we demand for ourselves. Relations within the in group conform more or less to
the model of a free society that Locke sketched out: we are all moral beings
who are entitled to freedoms and respect for our persons, property, and rights
from all others as long as we, too, respect their rights and freedoms. Freedom and democracy are the ideal forms that in groups take, in our world. But
relations to out groups and their members are much closer to the Hobbesian
model: they are lazy and dirty, sexually promiscuous, and their women
therefore are legitimate sexual targets for our men. Of different out groups
we say that they are greedy for money and will do anything to enrich themselves. Others are portrayed as fanatic adherents to an alien religion who will
not shrink from the most brutal acts, even including self-immolation, to
harm us, who have not injured them in any way. In each case they have no
moral sense. Their pursuit of their goals and desires is not tempered by moral
hesitations. They go after what they want and have no regard for the harm
they will do us. We even characterize them by derogatory names—just as we
do to our enemies in fighting wars. We are therefore entitled to take advantage of them, to despise and maltreat them before they can harm us. Our relations to them put us effectively into a Hobbesian state of nature, in a "war
of all against all."

Discussion Questions

*Think of the in groups you belong to and what the mutual relations are among
its members. Are they at all like the people in Locke's state of nature?*

*Think of an out group. How do you think about them? What are actual rela-
tions between you, and your group, and the members of that other group? Is
the distrust between you constructed by all concerned? Or does it have some
other source?*

CITIZEN AND GOVERNMENT

Previously in this chapter we discussed the relation of government to citizens, specifically what obligations governments have to enhance the freedoms of citizens through various redistributive measures. We now need to look at the other side of the relation between citizen and government and ask some questions about the contributions of citizens to the government and its continued functioning. Relations between citizens and their governments are complex. We are going to consider only two questions about those relations: whether citizens have an obligation to vote, and under what conditions citizens are allowed or even have the duty to disobey the government.

Is It Our Duty to Vote?

Many people believe that it is a part of the citizens' freedom to decide whether to participate in government or not. Voting, they think, is not an obligation; we are free to choose whether to vote or not. Freedom, so say the defenders of that point of view, is closely associated with choice. Our freedoms as U.S. citizens include our ability to choose whether to get married and to whom, where to live, where to work, and what sort of work we choose to do. It includes choices concerning religious observances, whether to go about armed, what to do with our property. In each case freedom seems to include the ability to choose for oneself without compulsion from other persons or from the government. If that is what freedom is, why does that not apply to the freedom to vote? Surely we should be free also in the political realm to participate or not as it seems best to us in our present life circumstances.

But, as we have seen many times before freedom is always limited. Our freedom does not permit us choices in all areas of life; it does not, for instance, allow us to restrict the freedoms of others; it does not allow us the choice whether to deal brutally with others or to defraud them. What choices are allowed us by our freedom cannot be decided once and for all but must be examined in each individual case. It will help us to clarify this matter if we go back to the question of why we have government at all.

In the social contract tradition, government is established by the citizens. Later generations who do not participate in the original contract, give their "tacit consent" by living in a country, paying taxes, and using its legal machinery to protect themselves. These governments established by citizens are not a threat to freedom because they merely put into effect the policies decided on by the citizens themselves; governments, according to the Lockian version of the social contract tradition, are merely executors of the popular will. In obeying the government, citizens merely obey themselves. Their freedom is not limited by obedience to the government because it is no more than obedience to oneself.

Clearly, if the citizens refuse to participate in the political process in which the government receives its instructions, the government will have to act on whatever policies it comes up with on its own. Such a government does not execute the will of the people because it does not know what the will of the people is. Instead, it imposes its own will on the citizens. It thereby becomes a threat to citizens' freedom instead of its protector. If we follow the Lockian version of the social contract tradition, it is clear that we have an obligation to vote.

Discussion Question

In the Lockian version of the social contract tradition, citizens must instruct the government of their will to preserve their freedoms. It is in their interests, if they love freedom, to instruct the government. They have an obligation to make their will known to the government only if they also have an obligation to preserve their freedom. Do you believe that we have a moral obligation to preserve our freedoms? Give reasons for your answer.

But now suppose that you reject the social contract tradition, and instead, hold a view closer to that of the anarchists. Government, you believe, is a device invented by the rich and powerful to keep the ordinary people in line, whose work made them rich and powerful. Governments have been established through war and other acts of violence. Governments maintain themselves by the threat or actual use of their military forces, including the police.

Discussion Question

If the anarchists are right about the nature of government, do you have any obligation to participate in choosing who will be running the government? Is it in your interest to do so? Give reasons for your answer.

Civil Disobedience

John Locke: Right to Revolution

In the opinion of Locke and other seventeenth-century social contract theorists, governments and the laws they promulgated served just one purpose: to preserve the persons and property of the citizens—that is, to create a peaceful society where all could thrive. For those purposes, citizens had united and established a government. But even Locke was fully aware that not all governments met those goals. Not all governments were at pains to better the lives of the citizens by securing their persons and their property and protecting them against the rapacious or the violent. Sometimes the governments themselves became a threat to the citizens' well-being by taking the citizens' property without authorization. Sometimes governments secretly tried to establish a particular religion; sometimes their dealings with citizens were completely unfair because the government played favorites. Sometimes governments, especially when they consisted of kings and their small councils, were not really interested in governing at all because they preferred fox hunting or other diversions to minding the affairs of state. The citizens' well-being was impaired by the government's neglect of the affairs of state.

What should citizens do then? Locke does not hesitate to answer this question by saying that a government that fails to serve the ends for which it was established has lost its legitimacy and needs to be replaced by means of a "revolution" or "rebellion." Governments that lose their legitimacy are, in effect, not governments at all, Locke says, and "when the government is dissolved, the people are at liberty to provide for themselves by erecting a new legislative, different from the other, by the change of persons, or form, or both, as they shall find it most for their safety and good."[15] How will they go about that? Locke does not really tell us, but the interpretation of his words by subsequent generations is clearest in the *Declaration of Independence* where Jefferson wrote,

> We hold these truths to be self-evident, that all Men are created equal and are endowed by their Creator with certain inalienable Rights, that among these are Life, Liberty, and the Pursuit of Happiness—That to secure these Rights, Governments are instituted among men . . . that whenever any form of Government becomes destructive of the those Ends, it is the right of the People to alter or to abolish it.

It is clear both from Jefferson's statements and from subsequent history that the intended revolutions might well be violent. Think of the Revolutionary War. But the political thinkers of the eighteenth century were not intimidated by that. Violent uprisings were reasonably common. In the late 1780s while the Constitution was being crafted in Philadelphia, a group of farmers in Western Massachusetts rose up in arms. They had fallen into debt, were in danger of losing their farms, or ending up in debtors' prison, but they had been turned down by the state authorities to whom they had turned for help. The uprising, known to history as "Shay's Rebellion," was put down. Jefferson commented on this rebellion in a letter to James Madison: "I hold it, that a little rebellion, now and then, is a good thing and as necessary in the political world as storms in the physical."[16] Such rebellions, he thought, were inevitable in a democracy even though a democratic government does not oppress its citizens as does an absolute monarchy, but more importantly, such rebellions also "prevent the degeneracy of government and nourish a general attention to public affairs."[17] Rebellions keep the government on its toes and citizens engaged in public affairs. And after all, the displacement of British rule required an extended war. It was a violent revolution.

Discussion Questions

Do you believe that people in a democracy have a right to revolution? Under what conditions could one justify a violent uprising against a democratic government?

Suppose we do not share Locke's theory about the origin of government in a social contract. Are revolutions still defensible? Give reasons for your answer.

Henry David Thoreau: Civil Disobedience

By the middle of the nineteenth century, the idea of revolution reappeared when Thoreau argues for "civil disobedience"—specifically not paying his taxes. He had some grave objections to the government's conduct: "when a sixth of the population of a nation which has undertaken to be the refuge of liberty are slaves, and a whole country [Mexico] is unjustly overrun and conquered by a foreign army, and subjected to military law, I think it is not too soon for honest men to rebel and to revolutionize."[18] He also objected strongly to the treatment of the remaining American Indians by his white fellow citizens. But *revolution* now is not the action of large numbers of people who replace the persons or also the form of an existing government by new personalities or a new form of rule. *Revolution* has changed into protest. What is more, Thoreau's protest was non-violent. From his action and his discussion of it in his essay "Civil Disobedience" this political tactic derives its name. Non-violence has been assumed to be an essential trait of civil disobedience.

Both Gandhi and Martin Luther King, Jr., who not only advocated civil disobedience but used it successfully to change oppressive conditions, claimed to derive their inspiration from Thoreau. But they were protesting injustices that they, personally, were suffering because India was occupied by the British, in Gandhi's case, or because the law forced African Americans into a painfully humiliating position, in the case of King. Thoreau refused to pay his taxes because he did not want to be complicit in the injustice of slavery, the Mexican American War, or the oppression of American Indians, by supporting the U.S. government. By not paying taxes, he believed, he was withdrawing his support from the government and thus could not be held responsible for the government's unjust actions. Thoreau was not protesting injustices done to him; he was trying to dissociate himself from those committing injustices—in this case the U.S. government.

Discussion Questions

1. *Perhaps in Concord, Massachusetts, in the time of Thoreau, in the 1840s, one met the U.S. government "once a year—and no more—in the person of the tax gatherer." But today the effects of the government are everywhere and not paying taxes will not suffice to withhold one's support from the government and its unjust policies. Consider what you would have to do today to withhold support from the government, in addition to not paying your taxes.*

2. *For what reasons might you seriously consider withholding your support from the government?*

3. *Many commentators refer to civil disobedience as "non-violent." But critics often point out that blocking traffic or disrupting the business in a drugstore by having black students sit in, even though they are banned from the lunch counter by law, is also violence of a certain kind.*

Do you think that that is a valid criticism of civil disobedience as a political tactic to claim that it is violent?

Many people object to acts of civil disobedience because, in a democratic country like ours, there are procedures for citizens to make their opinions known and to try to have them implemented as government policy. Practicing civil disobedience undermines democratic processes. But Thoreau was impatient of the electoral process. "Even voting *for the right thing is doing* nothing for it." Electoral majorities, he thought, are not firmly committed to doing what is right or to fighting injustice. "When the majority shall at length vote for the abolition of slavery, it will be because they are indifferent to slavery or because there is but little slavery left to be abolished by their vote."[19] Attempts to abolish grave injustices by means of the electoral process, Thoreau thought, were bound to fail. Civil disobedience was justified because the electoral process was unable to repair glaring injustices. The Mexicans, the slaves, and the Indians could not wait.

Discussion Question

Do you agree with Thoreau's assessment of the impotence of electoral reforms? Examine concrete examples. Give reasons for your answer.

In the summer of 1963, a federal judge ordered Vivian Malone and James Hood, two young black students, to be admitted to the University of Alabama. Then governor George Wallace stood in the door of the university's auditorium to prevent the two applicants from entering the university. He defied the federal government to maintain the law of the state of Alabama, which decreed segregated education. The governor clearly was committing civil disobedience. But was he justified?

That question—how we can justify our breaking the law for political purposes—has troubled advocates of civil disobedience or of revolution from the very beginning. Locke wrote:

> Who shall be judge whether the prince or legislature act contrary to their trust?
> . . . To this I reply: The people shall be the judge . . . But farther, this question, who shall be the judge, cannot mean that there is no judge at all; for where there is no judicature on earth to decide controversies among men, God in heaven is Judge.[20]

If the people replace their government by a revolution, how can they assure themselves that their cause is just? Locke has two answers: 1. if the majority agrees, and 2. in the end God will judge the revolutionaries.

The first of these answers is still being given today. Rawls added a second criterion that is used by many writers about civil disobedience: sincerity.[21] Civil disobedience is more likely to be justified if those who commit it are sincere in their belief that right is on their side, as is the majority of citizens.

Discussion Questions

Did Governor Wallace commit a justified act of civil disobedience? What criteria for justifying civil disobedience are you using in framing your answer? Give reasons for and against your opinion.

Gandhi and Martin Luther King, Jr.: Self-Suffering

In his *Letter from a Birmingham Jail*, King describes this method as follows:

> In any nonviolent campaign there are four basic steps: collection of the facts to determine whether injustices exist; negotiation; self-purification; and direct action. . . . You express a great deal of anxiety over our willingness to break laws. This is certainly a legitimate concern. Since we so diligently urge people to obey the Supreme Court's decision of 1954 outlawing segregation in the public schools, at first glance it may seem rather paradoxical for us consciously to break laws. One may well ask: 'How can you advocate breaking some laws and obeying others?' The answer lies in the fact that there are two types of laws: just and unjust. I would be the first to advocate obeying just laws. One has not only a legal but a moral responsibility to obey just laws. Conversely, one has a moral responsibility to disobey unjust laws. I would agree with St. Augustine that "an unjust law is no law at all.[22]

Discussion Question

Do you agree with Martin Luther King, Jr., that we have a moral obligation to obey just laws? Give reasons for your answer.

But how, we want to ask, do we differentiate between just and unjust laws? Were the segregation laws that Governor Wallace was trying to uphold just, and he, therefore, justified in barring Hood and Malone from the University of Alabama? King makes a telling point here: The laws the governor was trying to uphold were not passed by black voters because they had been excluded from voting in all the segregationist states since the end of Reconstruction in the 1870s. Citizens excluded from the political process cannot avail themselves of democratic means to redress the injustices committed against them. What is more, they never consented to the laws they are protesting. Neither of those is true of Governor Wallace and the laws he was trying to defend. It looks as if, in this case, King and the people with him had much stronger justifications of their civil disobedience than Governor Wallace.

We have now seen two different sorts of civil disobedience. Thoreau disobeys the tax law to disrupt his complicity in the injustices perpetrated by the government. At issue for him is his own moral integrity. He is not protesting injustices done to him as were the African American protesters in the 1950s and 1960s. Perhaps he was also making a political statement in the hopes of raising an issue and persuading his fellow citizens of its seriousness. That is a third kind of civil disobedience, one that neither maintains one's own personal moral integrity nor protests hard against injustices done to oneself and one's group by an unjust majority. The third kind of civil disobedience is a political tactic, a way of elevating a political conflict to a much more intense level in the hope that

a. no one can remain indifferent to the issue, and
b. a majority of persons will come to share the position of the protesters.

Common examples of that kind of civil disobedience are protests against war—the Vietnam War or the wars against Iraq—or more specific injustices committed in the conduct of those wars. An example of the latter are civil disobedience committed in protests against the School of the Americas, an institution at Fort Benning in Georgia where the U.S. military trains Latin American military and police officials. Graduates of the School of the Americas are regularly implicated in illegal, violent suppression of opposition parties in their home countries.[23]

In these protests, the protester needs to persuade the public that the civil disobedience is not committed rashly, on the spur of the moment. Hence,

King insisted that one of the steps in preparing oneself for civil disobedience is "self-purification." Gandhi spoke of "inviting suffering."[24] The civilly disobedient show their sincerity: that the issue they are protesting appear to them of exceptional importance, by willingly courting arrest, police assault, cruelties, and even death. The protester here is saying: "there are many important issues but this one is of such overwhelming urgency that I am willing to expose myself to considerable pain and inconvenience to bring it to the public's attention and to alter public opinion about it."

Discussion Questions

A few years after the summer of 1963, large numbers of Americans committed civil disobedience in the streets of U.S. cities to end the war in Vietnam. Did the same justifications apply here that justified the civil disobedience in Birmingham, Alabama, in 1963? If not, could those acts of civil disobedience be justified in some other way?

Review Questions

This chapter has shown that it is up to us whether we are a free people. Our freedom depends, in part, on our willingness to resist our own prejudices and those of others and to work hard to make "liberty and justice for all" not just a comfortable slogan but a reality.

In reviewing the chapter, summarize the views of Hobbes and Locke about human nature and government. Remind yourself of the different episodes of distrust of freedom in our history.

What can we learn from the experiences of Father Boyle?

When are acts of civil disobedience justified?

QUESTIONS FOR REFLECTION AND DISCUSSION

1. Many people believe that freedom consists of having many choices—the more choices, the more freedom you have. This raises two questions: do you think that the person who *chooses* to give up her freedom remains a free person? Think of persons who join organizations that minutely regulate individual behavior such as the military, a strict religious order, or some sort of religious cult run by a leader who determines for every member what he or she must do. Suppose a person is not forced in any way to join such an organization; are they free once they have joined?

   A second question concerns the importance of the choices we make. Is a person free who spends his days making fairly trivial choices—whether to have eggs or pancakes for breakfast, whether to wear the red or the blue tie, what radio station to listen to on the way to work, and similar choices all day long? If freedom is making choices, does it matter whether we choose things that are important or whether we make trivial choices? Consider this: you live in a country run by a dictator but there are no rules about what clothes to wear. Every morning you can pick out the clothes you will wear that day. Will you say that you are a free person?

2. Are all human beings competitive, trying to get ahead, selfish, wanting money and comfort? List the most familiar traits of human nature.

Now consider the Zuni character, as described by the famous U.S. anthropologist Ruth Benedict: "The most honored personality traits are a pleasing address, a yielding disposition, and a generous heart. All the sterner virtues—initiative, ambition, an uncompromising sense of honor and justice, intense personal loyalties—not only are not admired but are heartily deplored. The woman who cleaves to her husband through misfortune and family quarrels, the man who speaks his mind where flattery would be much more comfortable, the man, above all, who thirsts for power or knowledge, who wishes to be, as they scornfully phrase it, 'a leader of his people,' receives nothing but censure." Benedict added, "Even in contests of skill like their foot-races, if a man wins habitually, he is debarred from running. They are interested in a game that a number can play with even chances, and an outstanding runner spoils the game: they will have none of him."

What do you think about human nature now?

3. Here is another question about human nature.

Human nature refers to common traits of all human beings, regardless of where they live—in one of the world's mega-cities or in remote corners of Borneo—and when—ten thousand years ago in a cave or on Mulholland Drive in Hollywood, California. Do we, or does Hobbes, have sufficient information to make assertions about traits possessed by all six billion human beings alive today, not to mention all the billions that have lived before us in different countries and cultures?

4. The "English-only" movement has since the 1980s succeeded in persuading the legislatures of a number of states to pass laws declaring that English is the official language of the United States. Such legislation forbids use of any other language than English by all government agencies—federal, state, and local. This would, for instance, do away with all bi- or multilingual voting materials or government information literature. Often such legislation is also intended to abolish bilingual programs in schools.

Efforts like this to ban use of languages other than English in any official transactions have a long history. The first English-only laws were passed in the 1880s. The insistence that immigrants "Americanize" by adopting English as their primary language and in all other ways give up the customs and beliefs of their home countries have been a staple in U.S. history. Despite our habit of saying that we are a nation of immigrants, we have traditionally and to this day been suspicious of immigrants if they differed from the rest of us.

Does this demand that all people speak English in all their official transactions and that schools teach only English deprive immigrants of important freedoms? How is this demand for one U.S. language different from a demand that all Americans be Protestants? (Remember that John F. Kennedy was the first and only Catholic to be elected President!) Should we also demand of immigrants that they dress like us? The head scarf worn by Muslim girls and women has been declared illegal in French schools. Should we adopt similar regulations? What shall we say about people who eat ethnic foods? Should we close all ethnic food stores? What about African Catholics who use the music of their native country in Catholic masses or other religious ceremonies? What about sports? Can we allow people coming from abroad to continue playing cricket that they learned to play in their country of origin?

What do you think about singing the "Star Spangled Banner" in Spanish?

The basic question is this: should we allow ourselves freedom to have a variety of different customs and cultural traditions—language, dress, food, or should we demand that there be only one U.S. culture? If freedom involves being able to do what one wants, does that not also include the ability to fashion one's daily life as one chooses? Do your answers depend on your own heritage?

5. Do you think that breaking the law for the sake of "liberty and justice for all" is ever justified? How can you tell that yours is a just cause? Will this not lead to the breakdown of law and order and thus produce greater injustices for more people?

6. Look up Father Greg Boyle on the Internet. What do you think of his work with gang members and drug dealers? Do you have comparable experiences where persons respond with trust and affection for you when you treat them with trust and kindness? Will that approach work with all human beings? If yes, what's your evidence? If no, what reasons do you have for that opinion? Do you have any experiences to back up your answers?

How would Father Boyle's experiences apply to our treatment of persons in prison?

7. Split into small groups and make as extensive a list of everyone's prejudices against members of other groups. Do *not* hold back! It is important that we all be honest with ourselves about this. Then ask yourself where those prejudices come from. Do you know any members of these despised

groups? How well do you know them? Are they friends or distant acquaintances? If you do not know any members of this group, where did you get your beliefs about them?

8. Various newspapers carried a story not too long ago that reported that more and more states are passing legislation to force convicted sex offenders to bear GPS identification bracelets after they have served their prison term. Convicted sex offenders already have to register with the police where they live. Now they are being forced to be instantly locatable by the local police, wherever they are. This is clearly a limitation of the freedom that the rest of us enjoy of moving around anonymously without being under government supervision.

Opponents of this requirement point out that not all sex offenders that leave prison will reoffend. Tracking them by GPS is no more justified than tracking ordinary citizens. On the other hand, many drug dealers, murderers, thieves, con men, and kidnappers do reoffend after they leave prison. Why are they not being monitored in the same way?

Add to that, that the persons being monitored have already served their time. They have taken their punishment. Why can they not return to being like all other citizens and try to build a decent life for themselves with the same freedoms as everyone else and the same right to privacy?

Should we monitor everyone involved in serious traffic accidents, or people convicted once of driving under the influence? Should we put GPS bracelets on stalkers? If a woman takes out a restraining order against a violent boyfriend or husband, should he automatically be made to wear a GPS bracelet?

NOTES

1. "Mayflower Compact," retrieved June 1, 2006, from Answer.com website: www.answer.com/topic/mayflower-compact.

2. Thomas Hobbes, *Leviathan*, retrieved June 1, 2006, from Early Modern Texts webiste: www.earlymoderntexts.com/f_hobbes.html. This text has been modernized by Professor Jonathan Bennett to make it more accessible to modern readers.

3. Eric Foner, *The Story of American Freedom* (New York: Norton, 1998), 43.

4. "Loyalty Oath," retrieved September 12, 2006, from Answer.com website: www.answer.com/topic/loyalty-oath.

5. Retrieved October 1, 2008, from Human Rights Watch website: www.hrw.org/backgrounder/usa/qna1006/3.htm.

6. Studs Terkel, *Hard Times* (New York: Avon Books, 1970), 307–8.

7. John Locke, *The Second Treatise on Government,* retrieved June 1, 2006, from Early Modern Texts website: www.earlymoderntexts.com/f_locke.html. This text has

been modernized by Professor Jonathan Bennett to make it more accessible to modern readers.

8. Hobbes, *Leviathan*.

9. Locke, *Second Treatise*.

10. Noam Chomsky, *Notes on Anarchism,* retrieved January 5, 2008, from Z Communications website: www.zmag.org/chomsky/other/notes-on-anarchism.html.

11. Henry David Thoreau, *Walden and On the Duty of Civil Disobedience* (New York: Rinehart 1957), 281.

12. Robert Nozick, *Anarchy, State and Utopia* (New York: Basic Books, 1974), 43.

13. Celeste Fremon, *G-Dog and the Homeboys: Father Greg Boyle and the Gangs of East Los Angeles* (Albuquerque: University of New Mexico Press, 2004).

14. Fremon, *G-Dog,* 41.

15. Locke, *Second Treatise,* par. 107.

16. Thomas Jefferson, *The Life and Collected Works of Thomas Jefferson,* edited by Adrienne Koch and William Peden (New York: Random House, 1993), 383.

17. Jefferson, *Collected Works,* 383.

18. Thoreau, *Civil Disobedience,* 284–85.

19. Thoreau, *Civil Disobedience,* 286–87.

20. Locke, *Second Treatise,* pars. 240–41.

21. John Rawls, *A Theory of Justice* (Cambridge: Harvard University Press, 1971), 367.

22. Martin Luther King, Jr., *Letter from a Birmingham Jail* (Logan, IA: Perfection Learning Corporation, 1990), 13.

23. "Western Institute for Security Cooperation," retrieved February 27, 2008, from Center for International Policy website: www.ciponline.org/facts/soa.htm.

24. Ronald Duncan, ed., *The Writings of Gandhi* (Oxford: Fontana/Duncan, 1971), 66.

FURTHER READINGS

Eric Foner, *The Story of American Freedom* (New York: Norton, 1998). Chapter 8, "The Birth of Civil Liberties." The history of rising interest in the Bill of Rights early in the twentieth century.

Norberto Bobbio, *Thomas Hobbes and the Natural Law Tradition* (Chicago: University of Chicago Press, 1993). Chapter 2, "Hobbes' Political Theory," provides an overview of Hobbes's political theory.

Joy Kogawa, *Obasan* (New York: Doubleday, 1981). This novel vividly portrays the experience of Japanese American internees.

David Caute, *The Great Fear: The Anti-Communist Purge Under Truman and Eisenhower* (New York: Simon and Schuster, 1978). Provides a more detailed history of McCarthyism in the United States.

Studs Terkel, *Hard Times* (New York: Avon Books, 1970). An oral history of the early years of the Great Depression that shows the excitement of the early, hopeful years of the New Deal.

Richard Ashcraft, *John Locke: Critical Assessments* (London: Routledge, 1991). Provides detailed discussions of different aspects of John Locke's political theory, written by experts in the field.

Celeste Fremon, *G-Dog and the Homeboys: Father Greg Boyle and the Gangs of East Los Angeles* (Albuquerque: University of New Mexico Press, 2004). A moving portrait of Father Greg Boyle and his work with gangs in East Los Angeles.

Chapter Three

Property and Rights

The city of New London, Connecticut, situated near the mouth of the Thames River where it empties into Long Island Sound, has as long a history like most new England towns. Founded in the early seventeenth century, it reached its greatest glory in the middle of the nineteenth century when its whaling ships traveled far and wide. But in the 1850s, Benjamin Silliman, a Yale chemistry professor, discovered a method for extracting relatively clean-burning kerosene from petroleum. Soon kerosene replaced whale oil in lamps and whaling became less profitable. As the whaling industry declined, so did the fortunes of New London. Today, New London is a quiet shore town, home to some colleges and shipbuilding industries and a naval base. Tourism is a significant source of income. Economically, the town is always struggling. In the 1990s, the city conceived a plan to raze a working-class neighborhood on the shore of the Thames River to build a hotel and convention center, upscale housing units, and a park along the river's edge. Most of the inhabitants of the neighborhood sold their houses to the city, however reluctantly. Problems arose when seven families refused to sell their homes and a few small business owners also held on to their commercial properties. The city tried to take homes and some commercial buildings by eminent domain. The owners, forced to sell, sued the city, and their case wound its way through the courts until, in 2005, it reached the Supreme Court.

Taking by eminent domain refers to a procedure in which a government agency, in this case the city of New London, "takes" private property for public use. Owners are compensated; they are paid fair market value for their property, but they are forced to sell at the price offered by the government.

The Fifth Amendment of the Constitution states that "private property [shall not] be taken for public use without just compensation." The New London

115

property owners who sued the city for taking their properties argued that the Constitution allows the government to take private property, provided it pays market value for the property *and* the properties are taken for "public use." *Public use* is usually thought of as using land to build roads, a post office, a school, or a military installation. But the city of New London intended the land taken to be used for development by a private, for-profit company. Such development, they thought, would benefit the public by providing jobs, attracting more visitors to New London, and increasing the city's tax base. The plaintiffs claimed that their neighborhood was not a legitimate target for taking by eminent domain because the land taken would not be for public use. The Fifth Amendment to the Constitution did not allow, they thought, taking land from one private owner to give or sell it to other private owners.

In the 1950s, the Supreme Court decided that taking land by eminent domain for urban renewal was legitimate because it also constituted taking land for public use. These were cases where neighborhoods had a preponderance of poor, badly maintained, often unsanitary, and unhealthful housing. The government would take the properties, tear down the housing, and construct public housing instead. Presumably this was taking by eminent domain for public use because its intention was to improve the lives of the people who were to live in the newly constructed housing. It cleared out neighborhoods that were thought to breed crime. It might even improve the city's tax base.

Another alternative, taking land for the sake of economic development, is slightly different from taking it for the sake of urban renewal. In the case of taking land for the purpose of economic development, a government agency buys land from private individuals to give or sell it cheaply to other private parties who will then develop that land. These other private parties aim to make a profit because they gain the land at a good price. The original owners are forced to sell their homes to enable a private business to make a profit.

One example of such taking by eminent domain for the sake of economic development took place in Detroit in the 1980s. General Motors (GM) needed a new auto body plant. The company told the city of Detroit that it was considering building a new plant in the southern United States where labor costs were lower. They let it be known, however, that they would be willing to build the new plant in Detroit if they could find five hundred acres of open land. In response, the city of Detroit took a large neighborhood of working-class homes by eminent domain, paying about $200 million to the various homeowners, and then sold the cleared land to GM for about $8 million.[1]

This taking by eminent domain, one could argue, served a public use because it preserved six thousand jobs for people in Detroit, specifically for the workers at the Fisher body plant. On the other hand, the private property of individual homeowners was taken from them, even though they were paid market value, to increase the profits of the GM Corporation. Looked at in that perspective it is not clear that the land was taken for public use.

For economic development to be successful, the property needs to be taken from people with few economic resources and given (or sold at a reasonable price) to companies or enterprises that have good prospects of making significant profit on the properties. Taking by eminent domain for the sake of economic development often looks like taking from the poor and giving to the rich. Justice Sandra Day O'Connor raised this point when the New London case was being argued before the Supreme Court. "Would it be ok" she asked the lawyer for the city of New London, "to take a Motel 6 by eminent domain in order to have the land redeveloped for a Ritz Carlton?" Could, in other words, a city force the sale of a modest moneymaking motel to have the plot developed by a very fancy, upscale hotel that has a larger margin of profit?[2]

Discussion Questions

Should the government be allowed to take properties for private use even if private companies will profit from that transaction, while the persons whose property is taken lose the profits they might have made through future appreciation of their properties? Give reasons for your answer.

This controversy makes a number of important points about property rights:

The most ordinary property right is the security of one's private property. We have that kind of economic security insofar as we are protected against theft or as long as powerful private or public agencies may not appropriate land or houses or other property we own. Secure tenure of one's personal property is an important property right.

At the same time, we are reminded that the nature and limitations of property are defined by the legal system. Ownership and use of property are defined by laws. There are limits on what someone is allowed to own, sell, or rent out: Since the abolition of slavery it has not been legal to own other persons. Parents do not own their children; it is illegal to sell your children. The question whether it should be legal for women to rent out their uterus to carry someone else's child is still under discussion. Surrogate motherhood has been approved of by some courts, but the practice is not accepted by all as legitimate; ethical questions surrounding this practice are still under active discussion with many saying that surrogate motherhood should not be allowed. It is legal to sell one's blood; the question is less clear with respect to other bodily organs. Western European countries, Canada, and the United States prohibit organ sales; India permits them.

There are also limits on how one may *use* one's property. Ownership means, centrally, that one has control over one's property, and that one may therefore use it as one pleases. But in practice, these rights to use your property are limited. The law forbids you from running a "disorderly house." It also demands that you maintain your property. You may regard a half collapsed house overgrown with Virginia creeper and wisteria as consummately romantic and as a welcome interruption to the boring rows of neatly maintained bungalows with their postage stamp front lawns that your neighbors own, but the city health inspectors will soon come to force you to clean up the mess and to conform to prevailing standards of home maintenance.

Ownership rights include the right to sell, or barter, or give away property for money, for other goods, or for services. It includes the right to give away one's money to individuals, such as children and other relatives, or to charitable organizations. You may use your money, if you came by it legally, to buy all sorts of things. But that right to use or to sell or to exchange what is yours is limited by law. It is not legal to use one's money to pay bribes to legislators or to police officers. There are strict and complex limits on how I may help finance a candidate's political campaign with my own money. You may not spend your money on political campaigns in any way you please. You may not, in theory, buy political influence. It is not legal to use one's money to buy controlled substances or stolen goods. The uses to which I may put the money I earned legitimately are defined by law. Property rights are limited.

All of these limitations on economic freedom raise disagreements. Cat lovers who live with thirty or more cats in their house often raise the ire of their neighbors, as do those who raise pit bulls, or share their house with pythons. How far does one's right over one's house extend and where must it be limited by the desires of neighbors or of city ordinances? Limitations on what one may buy, whether it be alcohol—not permitted during Prohibition—or now marijuana, are sources of unending debate as are limitations on campaign spending or of doing financial favors for a disc jockey or game show host. (It is illegal to pay a disc jockey for playing a specific record.) Secure tenure of one's property is limited, as are the uses one may make of them. Most of these limitations are sources of conflict within the society.[3]

Discussion Questions

Property rights are limited, and those limitations are hotly contested. State the grounds on which you would forbid or severely limit, and the grounds on which you would allow

Using one's money to finance one's own political campaigns privately.

Using one's money to finance the political campaigns of another candidate.

Using your money to buy media outlets like radio or television stations.

Using private funds to pay judges and legislators, or government bureaucrats.

Definitions of property give rise to as much discussion and disagreement as do civil and political liberties or the relations of citizens to their government. The case of New London shows how complex these controversies can be.

In this chapter we will discuss these questions:

- How can one justify property rights?
- Is private property the source of peace or of conflict?
- What is the debate over socialism and the free market?
- Should we look to the government to protect us against ourselves?
- What is file sharing on the Internet?
- Should we be allowed to patent animals and plants?
- Is poverty a limitation on one's freedom?
- What are rights?
- How do we justify the idea that all people should have equal rights?
- Does the language of rights overlook the perspective of women?

PRIVATE PROPERTY RIGHTS

There is widespread consensus that the right to private property is among the most important rights we have. Philosophers have, however, given different reasons for considering property rights legitimate. We need to consider two different ways of justifying property rights.

Property Rights from Work

According to a common view, property rights derive from one's work. One earns property by working for it. That view was formulated by John Locke:

> [E]very Man has a property in his own person; this no one has any right to but himself. The labor of his body and the work of his hands we may say are properly his. Whatsoever, then, he removes out of the state that nature has provided and left it in, he has mixed his labor with and joined it to something that is his own and thereby makes it his property . . . for this labor being the unquestionable property of the laborer, no man but he can have a right to what that is once joined to, at least where there is enough and as good left in common for others. He that is nourished by the acorns he picked up under an oak, or the apples he gathered from the trees in the wood, has certainly appropriated them to himself; nobody can deny but the nourishment is his . . . the grass that my horse has bit,

the turfs my servant has cut, and the ore I have dug in any place where I have
the right to them in common with others, become my property without the assig-
nation or consent of anybody. The labor that was mine removing them out of
that common state they were in, has fixed my property into them.[4]

Locke justified the institution of private property by pointing to the fact that
each individual person is, in some sense, owner of him or herself. Each person has control over his or her body; each person owns his or her ability and
energy to work. Free persons may not be forced to work. The persons who
work for you need to be compensated for their labor because that is their
property and you may not use it without payment. As a consequence each of
us may claim as our property the land we worked or the produce we raised
(unless someone else paid us for our work). What I invest my strength and
ability in thereby becomes a part of me; it becomes mine.

Discussion Questions

How do you understand Locke's claim that "Every man has property in his
own person": *is it legitimate for me to sell myself?*

*Is it, on the other hand, legitimate for governments to decree that men wear
beards or women cover their heads? Do governments have the right to demand that I learn to read and write, or that I not sleep on a bench in the park?
Give reasons for your answer.*

The passage asserts that property rights are not assigned by God; as far as
God is concerned all things are common property. No property owner can
claim divine sanction for his possessions; neither wealth nor poverty are ordained by God. Things become private property legitimately when we work
for them; whatsoever you worked for is yours by virtue of the effort you
made. That is not so different a view from the opinion, held by many, that
what you work for is yours or, as people say more often, if you want something you need to earn it. It is not so different from the view of New England
Indians four hundred years ago or more. They, too, had personal ownership in
the tools they had made and the food they had raised in their gardens or
caught by fishing or on the hunt. The land, on the other hand, was not something they had made; it belonged to no one or it belonged to all in common.
One might use a piece of land for a while and during that time others needed
to respect the work one had put into a field or a garden and stay clear of it.
But one could not possess the land, trade, or sell it. Ownership rights and
working are somehow closely connected. Recent legislation in the United
States recognizes this principle. Company executives who enrich themselves
by illegal accounting methods, the law states, derived significant portions of

their income, not from work, but from manipulating numbers in their account books. If convicted, they must return that unearned income because they have no ownership rights to it.[5]

Discussion Questions

1. *How much do you need to work before you own something? When our example is gathering acorns or apples, that question is easily answered. But when we think, as Locke clearly does, about Englishmen taking a ship to the New World to find land for themselves, how much work do they need to do in order to acquire one, or ten, or a hundred acres of land?*

2. *If they work a piece of land do they gain property rights in the produce or in the land itself?*

3. *If they put a fence around their land do they own all the land fenced in or just the land on which the fence is built?*

4. *What about property I did not earn, like an inheritance? Is it illegitimate to inherit property?*

5. *Are persons not entitled to their winnings if they bought a winning lottery ticket? The attraction of gambling is, after all, that you gain money without a great deal of effort.*

6. *Granting that work confers ownership rights, does one gain ownership rights to borrowed tools used in repairing one's car? Give reasons for your answer.*

Property Rights for a Free Society

Philosophers who think about property differently from Locke justify the institution of private ownership on the grounds that it is good for the society. Property ownership, they argue, makes us into better citizens; it enables us to play a positive role in the political life of our nation and is, for that reason, an excellent institution. Property is a basis for a good society because it supports the independence of citizens.

This way of thinking about the institution of private property was popular among the founders of our nation. Thomas Jefferson repeatedly expressed his distrust of tradesmen and all others who were economically dependent on customers or on the persons for whom they worked. "Cultivators of the earth are the most valuable citizens. They are the most vigorous, the most independent, and the most virtuous . . . I consider the class of artisans as the panders [procurers] of vice and the instruments by which the liberties of a country are generally overturned,"[6] because they "for their subsistence depend . . . on the casualties [accidents] and caprice of customers. Dependence begets sub-servience and venality [immorality], suffocates the germ of virtue, and pre-pares fit tools for the designs of ambition."[7]

Economic dependence means that you are always trying to please some-body whether they are actual or potential customers of your business or ac-tual or potential employers. If you lack economic independence, you are for-ever under pressure to conform to the expectations of others, and you will hesitate to take stands that might alienate potential customers or employers. Only those who live off the land are economically independent. They do not need to make themselves agreeable to customers or employers; they can con-duct their lives as they see fit without fear that their independence or outspo-kenness might harm them economically.

The new nation that Jefferson and the other founders were constructing was to be a republic. It was to be a country governed by its citizens who elected those who were most public spirited—those who considered what was good for all rather than considering only their own well-being. Such a repub-lic required men—women obviously did not count in that whole reflection—who were independent, who could not be pressured, and who were not de-pendent on the thinking or the goodwill of others. They were men who stood on their own two feet and were beholden to no one. Because they did not need to cater to anyone for economic reasons, they did not need to support the pri-vate ambitions of persons interested only in their own advancement.

But men could display that sort of independence only if they owned land and sufficient land to owe no one for their livelihood. Hence property owner-ship was an essential precondition for the success of the new republic. A sec-ond precondition was the existence of a fairly large class of people who owned enough property to be economically self-sufficient, so that they did not have to work tilling the land every day but, instead, had sufficient leisure to educate themselves to become true statesmen and leaders of the new re-public.

According to this new and different conception, it is not work that justifies private property but the need of a free society for leadership by educated men with sufficient leisure to put their abilities in the service of their country and their fellow citizens. The justification of property did not lie in its origin—in the work of individual persons—but in its function as a necessary condition for the survival of a free country.

Discussion Questions

1. *How important is it for a republic that its citizens be independent thinkers rather than taking political stands that are good for their business?*
2. *What sorts of influences deprive us of our intellectual independence?*

3. *Are you an independent thinker in politics? Why are you, if your answer is yes, and why not, if your answer is no.*

4. *What role does your property play in making you more, or less, independent?*

Give reasons for your answers.

PRIVATE PROPERTY: BLESSING OR CURSE?

Plato's Condemnation of Private Property

It is today a matter of common sense that private property is a useful institution. When property rights are unambiguous, we believe, conflict is reduced over goods that are at all scarce. Everyone knows which is his or her house and car and everyone knows to leave the possessions of others alone. The conflicts that arise when two persons want to own or use the same piece of land, pick apples from the same tree, or harvest corn in the same field are avoided because the rules governing private property assign clear rights to different people. Everyone knows who owns this apple tree or that field of corn, and who, therefore, has exclusive right to the apples or the corn. Where ownership rights are certain, conflict is avoided. That assumption is so deeply entrenched in our thinking that it is rarely questioned. But in the Western tradition, doubts about the usefulness of the institution of private property have been raised from the very beginning.

Plato, a Greek philosopher who flourished in the fourth century BC, lays out an ideal state, in his book *The Republic,* as a vehicle for developing his ideas about justice. He thought that a far-reaching division of labor is essential to a well-ordered state. A state is in good health when everyone does what he or she does best and does not meddle in things that are less familiar. Where everyone is expert in their occupation, all jobs are well done and everyone is satisfied. No one wastes their talents by being a dilettante in many occupations and an expert in none. Every citizen is as highly skilled in some occupation or other as his or her native abilities permit. That principle extends even to government; governing, like everything else—being a doctor, a banker, or an athlete—is a skill that one needs to learn. It is best done by people who are really well trained. You buy your bread from the best baker and send your children to the school with the most professional teachers, and when you are ill, you seek out the best doctor you can find. In the same way, you would want to live in a state that is governed by those best trained, with the greatest aptitude for governing. Plato, a member of a wealthy and powerful family in Athens, abhorred democracy and argued for government by a talented and well-trained elite.

To avoid conflict in the leadership, the governing group, which Plato calls the "guardians," do not own private property because, as Plato said, "friends hold all things in common." Where property is privately owned, people are divided. Where all things are owned in common, you will find genuine unity because the well-being of any one individual is the well-being of all.

> This agrees with our principle that they [the guardians] were not to have houses or lands or any property of their own, but to receive sustenance from the other citizens, as wages for their guardianship, and to consume it in common. . . . [a guardian] will not rend the community asunder by each applying the word "mine" to different things and dragging off whatever he can for himself into a private home where he will have his separate family, forming a center of ex-clusive joys and sorrows. Rather they will all, so far as may be, feel together and aim at the same ends, because they are convinced that all their interests are identical.
>
>   . . . if a man's person is his only private possession, lawsuits and prosecutions will all but vanish, and they will be free of all those quarrels that arise from own-ership of property and from having family ties. . . .
>
> So our law will secure that these men will live in complete peace with one an-other [Plato actually proposed that both men and women who had the necessary abilities would be trained as guardians] and if they never quarrel among them-selves, there is no fear of the rest of the community being divided either against them or against itself. . .
>
> There are other evils they will escape, so mean and petty, that I hardly like to mention them: the poor man's flattery of the rich, and all the embarrassments and vexations of raising a family and earning just enough to maintain a house-hold; now borrowing and now refusing to repay, and by any and every means scraping together money to be handed over to wife and servants to spend.[8]

Private ownership, Plato thinks, divides the community of guardians because quarrels arise where interests conflict, and where the institution of private property exists, interests are different from one person to the next. Each of us has our own property; each has his or her own family and children; and that is where our heart is. Our interests center on what is our own. Under a regime of private property what is our own is different from what others possess, and thus everyone has different interests. Everyone wants things for themselves that others may also want and thus disunity, quarrels, and conflict arise that cannot be settled as long as possessions are privately owned. Contrary to what we all believe, namely that private property avoids conflicts, Plato asserted that, on the contrary, private property is the source of endless disagreements and contentions. Private ownership separates the interest of each one from those of everyone else and with distinct interests among citizens, unity can-not be easily achieved. Quarrels ensue.

Private property has other negative consequences as the final paragraph of the quotation from Plato points out: where there is private property, some people acquire a lot more than others, and societies are divided into different classes of people and are, most important of all, divided between the rich and the poor. Civic peace is not to be expected where those divisions exist, where the rich bear down on the poor because they are afraid of them, and the poor feel treated unjustly, envy the rich, and try to thwart their political power. Private property produces inequality, which is a fertile source of conflicts in any society. Unity, cooperation, and internal peace are not to be expected where there is serious inequality.

Discussion Question

We believe that property rights serve to avoid many conflicts and thereby make society more peaceful. Plato believed the opposite. Give reasons to support each side in this argument. (Recall the discussion in the preceding chapter of arguments that rest on assumptions about human nature.)

Later Critiques of Private Property

These criticisms of private property have been familiar since Plato's day. The early Christians in Jerusalem and in Rome, in the first and second century, believed that private property was a divisive institution that was not desirable for a community of men and women committed to loving one another in their common worship of God. In the early days, after the death of Jesus, his disciples and converts, "all that believed were together and had all things in common,"[9] and again "the multitude of them that believed were of one heart and one soul: neither said any of them that ought of the things which he possessed was his own: but they had all things in common."[10] In these early days, private property was avoided because it appeared divisive. Everyone believed that individuals preoccupied with the preservation and increase of their private possessions were bound to be distracted from their religious devotions and the community of the faithful.

Condemnation of the institution of private property became a commonplace in the Protestant Reformation on the European continent among the Anabaptists and other sects who were critical of the dominant Protestant churches. Having property was thought to deflect the faithful from what really mattered in life—namely to follow Jesus as a true disciple. Private property interfered with religious devotion and was condemned for that reason.

Jean-Jacques Rousseau, a French philosopher of the eighteenth century, shared that traditional distrust of private property. In his *Discourse on the*

Origin of Inequality, he paints a picture of the evolution of mankind from primitive times to the France of his day. From their early beginnings as little more than animals, human beings developed; they became more intelligent, more sensitive to each other, and their social life became much more complex. A great deal was accomplished that was good. But, on the other hand, Rousseau thought, there was much more conflict in the society of his day and a great deal more pretense and dishonesty. People were less satisfied because everyone wanted to be powerful and famous instead of being content if their life was decent and agreeable. One of the sources of this greater unrest and strife was the invention of private property. It aroused the desire to have more than others—that is, the desire for power to protect one's own property and to take away from others what was theirs—as well as a craving for fame and prestige. Restless desire, competition, deception, and conflict entered the society with the institution of private property.

> The first man who, having enclosed a piece of ground, bethought himself of saying "This is mine," and found people simple enough to believe him was the real founder of civil society. From how many crimes, wars, and murders, from how many horrors and misfortunes might not any one have saved mankind, by pulling up the stakes or filling in the ditch and crying to his fellows: "Beware of listening to this impostor; you are undone if you forget that the fruits of the earth belong to us all and the earth itself to nobody."[11]

Discussion Questions

1. *We believe that private property prevents many conflicts. But we also make considerable efforts to teach children how to share, instead of treating toys and other things as private property. Why is it important for everyone to learn to share? Are there situations when sharing is preferable to insisting on one's private ownership rights? Are there situations where it would be wrong to try to share?*

2. *Is our insistence that our children learn to share an acknowledgment that a world without private property would be preferable to ours because it would be much more peaceful? Give reasons for your answers.*

Property in Productive Resources

The seventeenth-century Civil War in England was motivated by many different conflicts; one of them pitted the owners of landed property against the rural poor who owned no land and starved because they could not find work or because the wages they earned in agricultural work were too low to support them and their families. The criticism of the institution of private property, voiced, for instance, by Gerard Winstanley, the leader of a sect that called itself "The Diggers," focused on private property as the right to exclude others from using land that one owned. In England of that day, large tracts of land, privately owned, remained uncultivated to serve as hunting preserves for the landed aristocracy, while families starved for lack of land on which to raise food for themselves. The Diggers wanted everyone to have access to land on which to grow food and to that extent wanted to restrict, if not abolish, private property in land.

No longer is it all private property that is the target of the critique but only private property in land. This significantly distinguishes the seventeenth-century critique of private property from previous versions. In an essentially agricultural country, like seventeenth-century England, not owning land condemned one not only to extreme poverty but often to starvation. Criticizing property in land amounted to advocating that everyone should have the necessary wherewithal for a decent living. In an agricultural society that meant that all should own lands, tools, draft animals, and seeds.

Discussion Question

Thomas Reid, an eighteenth-century Scottish philosopher, argued that all human beings had a right to life but that such a right was without value unless it included the means to life—either land or decently paying work. What do you think of that argument? Give reasons for your answer.

A second argument, also used by Winstanley, pointed out that ownership of land was closely linked to freedom. A person who had enough land was able to support the entire family if only he were willing to work hard enough. But the poor man who had no land was dependent on others for the opportunity to make a living. His willingness to work was not sufficient; he was dependent on owners of land to hire him to work for them. The landowner was his own boss; he could work when and how he chose. The landless laborer had to take orders. He had to work when he was told and in the way determined by his employer. He was dependent on others both for the opportunity to work and for the work he did and how he was to go about it. The landless had none of the independence of those with land. They were dependent on landowners for their very survival. They were considerably less free.[12]

Discussion Questions

Is it true that—in an agricultural society—ownership of land provides a degree of freedom not accessible to the landless? What provides comparable freedom in our society? Give reasons for your answer.

SOCIALISM

Between the days of Winstanley, in the middle of the seventeenth century, and the middle of the nineteenth century, when Karl Marx and Frederick Engels began to develop their socialist conceptions, England changed enormously. Many people moved from the countryside to the cities; industry had replaced agriculture as a major source of income. People without land could become rich by building and owning factories or businesses connected with industry—buying and selling industrial products or the raw materials used in industrial production. For those who owned no property, work was now available not only in agriculture but also in the new industrial enterprises. Land was no longer the necessary condition for a decent life.

But if the people in the 1700s who owned no land lacked independence and were often facing starvation, the same was now true of those who owned no industrial capital. Although in former times there had been people who owned land and the landless, the nineteenth-century society was divided into the classes that owned land *or* industry (or the capital to finance industry) and those who owned neither. All they had to offer was their ability to work and if no one wanted them, they starved. Nineteenth-century society—the same is still true of ours—was divided into two major classes of people: the owners of productive property—land, or capital, or businesses, or factories or trucks—and owners of nothing but their own ability to do work.

Marx, adapting the thought of the Diggers to the different conditions of the nineteenth century, argued that the distinction between the owners of productive property and those who lacked such property placed a great and unfair burden on the latter. The workers, or "proletariat"—as the latter were often called—were condemned to poverty and second-class citizenship by their lack of productive property. What is more, the owners of productive property, the capitalists, were not entitled to their property; it had been wrongfully taken from the workers who had produced it. The workers had been exploited because a portion of their daily work had remained unpaid. Underlying one version of the socialist argument is a moral claim: The capitalists who control productive resources are not entitled to that control because they did not acquire those resources legitimately. Capitalist control of productive assets rests on exploitation. Exploitation is clearly not legitimate. Capitalists are therefore not legitimate owners of the resources they, in actuality, control.

To clarify this claim we need to examine the idea of exploitation and consider the question of who is the legitimate owner of productive resources.

Exploitation

Persons exploit each other when one takes advantage of the other to get something that he is not entitled to. Take as an example the owner of a sweatshop who hires illegal immigrants and pays them a lot less than all the other workers in the place, knowing that this immigrant does not have a legal right to work. When the immigrant complains, the owner threatens to call the immigration service to come and arrest her. The immigrant is exploited because she is not paid what she deserves; she is not paid current market wages and the employer manages to force her to accept much lower wages by threatening to have her arrested and sent back to her country of origin. More generally, using compulsion to get something from another that the other is not properly compensated for is a standard form of exploitation. A woman may exploit the man who adores her by threatening to withdraw her love while extracting endless attention and expensive gifts from him. Men, similarly, exploit the love of women to get a great deal of attention and care while giving little in return. Leaders of cults often exploit their members by getting unpaid labor or cash donations from them by promising them eternal bliss in another life.

In all societies that have existed so far, some people were rich without doing a whole lot of work. Greek and Roman men spent their days exercising in the gymnasium or arguing in public places, while their slaves tilled the fields to support them and their families in style. Medieval lords built big castles where they feasted in the company of their knights, while the peasants labored in the fields to raise food and produce whatever the idle aristocrats called for. In capitalist societies like ours, the idea of exploitation is used to characterize rich people who do little if any work and spend their time, instead, at brilliant parties and public events where working people can admire them. The idea of exploitation is also applied to business leaders who may work hard themselves but are paid many times over what their employees earn.

Marx believed that workers were exploited by capitalists. A fair wage, he argued, amounted to the cost of keeping workers and their families in food, shelter, and other necessities to enable workers to come back to work another day and to raise a family whose children would come to work when they became adults. A part of the workers' day is spent earning what is needed to keep them and their families going. But, said Marx, the employers make workers work for more hours than are needed to earn their upkeep and for these extra hours they are not getting paid: they are being exploited to the extent that they are forced to work several hours of each working day which remain unpaid.

But this argument rests on an economic theory—the labor theory of value—which is no longer accepted by professional economists. According to contemporary economic theory, wage rates are determined by supply and demand in the labor market. Scarcity is an important determinant of wages: there are very few heart transplant surgeons and great demand for their services. As a consequence they become quite wealthy. There are a lot more people prepared to clean offices relative to the demand for cleaning services. As a consequence, wage rates for janitors and office cleaners are much lower. The janitor who cleans offices at Microsoft earns a whole lot less money than Bill Gates. But is he therefore being exploited? Is he like the illegal immigrant who is forced to take a smaller salary than market rate for the work he does? Gates's janitor is not forced to accept the job at its present pay rate. He is not under any threat to accept the wages he earns. Once one surrenders Marx's economic theory, the claim that workers are exploited is less easily proved. It becomes more difficult to support the socialists' claim that the capitalists have no right to the productive assets they own and control.

Accordingly, it seems today that the idea of exploitation has no place in our world. We may agree that slaves or medieval peasants were exploited, but workers today are not being forced to take the jobs they have. They are, after all, free to find a better paying job if they can find it. They are also free to get more education in the hope of finding a better paying job. Capitalists do not appear to be exploiting their workers. The profits from their businesses, their hard work, and invested capital seem to be rightfully theirs. They are entitled to own and control productive resources legitimately acquired.

But these arguments against speaking about exploitation in capitalist societies are inconclusive. Sons and daughters sometimes exploit their own mother's love when they, having reached adulthood, circle back to ask her for money or other help that she perhaps can ill afford. But they, knowing that she would do anything for them and make any sacrifice for them, callously take advantage of that love. They exploit their mothers by taking advantage of her boundless affection for them.

If employers take advantage of high unemployment to lower wage rates, could we say that they take advantage of the difficulties workers have in scratching together any sort of living to support themselves and their families? Is this not a situation that is similar to that in which a hardhearted child takes advantage of his mother's love? If the surgeon charges exorbitant fees from patients who, gravely ill, would be willing to pay anything to be allowed to live a bit longer, is that surgeon taking advantage of the straits the patients find themselves in?

At the heart of the debate about exploitation is the question of the freedom of wage earners to negotiate their wages and working conditions. To the extent that wage earners have limited freedom to find a new and better job, calling them exploited may have some justification. To the extent that they are not compelled by circumstances to take a poorly paying job but are perfectly free in their choices of employment, it seems inappropriate to call them exploited. On the one hand, few people are forced to remain in their current workplace if they want better conditions. (There are some: soldiers, prisoners, perhaps nuns and priests.) They can always look for a better job. Their employer can force them to accept the wages and working conditions in their present job only under special conditions, such as being an undocumented worker. But, on the other hand, employers often have the upper hand in negotiations over wages. Employees are right to feel that their employers take advantage of their greater power in setting wages and working conditions. We shall see some examples of that. The debate over exploitation in a capitalist society is directly connected to the other criticism of capitalist society, that the capitalists have more extensive freedoms than the wage workers.

Discussion Questions

If employers take advantage of the pressing needs of their employees to make a living, to pay their mortgage, and to feed their children, by paying them a low wage, are they exploiting them? If a businesswoman takes advantage of the financial difficulties of a competitor to buy that other business at fire sale prices, is she taking advantage and exploiting the other? Give reasons for your answer.

Who Should Control Productive Resources?

In capitalist societies, just as in all preceding ones, there exist great inequalities. But this inequality takes different forms. Some people barely survive, and even though they work, end up living in their cars while others own grand mansions in different places as well as yachts and other expensive playthings. But more important is this difference: the wealthy own productive resources. The poor do not.

Many owners of productive property are a lot richer than the people who work for them. But that was not the main criticism raised by Marx. He was well aware that many small business owners have a modest income for which they work very hard. What differentiates the business owner from the employee of the business is the greater independence and freedom of the business owner.

In their relation to each other, the employer has more power than the employee in at least two ways. To begin with, it is up to the employer whether there is work for the employee. Suppose I run a call center where my employees answer customer questions concerning a number of electronic devices whose manufacturers pay me for providing this service. Suppose also that I have located the call center in a small rural town in the United States where there are few employment opportunities and hence wages tend to be fairly low. After a while, competition heats up among providers of comparable services and other call centers can offer lower rates to their customers because they locate their call centers outside the United States where wages are a fraction of what they are here. My competitors force me to move offshore. I close my U.S. operation; my employees lose their jobs and because they live in an area of high unemployment they may have a hard time finding alternative work.

This story makes two important points. To begin with, it is up the owner of capital whether there are jobs in a given area or not. If I invest my money in a call center, say, in Appalachia, some people there get the opportunity to work. If I move my center, their job opportunities, never good, become even worse. Employers are more powerful than employees in this respect: they determine who gets the opportunity to work and who does not. For the same reasons, employers determine what sort of work will be available in a particular place. If only low wage industries move to your part of the country, only low wage jobs will be available to you. You may be exceptionally talented or be highly skilled and educated, but if there are no jobs for people of your ability and training you will have to work at what is available. The work you do depends on your employer, not on you or your capacities.

The other point made by the story is, of course, equally important. Individual employers are subject to systemic pressures. If I move my call center from Appalachia to a foreign country not because I hold a grudge against my domestic workforce but because I am losing out to my competitors, I, too, am subject to economic pressures. However reluctantly, I am compelled by market forces to relocate my business.

But here the employer is better off than the employee in another respect: if an industry moves to a small town in India, I do not need to uproot my family to move to India and send my children to school in a place where everyone speaks Urdu and few if any people speak English. I can remain where I have always lived. I just need to travel more. But if an industry leaves the town where workers live, they need to move, pack up their belongings, sell their house, and uproot their children to settle where there is work available.

If I get tired of running a call center, I can sell my business and invest my capital in some other business. If I am tired of business I can use my money to get retrained in a different occupation—perhaps to become a medical missionary in Africa, to run a travel agency, or to do whatever I please. As a worker, my ability to have steady and well-paying work has an equally important influence on my life, but I have much more limited influence over that because it is up to the employer to create opportunities for me to work. I have little power over those opportunities, and to that extent, have less power over my life than the owners of capital. If my income is modest and I just get by paying the bills for myself and the family, there are few opportunities for me to take off several years for a career change and retraining. My possibilities are much more limited than those of an owner of capital.

When it comes to the level of income, the employer, too, has much more freedom. His income depends on his hard work and his ingenuity in building his business. The employee is limited by the work available. The former employees in my call center are as likely as not to be either unemployed for a long period of time or, if they find other work, they may have to settle for a lower wage because that is all that is available to them where they live. Their power to determine their standard of living is a good deal more limited than the employers'.

Being a worker, a person who does not own capital, limits one's freedom to fashion one's own life in important ways. It provides considerable force to the accusation that employers, that is, owners of capital, take advantage of the workers' more limited freedoms, and thereby, exploit them. This problem, Marx reasons, would disappear if investment capital were not owned by individuals but were controlled by the society as a whole. A society in which investment capital is owned or controlled by the society as a whole is called *socialist*. The dream of a socialist society has an extended history that begins long before the nineteenth century when Marx and Engels did their work. It took many different forms but the central idea was always that of a society in which everyone commanded some means of production — whether that meant that everyone owned land, tools, or raw materials for industrial production, or whether all productive resources were to be owned by all collectively, and more importantly, were under everyone's joint control. The idea was always that in a good society no one should be coerced for lack of productive property and that no one should be less free than others because they had no control over such resources.

According to Marx, a socialist society is inaugurated when "capital is converted into common property."[13] A socialist society, as he envisaged it, would provide equal freedom for all and that would require that the control capitalists have over ordinary persons' lives in our society be abolished. A free, socialist society needs to abolish the private ownership of productive resources.

Actual social experiments to found socialist societies, notably in the Soviet Union and in China, interpreted this conversion of privately owned productive resources into "common property" as a transfer of capital goods from private to government ownership that produced a government with immense power so that the society, which was instituted to guarantee equal freedom for all, turned into one that was more oppressive than most. An alternative conception of socialism envisages a society in which productive resources are under the democratic control of all citizens. We will examine what such a socialist society might look like at the end of the next chapter.

Discussion Question

Marshal as many arguments as you can both for and against the claim that owners of productive capital have more freedom in our society than the workers who have nothing to offer for sale except their ability to work. Consult your own work experiences.

Defending Capitalist Property

Some theorists are ready to admit that existing economic inequalities do have an effect on the extent to which different persons are able to determine their own lives. Some go so far as to say that the existing system of private ownership of means of production does affect citizens' freedoms. The owners tend to have more freedoms than the employees. But at the same time, many argue that private ownership of productive resources is just. The owners of businesses have the *right* to use those resources as they see fit. Any attempt to give every citizen the right to participate in running the economy would violate the property rights of business owners. Such a scheme would be completely unjust. Before leaving the topic of socialism, we must consider this objection that, even if in some way attractive, the socialist project cannot be justified because it would violate the property rights of the business owners, that is, of the capitalists.

Let us consider an example. Rosalee Turan opened a bakery thirty-three years ago. Today she owns several bakeries at different locations in the city. Her business is thriving; she is a millionaire several times over. In her first bakery, the actual baking was done by Roger McEwan, who still works for her. He makes a decent living. He owns his own house and a nice boat. His two daughters attended the local state college because he could not afford to send them to a private school. With his wife also working, the two have managed to save enough money not to have to worry about their retirement now that the mortgage on their house is paid up. But his job has changed dramatically. Thirty-three years ago he made his own dough and then baked the breads, rolls, and cakes. Today the unbaked items are prepared at a central location by large, automated machines and brought to Roger's store frozen. He puts the frozen items in an automatic oven, keys in the right number, and waits for the oven to do its work. When the oven signals him, he takes out the finished baked goods. "I used to love baking," says Roger "but this job is really boring. I have become the servant to a machine. Any three-year-old could do it."

We need to ask two questions here: Is it unjust that Rosalee is a millionaire and Roger still has the same working-class lifestyle? And, secondly, is it just that Rosalee can completely turn Roger's work life upside down and transform a skilled profession he loved into routine and boring work? Defenders of capitalism give a number of different answers to this question.

1. Rosalee earned it. Roger worked hard all these years, but Rosalee may well have worked a lot harder. He baked, but she made business plans, advertised, bought buildings, ovens, flour, and other raw materials, and did whatever else was necessary to build her successful business. She showed imagination and business skill—qualifications much rarer than the ability to bake good bread. So we might well acknowledge that her hard work and her exceptional abilities are legitimately rewarded by a much larger income than Roger's.

But Rosalee not only earns a lot more money than Roger, she also has a lot more power in the business. Is that legitimate? Well, the defenders of capitalism point out, it is her business not only because she started it but she also supplied the capital needed to start it and to keep it going. Rosalee's ownership and control are justified by her hard work, her special ability, and her owning the original capital.

But of course, the contested question is just that: is it legitimate that private individuals own capital or other productive resources? Let us assume, for simplicity's sake, that Rosalee started her business with the money she had saved from a previous job. She had earned that money; why should she not be able to invest it in her bakery? But on the other hand, there was Roger and without his skill as a baker, Rosalee's business would not have been able to take off. Should he not also have *some* say over its conduct? To be sure, Roger did not invest any money in the bakery because on his pay he had no money to invest. Rosalee, on the other hand, earned a whole lot in her previous job and was able to save some. Should we conclude that control over the bakery belongs legitimately to the person who invested money in it? Saying that, we would say that the rich, people who earn more than they consume, should own all businesses and the working people who only earn enough to get by should have to take orders and have the rich organize their work life. Many people point out, at that point in this reflection, that Roger could have taken a job somewhere else. But of course, he would in that other job have been in the same situation where the business owner had the power to affect his work life and sometimes also his home life significantly by decisions about whether Roger would work at all, at what pay rate, and what sort of work he needed to do to earn his pay.

Discussion Question

Is it legitimate for people who have enough money to invest some of it to then, have power over the lives of their employees? Give reasons for your answer.

2. Rosalee is entitled to control her business because she did not have to invest her earnings from her previous job; she could have gone and spent them. Capitalist control over productive resources is often justified by the fact that capitalists make sacrifices when they save their money to invest it, instead of spending it. But could Gates spend the billions he owns? How great is the sacrifice of the hedge fund manager who just got a bonus of $20 million if he does not go and spend all his money and instead reinvests some of it?
3. Rosalee is entitled to control her business and with it have significant power over Roger's life because she took a risk in starting the bakery business. Some capitalists are entrepreneurs. They have a good idea. They think it will make money, but, of course, they cannot be certain of that. In starting up a new business, they are taking a risk; they might loose their shirt. Hence, if they succeed, they are entitled to owning and controlling the business.

    This third common argument in favor of legitimating capitalist ownership of productive resources overlooks the fact that Roger, of course, also took a risk. To be sure, because he had no money invested in the bakery he did not stand to lose any, but he could have lost his job if the original bakery idea had failed and he would then have had to start all over again. If a business goes bankrupt everyone loses, not only the owner.

Discussion Question

Considering these arguments for and against private ownership of the means of production, do you see any merit in the socialist position? Give reasons for your answer.

THE PHILOSOPHY OF THE FREE MARKET

We have examined a number of good reasons why we might be suspicious of the institution of private property, in general. Other considerations lead us to think that private ownership and control of productive resources is not conducive to equal freedom for all.

But opposed to these trains of thought is the contrary claim, that equal freedom for all is possible only in a society where the institution of private property—both of consumption goods and of productive resources—rules supreme. Unfettered owners must be free to buy and sell what they own without being confined by legislation or government regulations. The greatest freedom is available to all if private property is unrestricted and we therefore enjoy participation in a "free market."

These defenses of the free market take two forms. The first claims that only in the free market are all transactions voluntary; only free market transactions are not coerced. Hence a free market society provides the greatest freedom for all. A second argument claims that the free market harnesses the self-interests of all participants so as to produce the greatest prosperity for all. Prosperity increases the range of available opportunities and thereby freedom.

In Free Markets All Transactions Are Voluntary

The classic description and praise of the free market were provided by Milton Friedman and Rose Friedman in their 1962 book *Capitalism and Freedom*:

> The basic problem of social organization is how to coordinate the economic activities of large numbers of people. Even in relatively backward societies, extensive division of labor and specialization of function is required to make effective use of available resources. In advanced societies, the scale on which co-ordination is needed, to take full advantage of the opportunities offered by modern science and technology, is enormously greater. Literally millions of people are involved in providing one another with their daily bread, let alone with their yearly automobiles. The challenge to the believer in liberty is to reconcile this widespread interdependence with individual freedom.[14]

Whatever you buy in a modern, technological society results from a complex process of production. You can buy this car at a reasonable price because all the different subassemblies—parts made in different countries, all over the world—are available when needed in the auto plant. Each part is produced in a comparable process—manufactured on the right schedule, shipped out, and ready when needed. The raw materials and tools for its production must also be there at the right time. The men and women who produce these objects need food and shelter, clothing, education, and health care for themselves and their children. All of that must be readily available for them so that they can get what they need without spending too much time away from producing parts for the car you have just bought. It takes a great deal of organization to have all of these elements available when and where they are required, made by people who themselves must be able to readily procure what they need.

Fundamentally there are only two ways of coordinating the economic activities of millions. One is central direction involving the use of coercion—the technique of the army and of the modern totalitarian state. The other is a voluntary cooperation of individuals—the technique of the market place.

The possibility of coordination through voluntary cooperation rests on the elementary—yet frequently denied—proposition that both parties to an economic transaction benefit from it, *provided the transaction is bilaterally voluntary and informed.* Exchange can therefore bring about coordination without coercion. A working model of a society organized through voluntary exchange is a *free private enterprise exchange economy*—what we have been calling competitive capitalism.[15]

Government involvement in economic transactions tends to be coercive—witness the case of eminent domain in New London. Transactions in the free market are voluntary—or so the Friedmans and many other economists tell us.

Discussion Questions

A noted philosopher proposed this conundrum. Suppose as you sail your yacht a few miles from the ocean shore, it suddenly springs a leak and sinks. You find yourself desperately clinging to a piece of timber in a freezing ocean. A man comes by in a boat and tells you that he will rescue you, but only if you pay him a large sum of money. Is this person extorting money from you or making a generous offer? If you pay for being rescued, are you acting voluntarily? Give reasons for your answer.

Free-market transactions are of different kinds; it is difficult to maintain that all of them are completely voluntary. Suppose someone offers you a job that pays rather poorly, but it is the only job in sight, or other available jobs pay even less, or are for other reasons even less desirable. No one is putting a gun to your head, no one is threatening to put you in jail or to do serious physical harm to you or your family; but you know, and everyone else knows, that if you refuse the job, you will soon run out of money, you will be unable to feed your family, and you will be restricted in your activities due to lack of funds. Can we really say that you take that job voluntarily? Well, the Friedmans say, a transaction is voluntary if "both parties benefit." But so, of course, do the homeowners in New London who manage to stay out of jail by selling their house. What makes a transaction voluntary is not established quite as easily as all that because it is no clearer that a transaction "benefits" you than that it is voluntary.

In many cases, it is not easy to decide whether a transaction is freely entered into by all the parties. Imagine yourself in a situation where you have several utterly delightful alternatives. Whichever one you choose, you will, you think, be happy with the results and you clearly make your choice voluntarily. In other situations, you may have several choices open to you; one of them pleases you enormously, the others are more or less abhorrent. You choose the one that pleases you; you are happy and your choice is voluntary. But now imagine that you have a number of alternatives, but the one you hoped for is not among them. For instance, you applied to a number of colleges but do not get accepted at your first or second choice but only at one that you consider your "safety school." Or, you applied for a number of jobs and the ones you would really like are not offered to you, and you have to take one of the other ones that you would rather not take. Is your choice voluntary? No one forces you to take a job you do not like, but short of moving to a different city and trying your luck there, or maybe leaving the country and trying to find the work you really want abroad, you do not have another possibility; so you take the job you would prefer not to take, and you take it reluctantly. You are doing something that you would prefer not to do. If that is voluntary, it is certainly less so than if you really loved the job you are about to take. There are degrees of voluntariness.

Now consider the case where you are running out of money through no fault of your own; there has been serious illness in your family, a fire devastated parts of the family home, a drunk driver has demolished the family car, and both of your parents lost their job on the same day because the company they worked for moved offshore. The only jobs available to you are low-paying, dirty, dangerous, and exhausting jobs. You take one of them but you know you are going to hate it and you will still have serious money problems. Are you taking the job voluntarily? There are two ways of looking at your situation: one may say the employer who offers you a dirty low-wage job is a godsend because it allows you to earn some money when you really need it. The employer turns out to be your savior even though the job he offers is pretty unattractive, but it helps you out of a really desperate situation. The other way of looking at the situation says that your employer is taking advantage of your desperate situation. If you were not so hard up for money, the employer would have to offer you a lot more because you would not take the job as it is now. The employer is extorting work and money. You are forced to accept a really nasty job because your employer takes shameful advantage of your desperate situation.

Think about one other familiar scenario. You run a hardware store that your father started in your hometown. People know you, they like you, and you are friendly and knowledgeable about hardware so people come to you for advice and then buy from you. Your store is flourishing until a large chain comes into town. The town is small; it will not support two hardware stores. The newly arrived chain has deep pockets; they can afford to undersell you and so they do. You steadily lose customers and finally are forced to sell your store. Are you selling your remaining inventory voluntarily?

Discussion Questions

The homeowner in New London who is forced to sell his or her house gets money and stays out of jail. Those are "benefits." But is the transaction voluntary?

The unemployed single mother who accepts a minimum wage job because it is the only one available at this moment and she cannot afford to wait benefits because she has more money than before. But does she take the job voluntarily?

You are standing in front of the Justice of the Peace by the side of your pregnant girlfriend. Behind you is her father with a shotgun. Are you saying "I do" voluntarily?

You made a lot of money early and then retired. Now through some freak financial mishap, you have lost all your money, your house burned down, and both your parents fell seriously ill. The only job available demands back-breaking labor for little money. Do you accept it voluntarily?

List different senses in which these transaction are and are not voluntary. You should end up with a list of different senses of the word voluntary.

Many people believe that a free-market economy is preferable to all other economic arrangements. The most common argument in support of that points to the extraordinary productiveness of free markets. These arguments recommend the free market on the basis of its *results.* In similar ways, opponents of the free market point to negative results of the free markets—environmental degradation and progressively increasing economic inequality, for instance— to criticize it. These defenses and critiques raise complex issues in economic theories that we cannot discuss here.

But the argument we just examined advocates the free market not for its economic outcomes but because it realizes most perfectly the liberal political principle of economic freedom. Everyone who subscribes to the liberal political principle of equal liberty for all, and who believes that equal liberty for all is more fully realized when all have equal economic liberty must recognize, so the Friedmans argue, that the free market gives the widest scope to economic freedom because in the free market all transactions are voluntary.

Discussion Question

Assess the claim that in a free-market society all participants have the greatest freedom possible. Give reasons for your answer.

The Unseen Hand of the Free Market

A second argument in favor of free markets was supplied by Adam Smith. In his *The Wealth of Nations,* published in 1776, Smith wrote about the capitalist that:

> by directing that industry in such a manner as its produce may be of the greatest value, he intends only his own gain and he is in this, as in many other cases, led by an invisible hand to promote an end which has no part of his intention . . . by pursuing his own interests he frequently promotes that of the society more effectually than when he really intends to promote it.[16]

Free markets mobilize individual self-interest; the result is an improvement in everybody's condition. All are better off if everyone looks after his or her best interests. That was the claim made by Smith in the year of the birth of our American republic. There are still many people who believe that the market manages to transform individual, personal self-interest into a greater common good.

We need to notice here the conflict between Thomas Jefferson and Smith. Jefferson, as we saw previously, believed that the American republic could only survive if citizens were devoted to the common good rather than to their private interest. To be sure, Jefferson lived on his beautiful and luxurious estate, Monticello, supported by more than a hundred slaves in his opulent life. He was clearly not averse to looking out for himself. But in his role as political representative, as ambassador in Paris, and as president, he believed that reflection about the common good, rather than about his personal self-interest should guide his thinking. As against that Smith advocates, at least in economics, a policy of seeking out what is good for oneself—a policy which "frequently promotes [the interest] of the society more effectually than when he really intends to promote it." Deliberate efforts to guide the economy toward a better life for all frequently fail and have the opposite of their intended effects. The production, distribution, and consumption of goods in a society should not be regulated with an eye to the common good. Economic affairs thrive most when everyone considers private self-interest above all.

Discussion Question

Will you side with Jefferson or with Smith in the debate over self-interest versus devotion to the common good. Is selfishness or being public spirited better for all of us? Be sure to pay attention to distinctions between economic and political self-interest. Give reasons for your answer.

But there are reasons to be skeptical about this claim made by Smith. Consider this humble example: Joe Thomas has twelve children and his income does not quite suffice to keep all of them in sneakers, schoolbooks, and hats and gloves in winter. He is eager to save money wherever he can. His town charges for picking up garbage. He has to pay $1.50 for every bag of garbage collected, and twelve children produce a lot of garbage. Joe has gotten into the habit of dropping his garbage off in the park when he drives to work. Clearly that is in his own interest; but equally clearly, if everybody followed their self-interests in the same way, the park would soon be transformed into a garbage dump.

Every employer has an interest in lowering expenses for wages and salaries. All employers are, for that reason, eager to replace their employees with machines. Bill Wade may be able to increase his profit when he invests in a new machine that allows him to let three workers go. If everyone in the economy follows the same strategy, unemployment may rise sharply; consumers may have less money to spend. Demand for consumption goods may drop. Some businesses go bankrupt. Unemployment rises some more. Very soon the economy is in a recession.

There are endless examples of strategies useful for individual entrepreneurs that become disastrous if adopted by many. The pursuit of private self-interest is not always translated by the hidden hand of the market into collective well-being.

The problem lies in the idea of *self-interest*. We usually think of self-interest as what is good for me, or for you, or for some third party. But my self-interest, and yours, are, in fact, more complex: some things are in our common interest, such as having clean and safe streets, and traffic flowing smoothly without accidents, fights, and drivers swearing at each other. These common goods exist to the extent that all of us do not throw our trash in the street or that we behave as civilized human beings and are polite to our neighbors or strangers in the street. Traffic flows smoothly when everyone is civil to everyone else. The existence of these common goods depends on all of us and their existence is in everyone's interest.

But we encounter a certain amount of conflict in our own interests in the pursuit of these common goods. When I am late for work and stuck behind someone driving twenty miles per hour, I have an urgent need to vent my anger. That is one of my interests. I want to lean out the window and yell at the person holding me back. But I also have another, conflicting interest in traffic being smooth and everyone being civil. My self-interest is complex and there are conflicts between different aspects of it.

The unseen hand of the market seems to oversimplify the idea of self-interest. It is not always clear which self-interest I am pursuing—something that is only good for me, but not good for all, or something that is, in the long run, good for me but perhaps not my most favorite choice at this very moment. If everyone only does what is good for him or her now, at this moment, the whole will not always prosper. If everyone does what is best for all, we will, of course, be better off.

Discussion Questions

Consider some other examples of complex self-interests:

Are your interests identical with those of your employer or not?

What are your interests with respect to financing public schools when you have no children in school?

If you are able-bodied, what are your interests with respect to building access ramps for people in wheelchairs?

In the light of complexities like these, what do you think of the unseen hand doctrine? Give reasons for your answer.

PATERNALISM

Private property rights create a whole different set of questions once we look at questions about freedom in conjunction with issues of safety. Property rights have, in our time, created a cluster of problems when our rights to use our property as we please conflict with government measures to control how we use our property. These government regulations, of which mandatory seat belt and motorcycle helmet use are among the most familiar examples, are defended as being in our own interest because they make us safer. They often look as if the government were taking a parental role toward us even though we are adults ourselves and do not need parental supervision or guidance. Such measures are therefore often called "paternalism."

Protecting Us against Ourselves

In the late 1960s, the federal government began to pressure the states to pass laws making the use of motorcycle helmets mandatory. By now most states demand that everyone riding a motorcycle wear a protective helmet. Many states require anyone riding in a car to wear a seat belt. The government has taken it on itself to regulate how we will use our own property and protect ourselves against the dangers of driving motorcycles or cars. The government has not yet demanded that we protect our hearing against the noise of lawn mowers, not to mention of rock concerts, or that we use protective eye wear when building a bookshelf in the basement. But the day may soon come when those protective measure also become mandatory. All of these are limitations of individual freedom of property: the government demands on pain of legal

punishment that we take specific precautions before we use our possessions—motorcycles, cars, lawn mowers, or table saws.

Defenders of these paternalistic acts by the government remind us of the
statistics concerning rates of serious accidents and the costs of surgery and
hospital stays for their victims. They also draw attention to the fact that many
of us have insurance to pay for medical care. The effect of insurance is to
spread around the costs of injuries and hospitalization. If one person's carelessness leads to injuries and large medical bills, all the other owners of insurance policies will see their premiums rise. Everyone, therefore, has an interest in keeping medical costs low. The consequences of enforcing
paternalistic legislation may well be positive; it may save some of us a great
deal of misery and money.

But do these beneficial consequences of paternalism justify the government limiting our freedoms to use our property as we see fit? Opponents of
this protective legislation question the right of the government to limit the
freedom of citizens for the sake of protecting them against harm they may
be doing to themselves. To what extent, they ask, should we allow the government to protect us against the consequences of our own choices and actions? It is generally accepted that the government has a legitimate function
in enhancing security in a society by protecting citizens against one another.
But it is surely a different question whether the government should be allowed to limit the freedoms of individual citizens to protect them against
their choices for themselves. Should we allow the government to keep tight
control over what we eat? The New York City Health Department has recently issued regulations that prohibit all restaurants from using trans fats
in their kitchens. The Chicago City Council is considering similar restrictions on what people may eat and so are the leaders of other cities.[17] Consumers are being protected against their own choices of food. Will the government address sexual safety next and institute criminal proceedings
against persons found with sexually transmitted diseases as evidence that
they did not practice safe sex? Will bureaucrats prohibit high heels because
they strain leg muscles or forbid wearing chains around one's neck where
they could get caught on something and cause serious harm? One opponent
of motorcycle helmet laws points out that a much larger number of persons
die of heart disease than from motorcycle accidents. If we force the latter to
be as safe as possible, should we not prohibit the consumption of cheese-
burgers, cheesecake, and foods prepared with heavy cream? "Compare the
2,500 motorcycle fatalities with 720,862 from heart disease, and you could
make a pretty good case that riding a Harley each day for twenty years is
safer than eating a cheeseburger a day for the same amount of time. . . . Hey,
waiter, how about a tofu burger?"[18]

Discussion Question

Locke said, "Every man has property in his own person." Freedom to dispose of one's own body as one pleases is the basis for freedom of movement, and for the freedom to choose one's work, and for the rule that doctors must obtain informed consent from patients before surgery. Ownership of one's body is an important freedom. Soliciting sex for money and offering to sell sexual services are illegal in most places in the United States. Do these laws against prostitution infringe on personal freedom, specifically to make important decisions about one's body? Give reasons for your answer.

Liberalism and Paternalism

Considering these examples of actual government supervision of our private lives and the ways in which we use our own property, as well as possible areas into which the government might expand its concern for our safety, it becomes urgent to decide how we determine what are legitimate areas for government regulation and when the government oversteps the limits of privacy to which all of us should be entitled. What if the government, concerned about the failures of individuals to take good care of themself, moves to protect citizens against their own errors and weaknesses? Is a limitation of individual freedoms justified because it intends to protect citizens against themselves?

Life in modern industrial societies is quite complex. We cannot assess the safety or the dangers presented to us by many of the goods we consume. Examples are the medicines we take when ill or the safety of car bodies or of air bags. Other examples are the wiring in our houses or the safety of genetically engineered foods. In many areas of our lives regarding consumption, we lack the information to make reasonable choices without needlessly endangering ourselves. We need the government to inform us and to regulate the uses of medicines; we need guidelines for the safe construction of cars or of our houses. But the dangers of riding a motorcycle without wearing a helmet or driving without using a seat belt are known to all, as are the possible consequences of unprotected sex or of smoking cigarettes. In these cases, government interference with our freedoms for the sake of protecting us cannot be justified by our ignorance of the relevant facts. The question whether the government may protect us against our own choices needs to be confronted.

Discussion Question

The complexity of life in a technological, affluent society leaves many of us without the information we need to make consumer choices that will not endanger us or others. It seems reasonable to call on the government to be diligent in educating consumers. Is it also reasonable to allow the government to force consumers to adopt certain safety measures such as wearing safety goggles and ear protectors while mowing the lawn? Give reasons for your answer.

John Stuart Mill

This is not a new question, peculiar to our time or our circumstances. In his justly famous book, *On Liberty* (1859), the British political philosopher, John Stuart Mill (1806–1873) tried to determine the limits of legitimate interference in the life of any adult person by other adults or by the government. Liberal political principles claim a range of freedoms for everyone, among which are the freedom to acquire, to own, and to use property. How, Mill asks, can we determine when a government or other citizens are entitled to interfere with us and our freedoms to use our property, including our own bodies, as we choose, and when they, in interfering, are being tyrannical?

Early along in the essay Mill declares that "the sole end for which mankind are warranted, individually or collectively, in interfering with the liberty of action of any of their number, is self protection. . . . his own good, either physical or moral, is not a sufficient warrant" (8), and again, "To individuality should belong the part of life in which it is chiefly the individual that is interested; to society the part which chiefly interests society . . . As soon as any part of a person's conduct affects prejudicially the interests of others, society has jurisdiction over it." (66–67). Mill takes an uncompromising stand: it is not legitimate for the government to restrict the freedom of individuals to protect them from their own actions that might harm them. Only actions that harm others are a legitimate target for government control and restriction. If our actions threaten harm to others, the government may intervene to protect those others. If my actions merely threaten myself, government interference is not to be allowed.[19]

Discussions Question

Some people starve themselves; others overeat. Should we make anorexia and overeating illegal or do both of those belong in the private sphere? Give reasons for your answer.

Obviously many actions harm others. They may therefore be prohibited. But suppose what I do harms no one but myself? Should we call on the government to protect persons whose actions only hurt themselves against their own carelessness or self-destructive inclinations? People often reply that there are many actions with which individuals harm themselves but, at the same time, they inflict damage and pain on others. Drunkenness affects the drunkard's family; addicts often do serious harm to those near and dear to them, and often also to complete strangers. But, Mill reminds us, not all alcoholics do serious damage to others nor are all persons doing drugs a burden on society. If someone, when drunk, commits acts of violence, Mill thinks, the law may certainly demand of her that she stay away from alcohol. Failing to do so may invite punishment.[20] But we should not control alcohol and drugs preventively. Only those users who harm others are to be punished and their drug use restricted.

Restricting actions of persons who have shown that alcohol or drugs lead them to harm others is different from prohibiting the use of alcohol to everyone or making the use of certain drugs illegal. Such prohibitions aim to protect us against our own actions because they may be harmful to ourselves, but that, Mill insists, is not justified. Once protection against actions considered harmful to the agent becomes accepted, there are no more reasons not to limit also what they think, censor what they read, and restrict the ideas that they may be exposed to in schools or in the media. Recall some of the debates about censorship of school materials in the first chapter. If the government is to be placed in the role of protecting citizens, how much more should we expect it to shield children and adolescents against violent, sexually charged, or simply upsetting reading material, or music that might be interpreted as condoning drug use and unmarried sex? We might think that many adults too would be better off if they had no access to pornography or to portrayals, let alone glorifications, of violence such as in the old Western movies.

Citizens have been known to choose the wrong candidate for public office. Adolf Hitler, notoriously, was elected overwhelmingly by German voters in 1933 before he proceeded to suspend civil rights, abolish elections, and, in general, institute a harsh dictatorship. In that vote German citizens made a horrific mistake for which they paid dearly. They would perhaps have been better off had they never had the opportunity to vote a man into power who proved to be a brutal dictator and in the end left his country in ruins. Could it be that we should learn from such examples of the failures of electoral processes and abolish democracy in our own country, thereby protecting each of us against our own occasional errors of judgment? Allowing the government to keep us safe from our own bad judgment in the use of helmets, seat belts, alcohol, or drugs may well be only a beginning for far-reaching government control of all aspect of the lives of citizens. Serious questions need to be asked about the government protecting citizens against themselves.

Discussion Question

In 1945, the people of Boston voted Michael Curley in as fourth-term mayor after he had served time in prison for corruption and was then under federal indictment for more corruption. Why should it be illegal to ride without a

seatbelt on but be perfectly legal to vote for politicians that are known to be
excessively corrupt? Give reasons for your answer.

The final chapter of Mill's essay *On Liberty* discusses some concrete applications. One of them is government regulation of the sale of various drugs. Mill discusses, and condemns in no uncertain terms, early efforts in the United States at prohibiting the sale of alcohol. He is willing to allow licensing of bars and other drinking establishments to make sure that owners are upstanding citizens, but he condemns the use of liquor licenses for making access to alcohol more difficult. "The limitation in number, for instance, of beer and spirit houses, for the express purpose of rendering them more difficult of access . . . is suited only to a state of society in which . . . [citizens] are avowedly treated as children and savages."[21] Limiting access to alcohol is to treat the public as if they were incompetent, not fully adult and in need of supervision appropriate for children.

Discussion Question

Do you agree or disagree with Mill that the government should not limit the number of available liquor licenses as a way to discourage the use and abuse of alcohol? Give reasons for your answer.

The sale of drugs—medicines or recreational drugs, such as opium, morphine, heroin, marijuana—should not, Mill thinks, be prohibited outright or restricted only to those who have obtained a doctor's prescription. Preventing the sale of such substances on the grounds that using them leads, in some cases, to crime is not acceptable. Mill explains: "there is hardly any part of the legitimate freedom of action of any human being which would not admit, and fairly too, as increasing the facilities for some form or other of delinquency."[22] Whatever a person does may provide the opportunity for acting illegally or criminally. Drivers sometimes speed or run red lights, for instance. If the prevention of crime always justifies limiting freedom, the government might decide that we would be better off not driving. We would soon find ourselves without any freedoms at all. For those reasons, Mill thinks, drugs should be labeled to advise buyers of the dangers. He is willing to go so far as to have sellers of drugs keep a register of buyers with name, day, and time of sale. But regulation, let alone prohibition, of the sale of drugs seems to Mill a completely illegitimate restriction on individual freedom. It would violate your freedom to use your property and your money as you choose as long as you do not harm others.

Discussion Questions

Many people favor the legalization of recreational drugs because they want
to be able to use them without threat of arrest and imprisonment. Consider

Mill's defense of legalization which appeals to our personal freedom as reason instead of our individual desires. How plausible are Mill's arguments? Give three reasons for disagreeing with Mill's position.

INTELLECTUAL PROPERTY

Copyrights and Patents

Most common forms of property are tangible. They are material objects such as buildings, machines, cars, houses, and land. When one uses material objects, no one else can use them. I cannot build my house in the same spot where you are building yours. We cannot both drive your car at the same time and certainly not in different directions. The piece of pie you eat is no longer available for anyone else; all others are excluded from enjoying it. Because tangible property diminishes with use, there are ample sources of conflict over who gets to eat this apple or drink that glass of wine. The institution of private property is a way of assigning tangible goods to specific persons and excluding all others to dampen ready sources of conflict. Property rights allow some users to exclude others. You own your car; therefore no one else may use it without your permission. No one is unclear as to who has the right to drive your car and there is no confusion about that. Even the thief who steals your car knows that she has no right to it. She knows she is stealing and that she is breaking the law.

But not all property is material. There are intangible goods such as ideas in your head, a remembered poem you recite to yourself and your friends, songs to sing, and recipes you can rehearse in your mind before you combine the ingredients to make a loaf of special bread. Intangible goods are not diminished by being used. One poem may be recited innumerable times. The national anthem is not used up by being sung over and over again. Nor is there any less of the Pledge of Allegiance after it has been recited every morning by millions of school children. It is impossible to exclude others from enjoying such intangible goods. You can think what you please and no one can take from you the enjoyment of a tune that runs through your head or a line of poetry that you find inspiring. You can remember the plot of a film you love, or repeat to yourself some of your favorite lines from the movie and no one can stop you.

These intangible goods come fully into their own only when they find a material expression. The story is written down in a novel or made into a film. The lyrics and tune in your head delight listeners when played by your favorite band and preserved on a CD. We share with each other what is in our mind mostly through material objects: writing, speech sounds, or recorded (or live) music. The intangible ideas must be embodied in tangible, material objects to be shared. The achievements of science are preserved in books or in technological inventions, the creations of artistic minds as paintings and poems.

We call these material embodiments of ideas *intellectual property*: paintings, books, live performances or recordings, software of all sorts, but also machines, industrial processes (e.g., how to puff rice for breakfast cereals). These material embodiments of ideas are like all other material objects; they may be used up, and, if used by one person, they usually cannot be used by another at the same time. Different material embodiments give public existence to the same ideas.

Ideas need to be discovered. It takes considerable effort to discover new scientific knowledge. New inventions come to light after much time and concentrated work. Great novels do not write themselves and good music is only produced by those who dedicate their lives to creating it. Human life has become much richer and more comfortable because humans have proven themselves to be extraordinarily creative in the realm of ideas. In science and in the arts, in religion and in law, we have enriched our understanding of the world and our ability to organize social life in ever more complex forms.

Societies therefore place great value on the creations of the human mind; they are eager to encourage the discovery of new knowledge and new techniques in the production of goods, in agriculture, in medicine, and in the organization of social life. The favored technique for encouraging production of new ideas is the assignment of limited property rights in the form of copyrights and patents on the material embodiments of these new ideas. Copyrights were invented a long time ago and have a long and complex legislative and juridical history. In the United States, the institution of copyrights and patents rests on a sentence in the Constitution which says "the Congress shall have power . . . to promote the progress of science and useful arts, by securing for limited times to authors and inventors the exclusive right to their respective writings and discoveries." The underlying idea is clear: writing a book or composing a piece of music takes time and effort and people should be rewarded for those efforts. The same applies to useful inventions. It is therefore in everyone's interests to give artists and inventors a limited monopoly on the exploitation of their work. Grants of copyrights or patents have time limits on them. Patents usually expire after twenty years; copyrights end at the end of the author's life plus seventy years. For a limited time, the author is the only one controlling the text she has written. If anyone wants to publish her writings they need her permission. That enables her to charge publishers or buyers of her novel, so that she can live comfortably while she is writing her next book. After a period of time, determined by copyright laws, the copyright expires and the book enters the public domain. It may now be copied and sold by anyone without the author's permission.

In recent years, patents and copyrights have given rise to a series of controversies produced by new technologies of reproduction of works of art as well as by new technologies of plant propagation. We shall consider the controversy about Internet file sharing as well as questions about plant patents.

Discussion Question

Copyrights used to end after twenty-eight years. Then the law was changed—under considerable pressure from the Walt Disney companies and others—to extend the life of a copyright to the lifetime of the author plus seventy years. That is useless as an incentive for individual creative persons but advantageous for corporations. It also restricts the dissemination of new knowledge and artistic creation for much longer. How long do you think copyright protection should last?

File Sharing

The conflict between the recording industry—the music publishers and the artists themselves—on one hand, and users of Internet file sharing is a recent example of the conflict over the precise details of copyright protection. The music publishers are afraid that they will be unable to sell their CDs if music lovers can download the tracks for free on the Internet. Why would you pay for something that you can get for free? They therefore sued Napster, the original file-sharing site, and forced them to close down—to reopen later in a different format. New file-sharing systems were then invented, which did not themselves possess a copy of the file, but merely mediated downloads from one owner of a CD to another. When legal suits against those sites proved ineffective, the music publishers began to sue individuals who downloaded files.

Among the file sharers there are, undoubtedly, those who believe that the record companies charge too much for their merchandise and make too much money and that, therefore, downloading music without paying for it is justified. But many others agree with the music industry that the music publishers should be protected if file sharing produced losses, but they do not believe that sharing music over the Internet actually does financial damage to the music publishers. They agree that music publishers have the right to restrict the distribution of their product because they own the copyright. But they also believe that restricting free sharing of files is not in the best interest of the music industry or of the consumers. They tell stories in support of their position of completely unknown bands that became popular after their tunes were shared over the Internet. The bands sold a sizable number of CDs only after they had gained a following among music lovers. The conflict turns on a disagreement about a question of fact: does file sharing on the Internet deprive music publishers of revenue, or does it, on the contrary, increase their profits because file sharing provides a form of free advertising for particular bands?

Copyright came into existence as a means by which the kings of England could control publications. The king gave a monopoly to the Stationers' Company of London for printing books. Only the members of that company were allowed to produce books. That allowed the Crown extensive powers of censorship. Manuscripts, which were objectionable from the royal perspective could easily be withheld from publication. In the early eighteenth century, copyright legislation was first introduced to protect authors against unscrupulous publishers who put out unlicensed editions of a given work. Copyrights were set to expire after seventeen years—long enough to give the author revenue for a period and not too long to withhold books from being freely reproduced once they became popular.

Copyrights today last a lot longer—the author's lifetime plus seventy years—but still extend essentially the same protection. If I write a book, for a time no one else can print and sell copies of it without my permission. If you buy a legal copy of my book, you buy the right not only to own the book but also to read it. But it is perfectly legal for you to lend the book to a friend, and that person, in turn, may read the book, without having bought his or her own copy, and then lend the book to someone else who may also read it without having paid any money to me, the author and owner of the copyright. Clearly the other two persons can now read this book without buying a copy from the author or publisher, and thus it would be in the interest of the author to make it illegal to lend out books. But because the stated purpose of copyright protection is to "promote the progress of science and useful arts" and because that progress is promoted when as many people as possible have access to printed material, lending out books is not prohibited by copyright protection. Libraries, public, as well as private, allow many persons to read one and the same book. The owner and publisher of the work receive payment for one copy, which may allow hundreds or even thousands of persons to read the same book. Once persons have bought my book, they may also sell it to someone else. The buyer is now the legitimate owner, but he has not paid any money to me. He can also give the book away; the recipient now owns it without ever having paid money to anybody. Copyrights do not prohibit sharing intellectual property.

With the invention of computers, copying machines, and scanners, the technological situation is radically altered. It is no longer expensive to copy a book. It has become even easier to copy music. But how shall we think about that? The music industry, as well as publishers of books and other printed matter, insist that we must look at file sharing on the Internet as analogous to printing unlicensed copies of a book. But of course, the analogy between file sharing, on one hand, and printing a book or pamphlet without the author's permission is imperfect. When I send a piece of music to you, which I have just discovered and am excited about, I am not making a whole lot of copies nor am I selling them at a price that undercuts the price of the official CD in the record store. I do not get paid for the copy I send you. I am sharing; I am not trying to steal the music publisher's business. File sharers point to the analogy between sending a music file to a friend because one wants to share a piece of music one is particularly fond of and lending a book to someone or even giving as a present a copy of a book one has enjoyed reading. But obviously that analogy is not perfect either because when I lend my book to you, I do not have my copy any more, whereas the file shared with you leaves me free to keep listening to my copy of the song while you can also enjoy it.

Discussion Question

Consider the case of Bea, Rhea, and Thea, three close friends. They often buy music together and Bea listens to the CD for a week and then gives it to Rhea when she gets tired of it, who then gives it to Thea after a week. This is perfectly legal. Now new technologies make it unnecessary for them to pass the actual CD along; they can transfer the music electronically. Why is the latter method of sharing illegal while the former was not? Give reasons for your answer.

Common Goods and Goods Privately Owned

Not all things owned by individuals are protected by private property rights. Some are common goods. Common goods are of different kinds. On the one hand there are goods that cannot be privately owned due to lack of the requisite technology. As long as people got their water from the river nearby, it was difficult to privatize water so that those who did not pay could be excluded. Someone could own a piece of river frontage and demand payment from those who came to get water. But others, who did not want to pay, simply had to go to the river elsewhere. Today, drinking water comes in underground pipes which are easily owned by the city or a private company, and we all end up paying for the water we use. Private ownership of the air we breathe, on the other hand, is not technologically possible at the moment. Air cannot be privatized; it is a common good. National security is not easily privatized. It would seem impossible to defend only the suburbs, where the rich live, from enemy attack and leave the city center, inhabited primarily by less affluent persons, to an invading enemy. If the country is defended at all, security will be enjoyed by all regardless of wealth or social status. (We can privatize national defense by leaving the job of fighting attackers to private companies rather than to the military who are an arm of the government, but that is not privatizing national security.)

Other things, like roads, could become private property, but it would be incredibly inconvenient. If you had to stop at every block to pay toll, travel would become awkward, and transport would be slowed. That would have significant effects on the economy. But we can imagine a future in which surveillance cameras at every intersection photograph license plates, and drivers get a monthly bill for tolls in the mail. Schools or police protection could become private property but to do so would produce a society different from the sort of society we have chosen to live in. A society in which all schools are private might well be one where some children grow up without any education at all. In a society where all police protection was paid for by persons wealthy enough to afford it, some would be reasonably secure and others would live under anarchical conditions. This would aggravate social conditions, not unfamiliar to us today, which we regard as completely undesirable—insecurity in the cities that can never be contained in specific neighborhoods and stark poverty of those not able to get an education or find work. Although some common goods are common by virtue of available technology or of the sorts of goods they are, others are considered common because privatizing them would create a society we regard as undesirable. Often complex choices are involved in making some goods common property and privatizing others.

Discussion Questions

As it becomes more and more feasible to privatize natural resources and objects used by all, we face important policy questions: what resources should be allowed to be privately owned and to be sold to consumers and what resources should be open to all? What do you think about privatizing all roads?

privatizing all education?

privatizing all drinking water supplies?

privatizing the supply of all breathable air?

privatizing the supply of transplant organs?

Give reasons for your answers.

Patenting Plants

The private ownership of portions of nature has, in recent years, become a source of sharp disagreements. One's first impulse might be to say it is perfectly obvious that nature belongs to all of us and thus no part of it may become private property. But is that so obvious? After all, land, trees, plants, and flowers are all part of nature and are, in our society, all privately owned. The tomato plants in my garden are mine. I bought the seedlings in the nursery, planted them in my garden, and cared for them all summer, weeding the plants and watering them, and now the luscious tomatoes are also mine. Here are portions of nature that are clearly private property.

Patents are granted by governments to inventors in exchange for disclosing details about an invention. An inventor is protected for twenty years against anyone using the patent for making a better mousetrap of the inventor's design. Patents were instituted to reward creative persons and, at the same time, assure that their new ideas are available to others to learn from and to build on. To be patentable, an invention must be "useful" in a practical sense (the inventor must identify some useful purpose for it), "novel" (i.e., not known or used before the filing), and "nonobvious" (i.e., not an improvement easily made by someone trained in the relevant area). The invention also must be described in sufficient detail to enable one skilled in the field to use it for the stated purpose (sometimes called the "enablement" criterion).[23]

In 1990, the Winterboers, a farming couple in northwestern Iowa, discovered that they were being sued by the seed company from whom they had bought their soybean seeds. At harvest time, the Winterboers sold some of the seeds they had just harvested to their neighbors. They had always done that and so had their parents before them. Using a portion of a crop as seed for the next year and selling that seed to neighbors had been an established custom among farmers for many generations. But now the seed company claimed that this traditional practice was illegal.[24]

What had changed? The seeds used by all the farmers were genetically modified and the company that produced those seeds had a patent on them. That patent gave the company the exclusive right to sell the seeds. The patent gave its owner "the right to exclude others from making, using, offering for sale or selling the invention throughout the United States or importing the invention into the United States." A patented commodity may be sold only by the patent owner or someone else to whom the owner sold a license. If you do not own the patent and want to use this seed patented by the seed company, you will need to pay the company. If you grow soybeans from patented seed, you may not keep part of your harvest to use it as seed for the next year because that would be using the product without a license from the owner of the patent. You certainly may not collect part of your harvest at the end of the year and sell these seeds to others. The seed company has exclusive right even to seeds they did not "mix their labor with." The Winterboers had grown the soybean plants whose seeds they sold to their neighbors. They had paid the seed company for the original seeds; the company had not worked for the next year's seeds but still claimed property rights over those seeds also. Here the previous question arises again: supposing we acquire property rights by working, how much property does one acquire by how much work?

A Canadian farmer, whose neighbor had been using a patented seed from Monsanto, found that some of the neighbor's plants had contaminated his fields. He was now growing some of Monsanto's patented seeds in his field. He had not paid for those seeds. He had not wanted them in his field, but the wind had done its own job. Monsanto sued the farmer for more or less stealing their seeds without payment. The fact that this seed had been moved from one field to the other by the wind, Monsanto said, made no difference.[25]

These are just two examples of the complexities introduced into the life of farmers by the patenting of genetically modified plants. For many years patent offices in the United States had refused to patent plants on the grounds that plants and seeds were made by God or by nature and could therefore not earn patents, which were intended to give protection to *human* inventions. This attitude began to change in the 1930s when Congress passed legislation that allowed patent protection for some plants. By the 1980s, the Supreme Court declared that anything accomplished by human effort was patentable whether it involved mechanisms, plants, or animals.

These changes in the outlook of the U.S. patent law came about through the pressure from the seed companies as well as the development of new technologies. During the nineteenth century many improved seeds were produced by the government, which often distributed them to farmers for free. The twentieth century saw the rise of private, for-profit seed companies that pressured Congress to limit and then eliminate the government's free seed distribution to farmers. Until the 1970s improvements in seeds were brought about by a slow and careful process of selecting the most desirable plants and pollinating them with other equally desirable plants to breed a heartier and more productive variety. Since then, techniques of genetic engineering have been developed that allow seeds to be modified in the laboratory by directly introducing genes from other plants into the germ plasm of a given variety. This method is not only faster than the old-fashioned breeding, but it also allows for introducing genes from plants that would not crossbreed in nature. Thus, even animal genes have been introduced into plants and plant genes have been moved from different sorts of plants to others. *Bacillus Thuringensis*, Bt, which is an insecticide produced by bacteria found naturally in the soil, has been introduced into a number of agricultural plants, such as sunflower seeds, seed corn, alfalfa, and other agricultural crops. The Bt protects these plants against some insect plagues.

These techniques are labor intensive and very expensive. Seed companies claim the protection of patents for their products to finance the research and development needed to produce new seeds that are more productive and hardier. But the patenting of plants has created a good deal of dissension and legal controversy. Farmers are outraged when they may not use seeds they grew themselves or share them with their neighbors as they have done for generations. Others are made uncomfortable by the thought that natural products like plants and animals that belong to all of us should become private property. There are weighty arguments on both sides of this controversy over patenting plants, especially those that have been genetically modified. Different people are persuaded to different degrees by these arguments and hence the controversy is nowhere near abating.

Discussion Question

Is it fair to grant a patent to a seed company not only for the seed they produce and sell to farmers, but also for the seed that farmers produce using the seed purchased from the seed company? Give reasons for your answers.

Genetic modification of plants has produced different sorts of products. Some companies have produced plants that are not harmed by herbicides. When the weeds grow up between the rows of corn or soybean, the farmer can liberally spray herbicides to kill the weeds without fear that his corn or soybeans will be harmed. (But those poisons may enter the water supply or the food chain.) Other plant modifications introduce genes into a given plant, say tobacco, that make this plant resistant to certain diseases. Traditionally, tobacco plants have been attacked and destroyed by fungus. But now various laboratories have developed a strain of tobacco that is fungus resistant. Tobacco plants thrive and—that is the important part—do not need application of fungicide. The genetically modified tobacco plant resists fungus without the application of poisons.

Genetic modification of plants and seeds can either make it easier to apply various kinds of poisonous substances to the plants, thereby increasing the use of pesticides, or it can make applications of poisons unnecessary. The multinational corporations that have developed new genetically modified seeds often also own chemical companies that produce pesticides and fertilizers. In their research labs, scientists are not encouraged to develop genetically modified seeds that make the use of pesticides, herbicides, and fungicides unnecessary. After all, the multinational corporation that employs the scientists is not interested in undercutting their own subsidiaries that produce pesticides. The patent process enables the multinational corporation to make an important decision that affects all of us: whether to look for a reduction in the use of pesticides by producing plants that are disease resistant, and perhaps discourage the growth of weeds, or whether to breed plants which tolerate liberal administration of pesticides. If plant patents are owned by multinational corporations, they are most likely to decide to produce plants resistant to pesticides rather than producing plants resistant to pests. The power given to the corporation via plant patents excludes all of us from participating in a decision that has a serious effect on our lives. Plant patents thus shift the power to make important decisions, which affect all of us, to private corporations whose avowed goal is not to do what is best for everybody but to increase profits for their stockholders. Patenting plants in an economic environment dominated by large international corporations restricts the scope of democratic decision making.

Discussion Questions

Should decisions about increasing or decreasing uses of agricultural pesticides be left to private parties or be reserved to elected legislators? How would you assure that the policy you favor is enforced? Give reasons for your answer.

Newly Discovered Plants

Different problems arise when patents are granted for plants that have not been modified at all but had previously been unknown in the United States. About twenty years ago an American, Loren Miller, went to Ecuador, South America, and came back with a cutting from a local plant, the Ayahuasca, which had for a millennia been used by indigenous people in religious ceremonies and as medicine. Under U.S. patent law this plant could be patented because it was previously unknown in the United States. To be able to patent a plant you must have discovered it and reproduced it asexually—that means from cuttings rather than from seed. More important, in the present context, is the stipulation that the plant to be patented may not have been sold or released in the United States before the patent application. A new plant, under the current U.S. law, is a plant that is new to the United States—regardless of the fact that it may have been familiar to large numbers of people in other countries for a long, long time. What Miller did when he "discovered" the Ayahuasca plant was probably no more than take a few cuttings from a plant someone in Ecuador showed him, telling him that it was a sacred plant with important medicinal properties.

Miller and his small medical company are now the official owners of a patent on an indigenous plant from Ecuador known to and used by people there for thousands of years. Owners of patents can exclude all others from selling and using a patented plant. Patents were originally granted by national governments and apply only in the country that grants the patent. A U.S. patent would not constrain the actions of persons in Ecuador. But today patents apply worldwide with increasing frequency due to trade agreements between countries or due to the activities of the World Trade Organization. If the United States can impose its patent regulations on Latin America, as it is trying very hard to do, it may be able to keep people in Ecuador from using that plant without paying licensing fees to the owner of the patent, Miller. If Latin American countries accept U.S. patent law, they may find that they can no longer use native plants they have used from time immemorial because someone, often a foreigner, has managed to patent that plant in the United States.

Discussion Questions

1. *Does it seem right to you that plants and other resources used for centuries by people of a country should suddenly become inaccessible to them unless they pay a licensing fee?*

2. *Miller did not ask for or receive anyone's permission to take the plant he brought home to California. He did not even know how to find that plant until some local people showed it to him. Do you think that, if anyone should own a patent on this plant, it should be the people in Ecuador who know how to find and use the plant in question?*

Give reasons for your answers.

These are some of the controversies surrounding the rights to intellectual property. Once we begin to consider concrete controversies, we see that economic freedom is also a contentious topic. There are conflicting interests at work when we try to decide what limits to put on the property rights of producers of books and music or of genetically altered seeds, and how, on the other hand, we need to restrict the property rights of the purchasers of recorded music, printed texts, or of commercially produced seeds. Once again, freedom is the source of complex disagreements about the limits to be imposed on the freedoms of different actors in the marketplace.

DISTRIBUTIVE JUSTICE

Poverty and the Problem of Justice

In the first chapter we discussed the disagreement between two different liberal political philosophers, Robert Nozick and John Rawls, about the legitimacy of government action to redistribute resources from the rich to the poor. Nozick claimed that redistribution from the rich to the poor was unfair; it took from the rich what they had acquired legally. Rawls denied that economic in-equalities always reflect differential effort; often, he believes, the rich own property they are not entitled to. Redistribution is sometimes justifiable.

The disagreement, we saw, rested on different views about the legitimacy of profiting from exceptional abilities. Both authors agree that one has legit-imate property rights only to what one has earned by working. Nozick con-cludes that if one works hard and is successful, one is entitled to the fruits of that effort. Rawls points out that the work of those with specialized abilities is rewarded more highly than the efforts put out by others whose capacities are just ordinary. Because we do not acquire our talents but are born with them, Rawls thinks that differential income depending on exceptional talents does not yield legitimate property. He wants to say: most people work hard but incomes differ widely. One cannot justify those discrepancies by the ex-ceptional abilities of some persons because those exceptional abilities are not created by their owners but are theirs from birth. The difference between a player in the farm clubs and in the major leagues is not the intensity of their effort but native ability for which no one can take credit. It is a gift of God or of nature, not something anyone has earned. There exists a clear disagreement between liberal political philosophers over economic inequalities.

But not only the wealth of some, but also equally the poverty of others re-quires a justification. If the extraordinary rewards that some talented people earn must be justified, then also the small rewards that others earn even though they, too, work hard, must also be scrutinized. This section will ex-amine whether poverty in a generally affluent country is justifiable. Is it fair that some people are comfortable or much more so, whereas others are strug-gling to keep their head above water? Some persons in our country are unable to acquire the most limited amount of property. A certain, fluctuating per-centage of the population cannot find decent jobs that support them and their families adequately. Others do have jobs, often more than one, but can still not get through a month without running out of money.[26]

Are the Poor to Blame?

All humans have rights, but rights can also be forfeited. Convicted murderers forfeit their right of unrestricted movement and perhaps their life. Embezzlers forfeit some of their wealth when they are forced to make restitution and pay a fine. Professionals forfeit their economic rights to use their skills and ex-pertise to their best advantage when they neglect their duties. They lose their professional licenses when they are incapacitated by addictions such as the lawyer who shows up in court drunk or the doctor who, high on painkillers, misdiagnoses a patient. No one thinks that an injustice is done to those who have forfeited rights due to their own errors, bad choices, incompetence, or indolence. When forfeiture of rights is deserved, justice is done.

The poor are widely thought to be responsible for their own condition. They are thought to be lazy, without ambition, or without the will to better their condition. Their poverty is their own fault, people say. No one gets anything without an effort; property rights must be earned by hard work. All need to do what at times they would much prefer not to do. That is a part of exercising one's economic rights. Those rights do not entitle one to life in never-never land where roast chickens fly into your mouth and the brooks run with lemonade. Those who expect to get a minimally decent life without making the requisite effort have nothing to complain about if they end in utter poverty. The poor suffer the effects of their own indolence, incompetence, or shiftlessness.

Is That an Accurate Picture of Poverty?

Who Are the Poor?

Current statistics in the United States indicate that at least 11 percent of families are officially poor. Many experts believe, moreover, that the government definition of poverty seriously underestimates the number of the poor. The government uses a formula from the 1960s to calculate who is below the poverty line. At that time most families spent about one-third of their income on food. Ever since, the government has calculated the official poverty line by multiplying the cost of an average family's food budget by three. But since then many other costs—rent, medical care, education, and transportation—have risen much more rapidly than food costs. As a consequence experts estimate that food costs today constitute only one-sixth of the average family's budget. The poverty line should be calculated accordingly. If that alternative formula were used, the number of poor in the country would be twice the government estimate of 22 percent. Whether we believe that 11 percent or twice as many Americans are poor, either is a large number, considering the wealth of our country. Before we write off the poor and blame them for their condition, we need to inform ourselves about them. Different persons are poor for different reasons. Some may be responsible for their condition; others not.[27]

Politicians have given wide currency to an image of the poor as idling away their life on welfare, living comfortably on government handouts, while the rest of us slave to support ourselves and pay taxes to support the welfare programs. Many political figures have run for office by telling stories about people who cheated on welfare—stories that often could not be verified. Campaigning in 1980, Ronald Reagan frequently repeated a story about a "welfare queen" in Chicago who drove around in a Cadillac and received over $150,000 a year from the welfare system by drawing welfare under a variety of different names. Reagan was, in part, elected on his promise to end those abuses, but his stories turned out to be complete fabrications.[28] We cannot rely on politicians, especially when they are running for office, to give us an accurate story about poverty in our country. We need to get the facts for ourselves. Anecdotes and urban myths cannot replace serious evidence.

There are as many kinds of poverty as there are poor people. A significant number—between a third and a half of all officially poor persons—are children; they did not make any choices that landed them in poverty. They were born into poverty; they are poor for no fault of their own. Many of them have parents who work. In the mid-1990s, for instance, half the poor children lived in families with at least one working adult; 11 percent of those adults worked full time. A significant number of the poor have jobs that pay so poorly that their wages do not suffice to lift them above the poverty line. Wages for some jobs are not sufficient to maintain a family. Certain jobs pay, say, $8.00 an hour to whoever fills that job. Your local fast-food restaurant will not pay more to high school graduates than to dropouts. An $8.00 an hour job is an $8.00 an hour job. If that is the only job available, you work and are poor. Low wages are the doing of employers and of the government that fixes minimum wage levels. They are not to be blamed on the persons who, for whatever reason, end up filling those jobs.

In other cases, the parents are unemployed because their employer "downsized" or the business where they worked moved offshore. In the late 1900s, jobs in steel and other heavy industries moved mostly to Asian low-wage countries. In 2006, significant numbers of service jobs were leaving the United States for Asia.[29] For older workers—that is, men and women over 40—finding a new job comparable to what they had before often proves difficult. Jobs disappear as a result of technological change: agricultural work, for instance, has shrunk with the mechanization of agriculture. As a consequence families must leave rural areas to move into the city to find jobs they are not really prepared for. The skills that allowed them to live comfortably in the countryside are no longer in demand. They do not have the skills they need in the city.[30]

Unemployment has many different sources: a significant number of the poor did not finish high school or have limited or no work experience. Some, to be sure, have some college courses or even college degrees but are, nevertheless, unemployed. Others have a hazy sense of what sort of dress, behavior, or habits of punctuality are required by regular jobs. They are, in the jargon of social workers, not "job ready."

There are other causes of unemployment: a significant percentage of the unemployed have mental problems. Recent research strongly suggests that poverty is one of the effects of mental illness. Poor communities in Massachusetts tend to have three times the rate of mental illness than more affluent ones.[31] Many persons afflicted with mental illness, even when medicated, have limited capacities for steady work; they function poorly in stressful situations; their abilities are limited. They are not equipped to hold down any job that is at all demanding. Their ability to earn an income is, accordingly, limited. Many women who were sexually abused as children or raped, now suffer from posttraumatic stress disorder (PTSD). Careful study shows that women victimized by sexual abuse as children have a higher incidence of mental illness as adults; their educational and economic accomplishments are below average.[32] They tend to be psychologically fragile. Holding down a regular job, showing up at work five days a week and doing a day's work day in, day out, is more difficult for them than for most workers. As a consequence their income suffers. Veterans returning from active duty have similar problems in a significant number of cases. "Approximately 22% of homeless people suffer from chronic mental illness; 11% are veterans."[33] Unless they have families able to support them, those afflicted by mental illness, victims of sexual abuse, and veterans are likely to be poor.

Poverty is often accompanied by ill health. Poor people, especially if they work, often do not have health insurance because low-wage jobs do not provide medical benefits. These workers are absent from work more often because they are sick, and they are sick more often because they have no health care. Poor women get worse nutrition; often their prenatal care is inadequate and thus their children are, from birth, more likely to be ill. But sick children force parents to stay away from work. They may lose income and often their job if they are absent too often.

Poor people often do not have the money—let alone the insurance—to pay for dental care. Their teeth may be bad or some may be missing. When the time comes to look for a job, bad teeth are a serious handicap. Any job where they might meet the public is not open to people who do not have all their teeth. Other jobs also are often harder to get if your dental health is poor. Persons like that are caught in an impossible situation. Without a job that pays for dental care, they have a difficult time finding work. But as long as their teeth are not taken care of they cannot hope to find a job that will allow them to visit the dentist. They are caught in a situation not of their own making.

A certain portion of the poor have disabilities; they have a much harder time finding work than others and live in poverty at a much higher rate than persons not disabled. Although the Americans with Disabilities Act forbids discrimination against persons with disabilities, two-thirds of disabled people are unable to find work. Almost 30 percent of disabled persons earn less than fifteen thousand dollars a year. Often the problem is aggravated by inadequate education. In addition, for many disabled, transportation to and from a potential job is a serious obstacle to making a decent wage. And, as for so many poor persons, inadequate health care and the resulting poor health interferes with their job prospects and thus intensifies their poverty.[34]

More and more frequently the poor are single women, often with children. Some of them were never married; others are divorced or abandoned by a husband who does not provide for them and their children. Often the poor are members of racial and ethnic minorities who still experience discrimination on the job or find it more difficult to secure work than their white counterparts. Many, especially members of less favored minorities, are crowded into older parts of cities due to residential discrimination. Workplaces have moved away from the decaying parts of cities and its residents often do not have transportation—cars that will get them to work on time every day—and in many cities public transportation is inadequate. Some authorities believe that 90 percent of the poor are without working cars. Thus poverty is self-perpetuating: if you are poor you cannot afford a car; if you do not have reliable transportation you cannot find or hold on to a job.[35]

These facts are relevant to the question whether the poor are responsible for their poverty. They show, above all, that poverty is a complicated condition and that we cannot make any easy generalizations about the poor. Different persons arrive in poverty by different routes. Different persons are poor for different lengths of time. They manage to escape by different routes. Like all persons, the poor bear some responsibility for their condition and owe some of it to bad luck. As with all other persons, sometimes their condition is significantly affected by bad choices they made. At other times, their poverty is mostly the result of unexpected misfortunes. "According to the U.S. Census Bureau, a startling 37 million Americans currently live in poverty, and the average family [in that group] is a dangerous three paychecks away from homelessness."[36]

One final consideration is important. One terrible consequence of poverty is that the effects of mistakes are magnified by lack of resources. If the sons or daughters of middle-class families leave school after tenth grade against everyone's advice, they will discover after a few years that they have foreclosed the possibility of making a decent living without resorting to selling drugs or other criminal activity. Their family, however, will certainly be able to support them for the year or two it will take them to earn their GED and will be able to support them through college. For persons who never have quite enough to pay their bills for the essentials—food, rent, and transportation—there is no extra money to go back to school. If a middle-class teenager gets pregnant or is arrested for drugs, their family has the resources to help them overcome their problem and build a satisfactory life for themselves. For those who have never quite enough for the essentials, the extra money is not there to overcome a mistake they made. Poverty is unforgiving. It magnifies poor choices. The middle class gets second chances. Poor people rarely do.

Discussion Question

Write down what you consider to be the causes of poverty. Then go on the Internet to find facts about the causes of homelessness, about who is on welfare and for how long. Research the problems of single mothers and how they get to be single mothers as well as the causes of unemployment, under-employment, and the careers of low-wage workers. Do you need to reformulate or refine your initial ideas about the causes of poverty?

RIGHTS

Consequentialism

Plato's critique of private property rights asserts that it brings with it a lot of discord, selfishness, greed, and bitter conflict. This attack on the institution of private property condemns it for its consequences. Such an approach philosophers call "consequentialist"—the attempt to justify or reject a moral or a political practice or principle by reference to its consequences.

But some philosophers want to say that certain actions are simply right or wrong, regardless of their consequences. Imagine a group of teenagers hanging out in a shopping mall who keep away the customers by their loud and offensive behavior. Nothing seems to work to stop this nuisance until the police randomly arrest one of the young persons and charge him with resisting arrest and assault on a policeman. The young man arrested suddenly faces a ten-year felony conviction. Frightened, the teenagers move on. The charge against the young man is bogus; it would never stand up in court. The police know that. The person arrested was not guilty of anything more than being a public nuisance. It was clearly wrong of the police to arrest him and even more wrong to charge him with something he did not do—attacking a police officer. His rights were violated. But defenders of the police among the local merchants say "it worked." The trumped up charge and violation of rights finally persuaded the teenage gang to disperse. That is the consequentialist view of the matter. But opponents of consequentialism say that, whatever the consequences, violating a person's rights is always wrong. It is never justified. Certain actions are wrong regardless of their consequences.

Discussion Questions

Consider some other cases where consequentialism becomes controversial:

An inventor has developed a cure for a lethal form of cancer but demands an astronomical price for it that few can afford. In the meantime patients are dying painful deaths for lack of the cure. Someone breaks into the inventor's office and steals the invention. Lives are saved.

A software company using morally questionable tactics makes enormous profits. Some of these profits are then given away as grants to scientific research that develops important new medicines.

In both cases there are beneficial consequences of immoral acts.

What would you say about these actions of stealing or of winning business competition by immoral means? Give reasons for your answer.

Rights

Consider the role played by appeals to rights. Your neighbor does not like the looks of your car; it is old and rusty. He tells you not to park it in front of his house where people see it and may think that it is his. You point out to him that there are no street signs prohibiting anyone from parking in front of his house. You have, you say, a right to park in front of his house. Your right is more powerful than his dislike of your car. In another example a presidential candidate visits your town. You and your friends want to demonstrate against some position the candidate has taken publicly. The police want to prohibit you from demonstrating because your demonstration will make their job of keeping the candidate safe more difficult. You reply that you have a right to free speech and that this right is stronger than whatever problems the police may have in doing their job. When we can claim a right to do, think, or say something, we are in a strong position against people who dislike what we are doing or saying or who are inconvenienced by our action or speech. Rights provide strong support in conflicts with other private parties or the government. Your rights allow you to do what may well inconvenience or anger others. If you have a right to park in front of your neighbor's house, his possible embarrassment is of lesser importance. Your action is protected.

It is often said that the right of one person imposes obligations on others. Children's rights to be taken care of impose obligations on their parents, or if there are no parents, the state inherits the obligation. Societies have believed for a long time that taking care of orphans is an obligation of the state. Similarly, property rights impose obligations on others, for instance, not to trespass on private property, not to impair or destroy it. Parking regulations that allow parking for everyone on both sides of the street impose an obligation on my neighbor not to try to prevent me from parking in front of his house.

But this matter is, of course, complicated. Your right to free speech imposes an obligation, for instance, on the police not to interfere with your speaking out except under exceptional circumstances. It may also, in some situations, require of the police that they actively protect you and your ability to speak against protesters determined to silence you. But does your right to free speech impose an obligation on the newspaper to publish your opinions or on the television stations to give you free air time? Does it impose an obligation on anyone to listen to you? We tend to answer that question in the negative, but the reasons for that are not entirely clear.

These questions suggest the complexity of the concept of rights. But we now have a general idea of what rights are: a person's right to do something imposes on some others the obligation not to interfere with that activity under normal circumstances. Barring exceptional circumstances—for instance, when I am falsely shouting "Fire!" in a crowded theater—no one may interfere with my speech because I have a right to free speech. My rights to free choices in matters of religion forbid the government to insist that I join a particular religious organization. No one may make specific religious affiliations or practices a condition for employment in jobs that have no connection to religion. The Anglican Church may require of candidates for the priesthood that they be Anglicans. It is less clear that they can demand that the janitors in their church worship in the Anglican Church or have any religious faith at all.

The obligations imposed by rights range from mostly negative ones of not interfering with others to more positive ones of providing services or assistance. Sometimes, someone's right may involve obligations on others to provide certain services, such as schools or health clinics. The rights of wheelchair-bound persons to access to public buildings impose obligations to build ramps and elevators. Children's rights to an education obligate someone to build schools. Citizens' rights to life are often understood to obligate someone to provide health care for all. But it is not at all clear what the extent of these obligations is. Does every public building require ramps or only some? Do we need ramps in city hall but also at the city truck repair facility? Nor is it clear who is obligated to provide what others have a right to. Should the government or the owners of the building have to pay for wheelchair access in private office buildings? The same questions arise with respect to education and health care. How extensive is the education or health care citizens may lay claim to? Should health services include preventive measures? Should it pay for plastic surgery? And who should pay for all this: cities and towns, the federal government, or private charities?

Discussion Questions

We often say that everyone has a right to education or to adequate health care. But what sorts of obligations does that impose and on whom? Does that obligate private schools to accept students who are unable to pay private school tuition, without charging them? Does it obligate the authorities to open free schools for all children or only for children whose parents cannot pay tuition? Does that right to education include higher education? Do we have a right to get as much education as we can use and as we want or does it end at high school? And if so, why there?

Similar questions must be raised about health care. On whom does my right to adequate health care impose obligations: The doctor, the hospital, the local or state or federal government, or on the insurance company where my employer buys insurance for me?

Give reasons for your answers.

Rights often block actions that would be in the interest of the majority. Health-care costs are rising precipitously precisely because modern medicine is powerful. Human beings live longer; their final illnesses become more and more drawn out because new medical technologies and medicines delay the inevitable end. But all of these medical improvements are expensive and as more people live longer and their final illnesses last longer, the costs to the country rise steeply. We might do better not to extend the lives of the elderly as long as possible but instead to rebuild roads and bridges and improve the education of our children. Once persons reach a ripe old age, maintaining what is often a life of dubious quality is disproportionately expensive, and we might decide in the interest of the vast majority to refuse medical care to some of the sickest and most expensive patients.

Such a policy is prevented by an appeal to rights: every person has a right to life and that right is more powerful than the benefits the vast majority would derive from allowing our sickest patients to die. The appeal to rights will often produce serious disadvantage to a majority of persons in the country. It has significant disadvantages. It is therefore a pressing concern to discover how rights are justified.

Discussion Question

What do you think of this proposal to cap the expenditure on health care for the elderly and the very ill of all ages and instead use some of the savings from that on education and rebuilding the infrastructure of the United States? Give reasons for your answer.

Justifying Rights: Legal Rights and Human Rights

Rights have different origins. Some are clearly established by legislation. The law tells you where parking is allowed and where it is forbidden. Where parking is allowed for all, you have a right to park. In other places you may need a special permit that gives only you and other permit holders the right to park there. These rights depend on legislation. When the law is changed, you may lose or gain rights. Your rights as a motorist or as pedestrian are regulated by law as are your rights as a consumer. Some states have so-called "lemon laws," which give you the right, under certain circumstances, to receive reimbursement for a car you bought that proved seriously defective. In other states that do not have comparable laws, your rights are more limited.

We claim other rights which we regard as ours "by nature," as belonging to us merely by virtue of being human beings or as a gift from God. These rights are not created through legislation. They may not be abrogated by laws. On the contrary, lawmakers must make sure that their legislation does not violate such laws. Such *natural*, *human*, or *divinely given* rights are the touchstones by which we test the legitimacy of laws made by humans.

We encountered this contrast previously in this chapter in the discussion of the rights to private property. Locke and others, we saw, want to claim that the right to private property is absolute: Laws may not infringe on property rights. But Locke's arguments in favor of the idea that property rights are absolute or "natural" rights were not completely convincing and thus left an opening for the opposite view that property rights are instituted and defined by legislation and can therefore also be modified by legislation.

Discussion Questions

Legislators may not be arbitrary when they create new rights or alter or abolish existing ones. How do they justify proposals for new laws or for altering existing law? Consider these examples. How do legislators justify progressive income taxes?

drafting young men and women into the armed forces?

limiting the rights of Americans to travel to foreign countries?

Give reasons for your answers.

Rights established through legislation can be rescinded by legislation. If the city closes a road, you lose your right to travel on it. If Congress abolishes a government entitlement program, such as access to free education for veterans, you may, even though you are a qualified veteran, lose your rights to educational benefits. But not all rights can be abolished by laws; laws that try to abolish some rights are illegitimate. For many years after the Civil War, so-called Jim Crow legislation reduced the freedom of travel or rights to a decent education for African Americans. But these laws, we say now, were not legitimate. They did not extinguish the rights of African Americans to free movement or to education—they just prevented them from exercising those rights. Some rights may not be restricted by legislation because they are, in the words of the Declaration of Independence, "inalienable," because they are given to us by God. Rights we have from God may not be modified by humans. Today, rather than talking about *God-given rights* we often talk about *human rights*—rights everyone has merely by virtue of being a human being.

Discussion Question

The law limits the rights of specific groups: in many places convicted felons are not allowed to own guns or to vote. People lose their driver's licenses and the right to drive on convictions of driving under the influence.

Would it be acceptable for the government to prevent persons who had declared bankruptcy from borrowing money? Would it be acceptable to refuse marriage licenses to persons who had been divorced more than once?

In all of these cases, persons do poorly with certain rights—owning guns, driving, borrowing money, and marriage. Why are we prepared to accept restricting rights in the first two cases but not in the last two?

Give reasons for your answer.

Rights obligate others not to interfere with actions of the rights holder; sometimes they also obligate others to provide certain services. Rights have two disparate sources: legislation or gift from God or from nature. We also say that all human beings are equal in that all have the same rights, and all have rights to equal freedoms. That thesis, the heart of liberal political philosophy, gives rise to two further important controversies we need to examine next:

1. How can we support by reasonable arguments the liberal claim that human beings should be equal in their freedoms?
2. Suppose we accept human equality, what precisely does it consist of?

Both of these questions, as we shall see in the next section, raised controversies that have not been settled to this day.

EQUALITY

How to Argue for Equality

Things that are equal are sort of the same, but not quite. Joe and Bill, being twins, are equal in age, but they are not the same person because they are two distinct persons with their own bodies and their own minds. When we say that things are equal, we are comparing two or more things. What is more, when two things are equal, they are usually equal in some respect or another. Joe and Bill are equal in age, but that does not mean that they are equal in all other respects. They may well have different personalities, different abilities, and different goals for their lives.

Whether two things are equal in a particular respect is easy to ascertain when the respect can be measured. Things are clearly equal or unequal in size, in weight, in age, and in many other aspects that can be expressed in numbers. It is easy to determine whether this man is richer than that woman if we are only considering money and property. But if we are comparing a man who has a loving wife and adorable and talented children to a woman who owns a lot of houses and yachts and fancy automobiles, the comparison becomes a lot more difficult. Equality with respect to matters not easily measured or expressed in numbers is difficult to ascertain.

The preceding discussion of rights leads us to consider fundamental liberal principles that tell us that all human beings are "created equal," have equal moral worth, have equal dignity, and are all entitled to equal freedoms and to the same rights. Among liberal political philosophers in the last several centuries these expressions are commonplace. They all agree on it. But they do not agree on the reasons for these claims. They offer quite different defenses for attributing equal rights and freedoms to all.

John Locke and Thomas Jefferson

"All men are created equal," wrote Jefferson, echoing the thought of Locke who believed that "by nature," that is, not by virtue of any human institutions, humans are free and equal. By *equality*, Locke means all human beings have equal power—not as a matter of fact, but as a matter of entitlement. Whatever actual situations we may live in, each of us has the *right* to the same amount of power; no one should have more power than anyone else. No one should have power over any other person. Equality here does not describe what human beings are like as much as state what humans are entitled to: everyone is entitled to run his or her own life "without asking leave, or depending upon the will of any other man."

That is what Locke and Jefferson say, but what are their reasons for that? Are they right? We have been indoctrinated so thoroughly in the belief of equal freedom for all that it is difficult for us to ask whether it is true. Should all human beings be equally free and nobody have power over anyone else? What makes us so confident that we are right about that? Locke gives us these reasons for believing in equal freedom for all:

"For men being all the workmanship of one omnipotent and infinitely wise Maker . . . and being furnished with like faculties . . . there cannot be supposed any such subordination among us that may authorize us to destroy one another, as if we were made for one another's uses, as the inferior ranks of creatures are for ours" (5). Animals are inferior to us, and it is, therefore, all right for us to use them for our own ends, for instance, by domesticating them to work for us or by raising them for food. But, and this is a central tenet of liberalism, we are not allowed to use other human beings for our own ends.

Locke provides two reasons for that. The first is that humans are pretty similar; we are all "furnished with like faculties." We are dissimilar from animals to such an extent that we may use them as a means to our own ends. But we are not sufficiently dissimilar from other human beings to be permitted to use any of them for our own ends.

Discussion Questions

What does it mean to use another person for one's own ends? Give examples. What is wrong with doing that? Give reasons for your answers.

The first argument for human equality is the claim that human beings are not sufficiently different from one another to allow some to use others for their own ends. The argument rests on a factual claim, namely that human beings, however dissimilar we may be from one another, are similar to one another in what really matters, in all essentials.

Discussion Question

Consider the many differences between human beings, between Nobel Laureate scientists and people who are barely literate, between people who win marathons and people who can barely walk, and between persons who are really talented or are great leaders or are moral exemplars and those whom even their parents have difficulty loving. Is it plausible to say that the most gifted, the most splendid examples of humanity may not use the people who are their most opposite, who are marginal human beings, for their own ends? Give reasons for your answer.

But Locke has a second argument, which Jefferson then echoes—namely that we all are God's creatures, and therefore may not use each other for our private ends. What did they mean by that? It is tempting to think that being God's handiwork we are all, in some sense, sacred, and therefore must be treated respectfully and not be used by others for their own ends. But God created not only our ancestors, Adam and Eve, but all the animals and plants, the mountains and the oceans. If being God's creation renders us sacred, that holiness extends equally to animals and to all of nature. It would forbid us to use animals for our own ends, to dig into the earth to mine for coal or metals, or to reshape the earth's surface to build cities.

But perhaps we need to read Locke and Jefferson differently. Perhaps their reminder that humans are God's creatures serves to remind us that the defense of human equality does not rest on the claims about fundamental human similarities, which anyone can observe. Instead, they suggest that we differ from the rest of creation because we alone are created in God's image and are to that extent similar to each other. We partake to a limited extent in the majesty of the divine and hence must treat each other accordingly—namely not use others for our own ends. Whether we are exceptionally talented or marginally competent, we are created in the image of the deity, and therefore have the right to be treated as ends and not to be used for the purposes of others. Animals and plants, oceans and plains are God's creation but are not created in his image.

Discussion Question

More and more Christians and other believers are coming around to the view that all of nature, being God's creation, needs to be cared for by us because it is in some way sacred. If we accept the idea of Locke and Jefferson that human beings occupy a special place in creation because they alone are created in God's image, does that allow us to use the rest of nature as we please? Give reasons for your answer.

John Rawls

Rawls hearkens back to the social contract theory. But he does not regard a social contract as an historical event, as did Locke and the early Americans, but as a thought experiment. Suppose, he says, that people come together to determine the principles for a just society. If they come together as they are, different persons will have different personal interests because they are young or old, rich or poor, male or female, black or white. Because human beings differ from each other in infinitely different ways, people who come together to choose principles for a just society will probably not manage to agree. What is more, because some of them are more powerful than others, they will be able to impose their will on the assembly. The whole affair will descend into the dispiriting spectacle of endless arm-twisting and log-rolling and the result will not inspire any confidence that the principles chosen are the best for all, except for that small group whose interests dominated.

An assembly to find the principles for a just society, a society in which there is indeed "liberty and justice for all," must be one where, for a time, the members are ignorant of their specific personal characteristics and their position in the world. Rawls calls this condition of his imaginary men and women meeting together to outline a society just for all, the "original position." He proposes a thought experiment in which we imagine men and women who do not know what their actual situation is—they do not know who they are or what their position is in the world—deliberate about principles of justice. This ignorance of their own situation "converts what would, without it, be self-interest into equal concern for others, including others who are very different from ourselves. Those in the original position . . . think from the perspective of *everybody*."[37] Not representing oneself in this imaginary deliberation, everybody can only decide what would be the most just arrangement for everyone. The thought experiment would yield, Rawls believes, a reliable set of principles of justice.

Discussion Question

Does the justification of equal rights for all on the grounds that that is what people would choose under suitable conditions assume what needs to be proved—namely that when choosing principles of justice all are entitled to participate? Give reasons for your answer.

John Stuart Mill

A third kind of argument in favor of equal freedom for all comes from Mill who provides us with a consequentialist argument to say that if we are all equally free, we are all better off. The best result for all is achieved if everyone is as free as the next person. If some people have more power and thus more freedom than others, they can, for instance, suppress the ideas of those with less power. There are many examples—Mill cites the story of Galileo—where the more powerful have less knowledge than those without power and use their superior power to perpetuate ignorance. Galileo introduced the heliocentric theory of the solar system but was forced by Catholic Church authorities to recant to save himself from being burned at the stake. The church feared that the heliocentric theory would undermine the Catholic faith. In our day, governmental authorities sometimes try to use their superior power to suppress evolutionary theory because they fear that persons would lose their Christian faith if they believed that we are descended from other mammals. Mill cites examples like this to suggest that we all lose if some use their power to suppress well-founded scientific theories. The consequence of equal freedom for all is, on the contrary, that human insight grows the fastest because all opinions can be freely debated and subjected to critical examination.

We have now seen a number of arguments for demanding that all human beings have equal rights: we are more or less equal to one another—that is, we are God's creatures; if you asked everyone they would agree that all should have equal rights, and if some can suppress the opinions of others, we all lose. We have also seen that none of these reasons given for equal rights for all are overwhelmingly persuasive.

What Is Equality?

It is not altogether clear how solid our justifications are for demanding equal rights for all. That is not merely an abstract philosophical problem but has clear, real-world implications. Our government sends its emissaries around the globe exhorting other countries to adopt democratic constitutions and to allow all citizens equal freedoms. These recommendations are not always welcome in countries in which women are definitely second-class citizens or in countries in which ancient traditional caste systems are deeply entrenched in the culture and the thinking of ordinary people. To the extent that we understand that our dedication to equal freedom for all does not rest on irrefutable arguments, we may at least moderate the tone in which we exhort others to follow our example.

But whether we have solid arguments for our stance or not, we are deeply committed to equal freedom for all—even though we find it often difficult to practice what we preach. But what does this "equal freedom for all" mean? It turns out that the meaning of that formula is also seriously contested. Different philosophers understand it in different ways and important questions need to be raised about their interpretation of this very basic assumption of ours.

F. A. Von Hayek

F. A. Von Hayek, an Austrian economist who emigrated to the United States, wrote in the 1960s,

> Equality of the general rules of law and conduct, however, is the only kind of equality conducive to liberty and the only kind of equality we can secure without destroying liberty.[38]

By equal liberty for all, Hayek means equality before the law, and presumably that means, at least, that the same laws apply to all people, and secondly, that the laws are applied in the same way to all citizens. Laws are the same for all when they do not impose different rules on different groups of people, as did, for instance, the racial laws that restricted black persons to ride at the back of the bus. People are, in addition, only equal before the law if courts are truly impartial and the experience of citizens in the courts is no different for rich or for poor, for white or for black, for men or for women. This is the *only* sense of equality in which we can all claim to be equal "without destroying liberty." In that statement, Hayek refers to other forms of equality — equal rights to a decent life, to health care and education — rights that require government intervention in the economy and redistribution of wealth from the rich to the poor. Such conceptions of equality, if put into practice, Hayek thought, destroyed liberty because they infringed on the freedom of property of the rich.

Although equality before the law is a noble ideal, it is not without its own difficulties. Consider existing laws governing the paid work of children. They must have reached a certain minimum age before they can get paid work; for a few years they need parental permission before they can be employed, and they may not work later than ten o'clock at night on school nights. Or think of the Older Americans Act, which makes provision for the protection and support of older Americans and their families. Is passing laws that apply only to children between certain ages or only to older Americans different from passing laws that apply only to blacks?

But the demand that the same laws apply to all creates a second problem. Because citizens are different from one another, the effects of these laws on persons situated differently will be different. Applying the same laws to all may well create inequalities because the same law will have very different effects on persons living different lives. (Hayek admits that.) If the tax rate for a single professional person is levied on a worker with seven children it will bankrupt the parent of the large family, whereas it is no more than a slight annoyance for the single professional. If the same laws must apply to all, will all be taxed at the same rate? Equal laws for all, if interpreted in this way as Hayek wants us to interpret them, turn out to produce serious inequalities among different groups of citizens. Because different citizens are situated in different ways, the same laws will have different effects on them. Hayek's equality breeds inequality.

Discussion Questions

Is there a difference between racially restrictive legislation and laws aimed, for instance, at the paid work of children that try to protect children? If so, what is the difference? Are special laws, not applying to all in the same way, justified in some cases and not in others? Give reasons for your answers.

Suppose, furthermore, that we agree that existing laws must not exclude anyone unfairly or place unfair burdens on some groups. We may still worry that these fair laws are applied in unfair ways. The most obvious example of that is the experience of people who are brought into court accused of crimes. The legal system is complex; many technical details make a lot of difference to the outcome of a case. You need the help of a good lawyer, or better, of an entire legal team, to negotiate the system successfully, by escaping indictment, or making a deal with the prosecutor if you are indicted, getting acquitted, or escaping a prison term, or getting a light sentence, if convicted. That costs a lot of money, and few people, certainly not poor people who find themselves in court, can afford to hire a crack legal team. If they cannot afford a lawyer, the court will appoint a lawyer for them, but often these lawyers are barely competent or are overworked. In many cases they are ill prepared to defend their clients. The legal defense the poor receive is significantly inferior to that of the well-to-do.

In 2003, the American Bar Association held extensive hearings about the legal defense and advice received by indigent clients. Here is an excerpt from their final report:

> Overall, our hearings support the disturbing conclusion that thousands of persons are processed through America's courts every year either with no lawyer at all or with a lawyer who does not have the time, resources, or in some cases the inclination to provide effective representation. All too often, defendants plead guilty, even if they are innocent, without really understanding their legal rights or what is occurring. Sometimes the proceedings reflect little or no recognition that the accused is mentally ill or does not adequately understand English. The fundamental right to a lawyer that Americans assume applies to everyone accused of criminal conduct effectively does not exist in practice for countless people across the United States.[39]

Equality before the law requires that all laws be the same for all—and that, as we have seen, is not easily interpreted—and that laws be applied equally to all. But such equal treatment in the courts is impossible unless the legal representation accused persons receive is the same for all every step along the way from being arrested to being tried and perhaps convicted. To reach that goal the poor need substantial legal and financial assistance from the government. Public money, collected from the taxes paid by those who are not poor, must be used to equalize everyone's position before the law. Hayek is adamantly opposed to that. Asserting, as he does, that equality before the law is the *only* meaning of equality, he asserts that government measures that try to compensate for economic inequality are bound to violate individual freedom and must therefore be condemned. But it is difficult to achieve equal treatment by the legal system if you are not prepared to give extensive assistance to those who appear in court but have no money for legal representation. It is difficult to achieve the sort of equality—equality before the law—that Hayek recommends.

Discussion Question

Equality before the law is impossible unless everyone has legal resources of similar quality available. Because many poor people cannot afford the legal assistance available to persons with money, equality before the law requires economic assistance for the indigent accused. But that requires taking money from the rich and giving it to the poor. We face a dilemma: either deprive the poor of equality before the law, or deprive the rich of some of their money through taxation. Which of these alternatives is preferable? Give reasons for your answer.

Iris Marion Young

Some liberal political philosophers have fewer hesitations about government efforts to redistribute resources. Rawls, as we saw in chapter 1, interprets the idea of equal freedom differently from conservatives like Nozick or Hayek. All are supposed to have the same equal freedoms, such as civil liberties, and where resources are unequally distributed, that inequality is justified only if the poorest profit from it. If there are ardent sports fans among the poor, the fact that some star players make more in a year than poor people may make their entire working life, is justified because it yields enormous satisfaction to the poor who watch those players perform their athletic miracles. If rich men use one-hundred-dollar bills to light their expensive cigars, their affluence does not benefit the poor and is therefore not justified.

Other philosophers, such as Young, point out, however, that some citizens do not just need more money to be truly equal. Often it is lack of power, a limited ability to participate in decisions, that seriously affects lives of citizens and makes them unequal.[40] The college where I teach recently decided to arm its campus police. Originally that decision was going to be made by the college administration and the trustees. Some students were upset that they were not even informed about this impending decision. They held meetings and the opponents of arming the police won a vote sponsored by the student government by a small margin. The Board of Trustees and the administration were informed of that decision on the part of the students, but the original decision of arming the police was reaffirmed. The debates among students and their vote had no noticeable effect. The arming of police has an effect on students—more so than on the trustees who rarely, if ever, visit the campus. But the students were not consulted. The students clearly had less power; they were unequal in an important respect that had nothing to do with money or with equality before the law. They could not participate in decisions that had profound implications for their lives.

Discussion Questions

Assuming that we all believe in equal freedom for all, how do you think that the decision about arming campus police should have been handled? After a majority of students objected, what would have been the proper next step to take on the part of the college administration?

Are there other situations in your life—at work, in classrooms, or elsewhere— where decision-making power is unevenly distributed? Can this unequal distribution of decision-making power be justified? Give reasons for your answers.

We have looked at three different interpretations of equality: equality before the law (which has two parts: the same law for all and the same treatment in the court system), far-going financial equality unless the poorer profit from economic inequalities, and finally, equal power to participate in public decisions that affect one's life. Equality may be understood as mostly a legal condition, one having to do with distribution of economic resources, or as involving degrees of participation in public decision making.

Discussion Question

Considering these three views on equality which do you consider most important for a free country? Give reasons for your answer.

DO ANIMALS HAVE RIGHTS?

Most people look at that question in disbelief. Why should animals have rights? Are they not *animals*? Human beings have rights; animals are different from human beings and therefore are not entitled to rights. This question is interesting because it may encourage us to ask ourselves why human beings have rights. We saw previously that there are different opinions why humans are thought to have *equal* rights—none of them totally persuasive. But now we must confront an even more basic question: why do human beings have rights at all. Animals, we think, do not have rights and are we not also animals?

There is a long list of answers to the question about the rights of humans:

Human beings suffer pain; they have a right not to suffer needlessly.
Human beings are rational; rational beings should have the right to think for themselves and, within certain limits, act on their thoughts.

Human beings have a sense of morality; they should not be forced to do what
  they regard as being morally repugnant.
Human beings have the capacity of being persons, of leading their own lives,
  taking responsibility for their actions, and making plans.
Human beings have the gift of language; they should have the right to speak
  freely.
Human beings think about how best to live their lives; they should be able to
  live according to their chosen plan of life.
Human beings form strong attachments to other human beings; they should
  be able to nurture these attachments and to be secure in their enjoyment of
  them.

Here are some answers to the question of why humans should have rights.
They are all more or less of the same form: human beings have certain capacities. They should have the rights that protect the development and use of
these capacities.

Discussion Questions

*Which of any of these characteristics of human beings cited provide a good
reason for allowing human beings the sorts of rights we claim for ourselves?*

*Human beings also have the capacities for unparalleled cruelty. Should they
have a right to be cruel?*

Give reasons for your answers.

But are animals not entitled to the same or at least to *some* of the same
rights? Surely, mammals suffer. They no more like being in pain than humans; it is doubtful that they like living in cages so small they can barely
move. That principle is generally accepted. Many if not most localities have
laws against cruelty to animals. Dog fighting and cock fighting are illegal for
that reason. If we accept that as reasonable, can we in good conscience eat
animals?

Discussion Questions

1. *Dog racing is legal. Should it be?*
2. *Are laws against animal cruelty justified?*
3. *Should you become a vegetarian? If not, why not?*
4. *Are animals sufficiently like us that they should have other rights, besides
   being spared unnecessary pain?*

Give reasons for your answers.

Here is a real-life case where the question about rights of animals has serious implications for a pair of Austrian chimps. The case challenges the widely held assumption that only human beings are capable of being persons:

> VIENNA, Austria (AP)—A chimpanzee cannot be declared a person, Austria's Supreme Court has ruled, activists said Tuesday. An animal rights group had sought to have the chimp, Matthew Pan, declared a person in hopes of gaining guardianship of the animal. The shelter where Matthew has lived for 25 years is going bankrupt, threatening to leave him homeless. Donors have offered to help support him, but under Austrian law, only a person can receive personal gifts.
>
> The Vienna-based Association Against Animal Factories sought to have him declared a person and petitioned to be appointed Matthew's trustee. But the high court upheld a September ruling by a judge in the town of Wiener Neustadt rejecting the petition, the group said Tuesday. The rights group said it would take the case to the European Court of Human Rights. Matthew and another chimp at the shelter, Rosi, were captured as babies in Sierra Leone in 1982 and smuggled to Austria for use in pharmaceutical experiments. Customs officers intercepted the shipment and turned the chimps over to the shelter.
>
> Organizers said they may set up a foundation to collect donations for Matthew, whose life expectancy in captivity is about 60 years. But they argue that only personhood will ensure that he isn't sold outside Austria.

Discussion Question

Do these chimps have the right not to be used in scientific experiments? If you had been the judge in this case, how would you have decided? Give reasons for your answers.

THE FEMINIST CRITIQUE OF RIGHTS

Rights provide extensive protections for citizens. They protect against being forced to make sacrifices in the interests of the majority, and they protect one's opinions if they happen to be unpopular or offend the powerful. They provide a secure private domain where we are safe from the disapproval of governments or our fellow citizens. Rights ensure our safety in situations of conflict between the citizen and the government or powerful institutions such as the church, between citizens and their neighbors, between citizen and citizen. Rights are an important part of living free. Rights therefore play a central role in political philosophy and an especially important role in liberal political theory.

But talking about rights, standing on one's rights, and claiming one's rights is not central in all parts of our lives. Mothers and fathers care for their children, not because the children have a right to being cared for—which they do—but because the children are cherished. Lovers do not demand respect for their rights but give generously to each other from love. It is a sign that the family is not functioning well because of conflicts when family members begin to insist on their rights. In functioning families, children and adults share with one another from mutual affection rather than demanding that they receive the shares to which their rights entitle them. The language of rights is not central within families, among friends and lovers, or even in well-functioning communities. Rights do not play an important role in relations to persons we know, in families, among those we trust and depend on, in relations to persons dependent on our caring and goodwill. They are important only as symptoms of relations disturbed by conflict apparently so intractable that everyone falls back on insisting on their rights.

Second-wave feminists pointed out in the 1960s that Western philosophers had all been men, with very few exceptions. Most of these men had had families; women had taken care of their physical and emotional needs, had raised their children, and had maintained the emotional web that is the family, whereas the men had made few contributions to any of that. Their contributions had been perhaps economic and they had had the power to make important decisions in the family. But the day-to-day work of nurturing children, of creating a family as refuge from the hurly-burly of political and economic life for the men—that had been pretty exclusively the work of women. Consigned to this work of nurturing and caring, women had been unable to educate their minds to the extent that some men could. Their household chores, as well as social rules, had prevented them from going out in the world to debate philosophy with other women and men. Hence, not only because of their absence from the list of great works of philosophy, but also because women's lives and experiences had not been represented, their perspectives were lost.

Discussion Questions

1. *In the last fifty years, opportunities for women have expanded tremendously. To what extent do you think that the traditional division of labor still exists between women who take care of relationships and men who act in the realm of conflicting rights? Tell stories to support your opinion.*

2. *Is it true that family members are connected by ties of trust and mutual caring or is that a romantic distortion of a much harsher reality? Tell stories to support your answer.*

Political philosophy had reflected deeply about the rules governing public life—life between strangers—and how those impersonal transactions had best be governed. But political philosophy had little to say about relations in familial contexts. Written mostly by men, who had been silent partners in family life, as recipients of caring by women but not as providers of emotional support or as nurturers of the young and the old, ethics and political theory reflected the one-sided moral and political experience of its authors. Ethics and political philosophy raised questions—and tried to answer them—about how we may live our lives well and how best to arrange our life with strangers. But a political philosophy that limits itself to talking about rights is of limited use to us when we are trying to think about how to be good parents, what are the virtues of friends and lovers, or how to fashion the life in communities. In all these areas talk about rights begins only when the relationships are in serious trouble, when the participants in a web of relations begin to treat each other as if they were strangers because they are no longer able to live together in trust and affection. If we are going to do justice in ethics and political philosophy to the characteristics of intimate relations, we need to think about our relations to others not as relations governed by rights but by caring for one another. Feminist theorists, accordingly, developed an ethics and political theory that is often called "the ethics of care" as an alternative to ethics and political theories that put the concept of "right" in the center.

Discussion Question

Are there occasions when family members insist on their rights within the family that are not evidence that the family is dysfunctional? Tell stories to support your opinion.

An important milestone in the development of these attempts at alternative ethics and political philosophy was the work of a psychologist, Carol Gilligan, whose book, *In a Different Voice*, had a wide influence on feminist thought.[41] Gilligan asked children to think about Heinz, a poor man whose wife was desperately ill and only a very expensive medicine, which Hans did not have the money to pay for, could save her. What was Heinz to do? The answers given by the boys were quite different from those given by the girls. The boys thought about whether Heinz should steal the medicine and then debated what were the rights of Heinz and of his wife and those of the druggist from whom he might steal. The girls tended to think about trying to talk to the druggist. They thought about the problems by considering relationships between persons rather than their rights. Gilligan concluded that men thought differently about human behavior and about ethical issues than women. Men considered questions of rights and of justice; women focused on relationships.

Many readers of Gilligan's book concluded that there were two ethics—an ethics of justice and of rights and an ethics of relationships and of care—and that men usually used the first, and women the second. But other theorists

soon saw that for the exaggeration it is: obviously issues of justice and fairness, as well as of rights, have their important place within the family. After
all, one element of the political demands of the feminist movement was fairness within the family, a fairer distribution of the chores in the family as well
as the right and power to make important decisions. Out of these discussions
emerged an exceptionally rich literature reflecting about ethics and political
philosophy. We can discuss only one aspect of that literature.

Feminist Criticisms of Liberalism

At its most general, liberalism insists on the dignity of each human being.
Every last one of us has our own life to live; every one of us is valuable intrinsically, for our own sake, and not just as means to the ends of another.
These formulations are general; they need to be interpreted. Feminist political philosophy raises questions about liberalism's interpretation of the general
formula that each of us is intrinsically valuable and should not serve merely
as a means to the ends of another.

The language of liberalism interprets the equal value of everybody by saying that all have the same rights to property, to civil liberties, to political freedom, and to equal protection by the law and by the courts. In Rawls's original position no one knows their own or another's identity; the rights and
freedoms that persons in that condition choose are rights and freedoms we are
willing to yield to strangers and expect strangers to concede to us. But when
we take another person seriously because that other person is intrinsically
valuable, we do not merely treat them as a stranger. On the contrary, valuing
others requires that we know them as well as circumstances permit and requires that we establish a relationship to them. We value the others most
deeply when we have a relationship to them, not when they are completely
unknown to us. We value others when we care for them and that means both
that we like them—at least in some ways and to some degree—and that we
try to be helpful to them and try to contribute to making their life good. We
also value others when we accept the same from them—accept affection from
them and assistance in furthering our own goals. To value another, one must
understand who that specific person is, what she needs, and what she can contribute to me and I to her life.

In that relationship to the valued other, fairness does not mean that everybody gets the same rights and the same freedoms. Valuing that other person
means, in part, that their well-being is important to us, and we are willing,
within reason, to provide for them what they need and not only what is equal to
what we have. This is clearly true in relation to children, but also with our
friends. We do not say, "You listened to me for no more than an hour and now

it is time to stop because I have listened to you talk about your problems for an hour. We are even now." On the contrary, we try to make ourselves available to the other; fairness is not understood in quantitative terms. Among strangers, equal freedoms require a form of bookkeeping, to make sure that no one loses out. Among family and friends we do not keep books. Fairness among friends or lovers depends on whether everyone thrives, not on equal time or money or energy spent on one or the other or on equal freedoms and rights. Fairness among family and friends means something much closer to mutuality; each cares for the other. Each is alive to the other's needs and shares in the other's joys and pains. Each wishes the other well. Fairness in the familiar context or among friends has little to do with equal rights or equal freedoms.

Discussion Question

Consider the different members of a family—the old grandparents, the parents in the prime of life, and small children. How shall we make sure that all treat each other fairly and that no is being taken advantage of? Give reasons for your answer.

The feminist critique of liberalism points out that the inherent dignity of all human beings is understood only partially by established liberal theorists. A much broader and more important aspect of appreciating the value of each other requires that we do not treat others as anonymous others but have relationships to them. Fairness in those relationships is assessed in complex ways having to do with everyone doing as well as possible in their lives. It is much less important whether the rights and freedoms of everyone are equal. What matters, instead, is that each be attuned to the other, that they share weal and woe, that they help each other out where they can and are prepared to turn to each other when they need assistance or when experience is enhanced by being shared.

The upshot of this critique is that liberalism overlooks that fairness and justice are not always best understood by thinking about everybody's rights. In much of our lives we focus on needs, on providing for others, not only in the family but also in relation to friends and neighbors, to persons we like at work. Even in relation to strangers, for instance when there is an accident, we do not ask what rights the other has to receive assistance; we try to help. Liberal political theory with its exclusive focus on rights misses important portions of our moral and political life.[42]

Discussion Question

Liberalism demands that we recognize that each person has intrinsic value. List as many different ways of doing that as you can think of and give specific examples of each. Give reasons for your answer.

Review Questions

Three questions about property remain at the end of this chapter:

1. *Who should have private property?*
2. *How much should they have?*
3. *What sorts of things should be private property?*

Formulate your answers to these questions, consider your opponents' views, and show why their criticisms of your position are not persuasive.

   About the fundamental principles of liberal political philosophy, we need to ask

1. *In what does our equality consist?*
2. *What is it about us that entitles us to equal rights?*
3. *What rights belong to us intrinsically, as human beings, and what rights do we owe only to specific legislation?*
4. *To treat other persons well, what else must we consider besides their rights?*

QUESTIONS FOR REFLECTION AND DISCUSSION

1. In the wake of *Kelo vs. City of New London* many states have considered passing laws that propose to make it more difficult for local governments to take private property for development by private developers. These bills respond to the widespread feeling that it is legitimate for the government to take property by eminent domain in order to serve certain public functions such as building schools or courthouses, but that eminent domain should not be used to take private property that does not yield a lot of profit or taxes to give it to other private parties who will make a more profitable use of the property.

   But the details of these bills have shown that this matter is much more complicated than it seems at first.

   Many of the laws that have been passed prohibit taking by eminent domain to give property to private developers *unless* the property taken is "blighted." Although that seems reasonable insofar as it allows eminent domain being used in urban redevelopment, many observers object that *blighted* property is more often than not likely to refer to property in parts of town inhabited by African Americans or Hispanics, so that such legislation would encourage the taking for redevelopment along racial lines. White property would more likely be protected by such laws and property in minority districts would be open to redevelopment.

Bills that prohibit taking by eminent domain for transferring property from one private owner to another would make it much more difficult to redevelop storm-ravaged properties as, for example, in New Orleans and other Gulf Coast cities. Congress is therefore under pressure not to pass any anti-Kelo legislation.

Taking by eminent domain to develop properties that produce little revenue into ones that make a significant contribution not only to the cities' tax base but that attract new companies to the towns, create new jobs, and provide new and attractive recreational facilities is an important method for towns that are struggling economically to improve the life of all inhabitants. Anti-Kelo legislation cripples economically underperforming towns.

Eminent domain has sometimes been used when specific neighborhoods organized themselves to clean up empty lots and attract contractors to build new housing. The legislation limiting taking by eminent domain would impair the ability of neighborhood activism to turn neighborhoods around and breathe new life into them.[43]

Taking by eminent domain and transferring private property to private developers raises a host of questions. List as many of the conflicting considerations you can think of and try to develop what seems to you the most just policy.

2. In 2006, the U.S. Supreme Court declared invalid a law passed by the legislature of the state of Vermont that placed stringent limits on political campaign contributions. Giving one's money to a political candidate to help finance election campaigns, the Supreme Court had decided in the 1970s, is a form of free speech. The Court reaffirmed that opinion in 2006 and found that the Vermont law placed too strict a limit on this particular form of free speech.

   Consider whether it is legitimate to regard giving money to politicians as a form of free speech. How are political campaign contributions different from spending money in the liquor store or for illegal drug purchases? Are those not forms of voting with one's dollars? Can those not also be interpreted as instances of free speech?

   If we agree that political contributions are instances of free speech, should we abolish all campaign finance regulations?

3. Copyright gives a monopoly to an author or composer for their lifetime plus seventy years. During that time the distribution of their works is restricted and they and their heirs can reap monopoly profits because no one can publish their works or perform them without paying royalties. Copyrights limit the distribution of works of art of all sorts and the dissemination of important new ideas because one needs to pay—often a

great deal—for the books in which these new ideas are written down or for the CDs of new bands and composers.

Many people point out that these laws do not, as they were intended, benefit authors and composers. Writers write and composers compose because that is their chosen way of life and their favorite activity. They would do their work—they do in fact do it—even if there is not much money in it for them. The people who profit from copyrights are publishers and musical agents—people who are not creative but merely out for profit.

Do you think that copyrights serve the purposes for which they were instituted? Would the world be better off if we abolished them?

4. Look up information about surrogate motherhood on the Internet. Is hiring oneself out to have someone else's baby a legitimate use of one's property rights, particularly one's rights to make decisions with respect to one's own body? Give reasons for and against the legitimacy of surrogate motherhood.

5. For more than two thousand years, thinkers have objected either to the institution of private property or to significant economic inequality. Consider the reasons for and against projects to reduce economic inequality.

6. U.S. laws allow parents to bequeath their wealth and property to their children (or to anyone else they choose.) Two reasons have traditionally been given for putting severe limits on the rights to inheritance:

   a. If the wealthy can leave their wealth to their children, the country is in danger of developing a hereditary elite or ruling class that passes access to leadership positions in business and government from one generation to the next. Many people believe that that is contrary to our democratic and egalitarian traditions and therefore want to limit rights of inheritance.

   b. We firmly believe in the virtue of hard work and keep saying that people should have to earn what they get. But if a young person receives an inheritance of a million dollars or more, they have not earned that. Should we allow that?

   Argue for and against limiting rights to inheritance, giving reasons for your opinions.

7. Look up arguments for vegetarianism on the Internet. Find arguments having to do with the rights of animal as well as with the ecological impact of raising animals for food. Consider these arguments carefully and show in what ways they are or are not persuasive.

NOTES

1. Ellen Frankel Paul, ed., *Property Rights and Eminent Domain* (New Brunswick: Transaction Books, 1987), 32.

2. Linda Greenhouse, "Justices Rule Cities Can Take Property for Private Development," retrieved January 9, 2007, from New York Times website: www.nytimes.com/2005/06/23/politics/23wirescotus.html?ex=1277179200&en=15be 0deff62f7ed7&ei=5088&partner=rssnyt&emc=rss.

3. In the 2006 mid-term elections, voters in twelve states voted on amendments to their state constitutions restricting taking by eminent domain.

4. John Locke, *Second Treatise on Government* (Oxford: Basil Blackwell, 1946), 15–16.

5. Matthew Boyle, "They didn't earn it—they should return it," retrieved October 15, 2006, from CNN.com website: http://money.cnn.com/magazines/fortune/fortune_archive/2006/05/15/8376829/index.htm.

6. Thomas Jefferson, *The Life and Selected Writings of Thomas Jefferson,* edited by Adrienne Koch and William Peden (New York: Random House, 1993), 351.

7. Jefferson, *Selected Writings,* 259.

8. Plato, *Republic,* translated with Introduction by Francis M. Cornford (Oxford: Oxford University Press, 1954), 165–167.

9. *Acts,* 2:44.

10. *Acts,* 4:32.

11. Jean-Jacques Rousseau, *A Discourse on the Origin of Inequality* (New York: E. P. Dutton and Co., n. d.), 234.

12. Christopher Hill, "Gerard Winstanley, 17th Century Communist at Kingston," retrieved January 14, 2008, from Digger Archives website: www.diggers.org/diggers/gerard_winstanley.htm.

13. Karl Marx and Frederick Engels, "The Communist Manifesto," in *The Marx-Engels Reader,* edited by Robert Tucker (New York, W.W. Norton & Co., 1978), 485.

14. Milton Friedman and Rose Friedman, *Capitalism and Freedom* (Chicago: University of Chicago Press, 1963), 12.

15. Friedman and Friedman, *Capitalism,* 13.

16. Adam Smith, *An Inquiry into the Nature and the Causes of the Wealth of Nations* (New York: Modern Library, 1985), 225.

17. Monica Davies, "Chicago Weighing New Prohibitions: Bad-for-you-Fats," retrieved January 19, 2007, from New York Times website: http://travel2.nytimes.com/2006/07/18/us/18chicago.html.

18. "Hold the Cheese," retrieved January 19, 2007, from Bikers Rights Online website: www.bikersrights.com/press/cheese.html.

19. John Stuart Mill, *On Liberty and Considerations on Representative Government* (Oxford: Blackwell, 1948).

20. Mill, *On Liberty,* 73.

21. Mill, *On Liberty,* 91.

22. Mill, *On Liberty,* 86.

23. "Genetics and Patenting," retrieved October 25, 2007, from Oak Ridge National Laboratory website: www.ornl.gov/sci/techresources/Human_Genome/elsi/patents.shtml.

24. Seth Shulman, *Owning the Future: Inside the Battles to Control the New Assets—Genes, Software, Databases and Technological Know-how—that Make up the Life Blood of the New Economy* (Boston: Houghton, Mifflin Company, 1999).

25. "Monsanto vs. Schmeiser," retrieved October 15, 2006, from Percy Schmeiser website: www.percyschmeiser.com/.

26. Paul Krugman, "Summer of Our Discontent," retrieved October 17, 2006, from www.truthout.org/docs_2005/082605F.shtml.

27. Marlene Kim, "The Working Poor: Lousy Jobs or Lazy Workers?" *Journal of Economic Issues*: 32(1998).

28. "The Mendacity Index," retrieved January 19, 2007, from www.washington monthly.com/features/2003/0309.mendacity-index.html.

29. "Offshoring Statistics—Dollar Size, Job Loss, and Market Potential," from January 19, 2007, from www.ebstrategy.com/Outsourcing/trends/statistics.htm.

30. David L. Harvey, *Potter Addition: Poverty, Family and Kinship in a Heartland Community* (New York: Aldine de Gruyter, 1993).

31. "Mental Illness and Poverty: Does One Cause the Other?" Retrieved January 17, 2007, from www.boston.com/news/globe/health_science/articles/2005/03/08/ mental_illness_and_poverty_does_one_cause_the_other/.

32. Batya Hyman, "The Economic Consequences of Child Sexual Abuse for Adult Lesbian Women," *Journal of Marriage and the Family*, 62, no. 1 (Feb. 2000): 199–211.

33. "Food Assistance Is Critical," retrieved January 20, 2007, from www.food bankrockies.org/hunger.cfm.

34. *Worcester Telegram and Gazette,* April 5, 2006, E1.

35. David K. Shipler, *The Working Poor: Invisible in America* (New York, Vintage Books, 2005).

36. "Whitney Dibo: Homeless for the Holidays," retrieved January 21, 2007, from http://media.www.michigandaily.com/media/storage/paper851/news/2005/12/09/ Opinion/Whitney.Dibo.Homeless.For.The.Holidays1433667.shtml?sourcedomain=w ww.michigandaily.com&MIIHost=media.collegepublisher.com.

37. Susan Moller Okin, *Justice, Gender and Family* (New York: Basic Books, 1989), 101.

38. F. A. Von Hayek, "Equality, Value and Merit," in *Equality*, edited by David Johnston (Indianapolis: Hackett, 2000), 107.

39. "Gideon's Broken Promise: America's Continuing Quest for Equal Justice," re- trieved January 22, 2007, from www.abanet.org/legalservices/sclaid/defender/broken promise/execsummary.pdf.

40. Iris Marion Young, *Justice and the Politics of Difference* (Princeton: Princeton University Press, 1990).

41. Carol Gilligan, *In a Different Voice* (Cambridge: Harvard University Press, 1982).

42. Virginia Held, "Liberalism and the Ethics of Care," in *On Feminist Ethics and Politics*, edited by Claudia Card (Lawrence: University of Kansas Press, 1999), 288–309.

43. *Boston Sunday Globe*, April 16, 2006, D1–D3.

FURTHER READINGS

Andrew Reeve, *Property* (Atlantic Highlands, Humanities Press, 1987). An informa- tive overview of the idea of private property.

Ellen Frankel Paul, *Property Rights and Eminent Domain* (New Brunswick, Transaction Books, 1987). Provides a detailed discussion of the takings by eminent domain and the problems they have given rise to.

David Schweickart, *Against Capitalism* (Cambridge: Cambridge University Press, 1993). States the arguments for and against capitalist property rights and develops a socialist alternative.

Rochelle Cooper Dreyfuss, "General Overview over the Intellectual Property System," in *Owning Scientific and Technical Information: Value and Ethical Issues*, edited by Vivian Weil and John W. Snappers (New Brunswick: Rutgers University Press, 1989). A brief introduction to copyrights and patents.

Seth Shulman, *Owning the Future* (Boston: Houghton Mifflin, 1999). A critical look at the changes in patent and copyright law that favor ownership by large corporations over public access to the United States' innovations.

David K. Shipler, *The Working Poor: Invisible in America* (New York: Vintage Books, 2005). A carefully documented study of the working poor in the United States.

Chapter Four

Democracy

Societies in which the authorities impose rules on citizens are less free than those where citizens can participate in shaping those rules themselves. Where citizens participate in legislation they impose rules on themselves and are, therefore, more free than if the laws are forcibly imposed by the government. We call a system a *democracy* when citizens participate in legislating. What democracy consists of in detail is, however, much more controversial than we usually think. This chapter will examine democracy, the people's participation in the legislative process.

When Iraqis in large numbers went to the polls in January 2005, President George W. Bush welcomed the vote as an important step on the road to democracy. "The world is hearing the voice of freedom from the center of the Middle East," Bush said. "In great numbers and under great risk, Iraqis have shown their commitment to democracy. By participating in free elections, the Iraqi people have firmly rejected the anti-democratic ideology of terrorists."[1] The president's quote represents a widely held opinion that democracy amounts to a political system in which there are periodic elections. To be sure, the elections have to be honest and aboveboard and include a reliable count of the votes cast. The electoral campaigns have to be open to all and to be free of violence. If those conditions are satisfied, many people believe, the people enjoy a democratic system.

This chapter will examine in more detail what democracy is. We will ask

- Is democracy a desirable form of government?
- What is democracy?
- What is the condition of our democracy?
- What are some current proposals for improving our democratic system?

- If democracy is good because it contributes to the freedom of citizens, why do we not extend democratic processes to the workplace?

THE CRITIQUE OF DEMOCRACY

We have been brought up to believe that a democratic country is better than any other one. We have heard that so often it is hard to remember why we believe this. Could we be mistaken?

In the last two thousand or more years of Western history, the consensus of many thoughtful and informed thinkers has been that democracy is a thoroughly undesirable form of government. The most powerful argument against democracy was framed in Athens, Greece, in the fourth century BC. At the time, Athens had thriving democratic institutions. Not only did all the male citizens vote but everyone also took turns doing the work of government. There existed no separate government bureaucracy; instead citizens were assigned by lots to various government jobs that they would fill for a year and would get paid for if they needed to get paid. But during that period, Plato, one of the first great Western philosophers, a member of one of the wealthy, aristocratic families in Athens, argued against democracy as follows: if you need a pair of shoes, you go to the shoemaker to have him make a pair of shoes for you. You let the shoemaker make the shoes as well as he is able; you do not tell him what to do because you are not yourself a shoemaker. This is also true when you use the services of the cook, the doctor, or the lawyer. They are especially skilled in their work. Their customers do not tell them how to do their job. In any given society people have different work. If a society is well run, everyone is trained in their specialty and the untrained do not interfere with experts when they are doing what they have been trained to do. Democracy is a bizarre form of government, Plato thought, because governing is of course also a specialty that one needs to have learned to do it well. The idea that every Tom, Dick, and Harry should have a say in how a country is run makes about as much sense as having the patient on the operating table vote on how the surgeon is going to perform a triple bypass surgery or a facial reconstruction.

Discussion Questions

Plato seems right to insist that we should do well, whatever we do, but does that mean that we must have one specialty and leave all other work to other specialists? Being a good doctor or cook or car mechanic or diplomat does not only take training but a lot of time. You cannot be good at most occupations unless you devote a great deal of time and energy to them. If you only cook on weekends, can you rival professionals? If you only vote every other year, can you really run the country? What do you think? Give reasons for your answers.

A well-ordered city—and the same applies to larger states—is one where everybody is doing their job and doing it well. Those who govern must be specialists. They must be allowed to practice their statecraft as well as they can without being disturbed by the demands and instructions of people who are unqualified to give orders to the governing experts. That means that people do what they are trained to do and each stays out of the business of the other. Democracy, for that reason, is one of the least desirable political systems.

Some framers of our Constitution held similar views. Alexander Hamilton said that

> all communities divide themselves into the few and the many. The first are rich and well born; the other the mass of the people . . . the people are turbulent and changing; they seldom judge or determine right. Give, therefore, to the first class a distinct, permanent share in the government. They will check the unsteadiness of the second, and as they cannot derive any advantage by change, they therefore will ever maintain good government.[2]

Similar criticisms of democracy have been raised in our day by Joseph Schumpeter, a highly respected Austrian economist who taught at Harvard University for many years. In his *Capitalism, Socialism and Democracy*, he points out that many people have excellent judgments in matters bearing on their daily life. They are competent to make decisions in matters having to do with their families and their livelihood. But even in these matters, the public judgment is often unreliable because people see their immediate, short-run interest more clearly than their interests over the long run. A measure that is designed to protect the environment, for instance, may encounter popular hostility when it threatens jobs in the short run. It is voted down because short-run interest only too often trumps the long-run interests of everyone. Everyone votes for the politician who promises to lower taxes because everyone wants to have lower taxes and more disposable income. But then there is no money for schools or for the upkeep of roads and bridges. But nobody thought about that when they supported the tax-cutting politician.

In matters that are more distant from daily life—banks and the monetary system, foreign affairs, and the relations to distant peoples—ordinary people are poor judges of their own or the country's interests. They do not have the necessary knowledge of those other peoples or of the history of relations between their country and that other place to decide intelligently what policy the government should follow. Their votes should not be counted as decisive when the government decides what actions to take.[3]

Discussion Questions

In our industrial, technological society, many decisions must be left to the experts such as how much chlorine to add to the drinking water or what level of alcohol in the blood makes one an unsafe driver. Should such technical questions be voted on by the general public? Is it appropriate for people to vote on sex education in schools, on teaching evolution in biology classes, on whether the government should be allowed to run a deficit, or are those questions for experts to decide? Give reasons for your answers.

Plato's views, as well as those of Schumpeter's, are very much at odds with what we are accustomed to thinking about democracy. We need to consider them carefully before we decide that they are unacceptable and that we are right in thinking that democracy is a desirable system.

Was Plato Right?

Here is an example of the sort of difficulties with democracy that Plato emphasizes. The town where I live does not add fluoride to the drinking water. The question whether to change that policy appears on the ballot every few years and is promptly defeated by a coalition of right- and left-wing citizens. Those on the right believe that the proposal to add fluoride to the water is a communist plot to poison the children of our community. Those on the left consider the proposal a capitalist plot hatched by chemical companies to make huge profits from the sale of fluoride, which threatens the health of our children. Two questions face the electorate in this case: does adding small quantities of fluoride to the drinking water prevent tooth decay in children and would this endanger their health? Both of these questions have been widely discussed in technical journals dedicated to dentistry and to public health. As ordinary citizens we do not have access to these journals, we do not know their names, and we do not know where to find them. Were we to read them we would, most likely, not understand the technical discussions of the chemistry of preventing tooth decay in children or of the statistical evidence bearing on the dangers of introducing tiny quantities of fluoride into the drinking water. The question is a technical one. It requires expertise in dentistry, in chemistry, and in large-scale statistical public health studies to make an informed decision. Ordinary citizens, whether educated or not, are in no position to have an informed opinion about this.

Here we have a case of citizens voting to make a decision they are in fact not equipped to make because they lack the necessary technical expertise. Plato wants to say that *all* the decisions voters make in a democracy are of the same nature: citizens in an electoral democracy are repeatedly asked to decide issues that they are not equipped to decide. But as citizens, we do not believe that. We think that we know what is best for us and what is best for our country in a large range of areas. It seems clear, however, that we often overestimate our ability to judge matters of national interest. Consider the debates about the national debt. Does the ordinary citizen understand whether the national debt damages our economy or benefits it? Do we understand the far-reaching consequences of free-trade agreements with other countries? There are lively debates about problems in the environment but without being expert in environmental issues am I, as a citizen, really equipped to make the right choices here? Many people argue that we need to reduce air pollution and that we need to reduce our use of natural resources. But others warn that such a reduction in the use of natural resources would do fatal damage to our economy. I, for one, am not confident that I have a reliable judgment in these debates about the environment and our economy. I lack the necessary information, and I do not know how to evaluate the information I can find. Most citizens, I suspect, are in a similar situation.

Clearly Plato was not completely wrong. His objections to democracy are more powerful today in our highly technological society where many issues are only understood by trained experts. Many questions on which ordinary voters have firm opinions should be left to the experts. The opinions of ordinary voters may be definite but they are bound to be ill informed and irrational because ordinary citizens lack the training to understand what they are voting on.

Discussion Question

Make a list of political issues currently being debated. In which of these issues do you feel competent to form a reliable judgment? Give reasons for your answer.

But not all the questions confronting voters are technical questions to which only well-trained experts have reliable answers. In the United States today, there are acrimonious disagreements about abortion, about the death penalty, about the right of the terminally ill to die, and about euthanasia. We disagree about the role that religion should play in our public life and we disagree about the extent to which every citizen is entitled to a minimally decent living—to shelter, food, health care, and education. All of these are *moral* questions: whether a woman pregnant against her will may abort the fetus, and whether human beings have the right to punish their fellow citizens by taking their life. Sexuality and questions of life and death raise deep moral issues on which we disagree sharply.

Is every thoughtful citizen equally entitled to decide moral issues? Most people would say that each of us is as much of an expert in moral issues as everyone else. But surely many people look to their priest, minister, rabbi, or imam for moral guidance. Others trust their therapists or perhaps their parents or grandparents to steer them on the right moral path. In our daily life, we often distrust our own moral judgments and look to experts, whether religious or secular, to guide us. Today we even agree that majorities are often mistaken in moral questions. For many years the majority of Americans supported slavery and thought that "a woman's place was in the home." Today we think both of those were serious errors. It seems that Plato is at least partly right when he claims that even in matters of moral judgments, some of us are more expert than others. Allowing everyone who is a citizen to vote on moral issues is inviting trouble.

Discussion Questions

Are there not experts in morality also? We put more stock in the ethical teachings of Jesus or Mohamed than of some random person in front of us in the check-out line. Would you trust your six-year-old kid brother or your alcoholic uncle as much in questions of morality as your parish priest? Give reasons for your answers.

Plato's criticism of democracy is weaker when we consider another class of subjects for popular vote. Often in the heat of electoral campaigns we ask not about matters that only experts can decide or about moral questions but we ask about what we want. Do we want each of us to have our own car to be able to go whenever and wherever we want? If so, we would vote for more money to be spent on highways and highway improvement and perhaps for a reduction in environmental controls on automobile emissions. Or do we want to strengthen public transportation to allow people in the cities to travel comfortably and cheaply to and from their work or to and from their shopping without the expense of their own car and the damage private automobiles do to the environment? Choices of that sort are not choices to be made by experts because they are, at least in part, choices about what sort of life we want to lead and what sort of world we want to live in. Citizens are asked to decide whether they are willing to pay more taxes to help the poor, to finance and improve public education, or to ease the later years of retired people. Here expertise, whether technical or moral, is not the deciding factor. What decides us is our sense of what we want to do for other people, what perhaps we believe we owe to other people, and what we want the world in which we live to look and feel like. What decides us, in the end, is what we want for ourselves. No one knows that as well as we do. There are no experts who know better what we want than we do ourselves. Democracy is clearly the best system when it comes to deciding what citizens want for themselves.

But Plato is not finished yet. He has one more question for us: is what we want for ourselves always good for us? People overeat or they drink too much. They work, work, and work and do not enjoy their lives. They marry persons with whom, after a while, they cannot get along. From the beginning their friends and relatives knew that they would not be able to live together happily. There is an endless list of bad choices people make; they do what they want to do and the outcome is a disaster. That seems to suggest that allowing us to choose what we like most may not always be conducive to leading a good life. It is not even conducive to our happiness because many of our choices are really self-destructive. It seems that perhaps we would lead better lives, and more importantly, happier lives were we to entrust the government to people who know better what is good for us than we often do ourselves.

Discussion Questions

Are you always the best judge of what is good for you? Are there not people who know you and care for you deeply who are sometimes better judges than you about where you should live, with whom, and where you should work? Give reasons for your answers.

Here is a frequent reply to this observation of Plato's that many people consistently make bad choices in their own behalf: It is true that we often hurt ourselves when we do what we want because what we want is, in the short or the long run, not good for us. But, in most situations, there are few if any other people who know better than we do what job to pick, where to live, or with whom to share our lives. Yes, to be sure when your wife wants a divorce, everyone pretends to have known all along that your marriage would fail. There are always other people who think they know better than we do but there is no reason to trust them anymore than we trust ourselves. Their opinions are only the perfect knowledge everyone has in hindsight. There are no experts when it comes to choosing life partners or jobs or where to live because whether a marriage or a job will work out depends to a large extent on unforeseeable events.

Discussion Question

On balance, how powerful are the arguments against democracy? Give reasons for your answer.

When the Majority Proves Wrong

Often the people as a whole, the majority, make bad choices. Years later everyone sees that clearly, but at the time, in the heat of the current emotions, majorities are on the wrong side. Consider this example: in June 1963 at the height of the civil rights struggle, Vivian Malone and James Hood wanted to register as students at the University of Alabama. Because they were African Americans the law prohibited them from entering the then all-white University of Alabama. The federal government, led by President John F. Kennedy and the attorney general, Robert F. Kennedy, called out the Alabama National Guard to allow Malone and Hood to register. The governor of Alabama, George C. Wallace, stood in the door of the university to bar the two. This was clearly a symbolic gesture, but Wallace was, without doubt, representing the sentiments of the majority of the citizens of the state of Alabama. He had learned that from his own bitter experience. When he had run for governor for the first time, five years previous in 1958, he had refused the support of the Ku Klux Klan and had, for that reason, gained the endorsement of the National Association for the Advancement of Colored People (NAACP). He lost the election by a large margin. In Alabama, candidates endorsed by the major black organization lost elections. There is, in addition, good reason to think that the majority of the U.S. population at the time had little interest in the Civil Rights struggle.[4] The majority of Americans did not believe that the military intervention of the federal government in the conflict between the African American community and whites in the state of Alabama was justified. They may well have been rooting for Wallace and the white people of Alabama who did not want black people in the university. Wallace's gesture gained for him sufficient popularity not only in the Deep South but all over the United States to make him a plausible candidate for the presidency of the United States in 1964 and again in 1972. The federal government that enforced the black students' rights to study in any but all-black universities did not represent the majority opinion of the voters.

But that example raises a problem for us forty-odd years later. From our vantage point the two Kennedy brothers were the heroes of the day—not to mention Malone and Hood—and the villain was Wallace. But he may well have represented the majority and the government run by the Kennedys was a government of the minority. At that moment, it was once again the minority that used the power of the government for its own ends. It was not a democratic government as we have defined it so far. Yet, today, we think that the Kennedys were right. Does that show that democratic government is not always a good thing? Should it make us rethink whether democracy is under all conditions desirable? Perhaps we need to withdraw some of our enthusiasm for democracy and for government of the people.

In our day, we often hear the accusation that "activist judges" make decisions which should instead the made by all the people. The latest controversy in which this accusation has surfaced concerns the 2004 decision of the Massachusetts Supreme Judicial Court to allow gay couples to marry. Critics say that this decision should not be made by the judges but should, instead, be left up to the voters. The controversy brings to light a characteristic of our democracy that is not often discussed: decisions that are, at the time, unpopular may well be made by authorities that are only indirectly under a popular control such as the U.S. Attorney General in the case of black admissions to the University of Alabama or the Supreme Judicial Court in Massachusetts in the case of gay marriage. We are sufficiently uncertain about the virtues of democratic decision making in controversial issues to have allowed ourselves alternative routes toward the extension and protection of justice.

We might, considering how many bad choices we have made throughout our lives, entrust the conduct of our lives and of government to people whose judgment we have greater confidence in than in our own. But in so doing we would give up our freedom—the freedom to run our own lives as we see fit as long as we do not harm others by the choices we make. That thought raises an important question that we will not answer until later in this book. The question is how important is freedom? If we are free, if we run our own lives, we may well make bad choices and thereby impair our lives and our happiness. Is freedom worth a certain amount of failure, of poor choices, and of bad outcomes? We need to raise the question about the value of freedom explicitly. Everyone believes that freedom is terribly important, that it is important to live in a free country, and that it is very important to be able to live as you choose. We all take that for granted. But we need to ask ourselves why we believe that freedom is so important.

I will discuss possible answers to that question in the final chapter.

WHAT IS DEMOCRACY?

We have seen some reasons for distrusting democracy. It is time to clarify what we think democracy is. Plato thought it was a way for the poor to get some power over the rich and their wealth. Schumpeter thought that in elections, the people should fill open slots in the government and should, for the rest, leave the government alone to make policy. In these two views, democracy is neither a desirable institution nor is it important in the life of a nation.

Discussion Question

Winston Churchill—Britain's Prime Minister during the dark days of World War II—is often quoted as saying, "Democracy is the worst form of government, except for all those other forms that have been tried from time to time." What do you think he meant by that? Do you agree or disagree? Give reasons for your answer.

Most of the time, we make much bolder claims for democracy. A contemporary philosopher defines it as the "rule by the people, by way of voting."[5] This repeats a formula used by the earliest Americans as well as the framers of the Constitution more than two hundred years ago. "The people rule"—that has been the way we have described our political system to ourselves from the earliest years on this continent. Roger Williams described our form of government in those terms in 1644. Williams, a preacher and advocate of religious liberty, fell afoul of the rigid Puritans in Massachusetts and moved south to the head of Narragansett Bay to found what is today the city of Providence, Rhode Island. One hundred and forty years later, when the U.S. Constitution was being debated before its adoption, James Madison described the proposed democracy in the same terms. Madison wrote in *The Federalist:*

> we must define a republic to be . . . a government which derives all its powers directly or indirectly from the great body of the people, and is administered by persons holding their offices during pleasure, for a limited period, or during good behavior.[6] [See the following chapter for a more detailed distinction between a republic and a democracy.]

We have described our democracy in those terms ever since. The constitution that was officially adopted in 1787 begins with the words "We the People." The definition of democracy cited most frequently refers to a system "in which the supreme power is vested in the people."[7]

Discussion Question

Bill Gates and his associates run (or "rule") Microsoft. Do the citizens, you and I, run the United States in the same sense? Give reasons for your answer.

A democracy, where the people hold the supreme power, receives its structure from the people. They decide the precise forms of the government and may enshrine that definition in a written constitution. Moreover, through their elected representatives they make the laws the government will follow and will impose on the people themselves. In a democracy, in this sense, people remain free under government because the laws they obey have been made by the citizens themselves. The rules everyone must conform to are self-imposed and thus no one is coerced: that is, no one is forced to do what they do not want to do. Freedom, as we said at the beginning of this book, consists of being able to do what one wants. As long as laws are written by the people themselves or by their elected representatives, the people obey only those rules which they themselves have formulated and imposed on themselves. They only do what they want to do. Democracy is, for that reason, the only form of government compatible with individual freedom of citizens. Governments are inevitably coercive: they enforce laws. They threaten to arrest and incarcerate all those who fail to stay within the limits of the law. Governments are always a threat to citizen freedoms. But where the laws are made by those citizens themselves, the government only enforces rules the citizens imposed on themselves and thus—at least in theory—the citizens in a democracy can be subject to a government and still remain as free as before.

Discussion Questions

In our democracy, we say the power of the government derives from the people. Consider the cases discussed in the preceding section of instances where the government acted in ways disapproved of by the majority.

1. *Can you think of other instances where government policy contravenes the wish of the majority?*
2. *How can we square those cases with the definition of democracy as the rule of the people?*

Give reasons for your answers.

This is a much grander, more elevated picture of democracy—no longer, as Plato thought, a degenerate form of government or, as Schumpeter described it, a means for keeping government jobs filled and the masses of citizens pacified and out of the hair of the government. It is now an assertion that the people are the fundamental source of power in the society. It asserts the basic freedom of all of us to have our society run as we wish it to be run. According to this idea of democracy this society is ours to arrange as we think best. We, the people, are the ones who, in the final analysis, have the power to arrange matters as they seem best to us.

PROBLEMS OF ELECTORAL DEMOCRACY

Is This an Accurate Picture of the Political System under Which We Live?

If democracy is a political system where all government power is derived from the people, is ours a democracy? Recent opinion polls suggest that many Americans feel distant from the government. They do not feel that the government is theirs, that their own opinions and their needs and problems carry any weight with the decision makers in Washington, D.C., or in the state capitals. They do not see themselves as the sources of government power. Instead the government is more often perceived as an adversary; only rarely is it felt to be on their side. Citizens see it as an alien power, and sometimes even a hostile institution over which they have little control. Contrary to our common description of democracy, many people see themselves as powerless in the face of an all-powerful government. "[T]he majority of Americans feel disconnected from government and believe that government is no longer 'of, by and for the people,' according to a new poll sponsored by the Council for Excellence in Government and conducted by the survey research firms of Peter D. Hart and Robert Teeter."[8] This result comes from a survey taken during the 1999 election season. Polls taken in 2005 showed that the majority of voters considered their representatives to be corrupt and to be hanging on to power at all costs instead of doing their best to represent their constituents. They would serve anyone who would help them stay in office without regard to the express wishes, needs, or interests of their constituents.[9] Many Americans do not feel that the power comes from them or that the society is basically run by them through representatives who are instructed by voters and who must follow those instructions if they want to remain in office. They feel alienated from the political process, victims of government power rather than its source.

Discussion Question

Are the people mistaken who feel that the government is not theirs? Or has our government ceased being a democracy in which the people rule? Give reasons for your answers.

Many of us do not think that we rule. We are ruled instead, it seems, by politicians who call themselves our "representatives" but do not in fact represent our interests and opinions. Political theory responds to that complaint by drawing a distinction between "ruling" and "governing." Governing consists of running the affairs of the government—the schools, the roads, the army, and foreign relations—day to day. That is the job of the government. When we say that in a democracy the people *rule*, we are saying something much more general—namely that the power of the government derives from the people. It is all of us who empower the government to govern. What is more, we instruct the government in how to govern through the mechanism of elections. The people rule by drawing up constitutions and setting up the basic outlines of their government. They rule also by electing the leaders of the government and refusing to reelect them when they do not follow the wishes of the voters.

Discussion Questions

What is this power of the government that derives from us, the people? It is tempting to see the manifestations of that power in the armed policemen that direct traffic or give us tickets, or in the National Guard keeping order during strikes or large political demonstrations. Does the policeman's or the soldier's power come from us or from the weapons they carry? Give reasons for your answers.

This is the story we have been telling ourselves for several centuries; it is the story that we continue to repeat. Is this story accurate? We shall see many reasons for doubting that our government derives its power from us, that we rule our country. The story we have been telling ourselves for two hundred years about our democracy may well be mistaken.

Democracy, we think, is government of the people, and when we say that, we mean the government of *all* the people. But is that facile assumption justified, that every adult citizen is allowed to participate in ruling? We need to ask ourselves.

Who Are "the People"?

The government established in 1787 was quite definitely not a government of the people. Few women voted, nor did the slaves who formed a significant portion of the population, especially in the Southern states. Free blacks and property-owning white women, (who were rare and permitted only in exceptional circumstances) voted for a few years. But in the early years of the nineteenth century they were gradually disenfranchised. By 1850 no blacks or white women were allowed to vote.[10]

Among white men, only owners of property could vote. The delegates to the Continental Congress, which in 1787 wrote the new constitution, were mostly elected by the state legislatures, whose members had been chosen by white, male property owners. Once the constitution had been written, it was submitted to constitutional conventions in each state whose members also were elected but subject to the same limitations of other elections at the time. The complexities of the system—bicameral legislatures, indirect election of senators and of the president, and the right to vote limited primarily to owners of landed property—were all intended to temper the influence of the opinions and desires of ordinary people whom the mostly aristocratic framers of the constitution distrusted. Recall the quote from Hamilton we saw previously:

> all communities divide themselves into the few and the many. The first are rich and well born; the other the mass of the people . . . the people are turbulent and changing; they seldom judge or determine right. Give, therefore, to the first class a distinct, permanent share in the government. They will check the unsteadiness of the second, and as they cannot derive any advantage by change, they therefore will ever maintain good government.[3]

The U.S. democracy, born in Philadelphia in 1787, was not a government in which *all* the people had supreme power. It was more like an oligarchy—a government of the few—that gave limited power to some white men to participate in the shaping of our government. It did not hesitate to exclude the significant majority of the people, consisting of slaves and white women. It was a complete misrepresentation when the founders described the U.S. government of 1787 as a government empowered and directed by all the citizens through their elected representatives. The representatives, who were elected, represented only a small layer of the population.

> The democracy of the mid-nineteenth century America was hardly a democracy at all: women of all classes and colors lacked political and civil rights; most blacks were enslaved; free black men found political rights they once enjoyed either reduced or eliminated; the remnants of a ravaged Indian population in the Eastern states had been forced to move West without citizenship. Even the most expansive of the era's successful political reforms encompassed considerably less than half of the total adult population, and at best a bare majority of the free adult citizenry.[11]

Discussion Question

Given the definition of democracy as a system where the people rule, when did the United States become a democracy? Give reasons for your answer.

What Is Representation? Edmund Burke

Edmund Burke was an eighteenth-century Irish philosopher and politician, who supported the American colonies in their struggle against King George III, and ten years later became an ardent and eloquent critic of the Revolution in France. In 1774, when he was running for the seat in Parliament from Bristol, he was drawn into a debate about the proper role of the elected representatives in a democracy. Burke's opponent promised to be tightly bound by the wishes of the voters. The opinions of the voters, he thought, were binding on their elected representative. Burke disagreed:

> Certainly, gentlemen, it ought to be the happiness and glory of a representative to live in the strictest union, the closest correspondence, and the most unreserved communication with his constituents. Their wishes ought to have great weight with him; their opinion, high respect; their business, unremitting attention. It is his duty to sacrifice his repose, his pleasures, his satisfactions, to theirs; and above all, ever, and in all cases, to prefer their interest to his own. But his unbiased opinion, his mature judgment, his enlightened conscience, he ought not to sacrifice to you, to any man, or to any set of men living. . . . Parliament is not a

congress of ambassadors from different and hostile interests; which interests each must maintain, as an agent and advocate, against other agents and advocates; but parliament is a *deliberative* assembly of *one* nation, with *one* interest, that of the whole; where, not local purposes, not local prejudices, ought to guide, but the general good, resulting from the general reason of the whole. You choose a member indeed; but when you have chosen him, he is not member of Bristol, but he is a member of *parliament*. If the local constituent should have an interest, or should form a hasty opinion, evidently opposite to the real good of the rest of the community, the member for that place ought to be as far, as any other, from any endeavor to give it effect. I beg pardon for saying so much on this subject. I have been unwillingly drawn into it; but I shall ever use a respectful frankness of communication with you. Your faithful friend, your devoted servant, I shall be to the end of my life: a flatterer you do not wish for.[12]

Elected representatives are not merely representatives from East Podunk, sworn to uphold the parochial interest of the East-Podunkers but representatives to the nation's legislative assembly, whose task it is to make laws for the entire nation. The representative must be attuned to the needs, desires, and opinions of the people who sent him to the national legislature, but he must, once there, participate in the process of deliberating about what is good for the entire nation, and in that, must go beyond the specific interests of his local constituents.

Discussion Question

Should elected representatives be bound by the specific wishes of the electorate or feel free, once elected, to use their best judgment to make policies for the entire nation? Give reasons for your answer.

How Can an Elected Official Represent All the Voters?

Legislators must represent the electorate's views on the controversial issues of the day. But that creates another problem for most elected representatives: they face an impossible task. On the average each representative is elected in a district of six hundred thousand persons. It is fairly unlikely that all the voters among those six hundred thousand persons in the United States today are sufficiently similar to each other that one person could represent the opinions and interests of each of these constituents in the legislature. Even if the elected representative is deeply in tune with the lives of persons in the voting district, no one person can replicate the wishes, thoughts, and actions of each voter in the district because those are, most of the time, at loggerheads. Most electoral districts include cities, small towns, and country. They include ardently religious constituencies and other groups who "worship" in the shopping malls or on the golf course rather than in church. It includes young voters and the very old; the healthy and the sick; the able-bodied and the disabled. It includes young families with school-age children and older persons whose children are grown and have moved far away. It includes the rich and the poor; families with members in the military as well as pacifists, carnivores and vegetarians, gay and straight. The voters of any district have different needs and interests; they fear different threats and they hold incompatible opinions on many different subjects. A representative cannot represent all of those; representing the outlook of some voters cannot fail but to offend others. Not everyone in any given district can be represented.

Governments need clear and unambiguous instructions because they must act. Instructions recommended by different citizens that are contradictory cannot all be adopted. If they were, they would paralyze the government. Not everyone's opinions can be put into practice; only some of the people can see their favored policies adopted and executed by the government. As we shall see, our government today tends to resolve these conflicts in favor of the opinions of the citizens with the most money. Because its elected representatives cannot speak on behalf of all of the voters who elected them, they usually speak in favor of the rich. We will return to that point.

Discussion Questions

Suppose the representative you voted for is elected and then votes on every occasion for measures which you oppose, and opposes measures you favor? Are you represented in the legislature? Give reasons for your answer.

How We Control Our Representatives

In a democracy, we tell ourselves, the people rule by electing representatives and instructing them how they should govern. Every schoolchild knows that in our democracy people elect representatives who follow the voters' wishes. If they do not they will not be reelected.

But is this familiar story of the elected representative who is punished at the polls for not reflecting accurately the desires of the voters just one more myth about our democracy? It presupposes that voters are intimately acquainted with the voting record of their representatives and that voters, equally, know what issues are coming up in Congress, what laws are proposed, what laws are passed, and which proposals are defeated. But we all know that that is a completely unrealistic picture of what voters consider when they go to the polls. Only a small number of them have any sense of what bills this representative voted for. Most voters make up their mind on rather different grounds. Representatives do fall out of favor but rarely for their voting records in Congress.

Worse, most voters have an unclear idea of what representatives do in Washington or in the state capital. The prevailing mythology pictures the representatives busily going to committee meetings to examine proposed legislation or giving speeches and listening to speeches in the full House or Senate in the debates that precede voting new legislation up or down. A part of that picture are the legislators who have spent ample time acquainting themselves with proposed legislation, who have been briefed by staff on new laws under discussion. They have considered arguments for and against that legislation and have, perhaps, already decided which way their vote will go. The reality is quite different. Again and again, legislators vote on legislation they have not read.[13] Often laws cover more than a thousand pages. Legislators are not able to read all that material and to study it carefully. When they vote, they often vote blind and go on the recommendations of their party leaders or of lobbyists. Their main occupation is not studying the proposed legislation but to raise funds for their reelection campaign.[14] Robert Reich, Labor Secretary in the Clinton administration, wrote recently, "The system is out of control. It cost the average candidate three times more to run for Congress in 2006 than it did in 1990, adjusting for inflation. Members now devote most of their time to fund raising."[15] The public business suffers because the elected representatives spend an enormous amount of time raising money. The perception of many voters that their legislators are more interested in being reelected than in serving the voters seems fairly accurate.

Discussion Question

Common political wisdom has it that incumbents have a much better chance at winning elections than their challengers. Does that show that most voters do not elect a new representative because they are satisfied with the representation they receive? Give reasons for your answer.

How Voters Make Their Opinions Known

In the mid-term elections in 2006, voters put an end to the Republican majorities in Congress and replaced them with Democrats. There was a widespread feeling that the voting public had made an important statement about the state of the country and the direction in which they wanted the government to move.

But what statement did voters make? The answer to that question depends to a considerable extent on the opinions of the specific commentator. The opponents of the war in Iraq saw the election as a decisive rejection of the war; critics of government corruption read the vote as an expression of revulsion at several high-profile scandals. Supporters of gay marriage saw a softening of attitudes toward homosexuals. The apparent unanimity of the voters hides disagreements with respect to the key issues facing us at any given moment.

The plain fact is that electoral majorities tell us little about the opinions of the voters. People vote for a given candidate for a variety of reasons. I may vote for a candidate because I like the way she thinks about social problems. Another likes her firm stands on foreign policy issues. Others again hope that the candidate will vote to lower their taxes. Environmentalists support her because she promises to sponsor environment-friendly legislation. Someone else votes for her because she is a woman. Some people vote according to party affiliations; they would rather not vote at all than, say, vote for a Democrat. She gains the votes of other persons who would vote for any opponent of the other candidate because they hate that other candidate with a fierce passion. Some like the looks of the candidate. She looks nice and her children are awfully cute. Others know her name but not that of the opposing candidate and therefore vote for her. A further voter remembers meeting her once at a social occasion and liking her. Candidates, especially incumbents, receive support for bringing a lot of federal money into their districts. Other candidates lose votes if family members are arrested by the police. There are an endless number of other reasons why people vote for one person. Their voting for the same candidate does not indicate any kind of consensus among them. The voters who put one particular candidate in office may not agree on very much of anything. The votes for one candidate rather than another tell us little about the opinions or the mood of the people. All it tells us is that this candidate got more votes than her opponent.

Candidates understand this very well. If they are seasoned campaigners, they do not have the same message for every audience, but tend to tailor their message to the different groups they speak to. For a liberal, middle-class audience they will stress their record on education and equal rights for all; when they talk to a Catholic men's club they may mention something about the rights of the unborn or their opposition to euthanasia. They will talk about city problems in the city and deplore the high price of basic foods, while they stress their unwavering support for farm price supports when they speak to their rural constituents. If you write a letter to your congressperson, do not expect to receive a reply that disagrees with you. Whatever point you make, the reply will tell you that your representative has supported that point of view and has advocated relevant legislation for many years. The candidate does not look for opinions; the candidate looks for votes. Within more or less legal limits, candidates will say or do almost anything to get your vote. They will send you pictures of their families, give you pot holders with their name on it, or invite you to gatherings where you are expected to contribute to their campaign fund. If you have specific complaints they will try to take care of them—everything to get your vote.

Counting up the marks on ballots does not assure us that the selection of the candidate is, at the same time, an endorsement of a set of policy choices. Voting for candidates does not yield a set of policies endorsed by a majority of voters. A government set up by majority vote is not necessarily a government that represents the people. The policies followed by such a government need not be the policies favored by the people or a majority of them.

A frequently cited example of that is the increasingly restrictive policy toward abortion. On the one hand, poll after poll shows that a majority of Americans support a woman's right to decide whether to have an abortion or not. At the same time, these same people elect representatives who oppose abortion and who help pass legislation that makes access to abortions more difficult. How can we explain that? People do not always choose their representative for their positions on matters of public policy or, if public policy issues do motivate voters, it is not always the issue of abortion that decides them to vote for one candidate rather than another.[16] The representatives that get the largest number of votes do not always represent firmly held opinions of the public. Even a legislature elected by a majority does not always give you a government that represents the people.

Yes, by voting for a specific candidate, voters give some instructions to the legislatures. But the messages are often difficult to decipher because different voters chose a person for different reasons; often the legislature does not represent the opinions of those who elected them. Over the long run legislative bodies may respond to popular opinion. But representatives rarely receive specific instructions in elections.

Discussion Question

In electing candidates, voters supposedly provide instructions to their representatives. What instructions can the victorious candidates draw from winning an election? Give reasons for your answer.

An Informed Electorate?

However alienated they themselves may feel from the government, many Americans believe that the people rule in our democracy; voters elect persons to represent their own opinions and interests when laws are made and policies formulated to guide the executive. In the preceding sections we have seen a number of problems with this picture of the electoral process. It is not by any means clear that elections guarantee that the voters will find themselves faithfully represented by the persons they elect. Added to the difficulties already mentioned there is the fact that most people, if they vote at all, are quite ignorant both about the political process and current issues confronting the nation, its citizens, and its legislators. Political scientists have exhaustively documented the U.S. voters' ignorance about political issues.

> American voters possess scant information about politics and policy. Examples are legion; here are a few. Although Social Security receives ten times the funding of foreign aid, two thirds of the American people believe that the government spends more on foreign aid than on Social Security. Sixty-five percent of the American people in 2003 could not name a single justice of the U.S. Supreme Court. . . . And in perhaps the most dramatic example of our time, more than 40 percent of Americans continued to believe as late as 2003 that Iraq was deeply involved in the September 11 attack on the United States even though none of the hijackers was an Iraqi and no collusion between Saddam Hussein and Osama bin Laden has ever been found.
>
> It may be reassuring to realize that 40 percent of Americans can be induced to offer an opinion on whether the Public Affairs Act of 1975 should be repealed but it raises serious questions about the existence of an informed public when we learn that there is not, and never was, such a thing as the Public Affairs Act of 1975.[17]

In 2001 and 2003, the president prevailed on Congress to pass legislation cutting taxes. The top 15 percent of the population received 40 percent of that tax cut. The gains for poor and middle-class persons were negligible. This one-sided bonanza for the very rich could pass without stirring up a popular outcry because most of the voters were woefully misinformed about our tax system. "Asked whether Americans pay more or less of their income in taxes than Western Europeans, 40% said they did not know. Asked whether they had heard about a proposal in Washington to do away with taxes on corporate dividends—the centerpiece of President Bush's new tax proposal and a prominent feature of political debate in the months before the survey—61% said no . . . asked whether the cuts should be made permanent . . . 60% said they didn't know. Asked whether his speeding up the cuts and making them permanent will mainly help high income, middle income, or lower income people, 41% said they didn't know."[18] Many people support the abolition of inheritance taxes even though these taxes are actually only levied on very large fortunes. The majority of Americans already do not pay inheritance taxes but they don't know that.

The familiar picture of elected representatives acting on the wishes of their voters is clearly quite unrealistic. Most of us are very poorly informed about the issues facing the legislators. We have no opinions on these issues or if we do, they often rest on misinformation. The men and women in Congress cast their votes not as they have been instructed by their own voters. Voters have no instructions to give because they do not understand the issues much of the time.

Discussion Questions

Poorly informed voters damage democracy. Would you support efforts to allow only those people to vote who have passed an exam on the political process and current affairs? What would we want voters to know before allowing them to vote? Give reasons for your answer.

The "Power Elite": The Role of Money in Electoral Politics

Elected representatives cannot possibly represent all the electors in their district because the voters hold contradictory opinions on many subjects. How do representatives decide whose opinion they will take seriously and whose interests they are going to defend in Congress or in the state legislatures? Running for office in our day is extremely expensive. Few candidates for public office are sufficiently rich to be able to finance their own electoral campaigns. Most candidates depend on donations to their campaign funds and those donations come from the rich who have money to donate in significant quantities. The opinions and interests of the rich therefore carry the day when legislators decide whose opinions and interests they will represent.

Although it is an old tradition in the United States to say that we live in a democracy where "the people rule," there exists an opposing tradition that asserts that, on the contrary, the country is run by a "power elite" that not only makes the important decisions but also, mostly through the mass media, manipulates public opinion to support the choices of the persons who really run things.

This tradition was given forceful expression by C. Wright Mills, a Columbia University sociologist, who in his 1956 book, *The Power Elite*, argued that our country is run by a coalition of powerful groups from the largest corporations and the military. The leaders of the corporations and the military, often persons who move easily from highly paid, high-powered private jobs into the government and back again to private industry, are the ones who decide what are the pressing issues of the day and what should be done about them. They do not respond to popular opinion but, on the contrary, shape popular opinion through the mass media, produced by large corporations, eager to cooperate with the corporate and military leaders of the power elite.[19]

A few years after the publication of Mills's book, President Dwight D. Eisenhower, himself a much respected military man, issued a warning similar to that uttered by Mills. The departing president warned the nation in his farewell speech in 1960 that we not allow the "military-industrial complex"—a formation much like Mills's power elite—to destroy our democratic freedoms and decision-making processes. He said:

> Until the latest of our world conflicts, the United States had no armaments industry. American makers of plowshares could, with time and as required, make

swords as well. But now we can no longer risk emergency improvisation of national defense; we have been compelled to create a permanent armaments industry of vast proportions. Added to this, three and a half million men and women are directly engaged in the defense establishment. We annually spend on military security more than the net income of all United States corporations.

This conjunction of an immense military establishment and a large arms industry is new in the American experience. The total influence—economic, political, even spiritual—is felt in every city, every State House, every office of the Federal government. We recognize the imperative need for this development. Yet we must not fail to comprehend its grave implications. Our toil, resources and livelihood are all involved; so is the very structure of our society.

In the councils of government, we must guard against the acquisition of unwarranted influence, whether sought or unsought, by the military-industrial complex. The potential for the disastrous rise of misplaced power exists and will persist.

We must never let the weight of this combination endanger our liberties or democratic processes. We should take nothing for granted. Only an alert and knowledgeable citizenry can compel the proper meshing of the huge industrial and military machinery of defense with our peaceful methods and goals, so that security and liberty may prosper together.[20]

Twenty years later, another former president took up the theme of the power elite. President Richard Nixon warned in his 1980 book, *The Real War*, that the country was run not by the people but by a power elite. He believed that this elite was composed of professional intellectuals, academics, writers, and such, rather than by corporate and military leaders. But he agreed that democracy was decaying; instead we had government by a power elite.[21]

More recently this belief in a power elite has been transformed into the view that the country is governed by the people with enough money to be significant financial supporters of individual members of Congress and of the state legislatures. These claims are supported by obvious facts. Since the advent of television, elections have become even more expensive than before. Politicians no longer woo the voters in person or by distributing handbills and buying rounds of beer in the local bar. They must now produce advertisements on radio and television. They must pay a professional staff to produce the ads and then pay very high prices for prime-time advertisements. These funds come from wealthy donors, most whom are large corporations or the chief owners and managers of them. Corporations and wealthy owners hire lobbyists to distribute money for them in the right places.

Discussion Questions

Offering cash to a policeman about to write out a ticket is corrupt and, in fact, illegal. What about legislators passing laws that favor industries who have contributed to the lawmakers' campaign funds? How is that different from offering a bribe to a policeman? Should we make all private campaign contributions illegal? Give reasons for your answers.

Lobbying is an old institution in the United States and dates back to the period of the founders, when politicians had occasional dinners with New York merchants. It became a more serious project during the administration of President Ulysses S. Grant after the Civil War. Today, lobbyists must register with the government and their activities are restricted by legislation. But lobbying has become very big business. Since the year 2000, the number of lobbyists in Washington has almost doubled; there are now about thirty-five thousand lobbyists in the nation's capital, trying to get the legislators to see things their way and the way of the lobbyists' employers. The majority of important lobbyists are former members of Congress or former employees of the government who abandon their elective office for work that may pay as much as three hundred thousand dollars per year for a well-connected beginner. Former legislators, familiar with the ways of Congress and with the current legislators, give up their roles as politicians for the much better paying jobs of lobbyists. Often close relatives of current legislators—their wives or sons or daughters—become lobbyists, as do former assistants to the president or the aides of various congresspersons or senators.[22]

Lobbyists have several jobs. They must present arguments to advance their employers' points of view with respect to some projected piece of legislation and try to sway the legislator to adopt that point of view. These days lobbyists even write legislation for the legislators who are too busy to do that work themselves because they need to spend so much time raising money for their reelection. Because legislators have more constituents than they can ever talk to, the question of who will have access to the legislator is of extreme importance. Ordinary voters rarely get a chance to talk to their elected representatives. One job of the lobbyist is to gain access to legislators. They manage that by virtue of another service they provide to legislators, namely contributing significant amounts of money to the campaign funds of politicians. Elected officials are fund-raising every day to raise the enormous amounts of money needed to get reelected. Lobbyists enable them to reach their fund-raising goals. Many representatives and senators have campaign funds actually managed by lobbyists. Lobbyists have access, and what is more, will be listened to more seriously than ordinary voters. Even if a delegation of voters from the representative's home district get to speak to the elected officials to explain a problem they need help with, their presentation will not be taken as seriously as that of the lobbyists who cannot only present a point of view persuasively but can also back their presentations with significant campaign funds.

Here is just one example:

> Hewlett-Packard Co., the California computer maker, nearly doubled its budget
> for contract lobbyists to $734,000 last year and added the elite lobbying firm of
> Quinn Gillespie & Associates LLC. Its goal was to pass Republican-backed leg-
> islation that would allow the company to bring back to the United States at a
> dramatically lowered tax rate as much as $14.5 billion in profit from foreign
> subsidiaries. The extra lobbying paid off. The legislation was approved and
> Hewlett-Packard will save millions of dollars in taxes.[23]

Another example of the effectiveness of lobbyists and their money—

> As a result of an elaborate system of price support programs and import tariffs
> and quotas . . . Americans pay artificially high prices for sugar, a practice that
> cost US consumers $1.9 billion in 1998. . . . One of the large sugar producers in
> Florida, Fanjul, contributed $ 350,000 to the Democratic and Republican parties
> in 1998. Complaints about terrible working conditions in the cane-fields and
> chemical runoff from the fields into the Everglades came to nothing. . . . the Fan-
> juls undoubtedly have unusual access to the highest levels of government.[24]

This access of the Fanjuls and of many other wealthy donors to campaign
funds—both corporate and individual—makes government much more responsive to the interests of the wealthy than of ordinary people. Pollution of
the Everglades, terrible working conditions in the cane fields, and artificially
high prices of sugar—these are not in the interest of ordinary voters, but only
in the interest of the wealthy. But these interests of ordinary voters are not
taken seriously because they are unable to contribute generously to campaign
funds. The government serves the interest of the wealthy. It is not government
for the people but government for the rich.

It is important to realize, however, that money, even very generously given
money, does not always have the desired results. There are many examples of
Congress passing laws in the interest of most ordinary voters and ignoring the
interests of the firms that lobby them and contribute lavishly to campaign
funds. During the second administration of President Ronald Reagan, Congress passed a tax reform bill that abolished a lot of special tax loopholes that
favored only the rich or large corporations. The leaders in Congress on this
bill were all known to have been cozy with lobbyists for many years; they had
never before shown any scruples against taking the money of the wealthy and
of big business. But this time, the internal stresses of this legislative process
produced a bill less favorable to the big money interests. More recently, in
2005, an energy bill was about to pass that allowed drilling for oil in the Arc-
tic Wildlife Refuge in Alaska, and that, in addition, contained many tax
breaks favoring energy companies. This in a time when energy companies

were earning large profits and the ordinary citizens' transportation and heating costs were skyrocketing. But then, something happened in the complex legislative process and the bill that finally emerged was relatively fairer to ordinary citizens. The folks with money cannot always have it all their way.[25]

Under a genuinely representative government everyone's interest would count equally, every citizen group would get equal attention to their concerns and legislation would try to be fair and address everyone's needs at least part of the time. Such is not our government because the people who have money to spend on behalf of legislators are much more likely to get their needs attended to. Not everyone has money to spend on lobbying. Not everyone has an equal chance to have legislators respond to their needs and to legislate in their interest. Moreover, the dominance of the people with money is firmly entrenched in a complex network of institutions, in the existence of lobbyists, in the private financing of campaign expenses, and in a political culture where representatives have no qualms about being cozy with the rich and ignoring the middle- and working-class voters except when they want those voters to reelect them.

Discussion Questions

What does the role of lobbyists tell us about electoral democracy? Can the ordinary voter really affect government policy by going to the polls? Give reasons for your answers.

Absentee Citizens?

So Do the People Rule in What We Call Our "Democracy"?

Imagine an owner who runs his business by coming around every two years and choosing someone to do whatever is needed during his absence. For the rest of the time the proprietor is somewhere else, preoccupied with other things and pays very little, if any, attention to his business. Would you say that this person was running the business? Much rather we would say that this person is an "absentee owner" who is not really involved in managing the enterprise. To be sure, the owner has property rights and pockets the profits from the business but does not manage it.

The role of the electorate in modern democracies is like that of this absentee owner. Some of them show up every two years and select the leaders of the enterprise but for the rest of the time other concerns take up their attention. These absentee owners are often poorly informed. Their choices of managers are not always felicitous and their policy recommendations frequently not in their own best interest. Most importantly one cannot really say that voters rule, for they are too passive and too disengaged from the government and the nation that they are said to rule.

Our democracy was different in the early years of the American republic. Citizens, even those who at that time were not allowed to vote, actively participated in public debates and political deliberation. Citizen participation remained high in the 1830s when the French aristocrat Alexis de Tocqueville visited this country. He observed vigorous public participation in the political affairs of the young nation:

> No sooner do you set foot on American soil than you find yourself in a sort of tumult; a confused clamor rises on every side, and a thousand voices are heard at once, each expressing some social requirements. All around you everything is on the move: here the people of a district are assembled to discuss the possibility of building a church; there they are busy choosing a representative; further on the delegates of a district are hurrying to town to consult about some local improvements; elsewhere it is the village farmers who have left their furrows to discuss the plan for a road or a school. One group of citizens assembles for the sole purpose of announcing that they disapprove of the government's course, while others unite to proclaim that the men in office are the fathers of their country. And here is yet another gathering which regards drunkenness as the main source of ills in the state and has come to enter into a solemn undertaking to give an example of temperance. . . . It is hard to explain the place filled by political concerns in the life of an American. To take a hand in the government of society and to talk about it is his most important business and, so to say, the only pleasure he knows. That is obvious even in the most trivial habits of his life; even the women often go to public meetings and forget household cares while they listen to political speeches. For them the [political] clubs to some extent take the place of theaters.[26]

All through the nineteenth century and the early decades of the twentieth century, party organizations worked hard to keep ordinary citizens involved in political meetings, in political campaigns and in the actual work of getting out the vote and voting. But all of this has changed. Today citizens are either completely disengaged from the political process or support specific projects dear to their hearts by sending money to professional lobbying organizations. The local party organizations, the ward committees, and all the other clubs and societies and neighborhood groups that participated in the political campaigns and involved individual citizens in the electoral process have mostly disappeared.[27] Political activity has fallen into the hands of full-time professionals who send e-mails encouraging us to contribute funds or click on their website to send a letter, already written, to our senator or congressional representative. Political activity requires a minimum of time, no effort—and no information. It requires some money, a computer, and a mouse—money to send to the local political candidates of your choice and a computer to click on a website that sends your elected representative a letter written by some political organization you trust. Citizen participation in the electoral process has become minimal. For those who are still active in politics it has become a job, their livelihood. They do not participate because they regard it as their civic duty or from love of country; they participate to earn a living.

Discussion Questions

1. *Do you think that we are really no more than absentee rulers of our country?*
2. *If so, is it worth the expense of millions and millions of dollars for electoral campaigns?*
3. *Has the time come to put an end to this pretense of living under a democracy?*

Give reasons for your answers.

REFORMING THE ELECTORAL PROCESS

In the preceding sections, we have examined a number of different difficulties with the existing electoral system. The first of these consisted of voter apathy. The electoral process lacks widespread support; many people do not vote and those who do often do not trouble to inform themselves about issues or candidates. Although there are, no doubt, many different reasons for that, one reason often given is the fact that in winner-take-all elections, the losers have no influence on the outcome, and worse, have no representative in the legislature and thus tend to feel that their vote was ineffective. Not being represented, voters lose interest, and when the next election comes round, they stay home.

An additional reason for voter apathy is found in the two-party system. Where there are only two competing candidates, each must garner a large number of votes. That encourages candidates to keep their message exceedingly bland for fear of offending anyone. Serious issues do not receive careful consideration; everything is touched on lightly and the public is being fed familiar bromides. The two-party system discourages serious discussion of the issues. Moreover candidates tend to tell voters what they want to hear; their messages do not represent principled stands but are tailored to the prejudices of different audiences. As a consequence, everyone knows that there may well be a startling difference between the promises made by candidates before the election and the policies they adopt afterward.

All of this encourages cynicism about the political process among voters and thus apathy and disinterest. In many other democracies, the political parties number in the twenties or more. Many of these parties are marginal, but a significant number of them do elect a few representatives and its voters can rightly believe that their point of view is aired in the discussions in the legislature. They do not need to feel completely unrepresented as do the losers in elections in the United States. In addition, where there are a large number of parties, each must be clear about its principles to distinguish itself from competing parties. Political discussion gains a bit of clarity. Candidates must provide some clear principles they stand for.

Discussion Question

Consider these criticisms of the two-party system and of winner-take-all elections. Which of them seem plausible to you? Give reasons for your answer.

Must we despair of electoral democracy? The defenders of alternative voting schemes believe that if elections were structured differently we would not feel the adverse effects of the winner-take-all elections or of the two-party system.

Proportional Representation

The defenders of an electoral system called "proportional representation" argue that although their system may not assure full-fledged representation for all the people, it provides considerably better representation for more voters than the winner-take-all elections we hold currently. In our present system, the country is divided into electoral districts in which the person who garners the most votes gets the job of elected representative. If the candidate elected is a left-leaning democrat, all the middle-of-the-road Democrats and the conservative Republicans in the district remain unrepresented. Only those voters get any representation at all who agree more or less with the person who has been elected. But, as we saw previously, in the average electoral district of six hundred thousand persons, so many different views exist that only a small minority of voters receive representation on any single issue. Because under the two-party system there are only two candidates, and because only one of them is elected, there is a wide range of voter opinions and voter concerns that remain unaddressed and a large number of people remain unrepresented.

There are a number of different versions of proportional representation. But all of them involve an arrangement where your vote is made to count even if your candidate loses the election. As a consequence this system of voting is much more responsive to the many different opinions of any group of voters. Accordingly, proponents of proportional representation claim that electoral participation in countries that practice proportional representation is much higher than in countries that have winner-take-all elections.[28]

Under the most common version of the system of proportional representation, the voters cast their ballot for a political party. Not only the traditional parties, the Republicans and the Democrats, but anybody who has a pressing political concern can form their own party and field candidates. The Greens, the Libertarians, the vegetarians, groups opposing abortion and defending family values, or groups that advocate the legalization of marijuana—all these and many other organizations—can offer platforms and candidates to the voters. Each party puts up a list of candidates and depending on the proportion of the total vote any group gained, one or more persons on the list is actually elected. The effect of such a system is that people who have specific concerns can try to find other like-minded people, and if there are enough of them, they can send one or more representatives to Congress who will be certain to speak for their specific concern. A wider variety of views will be represented among the elected politicians. There is a better prospect for individuals to be genuinely represented by the people they vote for. Such a system is not likely to represent all concerns of all voters; it still allows people to vote without being properly informed or to vote for a candidate for the wrong reasons. But it gives everyone a better chance of having some important concerns represented in public legislative discussions than they have under the existing system.

The results, the advocates of proportional representation claim, are much great voter interest. More opinions find representation; more opinions are therefore debated and often in more detail, and with more care, than in our elections. Electoral contests are more exciting. More voters participate and those who do are better informed.

Discussion Question

Get more information about proportional representation on the Internet. Do you think that the U.S. political system would function better if we adopted proportional representation? Give reasons for your answer.

DIRECT DEMOCRACY

Town Meeting Democracy

Here is a second difficulty with representative democracy: In a large country, elected assemblies are large and even so, every representative is voted into office by such a large number of people that the connection between voter and elected representative is inevitably tenuous. Individual voters rightly feel distant from their representatives, whom they usually do not know in person, and who may take stands different from theirs. These problems in any representational system do not exist where citizens participate in person in political decision making. They do not affect government through their representative but have themselves a chance to talk to their neighbors and together with them make decisions about government policy. This sort of political decision making is called *direct democracy.*

Direct democracy exists where citizens meet periodically to decide the issues facing their community. Tax rates or proposals for spending money are put before all the eligible citizens and decided by them in a public meeting. This contrasts with representative democracy where government policy is made not by the citizens themselves, but by elected representatives. Direct democracy is still in use in small towns in New England and in other parts of the country, and many thoughtful observers prefer it to representative democracy. Citizens can actively participate in decisions rather than someone else speaking for them or, as happens only too often in a representative system, being ignored entirely. But most people also believe that direct democracy is suited only to small towns. The policies of the United States as a whole are too complicated to be managed by all citizens together; the country is much too large for us to meet together for discussions of our common concerns.

Discussion Question

What, if any, are the advantages of direct democracy over representative democracy? Give reasons for your answer.

Most discussions of direct and representative democracy assume that the two systems are mutually exclusive, that we need to opt either for direct or for representative democracy. But that is an error. Not only is it possible to mix direct and representative democracy, but we are, in fact, already doing that. Small towns will arrange their affairs through direct democracy in periodic town meetings, but the citizens of these towns elect representatives to speak for them in state and federal legislatures. Even more interesting examples of this mixture of direct and representative democracy are the caucuses in Iowa and Nevada and several other states in which the citizens of those state choose candidates for the presidential elections. Most states hold primary elections, where each person enters the voting booth separately and records his or her choice on a ballot or voting machine. In the caucuses, by contrast, neighbors meet to discuss the different candidates, to explain their own preferences and listen to the thinking of their neighbors. A vote is taken only after several hours of conversation and attentive listening, after sharing information and perspectives on the different candidates. The meetings are a fine example of direct democracy even though they are only small steps in the complex national effort to select candidates for a presidential election.

The next section will introduce other forms of direct democracy recommended by many theorists and practiced in different places.

Deliberative Democracy

Many theorists deny that majority rule voting makes a government democratic. A government represents the people only, these critics insist, when its policies reflect the opinions, needs, and wishes of the people. Because ordinarily these needs, wishes, and opinions differ widely among the people, democratic government is impossible unless the rich profusion of popular ideas can be forged into some reasonably unified conceptions, sufficiently clear and nonconflicted to be effective guides for government actions. The electoral process is incapable of doing that; voting only counts up the numbers of supporters for different opinions. No unified policies can possibly emerge by that method. Only open discussion among all the people can produce something resembling a popular consensus; acceptable government policy can only result from the deliberations of the people at large. Popular deliberation, not voting, is the proper method for overcoming the many disagreements in any given group of people. Only where all the people deliberate together can we speak with any justification of government by the people.

In the electoral systems most familiar to us, policies are proposed to the electorate by the executive, or by legislators. In our system, proposals are often put forward by lobbyists and the industries or other private interest groups they represent. The people at large have the opportunity to say *yes* or *no*, but they rarely propose policies. This puts the people at large at a much greater distance from governing. To propose policies intelligently, one must have an intimate acquaintance with a particular problem; one must be knowledgeable about the policy proposals. If one's role is no more than approving or rejecting policies, one can afford to be much more distant from everyday affairs and problems. One need be much less well-informed, much less interested, much less involved in the day-to-day business of governing ourselves. The question concerning popular participation in formulation of policy directly concerns the extent to which ordinary citizens are deeply involved in their own government, or are, by contrast, fairly indifferent to the entire process.

An example may bring out the underlying issues in the debate between democracy as a process of voting and democracy as a people deliberating together to arrive at policies that are acceptable to all. Imagine that you belong to the management team of a small computer business. The managers have adopted democratic procedures in its decision making. Year-end sales figures have come in and are not encouraging; sales have shown a steady downward trend over the last year. It is clear that the company will go bankrupt unless management can reverse recent trends. Your group needs some new and exciting ideas.

A meeting is called. When it convenes, the chair could call for a set of proposals from different members, which would then be voted on after each proposal has been presented. The proposal that gathers the most votes would be adopted. That is the procedure that the CEO would follow if she believed that democracy consisted primarily of voting. But it would not be what most persons invited to the meeting would expect. They would look for a detailed presentation of the known facts. Then there would be an extended debate about how those facts are to be interpreted. Where should we look for the explanation of the company's problems: in the production process, in the price-setting mechanism, in sales, or is the problem, perhaps, industry-wide, rather than specific to the company? Only once the group has carefully reached some kind of agreement as to the most likely causes of the decline in sales, would the discussion be opened to suggestions for reversing current trends. When a group of people work together to solve a problem, meetings do not consist merely of voting on alternative proposals. Instead the group has extended discussions to get a clear agreement about the facts, about the most plausible interpretation of the facts, and about the relative merit of different proposals for solving the problem that the group faces.

Often such group discussions have an aspect of *brainstorming*. The hope is—and often that hope is fulfilled—that as the members of the group think together new ideas will emerge from the conversation. One person's idea is taken up and developed by another, and that, in turn, inspires a third one to make a suggestion that is utterly unexpected but really valuable to everyone. Groups working together often produce results that each member thinking alone would not have found. Such collective creativity is more likely when everyone is fully focused on the goal of solving a collective problem. To the extent that some members of the group consider only their private interest instead of thinking seriously about what might be the best for the group as a whole, discussions are less likely to be fruitful and innovative. Group deliberations do not merely pit private interests against each other; all members make a genuine effort to consider what is best for the group as a whole, not just for themselves separately.

Creative deliberation and discovery of new perspectives on shared problems emerge only to the extent that everyone participates in the work of the group. Large assemblies are unlikely to be innovative when they are addressed by charismatic speakers, while the majority of the attendees sit quietly and are essentially passive until it comes time to vote proposals up or down; their thoughts do not emerge from the interchange of the thinking of individuals. They are simply the reflections of the insights of a few powerful speakers that are accepted or rejected by the membership at large. Such large assemblies lack the yeast of widespread active participation.

Advocates of democracy as deliberation argue that if a nation faces problems, it, too, had best debate the issues extensively rather than subjecting different proposals to a vote or voting for different persons to resolve the problems. Procedures reasonable in solving concrete problems of private businesses are just as reasonable when an entire nation faces problems. The active participation of as many citizens as possible, talking with one another, striving together to understand their problems, and looking disagreements boldly in the eye are more likely to produce novel and useful solutions than simple up and down votes of proposals that did not emerge from group discussion.

This proposal for deliberative democracy takes different forms, but all inject an element of direct democracy into the democratic process. They all demand that, in one form or another, local groups meet together to discuss a problem. The policy-making work is not handed over to the elected representatives, or as is so often the case, to professional bureaucrats but is reserved for the citizens themselves who come together regularly to make policy for their community.

Is Deliberative Democracy Possible?

But with an estimated two hundred million voters in the United States that seems to be an unworkable idea. How can such large numbers of persons meet and deliberate with one another? This is a serious problem but is not as devastating an objection against the proposal of deliberative democracy as it may seem at first.

In the Jacksonian era of the 1830s, according to de Tocqueville, most citizens participated actively in political discussion and action. No decisions were made unless they had been discussed publicly first; policies emerged from these public discussions. Votes only came at the end of widespread, complex discussions in public meetings as well as in casual meetings around the kitchen table, near the town pump, or at the barbershop. Political deliberation was constant in everyday U.S. life. These discussions were not limited to official meetings called to decide matters of public policy but were an integral and important part of ordinary life; wherever two Americans met they continued the process of political deliberation. Participation in the decisions affecting the common good was everyone's work that all carried on in different forms, in different places.

That, you say, was a long time ago, when life was simpler, when the U.S. population was more homogeneous, and when there still was time for conversation in public. Today, many people say, everyone is too busy, too distracted by an affluent material culture and its attractions, and by many alternative forms of diversion. But in recent years, a variety of experiments have been made in different countries with a democratic budgeting process. Best known among those is the budgeting process in Porto Alegre, Brazil. Here, in a city of 1.3 million persons (or counting the population of greater Porto Alegre, of more than 3 million), the annual city budget is produced in a series of meetings in different parts of the city where ordinary citizens discuss and *decide* spending priorities for the city for the coming year. The budgeting process is taken out of the hands of the financial experts and professional politicians and entrusted to the citizens of the city at large:

> Participatory Budgeting (PB) programs are innovative policy making processes. Citizens are directly involved in making policy decisions. Forums are held throughout the year so that citizens have the opportunity to allocate resources, prioritize broad social policies, and monitor public spending. These programs are designed to incorporate citizens into the policy making process, spur administrative reform, and distribute public resources to low-income neighborhoods. Social and political exclusion is challenged as low income and traditionally excluded political actors are given the opportunity to make policy decisions. Governments and citizens initiate these programs to (i) promote public learning and active citizenship, (ii) achieve social justice through improved policies and resources allocation, and (iii) reform the administrative apparatus.[29]

Discussion Questions

Consult the Internet for information about participatory budgeting in Porto Alegre and elsewhere. What do you think of these experiments as alternatives to our representative democracy? What would it take for your hometown to adopt a similar budgeting process?

Give reasons for your answers.

This is one possible way of reintroducing an element of direct democracy into the democratic processes of large countries, such as Brazil, by using direct democracy to address only one of many tasks confronting government. The participatory budgeting process is employed with respect to only one, although a very central task of city government: making a budget. The city government has many other jobs such as maintaining public safety, building and maintaining roads and schools, securing public health through inspections of eating places and food stores, building and maintaining parks, and many, many more. All of these different tasks are only peripherally affected by the direct democracy of budgeting. In that way direct democracy can play a part in the government of very large countries. The Brazilian experiment is not the only one. There are many others.[30] Iris Marion Young, for instance, has pointed out that purely representative institutions can also take different forms. Voters can choose representatives but be otherwise totally uninvolved in the political process. Or alternatively, voters cannot only choose their representatives but have regular meetings with them to consult about current policy debates, to suggest ways to think about those debates before the vote, and to hear the representatives account for their actions after a policy has been adopted. In this second version of representation, elements of direct democracy are introduced into the electoral process.[31]

Discussion Question

Would you agree with Young that a representative system that includes extensive consultations between voters and representatives is preferable to one in which voters are essentially excluded from the political process once they have cast their periodic votes? Give reasons for your answer.

DEMOCRACY WITHOUT ILLUSIONS

Who Runs the Show?

So far we have discussed the ideal of democracy in which people govern themselves by going to the polls at regular intervals. The quotation from President Bush with which this chapter opened is just one example of this popular identification of democracy with regular elections. But we have seen, in the meantime, that this electoral democracy does not yield a full-fledged popular self-government. Nor is it altogether clear that the different remedies proposed will work to enable this sort of democracy to serve the purpose of citizens' self-government better than it does at present.

The identification of democracy with an electoral system paints a picture of our society as an association of people who vote periodically for representatives. The underlying assumption is that the citizenry is homogeneous; although specific groups may have different interests, no one has substantially more power than anyone else. Not only does every citizen have only one vote, but also all are more or less equal when it comes to political and economic power. The representatives elected by the citizens watch over and instruct the executive—the government that taxes, conducts wars, builds roads, and educates our children. All citizens work together to instruct and supervise their government.

But that is a grossly oversimplified version of how our society is put together.

Previously we considered the role money plays in our electoral system. That story suggested that the electorate consists of quite different groups: there are the common citizens who may vote but do not have much to say most of the time. But there are also people who have a great deal of power, either because they are rich or because they are prominent in the world of business and thus have means of pressuring the government. They exert pressure through campaign contributions or lobbying or by coercing local governments with threats of moving their plants elsewhere. Recall the story, in the preceding chapter, of General Motors (GM) threatening to move the Fischer Body Plant to a different state. Using this threat, GM prevailed on the city of Detroit to subsidize a new plant with cheap land in the city. A considerable number of ordinary working people lost their homes and were forced to move to make this land available to GM. The project might well have been defeated had ordinary people had a voice in the decision.

So our society does not only consist of the common voters and the government, but also of a group of persons who have a great deal of power and who shape national policy, mostly behind the scenes. The rest of us get glimpses here and there of their activities and influence when the wishes of the majority are being blatantly ignored in favor of a different policy. Clearly there are other persons and groups whose will the government follows before it follows the wishes of the common people.

But a more complete picture of society must also reckon with the government bureaucracy. In 2007, the federal government alone employed roughly three million people, working in a multitude of federal programs, bureaus, commissions, and offices. Joined by state bureaucracies and the bureaucrats of cities and towns, all these public employees keep control of citizens. Bureaucrats give permissions—licenses to get married, to parade down Main Street, to have a dog, to carry a gun, to sell liquor, to drive a cab, to run a restaurant, to add a room to your house, or to modernize your bathroom. Bureaucrats follow rules; they keep telling us that they do not make the rules. Although that may be true of the low-level bureaucrats that deal with the public, it is not true of the higher echelons of the government bureaucracy. Legislatures make laws that outline federal or state policies, for instance, for the protection of endangered species of animals and plants. One part of that legislation assigns the task of enforcing the law to an existing government agency or creates a new one. Before it can enforce that legislation, the government agency must issue detailed regulations; it must supply the specific details for enforcing the new law. Before, say, a logger can harvest trees in an area, studies have to be made to find out whether the logging threatens endangered species. If such species are found, the regulations prescribe what other steps are to be taken, what other permits have to be obtained, what are the methods of enforcing compliance with the law, what the procedures are preparatory to punishing infractions. These regulations are often only issued after first being published with public hearings held. But the bureaucrats who make the final decisions are not elected; they are not under control of the electorate. Public control over bureaucracies is extremely tenuous.

Discussion Question

Make as long a list as possible of all the records kept and regulations enforced by federal, state, and local bureaucracies. Do not forget libraries, taxi medallions, and liquor licenses. Do these bureaucracies limit the self-determination of voters?

When elections change the party in power and the individuals who fill prominent leadership positions, the federal bureaucracy remains unchanged except at its very top—the Secretary of Defense or the Secretary of State and other jobs of cabinet rank and their immediate deputies. The same is true of state and local administrative offices. When the people express opinions and desires through the electoral process, the bureaucracy remains unaffected. They do not have to pay a lot of attention to the will of the people. The bureaucracy is another center of power in our society and one that is only to a limited extent responsive to popular opinion as expressed in votes.

Discussion Question

Does this picture of our government being mostly run by the rich and powerful, as well as by the bureaucracy and its professional experts, strike you as plausible? Give reasons for your answer.

To the extent that real power is wielded by the rich and the leaders of large international corporations on one hand and by the bureaucracy that is minimally affected by elections on the other, the picture of our country as a democracy where the citizens run the government through the mechanism of periodic elections loses a good deal of plausibility. It pushes us to look for a different understanding of democracy, one that does not put much weight on the efficacy of elections or on the citizens' ability to determine current government policy.

Elections Do Not a Democracy Make

Democracy has existed since the early days of our republic. This is what it has looked like: sizable, well-organized, patient, and persistent groups of the people have been able to protest government policies and to change them, often only after *several generations* of protests. Democracy, in that sense, is a system in which the population at large is able to express its opinions and to try to win new converts to its views and is protected in its demonstrations and agitations against violence from other citizen groups and from the government. A democratic society is one in which freedom of speech, of assembly, and of petitioning the government are carefully protected even though the majority frequently abhors the opinions put forth by dissenting groups. Much of the time, many citizens have been able to express their views freely and have been able to practice the religion of their choice without having to fear violent reprisals.

To be sure, movements for the abolition of slavery, efforts to achieve equality for African Americans and for women, and struggles for working people to bargain collectively encountered their share of brutality and violence. Often the violence was from unruly mobs; sometimes the government itself, most spectacularly but not only in the case of Japanese Americans, used its power to incarcerate citizens regarded as a threat. We saw other examples of that in chapter 2. Without denying the constant threat of violence against persons unwilling to accept their oppression, especially against black persons, our country has been, compared to other countries, relatively free of constant supervision by secret police, by informers, and by the constant threat of imprisonment and death for those who were critical of existing economic and political systems. U.S. democracy is at its best when it provides relatively more security and a greater hearing for dissidents than many other countries. It enhances our freedom not so much by allowing us to vote but by allowing us to plead our case in the public arena *inside as well as outside* the electoral process.

Under this different conception of democracy, we are not flattering ourselves that each of us, each ordinary man or woman, rules the country through our elected representatives. But we understand that on issues that are deeply felt and unstintingly supported by sizable groups, the government will, sooner or later—often later rather than sooner—yield and follow the heartfelt will of the people. That is made possible by certain laws and constitutional guarantees, by institutions supporting the enforcement of these laws, and by a political culture without which the laws would be dead letters. We must examine each of these parts of this alternative conception of democracy in turn.

Violations of constitutional protections of citizen participation are illustrated by this report from Freedom House summarizing events in 2007 and 2008:

- In Russia, parliamentary elections were held under patently unfair conditions.
- Democracy in Georgia (once a part of the former Soviet Union), . . . was sullied by the imposition of a state of emergency and a violent police crackdown on demonstrators.
- In Pakistan, Benazir Bhutto was assassinated in the context of a recent state of emergency, intense pressure on civil society and the judiciary, and rising terrorism by Islamic extremists.
- In Kenya, hundreds were killed in rioting and mayhem in the wake of highly credible reports of vote rigging by the government in the country's presidential election.[32]

One of the favorite techniques of authoritarian governments is election rigging by stuffing ballot boxes or cheating on the vote count by preventing popular opponents from standing for election (putting them in jail on trumped-up charges or placing them under house arrest) or through political assassinations of opponents. Dissenters are prevented from openly presenting their views of the government and its policies. This is often accompanied or preceded by declaring a state of emergency when citizens no longer have the rights to assemble peacefully, to complain to their government, to form political parties and put forward candidates, or to hold rallies and do whatever else a political campaign requires. Under states of emergency the government can arrest citizens and keep them in prison for indefinite periods. If the courts are not independent from the ruling party, opponents of the government are unlikely to receive a fair trial, if they are tried at all. Populations are intimidated and the democratic process weakened by censuring media, closing down opposition newspapers and broadcast media, and prosecuting citizens who distribute political literature—all violent suppression of freedom of expression. Citizens intimidated in these ways have enormous difficulties creating and maintaining opposition movements.

For a democracy to work, citizens must have all the rights necessary for the political process to function: rights to assembly, to free speech, to vote, and to petition the government. But as the preceding examples of suppression of democracy show, none of these rights written down in a constitution is of much use to a population not protected by an independent judiciary—a judicial system that is not controlled by the party in power or by any political party. The right to assembly—which includes organizing political parties or holding campaign rallies—or the right to free speech—which includes criticizing the government and supporting opposing candidates—is worth little unless citizens who are arrested for assembling or speaking out will be defended against the government by an independent judiciary. Specifically important is the right of habeas corpus: if you are arrested, the police may not keep you indefinitely. You need promptly to be brought before a judge and arraigned. You must be told why you were arrested and you must be able to confront your accusers. You must be represented by an attorney and tried by a jury within a reasonable time. In many countries, where democratic institutions are feeble, the right of habeas corpus does not exist.

These protections are written into the U.S. Constitution:

Article 1, Section 9: The privilege of the Writ of Habeas Corpus shall not be suspended, unless when in Cases of Rebellion or Invasion the public Safety may require it.

Article 3, Section 2: The Trial of all Crimes, except in Cases of Impeachment, shall be by Jury;

Amendment 1: Congress shall make no law respecting an establishment of religion, or prohibiting the free exercise thereof; or abridging the freedom of speech, or of the press; or the right of the people peaceably to assemble, and to petition the Government for a redress of grievances.

Amendment 4: The right of the people to be secure in their persons, houses, papers, and effects, against unreasonable searches and seizures, shall not be violated, and no Warrants shall be issued, but upon probable cause, supported by Oath or affirmation, and particularly describing the place to be searched, and the persons or things to be seized.

Amendment 5: No person shall be held to answer for a capital, or otherwise infamous crime, unless on a presentment or indictment of a Grand Jury, . . . nor shall any person be subject for the same offense to be twice put in jeopardy of life or limb; nor shall be compelled in any criminal case to be a witness against himself, nor be deprived of life, liberty, or property, without due process of law. . . .

Amendment 6: In all criminal prosecutions, the accused shall enjoy the right to a speedy and public trial, by an impartial jury of the State and district wherein the crime shall have been committed, which district shall have been previously ascertained by law, and to be informed of the nature and cause of the accusation; to be confronted with the witnesses against him; to have compulsory process for obtaining witnesses in his favor, and to have the Assistance of Counsel for his defense.

The proper protections are all there, but as we saw in chapter 2, the Constitution as written does not enforce itself; if it is not widely supported among government officials, among judges, lawyers, and citizens, it can be violated by the government, and by a judiciary that lacks independence. A government is bound by a constitution only to the extent that it knows that attempts to manipulate elections or to deprive citizens of their constitutional rights in other ways will be met by massive popular resistance inside and outside the government. When, in times of national panic, as at the beginning of the war with Japan, most Americans are too frightened to worry about civil liberties, especially about the civil liberties of distrusted groups, the government is free to ignore constitutional protections of citizens. Democracy, electoral or otherwise, is safe only as long as there exists a powerful political culture supporting constitutional guarantees.

This culture is relatively stronger with us than in other countries that have different political traditions, but we know that it has repeatedly faltered in frightening situations. For a hundred years after the Civil War, African American efforts to win the same rights as white citizens were met with lynchings and state laws that clearly flouted constitutional guarantees, particularly the three Amendments to the Constitution passed after the Civil War, which were intended to assure former slaves not only of their freedom from slavery but of full citizenship. They had to fight for full citizenship for another hundred years and the fight is still not completely over. The U.S. political culture guaranteeing equal freedom to all failed seriously in relation to African American rights. Nor was that its only failure. Most recently there have been plausible allegations that before the 2000 presidential election in Florida, the state purged twenty thousand voters from its voter lists—most of them black and Democrats—on the grounds that they were convicted felons, whom Florida law does not allow to vote. Partial checks of those lists of supposed felons, however, show that 95 percent of the persons removed from the voting rolls had never been convicted of a felony.[33]

Discussion Questions

What are the contributions of individual citizens to a political culture that strongly supports democratic rights and protections? Do citizens have a moral obligation to contribute to this political culture?

Give reasons for your answers.

At the same time, our history has seen many conflicts over equal rights that improved the situations of those waging the battles: African Americans have managed to improve their situation, white women got the vote in 1920, and working people won the right to organize labor unions in 1934. War efforts in World War I and World War II won widespread support. The Vietnam War was soon intensely unpopular and that popular opposition contributed to ending that war after about fifteen years of protest and military failure in the field. Prohibition was widely hated and was finally ended due to that opposition.

An exclusive focus on electoral politics completely overlooks that U.S. democracy is at its best when minority opinions, the desires of the excluded and disrespected, are allowed to be heard and are able, sometimes only over a span of centuries, to alter public opinion in their favor. The people may not rule through elections in our country. They exercise limited power largely outside the electoral process because our political system allows them—most of the time—to do that. Those who are held at a distance from political power can make themselves heard—with reasonable safety. Elections should not be understood as mechanisms through which citizens rule, but as only one way in which ordinary men and women can state their opinions about the state of the country and its policies.

Discussion Questions

What do you think of this alternative conception of democracy? How responsive is our government to the views of the majority?

Give reasons for your answers.

KARL MARX AND ECONOMIC DEMOCRACY

Many theorists tell us that a free society can only exist if its economy is also free because it is organized around a free market in which all transactions are purely voluntary. In the preceding chapter, we examined some of the questionable aspects of this claim.

In that chapter we also examined the opposite position, that of the socialists, who argue that freedom of working people in a capitalist society is inevitably limited because only the capitalists have a say over the organization of workplaces; whether people work or not, the shape of their work life, and how much they earn is under the control of the capitalists. The outcome of that line of argument is that a socialist society provides greater freedom for all. The central impulse for socialist theories is the desire for a society where all are equally free and no one has power over the life of another. This was certainly the picture painted by Marx: the picture of a society in which everyone jointly ran not only the political system but also the economy. Although in a capitalist country the capitalists own and control the economy and run it for their own profit, Marx envisaged a socialist society where all the people also make economic decisions to meet the needs of all citizens.

In previous chapters, as well as in this one, we have seen some evidence that we are not all equal as citizens but that, on the contrary, in our society some groups of people have a great deal more economic and political power than others. The working life of many citizens is not so much shaped by them as by their employers (chapter 3); in politics the rich and the leaders of large corporations have disproportionate power (chapter 4). But actual socialist experiments as, for instance, in the Soviet Union and in China failed to increase citizen freedoms. Other regimes that have used the label "socialist" to describe themselves have often been thinly disguised dictatorships. In these systems, the idea of a socialist society in which all participate in running the economic system was transformed into an economy entirely run by the government. That increased the government's power enormously and allowed it to become plainly authoritarian. Both in the Soviet Union and in China, the hope that socialism would inaugurate a more ample democracy was soon disappointed. In its stead there developed a government that supervised all aspects of people's lives and enforced its often arbitrary will with widespread violence. The history of actual socialist regimes is not encouraging.

We face a dilemma. On the one hand capitalism seems to put serious obstacles in the path of genuine democracy. On the other hand, the experience with actual socialist regimes is extremely discouraging. The question remains whether actual economic democracy is possible.

Economic Democracy

Most of our waking time is divided more or less evenly between leisure time and work. Among the many things we do in our leisure hours, one is participating in the democratic process by informing ourselves, attending meetings, or going to the polls. We are free citizens during time away from work. Not so when we are working. The vast majority of workplaces are arranged in a pyramid of power: all important decisions are made at the top; from there directives pass down from manager to manager. The employees at the bottom take orders but have nothing to say. They are not free at work because they must do what they are told to do or be fired. The threat of losing one's job is always there. Employees are forced to obey their supervisor; in most workplaces they have little or no freedom.

Discussion Questions

If the company you work for pollutes the air, increasing environmental threats to you and your children, are you free to protest and demand that the company alter its policy? Does it matter whether you protest at work or away from work? Should you be able to protest and demand changes?

Give reasons for your answers.

But if democracy is so important, why do we limit it only to half of our waking lives? How can we proudly proclaim that ours is the land of the free when during every working day we are, in fact, taking orders and are forced to follow orders for fear of losing our jobs? Maybe we should amend this self-congratulatory formula and say that we live in the land of the free after work. Yet most people accept that state of affairs. Why does it seem so obvious that the boss in the workplace should give orders and not consult you and that you should have nothing to say over the conduct of the business you work for? Why should Rosalee have exclusive power over Roger's job, which is becoming more and more monotonous? (See chapter 3.)

When asked why workplaces should not be run as democratically as our political system, most people argue that the political arena is public, it belongs to all of us, whereas workplaces are, most of the time, privately owned. (Of course, even people working for the government do not participate in managing their jobs.) The business you work for is private property and its owners have the same rights to control their private property that all of us claim with respect to our own possessions. Workers' control over their workplaces conflicts with the owners' property rights.

But—as explained in the preceding chapter—private ownership of a house or a car is different from ownership of productive resources because they give one power over the work lives of employees. Consumption goods are used to feed and clothe people and otherwise to support their life. A house, one or more cars, a summer house, a boat, clothes—simple or fancy—affect the owners' own life, but do not give them any power over others. To be sure, the people who live in the fanciest houses in town, who wear the most elegant (and expensive clothes), and whose cars are the envy of all may be treated with a bit more respect in city hall or be listened to more carefully than homeless persons who appear before the city council in rags. But the real power of the rich rests not on their owning elaborate consumption goods but on their control over productive resources. The rich man not only impresses the city fathers and mothers by his custom-made suits but can get a respectful hearing for his ideas because he is always at liberty to move his business to a different town and take the jobs of a number of locals. The owners of productive capital can affect the lives of young people by contributing to summer jobs programs or by refusing to participate. They shape the physical appearance of the city by building malls downtown or perhaps contribute to the slow death of downtown areas by making large investments in shopping centers in the suburbs. They have many avenues for affecting the lives of fellow citizens; in many cities the clubs of the business owners have disproportionate political power because of their ownership of productive resources.

Ownership of consumption goods is altogether different from ownership of productive assets that give owners far-reaching political as well as economic powers—powers that do not come with owning consumption goods. One cannot defend the private ownership of factories, offices, and farmlands as instances of owning consumption goods because they are not. To defend private ownership of productive capital and installations one must justify a few persons having extensive powers over the lives and incomes of the majority of us. Advocates of workplace democracy recognize the power implicit in privately owning productive capital. They, therefore, advocate that workplaces not be owned by private individuals but by everyone who works there. Workers' control in the workplace requires worker ownership; worker managed workplaces must also be worker owned.

Discussion Question

Freedom, in a free country, should be equal for all. One person's freedom is limited by the equal freedom of all others. Why does that freedom end at the gate of the factory or the office door? Give reasons for your answer.

Worker-owned businesses have always existed in the United States. There are two forms of such worker ownership. One is a cooperative where a number of persons pool their resources to start a business and then run it jointly with every owner having one vote. If the business expands, and more workers are needed, the newly hired persons are usually expected to buy into the cooperative after a certain trial period. Except for some notable exceptions, most cooperatives are quite small with an average of thirty owner-workers.

Discussion Question

Look up the Mondragon Cooperatives on the Internet. Does that seem to you a good business model? Give reasons for your answer.

The other form of worker ownership is called an employee stock ownership plan (ESOP). These plans are supported by the government through various tax breaks both for the companies and the worker-owners. ESOPs are often started when the owners of a family-owned firm want to retire and sell the firm to the persons working for it. In this case, a trust fund is set up that holds all the stock in the company. Workers acquire ownership rights in some of the stock by investing their own money and by working for the company and getting stock ownership rights instead of cash wages, retirement, or other benefits. As time goes on, the employees own more and more of the stock.

Not all ESOPs are the same. In some companies, employees own only a small percentage of the company's stock; in others they own most or all of it. More importantly, in some ESOPs management is as top down as it is in other companies. But in others worker ownership is accompanied by workers participating in the management of the firm. In some, workers elect some members to the board of directors. In others, managers are elected by the workers, and workers participate in managing the workplace by participating in work teams and labor-management committees, and by discussing the current state and future of the firm in quarterly or annual meetings.

Many worker-owned businesses are small co-operatives—groups of ten to twenty persons who run a bakery, a print shop, or a small factory making T-shirts. But there are also large companies, well known to all, that are mostly owned by everyone who works for the company—from the cleaners to the CEO. Examples are United Parcel Service (UPS) and for a period United Air-lines. UPS has been thriving for many years and has made a successful tran-sition into the electronic age. United Airlines went bankrupt. Worker owner-ship has its ardent supporters and equally vocal critics. The critics point to United Airlines to show that worker ownership does not have any advantages. It does not make a company more efficient let alone more profitable. Sup-porters of worker ownership like to talk about UPS.

Thoughtful observers of worker ownership use the contrast between suc-cessful worker ownership and failed attempts to show that worker ownership needs to be done right. When it works well, workers are indeed owners not only because they own stock in the company, but because they know what they need to know to participate in managing their company. They are famil-iar with financial statements; they can read and interpret them. They are knowledgeable about the competitive pressures their company faces and have an informed opinion about the problems confronting it. Everyone in the com-pany must be committed to full participation of workers in the management of the company. Everyone must have opportunities to learn what they need to learn; essential information must be made available to all, and everyone must pull together to make their company succeed. That seems to be what is hap-pening at UPS.

At United Airlines, on the contrary, ESOP was a strategy used by some unions to gain greater control over management of the company. No one ever took the idea seriously that *all* employees would become full participants in the management of the company. Worker ownership as collective manage-ment was never tried and whatever benefits worker management may have, if it is done right, was not available in this case. Add to that that airlines are cur-rently going through a difficult time and that there are many bankruptcies in the industry and the failure of United Airlines does not imply that worker management can never work.

Discussion Question

There exists a good deal of actual experience with worker control. Look up a successful case and one where worker control failed and try to find out whether worker control is a good project or not. Give reasons for your answer.

About 8 percent of U.S. companies are worker owned in the form of ESOPs. In some cases these are simply devices to get some tax reduction for the private owners and management. In about a third of the ESOPs, however, workers participate to varying extents in the management of the company. A number of studies, including one by the Government Accounting Office (GAO) tend to show that ESOPs where workers participate in company management are more efficient and more profitable than comparable traditional companies. Workers who participate in managing their own work tend to work better, smarter, and more profitably. Worker management works.[34]

That serves to meet another frequent objection to worker management: namely that workers do not have the technical expertise to manage their workplaces. Experience shows that objection to be groundless. Any attempt at sharing the running of the company with everyone who works there requires, obviously, that everyone in the company have a lot more information about the health and well-being of the company than workers have in traditional companies. Worker control succeeds only if workers gain a good deal of information and skills which, in traditional businesses, are withheld from them. Workers in worker-controlled businesses become better educated. They learn whatever they need to know to participate effectively in running their workplace.

Worker control extends the freedoms offered by democracy to all of our waking lives. As long as the ordinary employee has the option of participating in the political process, however limited, in the ways examined in this chapter, but is no more than a cog in a huge machinery at work, we can hardly claim with a straight face that we are free. Today we are free in our leisure hours; when we work for wages we take orders and have no right to participate in setting policy. Freedom, as running one's own life, together with one's fellow citizens and fellow employees, is a real possibility only where democracy is extended to one's work life.

Discussion Question

Democracy in the workplace, like democracy in the political sphere, takes work and effort on everybody's part. Consider what you would have to learn to be able to participate in running your workplace. Do you believe that it would be worth your time and energy to learn to do that? Give reasons for your answer.

Review Question

Democracy enhances freedom. What form of democracy would provide the greatest freedom for citizens? Give reasons for your answer.

QUESTIONS FOR REFLECTION AND DISCUSSION

1. Consider this description of the electoral process in a small village in
   Afghanistan: "But walk down the main street of this bustling village
   south of Kabul, past the small shops near the main road, along the
   stream that feeds the small fields that provide much of the village's
   livelihood, out into the open desert where an arid wind whips the tat-
   tered flags that fly over old graves, and you meet Najibullah. His home
   is a large, square compound that looks like a medieval fortress. Behind
   these high, thick, sand-colored walls live extended families, the women
   kept out of view and everyone protected, once the metal doors shut,
   from the dangers of the night.

   "Najibullah, twenty-eight years old, was busy with preparations for
   his nephew's upcoming wedding, and it seems he had not gotten the
   word about how one talks about these first elections in Afghanistan.

   "'Karzai,' he said when asked whom he thinks people will vote for. But
   he was waiting to get word from the leader of the village council. Later on
   election eve, he said, an announcement from the loud speakers of the
   nearby mosque would summon the men to confer with Dr. Ziaulhaq. And
   then they would make their final decision. 'He is the elder of this village,'
   said Najibullah. 'Everyone will obey him, what he decides.'

   "Democracy, if you can call it that, collides in strange ways with the
   tribal system of Afghan village life. Dehnow is a mostly Pashtun village, and Hamid Karzai is a Pashtun. Even without the instruction of the
   leader of the village council, Dehnow would probably come out for
   Karzai. In Dehnow, like many villages across this remote and isolated
   country, decisions are made collectively, bubbling up from the three
   thousand families that live here, and trickling down from the elders who
   are village council members."[35]

   Question: The people in this Afghan village voted. The election was
   reasonably clean. Are they living in a democracy? Give reasons for your
   answer.

2. "Even a smart and hardworking person can rationally decide not to pay
   much attention to politics. No matter how well-informed a person is, his
   or her vote has only a tiny chance of affecting the outcome of an election. Since that vote is almost certain not to be decisive, even a citizen
   who cares greatly about the outcome has almost no incentive to acquire
   sufficient knowledge to make an informed choice."[36]
   a. Do you agree that it is a waste of time to vote in elections?
   b. If you agree, do you also think that democracy is an impossible dream?
   c. If you do not agree, why not?

3. In a nation of drug addicts, a referendum on legalizing drugs would predictably be approved. Suppose the majority of the U.S. people were addicted to hard drugs. Would it make sense to hold a referendum on legalizing hard drugs? Should the government do what people want or what is good for them?

4. Were President John F. Kennedy and his brother the attorney general, Robert F. Kennedy, justified in 1963 in nationalizing the Alabama National Guard to allow Vivian Malone and James Hood to enter the University of Alabama against the wishes of the majority of citizens of Alabama, whose taxes supported the university?

5. How do you know that your congressperson is doing a good job representing you in Congress?

6. In a book published about fifty years before American Independence, the great French Philosopher, Jean-Jacques Rousseau wrote, "No citizen should be rich enough to be able to buy another, and no one poor enough to be forced to sell himself."[37]

   a. Do you agree or disagree with that? Give your reasons.

   b. How does this saying reflect on the possibility of freedom and democracy in our present society?

   c. What are the implications of that view for government economic policy?

7. What is your assessment of the condition of democracy in the United States today?

NOTES

1. Robin Wright, "President Hails Election as a Success and a Signal," retrieved July 15, 2006, from Washington Post website: www.washingtonpost.com/wp-dyn/articles/A49115-2005Jan30.html.

2. Arthur M. Schlesinger, Jr., *The Age of Jackson* (Boston: Little, Brown and Company, 1945), 10.

3. Joseph Schumpeter, *Capitalism, Socialism and Democracy* (New York: Harper Torchbooks, 1947), 260–61.

4. Ira Katznelson, *When Affirmative Action Was White: An Untold Story of Racial Inequality in Twentieth Century America* (New York: W.W. Norton and Company, 2005).

5. David Estlund, "Democracy without Preference," *Philosophical Review* 49 (1990) 397–423.

6. Alexander Hamilton, John Jay, and James Madison, *The Federalist* (New York: Modern Library, n.d.), 243–44.

7. "Definitions of Democracy on the Web," retrieved October 21, 2006, from Google website: www.google.com/search?hl=en&lr=&defl=en&q=define:democracy&sa=X&oi=glossary_definition&ct=title.

8. "Trust in the government on the decline again," retrieved August 8, 2006, from www.govexec.com/dailyfed/0799/071399b1.htm.

9. *Worcester Telegram and Gazette*, December 9, 2005, A4.

10. Alexander Keyssar, *The Right to Vote: The Contested History of Democracy in the United States* (New York: Basic Books, 2000).

11. Sean Wilentz, *The Rise of American Democracy: Jefferson to Lincoln* (New York: W.W. Norton and Company, 2003), viii.

12. Edmund Burke, "Speech to the Electors of Bristol," retrieved January 29, 2008, from Electronic Resources of University of Chicago Press website: http://press-pubs.uchicago.edu/founders/documents/v1ch13s7.html.

13. "Congress should read Bills before Voting," retrieved March 27, 2008, from Fox News website: www.foxnews.com/story/0,2933,140204,00.html.

14. Jeffrey H. Birnbaum and Alan S. Murphy, *Showdown at Gucci Gulch: Lawmakers, Lobbyists and the Unlikely Triumph of Tax Reform* (New York: Vintage Books, 1987).

15. "Reich: Superficial Ethics and Voting Reform from Democrats," retrieved February 29, 2007, from Economist's View website: http://economistsview.typepad.com/economistsview/2007/01/reich_superfici.html.

16. *Boston Globe,* Monday, January 27, 2006, A1.

17. Alan Wolfe, *Does American Democracy Still Work?* (New Haven: Yale University Press, 2006), 24–25, 29.

18. Wolfe, *Does American Democracy Still Work?* 145–146.

19. C. Wright Mills, *The Power Elite*, (Oxford, Oxford University Press, 2000).

20. "Military-Industrial Complex Speech, Dwight D. Eisenhower, 1961," retrieved October 15,2 006, from Michigan State University, Matrix Courses website: http://coursesa.matrix.msu.edu/~hst306/documents/indust.html.

21. Richard M. Nixon, *The Real War* (New York: Warner Books, 1980).

22. Marion Nestle, *Food Politics: How the Food Industry Influences Nutrition and Health* (Berkeley: University of California Press, 2002).

23. Jeffrey Birnbaum, "The Road to Riches Is Called K Street," retrieved January 30, 2006, from *Washington Post* website: www.washingtonpost.com/wp-dyn/content/article /2005/06/21/AR2005062101632.html.

24. Nestle, *Food Politics*, 109.

25. Birnbaum and Murphy, *Showdown at Gucci Gulch,* 87.

26. Alexis de Tocqueville, *Democracy in America* (New York: Harper Perennial Library, 1988), 242–43.

27. Matthew A. Crenson and Benjamin Ginsberg, *Downsizing Democracy: How America Sidelined Its Citizens and Privatized Its Public* (Baltimore: Johns Hopkins University Press, 2002).

28. Ed LaBonte, Jr., "Proportional Representation," retrieved January 30, 2008, from http://ed.labonte.com/pr.html.

29. Rebecca Neaera Abers, *Inventing Local Democracy: Grassroots Democracy in Brazil* (Boulder: Lynne Riener Books, 2000).

30. Boaventura de Sousa Santos, ed., *Democratizing Democracy: Beyond the Liberal Democratic Canon* (London: Verso, 2005).

31. Iris Young, *Inclusion and Democracy* (Oxford: Oxford University Press, 2000), Chapter 4.

32. "Freedom in Retreat," retrieved February 5, 2008, from Freedom House website: www.freedomhouse.org/uploads/fiw08launch/FIW08Overview.pdf.

33. Greg Palast, "What Really Happened in Florida," retrieved February 5, 2008, from BBC News website: http://news.bbc.co.uk/2/hi/events/newsnight/1174115.stm.

34. John Logue, Jaqueline Yates, *The Real World of Employee Ownership* (Ithaca, NY: Cornell University Press, 2000).

35. "Staying Calm and Collective," retrieved August 8, 2006, from *Washington Post* website: www.washingtonpost.com/wp-srv/world/interactives/afghandispatch/afghan101004.html.

36. "Are American Voters Stupid?" retrieved August 8, 2006, from Cato Institute website: www.cato.org/research/articles/somin-040927.html).

37. Jean-Jacques Rousseau, *The Social Contract* (New York: E. P. Dutton and Company, n.d.), 11.

FURTHER READINGS

Paul Woodruff, *First Democracy* (Oxford: Oxford University Press, 2005). A readable and enthusiastic description of the democracy in Athens, Greece, that Plato was so critical of.

Alan Wolfe, *Does American Democracy Still Work?* (New Haven: Yale University Press, 2006). A summary of a large body of work in political science that documents the difficulties in our U.S. democracy.

James Fishkin, *Democracy and Deliberation—New Directions for Democratic Reforms* (New Haven: Yale University Press, 1991). A discussion of and argument in favor of deliberative democracy.

Rebecca Neaera Abers, *Inventing Local Democracy: Grassroots Democracy in Brazil* (Boulder: Lynne Riener Books, 2000). The participatory budgeting process in Porto Alegre, Brazil, and its political and historical background.

Jane J. Mansbridge, *Beyond Adversary Democracy* (Chicago: University of Chicago Press, 1983). A detailed study of direct democracy in small New England towns showing the complexities, advantages, and defects of such a form of government.

Lawrence Thornton, *Imagining Argentina* (New York: Doubleday, 1987). A harrowing fictional, but nonetheless realistic, account of life under the 1970s military dictatorship in Argentina.

John Logue and Jaqueline Yates, *The Real World of Employee Ownership* (Ithaca, NY: Cornell University Press, 2000). Worker ownership when it works well and when it fails and why.

Chapter Five

Why Is Freedom Important?

Vernon, California, is a small "city" southeast of downtown Los Angeles. Its five square miles are mostly industrial property with a workforce of over forty thousand during the day but a population of only ninety-one residents (according to the 2000 census). At the end of the working day, most of the inhabitants return to their homes in other sections of the greater Los Angeles area. Only the ninety-one actual inhabitants of Vernon remain. The city's website notes that it has a police department of over sixty officers who provide "high level security and a quick response time." That adds up to one police officer for every one and a half inhabitants, but the 5.2 square miles of industrial property must be patrolled even when no one is working there. The remaining third also works in city hall, the fire department, or the municipal power and light company. The city owns all the housing within its borders and subsidizes the rent of the city employees who live there.

Founded in 1905, Vernon has had only three mayors in its one-hundred-year history. The current incumbent was first elected mayor more than thirty years ago, in 1974. He is the grandson of the original founder, the first mayor of Vernon. The last election was held in 1980. The city has not held an election since then.

But all of that changed in 2006 when three persons moved in from outside Vernon trying to challenge the established power structure of this tiny town. The three candidates set up residence in a warehouse to run for office, only to have the city condemn the property and evict them. On at least two occasions, they were trailed by private investigators carrying unlicensed firearms. When that did not stop the campaign to bring democracy back to Vernon, the city called off the vote. The three challengers went to court and a judge ordered Vernon to hold a long overdue election for mayor and city council. After the election on March 11, 2006, for its eighty-six registered voters, the city clerk brought the locked ballot box to the city council chambers, and alleging challenges over voting irregularities, refused to count the votes.

The democratic system has completely broken down in Vernon. Its ninety-one adult citizens, living in city housing and employed by the city, are beholden to the mayor and the city council. They refuse to rock the boat; they do not demand elections because their economic security is more important to them than their freedom. They have willingly jettisoned democracy in their little town for the sake of keeping on the good side of the people who run it. For fear of offending the city fathers, from whom their paychecks come as well as free housing and other economic rewards, they surrender an important part of their freedom: the ability to choose their government. They have given up their right to participate, if only indirectly, in deciding how the city is to be run. In this chapter we will ask

- What moral commitments are required of citizens in a free society?
- Is freedom compromised when certain moral demands are made on all citizens?
- Can a society be truly free if citizens pursue only their self-interest?
- What is the role of the citizen in a liberal democracy?
- Why is freedom important?
- What is the price of freedom?
- What are the relations of freedom and violence?

Discussion Question

Because they all worked for the city, the people of Vernon saw that it was not in their interest to force the mayor and the city council to stand for election. If they annoyed the mayor, they might lose their job. Besides, things seemed to be going well for them, so why rock the boat? Were the citizens of Vernon right to give up electoral democracy because it was of no economic advantage to them? Give reasons for your answer.

THE GOOD CITIZEN

Toward the end of the last chapter, we encountered the idea of a political culture. The legal system of the United States tends to protect citizens' organizations and protests. Even when citizens challenge the government or powerful private groups, the legal system will protect them only to the extent that it has the wholehearted support of the courts, the legal profession, and many private citizens. The rock bottom foundation of our democracy is this political culture that values freedom and equality highly and is, in many situations, prepared to defend it. The health of our democracy depends, ultimately, on the citizens and their support. They remain free as long as they support their legal system in defense of critics, of unorthodox opinions, of dissident groups, and of open and uncoerced political debate.

There is little disagreement about the contributions good citizens make to the stability of the institutions of free societies. Everyone agrees that societies are strong and healthy when their residents are prepared to take their roles as citizens seriously. But what is the proper role of the citizen in a democracy? There exist at least three distinct conceptions of that in our political tradition. The first of these insists that good citizens must be morally good human beings. The second, quite different view holds that a democracy can thrive when all pursue their individual self-interest. Liberal political principles steer a middle course between these two extremes. We shall discuss these different views in order.

Good Citizens Seek Moral Excellence

The founders of the American republic would have been critical of the people of Vernon. They believed that a free society can only maintain itself if its citizens share certain important values and that those shared values need to be *moral* values. A free society, they thought, can sustain itself only if its citizens strive to be morally as good as they are able.

> Most of the debates in the Constitutional Convention centered around the structural allocation and balancing of political powers in the new government. There was no debate over the importance of religion and morality to the new government; . . . However angrily they might argue over points of constitutional structure, the American spokesmen agreed unanimously that it would take more than a perfect plan of government to preserve ordered liberty. Something else was needed, some moral principle diffused among the people to strengthen the urge to peaceful obedience and hold the community on an even keel. . . . Which were Americans to choose?
>
> The answer, of course, was virtue, . . . Samuel Adams spoke for all American thinkers when he reminded James Warren:
>
> "We may look up to Armies for our Defence, but Virtue is our best Security. It is not possible that any State should long remain free, where Virtue is not supremely honored."
>
> In addition to approving all recognized Christian, Roman, and English virtues, Americans singled out several attitudes or traits of special consequence for a free republic:
>
> * first, the willingness to act morally without compulsion, to obey the laws of nature as interpreted by reason and the laws of man as established in consent;

* second, the love of liberty, the desire for the adventure and sacrifices of free government rather than the false security of tyranny;

* third, public spirit and patriotism, defined by A Native in 1776 for the enlightenment of his fellow Virginians as 'a disinterested attachment to the publick good, exclusive and independent of all private and selfish interest.[1]

Discussion Questions

Do citizens in our democracy have any special obligations? Do we have an obligation to vote and to obey the law willingly (even if there is no chance of being caught breaking the law)? Are we obligated to consider what is good for all before we ask ourselves what would be good for us in any particular situation? Give reasons for your answers.

In our reflection about the role of the citizen in a democracy, we need to confront the opinions of the framers of our Constitution. We need to ask ourselves whether their demand for making morality central in the thinking of free citizens is legitimate. Before we can raise that question, however, we need to give some attention to the concept of morality itself. What is morality?

What Is Morality?

Most people will say that morality has to do with how we treat other persons, and if asked for examples, they often say that being morally good has to do with being kind to others, not doing them harm if that can be avoided, being truthful, and respecting the life, person, and property of others. There is disagreement whether it is allowed, morally speaking, to harm those who harm you.

But if you are kind to someone you love, are you doing what is morally right? Most likely not; consider this example. You are madly in love; you do whatever the other person wants and try, even, to anticipate his wishes. But then, just as the two of you are planning to go on a picnic, your grouchy Aunt Doris, who no longer drives, asks you to take her shopping. That is the last thing you want to do. You have never liked Doris a lot; she whines a great deal. But she is old, her kids live far away, and she is your mother's sister. Your mother has asked you for some help with looking after Doris. There is no moral issue about going on the picnic, but there is a question of whether it would not be right to go picnicking another day and go and help Doris do her shopping today as she and your mother asked you. Moral goodness has to do with doing what is right, such as being kind, even when you would prefer *not* to be. Perhaps you are really angry at someone and want to hurt him, as he has hurt you. You want to lash out blindly but then you restrain yourself and treat the other person as he deserves to be treated. You speak to him as calmly as you can at that moment and explain how his actions have hurt you. You control your anger. Now you are being morally good; you are doing what is right even though all your emotions cry out for harming the other.

Morality has to do with doing what is right (or wrong) in relation to other persons, especially when your emotions counsel a different action. Doing what is morally right is different from doing what you like or what you want to do from love. It is also different from being merely prudent, from doing what is in your own long-range interest. You would dearly love to borrow this sports car to feel how it drives, to glory in the wind ruffling your hair on this sunny afternoon. But the local police are good at tracing stolen cars. The joyride in the stolen sports car might cost you dearly and, you think, is not worth the months or years you might end up spending in jail. You are doing what is good for you. You are being prudent. But insofar as you follow the counsels of prudence you are not necessarily being morally good.

Morality is, above all, complicated. You may refrain from stealing the car because you figure it is not in your interest. But you may have additional reasons: You have promised to take care of your nephews and nieces—the children of your brother who was killed in the war. You cannot afford to get arrested because these kids need taking care of. Someone has to be there when they come home from school. One reason for not stealing the car is purely prudential—it is not worth the risk of going to jail. Another is moral—you have obligations to your nieces and nephews; for their sake you cannot afford to get arrested. Many acts can be viewed from various positions and sometimes people do the "right thing" for the "wrong reasons."

The subject of morality is full of disagreements and controversies. One of those concerns the difference between doing the prudent thing and doing what is moral. Clearly they are different. But can the same action be both prudent and moral, or are actions moral only if they are not motivated by self-interest? Philosophers disagree about that. Some think that duty, what we ought to do, is the essence of morality. Ethical systems resting on that central assumption are called *deontological* ethics. An act is moral if it is done because it is my duty, not because I want to do it, because I love you, or because I am very angry at you. Moral acts are also not done from self-interest. If I refrain from stealing a car because I know that stealing is wrong, I am acting morally, these philosophers say. If, on the other hand, I consider the likely consequences of stealing the car, I am being self-interested, rather than acting from my sense of moral obligation.

Discussion Question

Three men moved into Vernon from outside to challenge the failure of the city of Vernon to hold regular elections. Was that morally justified? Give reasons for your answer.

Not all philosophers agree that to be morally good, one must be acting from a sense of duty and from nothing else. Many think that when considering questions about morality, one may well consider consequences and thus an action may be morally right even though it is also prudent. Such conceptions of morality are, not surprisingly, called "consequentialist" ethics. The morality of an action depends on the consequences of the action. But there is a difference, these philosophers say, between choosing an action that is good only for me and one that is good for everybody or, at least, for the majority of people. Actions that are only good for me may be prudent but are not moral. Benefiting oneself only is being selfish; selfishness is not morally justified. Actions that have good consequences for many or for most people are moral—especially if what I do is best for the majority but not, in this particular case, for me. Philosophers who assert that those actions are good which have the best consequences for the largest number of persons possible are called *utilitarians*. Utilitarianism is one version of consequentialism. Deontology opposes all versions of consequentialism (see chapter 3).

Many philosophers insist on another characteristic of morality: its rules do not allow exceptions. Lying or stealing is widely considered morally unacceptable but when you make a mistake at work it is tempting to try to avoid a serious dressing down from your boss by telling a lie. The temptation to take something that does not belong to you is sometimes irresistible and one tries to explain how it is wrong to steal but that this case is different—one tries to make an exception. Moral rules do not allow that.

Discussion Questions

There are different kinds of exceptions to moral rules. We often make exceptions for small infractions. Telling what we call a "white lie" not to hurt someone's feelings seems all right to most people. But what about a different kind of exception, where I insist that everyone else must be truthful but I am willing to tell lies myself? In this case all the exceptions are for me; everyone else is obligated to follow moral rules in every case. What do you think of these two kinds of exceptions to moral rules? Are small infractions allowable as long as we observe moral rules in the big cases? Is it okay to demand strict adherence to moral rules from others but make exceptions for oneself? Give reasons for your answer.

The familiar Golden Rule has much the same implication: If you do not want people to deceive you or use your property without your permission, you may not lie or steal either. What you do not want others to do to you, do not do to them. What you think is immoral when other people do it to you, is equally immoral when you do it to them. There are no exemptions from moral rules.

What you expect others to do for you, you have to do for them. You are no different from everyone else. The same rules apply to all of us in the same way. They apply to all; they apply all the time. There are no days off in the moral life.

When we consider moral rules, we look at human conduct not merely in the perspective of our personal self-interest but from a more global, more impersonal and even impartial perspective. We consider what is right and wrong, understanding that moral rules apply to everyone and exceptions are not permitted. We distance ourselves from considering what is best for us by looking at what is right for everyone. Individual needs and desires that might tempt us to make exceptions for ourselves are discounted because we know exceptions will not be granted. We consider right and wrong independently of individual wishes. Some philosophers have referred to that as considering actions from a moral point of view.

The Founders Argue for Their Demand for High Moral Standards

Consistent with their belief that freedom requires high moral standards from its citizens, the founders feared that a society whose citizens are mainly selfishly motivated will not long keep its freedoms. We do not share that belief, on the whole, but it still resonates in our political discourse when we criticize politicians as being hostages to "special interests." We accuse them of serving particular groups rather than the common good. We talk as if we disapproved of self-seeking in political conduct even though, in actual fact, we accept it as a given that all political actors are primarily seeking the good for themselves and those who support them.

This issue whether democracy concerns itself only with the compromises between the self-interest of different parties, or whether democracy is about doing what is good for all, was central during the discussions of the Constitution in 1787. In chapters 9 and 10 of *The Federalist*, Alexander Hamilton and James Madison take up the issue of what they called "factions." Madison defined them as groups, either majorities or minorities, who support policies that are in their members' own interests rather than serving the public good. At times, factions support decisions detrimental to other groups and threaten the rights of those other groups. What they, at the end of the eighteenth century, called the problem of factions we call the conflict between private interest and the common good. Ideally we would like a political system where the elected representatives decide on the basis of what they consider to be good for all. In practice we are well aware that many decisions are made to benefit specific individuals or groups, even if those decisions are threatening the interests of the majority of citizens. We saw many striking examples of that in chapter 4, in the discussion of democracy and the special government programs to aid corporations.

Madison believed that the proposed federal republic whose blueprint our Constitution contains was designed so as to reduce the problem of factions as much as possible. He gives us several reasons for that. In the first place, the Constitution establishes not a democracy, as that word was used at the end of the eighteenth century, but a republic. Madison and his friends used the word *democracy* to describe a political system where the government was run by all the people. That meant that decisions about government policy were made in popular assemblies, which all citizens were entitled to attend. Everyone participated in popular decision making. Today we call that a *direct democracy*, contrasting it with a system in which the citizens do not run the government but elect representatives who do. A republic, by contrast, was what we call a *representative democracy*. The term *republic* referred to a system in which ordinary persons elected representatives periodically, and those representatives, not the citizens themselves, actually made laws.

Why did Madison and many others among the founders believe that a republic, or as we would call it, a representative democracy, would have fewer troubles with factions than a direct democracy? Why would interposing the representatives between ordinary citizens and the process of legislation protect everyone against the danger of private interests taking precedence over the public good? Madison believed that the electoral system would send the wisest, the most public-spirited representatives to Congress. Electing representatives, Madison thought, would "refine and enlarge the public views, by passing them through the medium of a chosen body of citizens, whose wisdom may best discern the true interests of that country, and whose patriotism and love of justice will be least likely to sacrifice it to temporary or partial considerations."[2] The people at large would elect representatives of exceptional wisdom, or as we might say today, people who were unusually intelligent and knowledgeable about political affairs. But what is more, the people would choose for their representatives persons of unusual "patriotism and love of justice"—women and men of exceptional personal integrity. If the elected representatives were exceptionally patriotic, if they were motivated by love of country, they would put the well-being of the entire country ahead of their own personal self-interest or the self-interest of some of their supporters. If they were persons of unusual love of justice, they would not pass laws that deprived some people of their rights or distributed resources unfairly. They would not, for instance, allow tax money to be used to enrich individual persons for that would do an injustice to the people who paid taxes.

The founders believed that a republic would be less likely to be seriously disturbed by factions, by the rule of groups we today call *special interests*, because the representatives elected in such a system would be persons of exceptional moral rectitude. They would be more firmly dedicated to the common good than the rest of us and more insistent on justice for all than we are. They would get elected, for that reason, and they would protect us against our inclination to put self-interest above public interest and to treat others unjustly if that turned out to be in our own private interest. The republic is protected against the evil of factions, of special-interest legislation, by the exceptional moral character of the representatives it elects.

The laws of a country will aim as far as possible at what is good for all or for the majority depending on the moral rectitude of its elected representatives. In this way the founders acknowledged that freedom and free institutions would work well only if the elected officials held tightly to certain moral values, to the overwhelming importance of pursuing the public good rather than private interests, and to the equally powerful role and importance of justice in the distribution of the benefits and burdens of government. Only if the elected politicians refrain from placing more burdens on some citizens than on others, and avoid distributing the benefits of government unfairly, will the republic remain untroubled by partisan strife and the disunity that flows from a government dominated by special interests.

Discussion Questions

Do you think that we and our country would be better off if our elected representatives were unselfish and public spirited as Madison demanded they be? What, do you imagine, might be done or what changes would we see if legislators refused to be swayed by the lobbyists of "special interests"? Give reasons for your answers.

Against the Founders' Demand for Moral Citizens

Government-Sponsored Morality Is Coercive

A society that believes that certain moral values need to be held by all will inevitably use legislation and government enforcement powers, or nongovernmental social pressure to assure that the desired moral ideas are shared and honored by all. The moral republic clearly threatens individual moral decisions and freedoms. Our history gives us many examples of the dangers of governments demanding that a particular morality be observed by citizens, and especially, by politicians.

The Puritans of the Massachusetts Bay Colony were quite ready to have the government limit the freedoms of citizens to aid them in their efforts to lead moral lives of self-denial. In colonial America, writes Columbia historian

Eric Foner, the idea of freedom was closely connected with Christian religion. "In the ancient world, lack of self-control was understood as a form of slavery, the antithesis of the free life. . . . This understanding of freedom as submission to a moral code was central to the Christian cosmology that suffused the world view of the early colonists. Christianity enshrined the idea of liberation, but as a spiritual condition rather than a worldly one. . . . the Puritan settlers of colonial Massachusetts, who believed their colony to be the embodiment of true Christianity, planted this spiritual definition of freedom on American soil. . . . this definition of freedom as flowing from denial and moral choice was quite compatible with severe restraints on freedom of speech, religion, movement, and personal behavior. Individual desires must give way to the needs of the community, and 'Christian liberty' meant submission not only to the will of God but to secular authority as well, and to a well understood set of interconnected responsibilities and duties, a submission no less complete for being voluntary."[3]

Freedom, in this traditional Christian view, consists above all of the self-discipline of Christians to resist temptation. They will honor God and their fellow human beings even when the temptation is overwhelming to stay in bed on a Sunday morning instead of going to church. Good Christians are free because they are not slaves to their selfish impulses or their bodies. Whatever forces may be assailing the Christians in pursuit of a holy life are overcome by the truly free. They are not obstructed in their pursuit of goodness by selfish emotion or the frailties of their bodies.

In a society where religious authorities were most intimately allied to political power, this conception of the freedom of the Christian easily flows over into political regulations of private life. The American Puritans were not an isolated example of governments that used coercion for the sake of supporting a distinct set of moral values. One hundred and fifty years later, the founders of the American republic held similar views, albeit a bit more moderate, to those of the Puritans.

The Massachusetts Constitution of 1780 "indicates something of the importance of government as a promoter of virtue. Not only did it nourish morality indirectly by encouraging and protecting, and perhaps supporting, the instruments of religion and education; it was expected to make a number of direct contributions: by passing sumptuary laws [laws regulating dress as well as consumption of food] 'to discourage prodigality and extravagance, vain and expensive amusements and fantastic foppery, and to encourage the opposite virtues'; by making proclamations from time to time of days 'of public humiliation, fasting and prayer'; and by itself operating at the highest level of justice, virtue, and incorruptibility. Preachers never tired of exhorting legislators and judges to be men of spotless integrity in both public and private dealings. Orators never tired of reminding the public that it should look for virtue before all other qualities in selecting candidates for public office."[4]

The founders had no doubt that high moral standards were indispensable to the continued health of their republic. They were also quite certain that the government played an important role in maintaining high moral standards of the citizens. Sometimes, the role of the government was direct, for instance, by passing laws that controlled consumption. Political leaders did not hesitate to exhort citizens to strive more earnestly for moral excellence. The citizen's morality was not regarded as a private matter but was instead an intrinsic feature of citizenship. At other times the government played an indirect role when it supported schools and churches whose task it was to shape the moral character of a new generation and to nurture the morality of current generations of adults.

Schools Should Build Character

The University at Cambridge, now known to everyone as Harvard University, was established faithful to the instructions written by John Adams. It considered one of its main tasks the moral education of the young men that attended the college, to "inculcate the principles of humanity and general benevolence, public and private charity, industry and frugality, honesty and actuality in all things, sincerity, good humor, and all social affections and generous sentiments among the people." U.S. colleges before the Civil War had two clear objectives: They aimed to build character and to instill mental discipline. To this end students had to learn classical languages as well as to learn to solve mathematical problems. Character was built by laying down extremely specific rules for behavior and requiring daily attendance at chapel services. "Rules of behavior were written in exquisite detail: Columbia officials took two full pages merely to describe the proper forms of behavior during compulsory chapel. Yale turned 'Sabbath Profanation, active disbelief in the authenticity of the Bible, and extravagant [personal] expenditures' into campus crimes."[5] Clearly educational authorities were concerned about the personal freedom of their students. They had no doubt that it was their job to instill values in the young men entrusted to their care.

Until the early decades of the last century college education had a distinctly moral cast, and it unabashedly tried to shape students to be moral persons. (Even today we hear many voices demanding that schools and colleges teach moral values to nurture good moral character in their students.) The ideal of the moral citizen was still dominant and had a clear effect on the extent to which educational institutions were prepared to supervise and limit the freedom of their students even though they were more or less adults.

Discussion Question

Provide as many arguments as you can for and against the view that it is the task of schools and colleges to mold students into human beings of excellent moral character.

The founders were willing to allow a direct and an indirect role to the government in producing moral citizens so that all could assure themselves of the integrity of elected officials. To nurture public morality, the government, in the past, was prepared to put some limits on public display of wealth by legislating what clothes people could wear. There was copious legislation regulating sexual matters—making adultery illegal, for instance, and even forbidding the sale of birth control devices or providing information about birth control methods. The government was also ready to encourage morality indirectly through support and financing of churches and schools. The effect, as some of the previous examples have shown, was to limit personal freedom. The founders faced, and we still face a dilemma: promote morality to have a more representative democracy or respect personal freedom and incur the risk of more self-centered and more easily corruptible elected officials who represent special interests rather than the bulk of their voters. It is pointless to demand high moral standards from public officials if one is not willing to promote those standards. But often efforts to foster morality infringe on what we consider today as our personal freedom—choices of styles of clothing, sexuality, birth control, personal conduct, or religion. Schools that promote morality may get praise from some parents, whereas others resent the school taking on a job which some parents believe to be theirs exclusively.

Discussion Questions

Which do you regard as more important: improving the efficacy of our democratic institutions through raising the level of honesty and public spiritedness of elected officials or the promotion of personal liberty?

Can we improve our democratic institutions without public meddling in matters of private consumption, lifestyle choices, and morality?

Give reasons for your answers.

Does the Common Good Exist?

Democracy can function well only if the representatives elected consider what is good for the majority—or so the founders believed. According to them the best political leaders care about the common good, not about their own interest. We have just seen one difficulty with that stance—namely that the price for producing public-spirited officials may be high in terms of personal liberty.

But another objection is often heard—namely that there is no such thing as an identifiable common interest. Especially in modern societies that are large and whose populations hail from different countries and bring different cultures with them on their migrations, it is impossible to find a set of values and goals that all groups would acknowledge as their ideal of a good life and a good society. Joseph Schumpeter formulated this difficulty clearly:

> There is, first, no such thing as a uniquely determined common good that all people could agree on or be made to agree on by the force of rational argument. This is due . . . to the much more fundamental fact that to different individuals and groups the common good is bound to mean different things . . . because ultimate values—our conceptions of what life and what society should be—are beyond the range of mere logic; . . . even if a sufficiently definite common good . . . proved acceptable to all, this would not imply equally definite answers to individual questions. . . . Health might be desired by all, yet people would still disagree on vaccination or vasectomy.[6]

No one set of general values exists that rational argument can show to be the best, the most desirable. Even if we could produce by rational reflection one set of general values that all would accept, endless controversies would erupt again once we tried to apply these general values to individual cases. Even if an abstract idea of the common good existed, there are no concrete understandings of the common good that all would share.

The common good to which the founders thought political leaders must be dedicated does not exist. What, in any given society, the leaders regarded as the *common* good was most likely a reflection of the ideas of the dominant classes of that society.

Discussion Questions

Do you agree with Schumpeter that there are no values that everyone would subscribe to? Do you know anyone whose conception of the good life includes ill health, falling victim to violence, poverty, and early death? Give reasons for your answers.

The ideal legislator, in the view of Madison, has his eye on the common good. The laws he draws up or votes for are intended to serve the advantage of the nation as a whole. He dedicates himself to the promotion of the good of all. A frequent criticism of this view points out that it is difficult to ascertain what the common good is. Particularly in a free society, there exist, as we saw in the first chapter, many controversies about the best policies to be adopted in

different areas. The situation in Vernon illustrates the difficulties of identify-
ing a common good. The democracy the three outsiders tried to restore in Vernon was not perceived by the majority as being in their interest. For the vast
majority, the existing suspension of the democratic process was not only acceptable but preferable. Until the outsiders came in and demanded regular,
democratic elections, the inhabitants of Vernon believed that their arrangement served the common good. Now three people are added to the ninety-one
inhabitants. Does that change the common good? Is the common good something that is literally good for everyone? Before we speak too comfortably
about pursuing the common good and how a politics that pursues the common
good is preferable to interest politics, we need to ask ourselves more carefully
what a politics of the common good pursues. Considering concrete situations,
we see again and again that anything like a common good is quite elusive.

Bitter struggles have always characterized our history. The disagreements
between abolitionists and slave owners were only settled by a bloody civil
war. The conflicts between large corporations and consumers continue to produce controversies, as do the conflicting interests between city and the agricultural countryside. The diverse interests of men and women have not been
laid to rest and neither have been the debates about abortion, pornography,
nor the conflicting claims of the environment and private property. Under
such conditions, does it make sense to ask representatives to legislate with a
view to the common good? Can they be expected to ascertain what that common good is?

The idea of a common good seems unobjectionable as long as we speak in
general terms. We know that liberty, prosperity, good health for all are important and that, insofar as we can promote them, we are promoting the common good. But of course we never promote liberty, for instance; in general,
we always do so by adopting specific policies. But when specific policies are
under discussion, agreement about the common good is often elusive. Not too
long ago, we discovered that the government had been listening in on over-
seas telephone calls of ordinary citizens without going before a judge and obtaining the warrants required by law. There is no reason to doubt that the authors of this policy believed it necessary to protect U.S. liberty. The policy's
opponents, on the other hand, were equally certain that warrantless spying
was a serious threat to liberty and therefore not in the common interest. We
may all agree that liberty is central to our way of life and we may all agree
that we must protect it. But here our agreement comes to an end. The *means*
necessary for protecting liberty are not self-evident. Different groups have
different proposals. It is difficult to decide between them.

In similar ways, persons of goodwill disagree on the best means for protecting and enhancing the well-being of our country. For many people it is of

the essence of protecting our way of life that ours be a "Christian nation." What is more, the advocates of such a view usually have a particular version of Christianity in mind that all Americans should, ideally, adhere to and practice. For others, on the contrary, it is of the essence of our way of life that people be free to practice different religions, or if they so choose, practice no religion at all. All agree that freedom of religion is important for the common good, but interpret that freedom in diametrically opposed ways.

There are similar disagreements about economic policies. For some a free market system with minimal government regulation is of the essence of the U.S. way of life. For others, the United States betrays its mission if the government does not remedy the excesses of capitalism displayed, for instance, in environmental degradation, in sharp inequalities, and in the suffering of the poor and the elderly. Different groups of the population have different visions of the good life. For some, rural communities with their center of gravity in the family and in local religious congregations are the epitome of what is best about our country. Others, more urban, more solitary and disconnected, praise the anonymity of city life. The individual's freedom to arrange his or her life is what matters most to this view of our country. Given those many disagreements, can we still urge everyone to make choices based on the common good?

These are powerful reasons for being skeptical of the traditional belief that a free country can exist only if citizens and the government pursue the common good. But perhaps that objection misunderstands what the concern for the common good consists of.

Rethinking the Idea of the Common Good

Regard for the common good means, in the first place, that we must be careful not to allow our self-interest to loom excessively large in our political deliberations. When we decide on policies, when we vote, we must do more than ask ourselves—is this good for me? We must consider the needs of our neighbors and the needs of other citizens and not just look at what will enrich us and those close to us. But once we consider the needs and interests of our neighbors, we need to consider them not only as they appear to us but also as those other persons understand what is good for them and what they see as being good for us. If democracy is not merely about everyone trying to get what they want, we must be prepared to discuss what is the best for all of our fellow citizens, particularly those who approach any particular course of action or proposed legislation from different perspectives than our own. Because it is by no means clear what, in individual cases, will promote the common good, and because different citizens have rather different ideas about that, a genuine dedication to the good of all centrally involves the willingness to discuss different ways of achieving the common good to reach agreement among as many people as possible about what we can best do to benefit everyone. The alternative to a democracy of self-interest is a democracy where public discussion is at the center. Political theorists often refer to this vision of democracy as *deliberative democracy* (see chapter 4).

It may well be true that rarely, if ever, a country as large as ours will find a common good—a concrete goal that all can agree is the best for all. But for all that, the idea of a politics aiming at the common good might still have some use. It remains an important goal for any political community to formulate policies and make laws that are, as far as possible, good for all as the different members of the community see it. It remains true that political leaders animated by the desire to come as close as they can in any given concrete case to a policy that is for the common good are more desirable than leaders that consider politics as the exclusive pursuit of their private self-interest.

The community that is seeking for the common good will conduct its political process rather differently from one in which politics is no more than the clash between different private interests. A political community in which the common interest moves people more often than their private desires is one in which there is genuine political dialog. In a society in which there are many sharp disagreements, the common good can be pursued only where the disagreeing parties speak openly and patiently with each other. Dedication to the common good requires a specific sort of public political discourse.

Discussion Question

Consider the common good as a goal, known to be unattainable but still good to aim at. Pursuing it will urge us to have conversations with our political opponents, which will clarify common goals even though we disagree in important respects. This will require genuine listening, tolerance of different opinions, and willingness to learn and to change. What do you think are the chances of establishing a democracy dedicated to the common good in this sense, where citizens are prepared to have productive conversations to thrash out important disagreements about ways of reaching the general aims everyone shares? Give reasons for your answer.

Good Citizens Pursue Their Own Self-Interest

There is a real conflict between the conception of the citizen held by the framers of the Constitution and the attitudes toward citizenship that are widely held in the United States today as exemplified by the people of Vernon. The people in Vernon considered democracy a system in which everyone pursues his or her interests and the resulting conflicts are resolved peacefully through negotiation and compromise. Citizens of democracies do not have any special obligations, certainly not *moral* obligations, as citizens. Perhaps—although even that is open to controversy—citizens have an obligation to go and vote. And, yes, they owe each other respect; they are obligated to be peaceful, honest, and willing to resolve conflicts through negotiation rather than through violence. Many Americans today have distanced themselves from the traditional belief that our liberties require from us a certain shared morality, a dedication to the common good as more important than private interest, a passionate commitment to freedom for all, and a firm determination to do what is right without being compelled by law or government. For us, the pursuit of self-interest often seems legitimate and dedication to the common good quixotic.

Democracy and Capitalism

Our ideas about our democracy have changed radically since the 1770s when our Constitution was crafted. One of the sources of this change was a book published in England in the year of the adoption of the Declaration of Independence. In 1776, Adam Smith published *The Wealth of Nations* in which he formulated some central economic principles of the capitalist system that was developing in England at the time. He believed that the division of labor—different people specializing in different work—and the free market promised a new and a more productive economy than the systems that preceded it. By specializing, people got to be more adept at their work. They could therefore produce more in less time. By adjusting supply to demand through the price mechanism, the market assured everyone that they could buy whatever they wanted as cheaply as possible and could, on the other hand, get the best price for their own products. What struck Smith about this market mechanism was that everyone who participated tried to do as well as they could for themselves. Everyone tried to meet their own needs and interests; by everyone looking out for themselves, everyone was better off. A system of enlightened selfishness, he thought, would produce better results than a system where most people tried to do good to others. Smith wrote:

> It is not from the benevolence of the butcher, the brewer, or the baker, that we expect our dinner, but from their regard to their own interest. We address ourselves not to their humanity but to their self-love, and never talk to them of our own necessities but of their advantages. Nobody but a beggar chooses to depend chiefly on the benevolence of his fellow citizens.[7]

The thought of Smith was restricted to the economy; he did not believe that all of our lives would or should conform to economic rationality and the pursuit of self-interest. But his economic principles soon were applied beyond their limits to different areas of everyday existence. Previously in this chapter, we encountered the moral doctrine known as *utilitarianism* whose point of departure is the thought that every human being seeks happiness for herself and that moral actions are those that satisfy this desire for happiness of the largest number of people. Here the picture of Smith's economic man who seeks economic advantage by buying cheap and selling dear is generalized into the entire moral universe, which is now described as a world where everyone pursues his or her own happiness. A bit later in the nineteenth century, after Charles Darwin's theory of evolution had been published, there arose a social theory often linked to the author Herbert Spencer that regarded all of human society as a battlefield. Here everyone tried to survive, if necessary, at the expense of their competitors, and in this struggle of all against all, so the theory went, the fittest would survive. Transactions in the society as a whole were only economic competition in a different guise, embellished with Darwinian conceptions that applied to finches in the Galápagos Islands but not so unproblematically to citizens of a free country. The ideas of Spencer are still with us. Some economists, for instance, have argued that families are best understood if we consider their members as independent economic actors who "invest' in the family with the expectations for certain "payoffs." Thus, Gordon Tullock argues that we can treat the family as a firm. Marriage is a contract between a man and a woman in which they commit themselves to certain rules. Making divorce difficult makes sense because no one would invest in the "firm" if they did not have some assurance that they have stable property rights in the enterprise. The difficulty of divorce assures the equivalent of that. The benefits of marriage are production of goods and services such as sex and children.

Discussion Questions

Would you be willing to rewrite Smith to say "it is not from the benevolence of the father, or the mother, or one of the children that we expect our dinner, but from their regard to their own interest. We address ourselves not to their humanity but to their self-love, and never talk to them of our own necessities but of their advantages"? In what ways does it make sense to consider marriage and the family as just another business contract? Where, if anywhere, does the analogy break down?

Give reasons for your answers.

This picture of more or less ruthless competition in the pursuit of one's own goals also, of course, affects our understanding of our electoral democracy. Writers about the economy glorify enlightened self-interest. Followers of Spencer (even if they have never heard of him) glorify competition as the best way to select the most competent, the most gifted, and the most valuable members of the society. Those notions affect how we understand democracy. In the eyes of Madison, elections serve to select the candidates that are most intelligent and most morally decent, who are thought to be most sincerely dedicated to the well-being of the nation as a whole. But today we believe that in elections, winning is everything, and we simply assume that those who are elected are the best candidates. Or if that is too absurd an assumption, we fall back on the idea that this candidate was the person whom his constituents wanted, or cynically, "the lesser of two evils."

The framers of the Constitution imagined a democracy where citizens elected the most public-spirited, intelligent, and farsighted candidates. Representatives were expected to possess exceptional integrity and devotion to the public good. Our view of a free society is different. We are content to have every person pursue his or her private interests and then hope that in the process of negotiation between conflicting interests compromises will arise which benefit the majority, if not all. When we consider the dominant political ideas of the late eighteenth century, we are tempted to accuse our ancestors of idealism, of being excessively optimistic about human nature and rather unrealistic about the ways of the world.

Madison and some of his contemporaries would point out to us that the politics of self-interest have many disadvantages — above all, that they do not produce a free country. A system like ours, they would insist, produces corruption and injustice.

Politics of Self-Interest: The Problem of Corruption

Many theorists believe that in a system of self-interested politics, corruption is the order of the day. If we are given license to do whatever is best for us — so the argument goes — we will not hesitate to take unfair advantage when that will bring us profit and property. A democracy that accepts the persistent pursuit of private interests virtually condones corruption. There are, of course, many different versions of corruption. Some are clearly illegal, such as paying legislators to vote the way one wants them to vote. Our democracy is plagued by a great deal of such illegal corruption. A recent report revealed that in the four years after September 11th, Federal Bureau of Investigation (FBI) efforts to uncover political corruption led to more than two thousand investigations of both national and state legislators and public officials. Plainly illegal corruption is rampant.[8]

But legislators decide what is illegal; they allow themselves practices which the rest of us may well consider questionable, such as receiving cash for their political campaigns as rewards for supporting legislation that favors specific individuals. Legislators have made it illegal to give money to elected representatives or other public officials for their personal expenses, but they allow attempts to influence elected officials in more subtle ways: by buying them dinner, taking them on trips, or collecting significant sums of money from supporters for the representatives' campaign funds. If legislators and citizens are motivated by their own self-interest, they may well throw their support to individuals and groups from whom they can expect wealth and power. They will be tempted to vote for the interests of large donors to their reelection campaigns; they will be likely to support legislative projects that will enhance their own wealth and standing in the world. When legislators vote their own interest, corruption is a genuine threat. Legislators may vote for the pet projects of persons from whom they can expect future benefits. The interests of the voters they represent may be pushed to the background; their votes are swayed by their own interests to maintain and enhance their power.

A study of the correlation between campaign contributions and state aid in Wisconsin between 1993 and 2004 showed that

> Overall, the 3,454 recipients of state grants, low-interest loans and tax credits received $771.3 million averaging $223,318 each.
>
> WDC [Wisconsin Democracy Campaign] found that 3,098 recipients, or 90 percent, who did not make campaign contributions received $402.7 million, or 52 percent, of the programs benefits averaging $129,990 each.
>
> Only 356 recipients, or 10 percent, had a track record of making large individual campaign contributions to candidates for the Legislature and statewide office. However, those recipients hauled in $368.6 million, or 48 percent, of the grants and loans doled out by the programs averaging $1,035,476 apiece.
>
> The campaign contributions from those recipients totaled $2.1 million from 1993 through October 18, 2004.[9]

Discussion Question

Giving a present to the letter carrier at Christmastime is not usually thought of as corruption, but giving a present to a policeman is suspect. Giving a bonus to your employees is surely acceptable. Giving a present to a legislator is questionable. Consider these and other cases to clarify the concept of corruption.

What we commonly refer to as *pork barrel legislation*—laws that favor specific constituencies in the district of a particular legislator and that do not even pretend to provide benefits for a larger group of people—is another familiar example. The representative from a particular district proposes a rider to a law authorizing spending a substantial amount of government money for some purpose that will please some of the representative's supporters. Representatives from other districts vote for that legislation in the hope that when their day comes to send some government money to their own district, other representatives will be supportive of that. The public interest is not at issue here. These pieces of legislation are intended to benefit the representatives who like to be reelected and, to achieve that, do special favors for important persons in the representative's district. Large construction projects—highways, bridges, sports palaces—are often built to benefit the construction industry and its workers. A recent and particularly startling example of that occurred when an Alaska legislator succeeded in having Congress vote more than \$320 million for a bridge connecting a town of eight thousand inhabitants to an island that is home to fifty persons. (The fifty inhabitants of the island currently reach the mainland by ferryboat.) The well-being of the entire population of the United States is not promoted by such a bridge. On the contrary, \$320 million are wasted which all the taxpayers of the country have to pay for.[10]

Discussion Question

According to Smith and most economists, everybody is better off in the marketplace if everyone looks out for himself or herself. Is that also true in politics, or does the pursuit of self-interest lead to benefits for the few to the detriment of the many? Give reasons for your answer.

Interest Politics Are Often Oppressive

When a government is dominated by factions or, as we say, dominated by the pursuit of self-interest, "the public interest is disregarded and . . . measures are too often decided not according to the rules of justice and the rights of the minor party but by the superior force of an interested and overbearing majority."[11] When the competition between different political groups aims at getting everyone what they want for themselves, the stronger party will not care about what is fair, or about the rights of the people who are weaker. If they can get away with it, they will perpetuate glaring injustices; they will, when possible, limit the freedoms of those who are losing this competition. Interest politics does not merely encourage corruption—both illegal and legal—but it threatens the freedoms of those who lose out in the competition, for when self-interest rules no one cares whether arrangements are fair to those who have less power; everyone only cares for their own good. Interest politics in that way are a threat to the freedoms of the weak, the unorganized. U.S. history provides familiar examples of that: slavery was enforced by laws made by elected representatives. It was enforced by U.S. courts and various arms of the government. The Jim Crow segregation that followed the Civil War into the 1960s was enforced by laws and state governments. The second-rate status of women and their lack of citizenship was similarly enforced by the law and the government. In each case the interests of a dominant group that had power deprived the politically weaker group of its liberties. Interest politics is a direct threat to freedom for all. The shameful treatment of American Indians over centuries was again and again endorsed and sanctioned by various legislatures and by the courts.

Discussion Question

Do you agree that a political system that encourages all to look out for their own interest is likely to be oppressive to the weakest group in the society? Give reasons for your answer.

The Citizen under Liberalism

It is difficult to determine what moral demands democracy makes on its citizens. The founders believed that moral excellence and dedication to the common good are essential if a republic is to flourish. But such a view easily degenerates into morally repressive regimes. The contemporary view that citizens need to look to their own interests, on the other hand, tends to foster democracies that are corrupt and oppressive to the weak.

Contemporary liberal political theorists address these dilemmas (see chapter 1). They side with the founders in their insistence that some moral qualities are essential to a just democracy, but, at the same time, they are aware of the dangers of a government trying to mold the moral character of its citizens. A healthy democracy, they therefore argue, requires only a limited set of commonly shared and observed moral values and is, on the other hand, adamantly opposed to what they call "perfectionism"—the idea that the moral character of citizens is a legitimate concern of the government. All persons have "life plans"—conceptions, more or less clearly articulated, of how they want to live, what is most important in their individual lives, and what will allow them, at the end of their days, to regard their life as a good one. An important mark of a free society is that our separate life projects are a part of our private domain and may not be judged or regulated by the government.

Citizens of a free society need to agree with each other that freedom is of central importance and that everyone is entitled to equal freedom, including an equal access to opportunities. John Rawls and his followers add that where inequalities between citizens exist, they must be justified by showing that they are in the interest of the worst off. It is in the interest of janitors, maids, and others who work for a minimum wage, that good health care be available to all. Thus we can justify paying doctors a lot more than minimum wage.

Beyond these basic principles of justice, which everyone must accept, each is able to choose a life plan and to adhere to it throughout their life unmolested by government pressures to live according to a different plan. But what if one's outlook on the world is inconsistent with the basic principles of justice? Take as an example a patriarchal subculture that assigns husbands a dominant role in the family, while women are no more than handmaidens to the man who has all the power and makes all the decisions, while his wife and daughters cater to him devotedly. Such a way of life will mesh uneasily with a political culture that insists on the government taking measures to assure full equality for women. The patriarchal family is characterized by property arrangements that leave women economically dependent on their husbands, restrict their capacity for working outside the home, or deny them having money and property of their own. As a result, a significant number of women find themselves impoverished when their husbands leave them after fifteen or twenty years of marriage, with several children, no work experience, and few skills for making an independent living. According to Rawls, the most illustrious representative of this political liberalism, "It seems intolerable that a husband may depart the family, taking his earning power with him and leaving his wife and children far less advantaged than before."[12] Clearly that sort of inequality calls for some government action, but prohibiting patriarchal families is not an option. To do so would be to allow the government to take sides for and against alternative ways of living one's life, and that, political liberals insist, is unacceptable. A government fully committed to equal freedom for all, as well as to respecting individual life choices, will have to negotiate many conflicts between public dedication to equal freedom for all and the respect for the private life choices of citizens. Rawls recognizes that but appears hopeful that these conflicts can be resolved fairly in all cases.

Discussion Question

Consider in detail what a government must do to assure equal freedoms to women, within the family, without interfering with the life choices of those who want to live in patriarchal families.

WHAT IS FREEDOM?

We began this book with the idea that to be free is to be able to do what you want. This refers primarily to *personal* freedom—the freedom to decide, for instance, what to wear, whom to marry, and where to work and to live. But this kind of personal freedom, the ability to make choices about one's everyday life, is actually compatible with being quite restricted in one's life. Even prisoners may have a range of personal choices: whether to write home or not, what to do with their leisure—watch television, read books, work out in the gym—who to make friends with, and how to deal with hostile inmates. There are many situations in which prisoners may choose to do what they want even if, overall, they are not free. Even persons whom we would not ordinarily regard as free, such as inmates of prisons, often can do as they please.

Discussion Question

Many people tend to define freedom as "being able to do as one pleases" without realizing that even people in prisons who are not free for other reasons can often do what they please. How would you amend this popular definition of freedom to render it more adequate? Give reasons for your answer.

A different kind of personal freedom was mentioned in the preceding section: the freedom to choose one's way of life. This freedom concerns fundamental choices—whether to live a religious life or not, and if so, what religion one will follow; whether to live in the city or in the country; whether to be always at the edge of the latest fashion as opposed to following one's own sense of dress and home decor, oblivious to what the taste makers decree. Some lives are turned inward, focused almost exclusively on the family; other persons seek to become leaders in their community or to play a role on the national scene. Some do this for the sake of fame; others want to make the world better for their fellow citizens; they seek a life of service.

Discussion Questions

What is your chosen life project? To what extent do you make choices to shape that plan on your own, and to what extent do you inherit it from your family and social environment? What deliberate choices are you making to direct your life according to a definite plan?

Freedom requires more than the ability to do what one wants: such personal freedom exists only where social and political institutions make it possible. Guarantees of free speech or of freedom to be politically active count only where institutions exist that protect and enforce these freedoms. Where law and order have broken down, citizens are limited in what they can do. They are always threatened with sudden and unforeseeable assaults and robberies; they may need to flee at a moment's notice. Living in abject poverty, homeless, or persecuted for one's race or religion, one's personal freedom is limited, as is the personal freedom of persons physically limited when their society does not provide special access to buildings, signing for the deaf at public events, or special assistance for the blind. All of us depend on the social institutions around us for our personal freedom. The question of what freedom is can only be answered satisfactorily by talking about the society in which one lives and how it manages (or fails) to assure personal freedom to its citizens.

Discussion Questions

What personal freedoms do you possess? What social institutions make those personal freedoms possible? What further personal freedoms, if any, would you like to have? How would existing institutions have to change to enhance your personal freedoms? Give reasons for your answers.

The founders, as we saw previously, were not primarily interested in personal freedom. Hence they cared little about government influence on one's way of life, one's religion, one's sexual behaviors, and even one's ways of spending one's money. The freedom of individuals, they believed, depended on the freedom of their society. Societies were free if, in external relations, the nation did not have to submit to the will of any other nation. Internally citizens were free if they, too, were not subject to the will of another. For that purpose, they needed to be able to participate in running the government through democratic institutions, and they needed to be protected against the possible violence of their neighbor by the government which they helped run. Of central importance to the founders were two kinds of freedom: political freedom—participating in republican government—and freedom of property—having one's ownership rights firmly protected. Other kinds of personal freedom counted for relatively little.

When asked what freedom is, many people answer by mentioning political freedom. They answer that to be free is to be able to vote—that is, to speak one's mind even if one is critical of the government or other powerful persons. Political freedom includes the ability to have meetings without being molested by the police or by bottle-swinging thugs; it includes the ability to organize political parties, to present grievances to the government. All of that presupposes, as we saw in the preceding chapter, a political culture that is vigilant in its defense of political freedom and a court system that is not subservient to one political party or another or bought out by the rich.

Another kind of freedom is freedom of property (see chapter 3). Everyone wants secure tenure of their property. One wants to be safe from home invasions, car theft, muggings, as well as identity theft and other newer, more high-tech forms of invading one's private property. In addition, property freedom also refers to the existence of a free market where all transactions are voluntary and uncoerced. The freedom of the marketplace may be impaired by government regulation, and also by private violence—the cop on the beat who takes it for granted that he gets free cups of coffee at the diner; the local crime family that breaks the plate-glass windows on stores that do not pay for protection.

Freedom presents itself in other guises. Artists and writers want creative freedom; they detest having to defend themselves against legislators or government bureaucrats. They do not want the government to decide what art is obscene or in some way politically incorrect. They do not want to be pressured by authorities closing exhibition space to artists or musicians or denying paper to writers to print their books or articles. Nor do they want to be hounded by ecclesiastical authorities for producing images or texts that offend the priests, rabbis, or imams.

Discussion Question

Compare the relative importance of personal and political freedom. As you think about your freedoms, which seems more important: participating in the common government or being able to make a range of personal choices about clothing, food, sex, the family, and so on? Would you be willing to live under a dictatorship if only your personal freedom were intact? Give reasons for your answers.

Republican and Liberal Conceptions of Freedom

The republican conception of freedom originated in the republics in Northern Italy in the fifteenth century. Freedom in these city-states referred, in the first place, to the external independence of these small states. Citizens of Venice or Florence considered themselves free when they were not dominated by other states. Citizens *within* these city-states were free if they were safe in their homes and if their possessions and their families were safe from those who governed the city-states or from others who were richer and more powerful. Freedom of the citizen meant, above all, the personal security of each citizen. But that personal security required that no one be excessively powerful and able to threaten the security of others. Thus the republican freedom, in the sense of security, came to be connected with various arrangements where these republics were governed, subject to some decisions of all male citizens. The Italian republics in that era contained different classes of citizens who differed in their occupations, their wealth, power, and social status. A free republic was one that was not only self-governing, instead of being governed by foreigners, but also one where the different classes were well balanced so that none had excessive power and all could feel secure in their families and possessions. These republicans agreed with one another that such a state of balance between different classes of citizens required citizens who for love of their city-state put aside all ambition for greater wealth or power. Civic peace and security was possible only where citizens were public spirited, where their love of country held in check their personal ambition and greed. Civic peace required citizens who were honest with each other, who possessed the integrity not to take or offer bribes or indulge in other forms of corruption. Civic peace also called for citizens who put the well-being of the entire republic over the advancement of their specific family or clan.

Republican freedom, personal security, was attainable, they thought, only in a city-state whose citizens were equally balanced in power. Such a balance could be maintained only if citizens shared a set of moral values with one another: they needed to be honest and incorruptible; their devotion to their country and to the good of all must outweigh personal ambition or ambition on behalf of their extended family. Republican freedom could exist only among men who subscribed and practiced a clear set of moral virtues. Among republican theorists, then and now, the word *virtue* was and is in frequent use and plays a central part in the conception of republican freedom.

It may appear that this idea of freedom is much like the liberal idea of freedom more familiar to us. But this appearance is misleading. Missing from republican freedom is the stress on *individual* freedom. Liberalism is focused on the individual and her freedom. A society aspiring to liberal freedom will be at great pains to leave a large space for individual choice. Where liberal freedom prevails, individuals choose their own occupation, their friends, and mates, and the place where they live. They choose their own religion and the moral values they adopt and decide to observe. A liberal government will stay out of moral controversies; it will not demand that citizens adopt a particular way of life. It will not demand that citizens put the well-being of the country above their own interest because it will not make any moral demands on its citizens at all. In this way, the individualism of liberalism, with its insistence that individual choice, for instance, of moral values is essential to freedom, differs sharply from a republican conception of democracy where it is taken for granted—as it was among the founders of our country—that freedom can only prevail when the citizenry shares a set of clear moral values.

Autonomy

One kind of freedom not previously mentioned is *autonomy*. The forms of freedom discussed so far all depend on societal institutions that facilitate personal freedom as well as property freedom and political freedom. The concept of autonomy draws attention to the fact that institutions make freedom possible, but actual freedom also requires the deliberate efforts of individual citizens. Populations that revere a leader, who not only shapes their opinions but makes important choices on their behalf, have surrendered their autonomy. They repeat what the leader says without thinking for themselves; they are happy to play the roles assigned to them by the regime. They do not want to run their own life but prefer to have someone else tell them what to do.

Political freedom depends on societal institutions but also needs individuals willing to make thoughtful choices instead of allowing others to make choices for them. Political freedom does not only require citizens who think independently of the government. It also needs citizens who are willing to act to maintain free institutions. Political freedom cannot exist if citizens do not want to participate in the political process; if they are too busy with other things to inform themselves about the issues that face their nation; if they have no time to go to meetings or to go and vote. Today many people say that they have no time to participate in making public policy; other things are more important. Their political freedom is of relatively little importance to them; they are willing to have others run their lives for them. They have chosen not to be autonomous. If the government chooses to restrict personal freedom, to limit choices of available goods, to decree how citizens should dress—think here of the Muslim headscarf for women or mandatory beards for men—or how they should conduct their private affairs, these citizens, who have given up their political freedom, may have no alternative but to surrender their personal freedom also.

Autonomous persons think for themselves. They do not allow others to run their lives but try to make their own decisions. They do not defer to political authorities, to cult leaders, or to the head of a sect. Nor are they dominated by their passions. They are able to resist desires of the moment if they believe that their long-term goals are better served by not spending money now, or by staying at work rather than taking the day off. Autonomy requires that one be able to choose the less pleasant alternative of the moment for the sake of reaching long-range goals one has set for oneself. One must be able to contain one's rage, to keep opinions to oneself rather than blurting out whatever comes to mind; one must consider other persons and not only the urgency of one's own needs. Autonomy requires a certain amount of self-control that allows one to be independent of the emotions of the moment.

Another version of autonomy draws attention to the fact that our freedom also depends on us in this other sense: my freedom is limited to the extent that I am not able to overcome emotions and desires that threaten to interfere with what I would like to do. Obvious examples are addictions: I would very much like to be a good parent to my children but am hopelessly addicted to alcohol and that makes me as bad a parent as my father was to me. Some persons are excessively fearful and thus cannot pursue the projects they have chosen for themselves because of the risks involved. Being excessively timid, one is unable to stand up for oneself against the insults of a boss or a domineering parent or sibling. Lack of self-confidence often interferes with choices one would like to make; one sabotages oneself by one's fear that one would not be able to bring the project to a successful conclusion.

It is difficult to live free without encountering conflict. If I exercise the freedoms guaranteed me as a citizen in the political process, I will certainly encounter others who disagree with me. I will find myself embroiled in sharp disputes or perhaps in physical violence. If I am serious about everyone's freedom, not only my own, I will clash with those who profit from the oppressions of others, and once again I have made enemies. In the workplace, being morally demanding of one's self and others may lose one a job or make one sufficiently unpopular to ruin one's career. Sticking to one's determination to live free is often frightening. One must be brave, one must be fearless, and one must trust one's own perceptions and must be willing to make considerable sacrifices if one is really to live free in our world. One must be able to overcome one's fear of opposition, of losing one's job, of the hostility of opponents, and of being ostracized in one's community. Resisting all those emotions so that they do not deflect one from the path one has chosen for oneself requires self-discipline and self-control. Living free requires a strong character and the willingness to brave opposition, dissent, and difficulties. One must overcome one's fears, one's desire to be loved by all, and one's desire for a life that is smooth and free of conflict. One must be self-disciplined and have one's emotions under control.

In the era after World War II, the United States experienced a long period of prosperity. The middle class grew and moved out to the rapidly expanding suburbs. Consumption, seriously restricted during the war years, became a major preoccupation. Pressures for conformity grew; political dissent came under sharp attack. (See the discussion of McCarthyism in the 1950s in chapter 2.) At the same time, many complaints were heard about a numbing conformity spreading through the country, making us uniform, no more than passive consumers. Americans, many commentators thought, were losing their individuality and autonomy. They were forgetting the enthusiastic advocacy of being different, of thinking for oneself, and of living as one chose by U.S. writers of the late nineteenth century—writers like Ralph Waldo Emerson, Henry David Thoreau, and Walt Whitman. Instead, we had become time servers, fearful conformists, unthinking, timid, and lacking in imagination.

In the streets, the young rebels of the 1960s took on this conformist version of the United States by proclaiming that all must "do their own thing." Philosophers responded to these anxieties about lacking autonomy with more esoteric discussions that urged us to seek autonomy in order to be "our own" persons or to "own oneself." These discussions soon made clear that autonomy is a complex idea that may be described in quite different terms. "In these different works 'autonomy' is used in a variety of senses: as an equivalent to liberty . . . as equivalent to-self-rule or sovereignty, . . . as identical with freedom of the will. It is equated with dignity, integrity, individuality, independence, responsibility, and self-knowledge . . . qualities of self-assertion, with critical reflection, with freedom from obligation, with absence of external causation, with knowledge of one's own interest."[13] Another author describes autonomy as follows:

(1) the wish to be different; the wish to be unique; the wish to go off in one's own directions; the wish to experiment, to wander, to float;

(2 the wish to be left alone; the wish to be uninvolved in somebody else's game; the wish to be unobserved; the wish to be mysterious, to have secrets, to be thought undefined;

(3) the wish to be unbeholden; the wish to own oneself;

(4) the wish to think, judge, and to interpret for one's self;

(5) the wish to feel real, not dazed and the wish to live, not to play just one life-long role, or perform just one lifelong function; . . .

(6) the wish to find one's self, to find the 'real me'; to be oneself rather than somebody else's idea of that self; the wish to be reborn as one's self.[14]

The idea of autonomy is complex. It includes thinking for one's self rather than depending on others to make decisions for one; living according to a life plan that one has made oneself; being independent, and not owing anyone anything; being different from others, being unique; and being in charge of one's own life; knowing what one wants and pursuing it; being "real" or "authentic" rather than play-acting to please others. Autonomous persons are said to "own" themselves; they are thought to be in control of their lives. These different aspects are distinct. One may think, and think logically, for oneself but be dependent on others, for instance, for a job or emotional support. Many people have definite ideas about how they should live and are vocal about those ideas, but when they come home at night they expect their spouses to serve them dinner, bolster their self-esteem, and take care of the children. They have their own life plans, but they are also dependent on others. People who think for themselves, on the other hand, do not all have clearly formulated life plans. They may think well but do not have a clear idea of what to do with their lives. Other people's thinking is chaotic and does not come to clear conclusions about what they would like their life to look like. They think, but their thinking is disorganized. Others may know what they want, but are not always able to pursue it. "I would like to travel and find romance in exotic countries far away but I am stuck in a low-paying job because I have to support a retarded sibling." We must think of autonomy as a complex bundle of fairly vague aspirations rather than as a single clear idea.

How much autonomy should one aspire to? Some people choose quite deliberately to limit their freedom for the sake of living and working in a hierarchical organization where they take orders and follow the commands of their superiors. Such choices are required if you join the military, if you join one of many religious orders, or if you subject yourself to the leadership of a cult. Some religious women believe that their role as wives demands subjection to their husbands, taking orders from them and being subordinate to them. Such roles are often chosen after careful deliberation. Shall we say that persons are autonomous who, on considering the matter with great care and as rationally as possible, decide to subordinate themselves to a religious order, to the upper echelons of any group, or to one specific individual—a leader or a husband? Choices of this sort meet some of the requirements for autonomy: they have been made deliberately after careful reflection. They are not imposed from the outside; they are not made carelessly or from a desire to do what others expect of us. They are the person's own choice, even though the choice consists of restricting one's own ability to choose freely.

There are many kinds of freedom and those who treasure freedom may well treasure different conditions: the freedom to make personal choices, to participate in government, to trade freely in uncontrolled markets, to run one's own life, and to be sufficiently self-disciplined to withstand one's own impulses and desires. Many of these freedoms presuppose a complex institutional framework of more or less impartial police forces and a court system that serves the demands of justice instead of a specific political party or powerful social group.

Discussion Question

Which of these freedoms do we have in mind when we call the United States "the land of the free"? Give reasons for your answer.

Feminist Critiques of Autonomy

These different versions of autonomy have been a powerful force in U.S. history and in our reflections about our lives. Autonomy has been an important ideal. But beginning in the 1970s, feminist theory has raised some important criticisms of this ideal. Women have pointed out that many of the most vocal advocates of autonomy were married men. After they finished their days, for instance, writing eloquently about autonomy and individual independence, they returned home to a dinner cooked by their wives who had, in the meantime, looked after their children all day, sending them off to school in the morning, and then supervising homework and play in the afternoon. These same wives were expected not only to have and raise children, but also to make a comfortable homes for their husbands, to help these husbands in their lives—think about politicians' wives expected to stand by their man during electoral campaigns regardless of the man's infidelities—by entertaining their friends or customers, and by being supportive to their autonomous husbands when life challenges them. The ideal of autonomy and personal independence, the feminist theorists have pointed out, is advocated by men who completely overlook the many different ways in which they are dependent on their wives and children, on their friends and coworkers. This ideal distorts the real situations in which we work and live in complex social networks that shape us as much or more than does our independent thinking. The ideal of autonomy misrepresents the social situation on which everyone, even the most autonomous man, depends for their thinking as well as their personal, material well-being.[15]

Another important aspect of this critique of autonomy is more political. The traditional praise of autonomy was implicitly limited to the autonomy of men. Married women did not have the same autonomy. They were not thought—until the last fifty years—to be deserving or capable of autonomy. Their role was, and to some extent remains, to be the providers of comfort and warm family life for their husbands and to care for children. The entire conception of autonomy was, according to the feminist theorists, a means for claiming freedoms for men which were not equally open for women and to assure men of the continued services of women. It was at the same time a theory to justify the glaring inequality between men and women where women provide support of many different kinds to men, but men, most of the time, are pretty oblivious to the needs of these women and to the great debts they, as men, owe to women. The ideal of autonomy was often a thin disguise for male neglect of the women they depended on, for glaring ingratitude women without whom their lives would be pretty miserable.

Discussion Questions

Can you be a good parent, willing to make serious sacrifices for the sake of your children, and still be autonomous? Is there a conflict between being a good parent and freedom?

Can the autonomous person take the advice of an older person about important decisions such as choice of job, of life partner, or concerning one's relations to one's parents?

If you share your life with another person, can you still be independent? If you love other people your well-being depends on theirs. Does that compromise your autonomy?

Give reasons for your answers.

WHY IS FREEDOM IMPORTANT?

Americans do not ask about the importance of freedom because we assume that the answer to this question is self-evident. Freedom, we think, is obviously important. What is more, its importance is so incontrovertible that asking for reasons to support it sows doubt where none is appropriate. We might just as well ask why love is good for raising children, or why it is good to enjoy a good meal or a sunny spring day.

But philosophers, as I said at the end of the first chapter, see their task as asking questions where most people do not think that questions are in order. What is more, we saw at some length at the beginning of chapter 4 that some philosophers have raised serious doubts about the value of freedom. Freedom, Plato argues, is not good for those who are unable to make the right choices. Most of us are competent to make good choices in some areas but are not equipped to make good choices in others. This applies most obviously in political matters, but also in one's personal life. We do not always understand what is good for us—witness the fact that half the marriages in the United States end within a few years. Half of us make the wrong choice when we choose a partner for life and many do that more than once. We are willing to admit our inability to make good choices in matters of morality or political principle; in religious worship the faithful acknowledge the superior stature of, say, Jesus, Mohammed, or the rabbis as teachers of morality. We are willing to subordinate our freedoms to great teachers of morality. We would often do better to allow others to make important life choices for us.

Despite these opinions, discussed previously, we persist in the confidence that freedom is undeniably good—so good, in fact, that its goodness does not need arguing. If philosophers insist that we give them a reason for believing that freedom is good, we give the obvious answer that being free consists of being able to do what one wants and being able to do that is preferable to having to do what one, often, does not want, but is forced to do. Freedom allows one to please oneself and pleasing oneself is preferable to pleasing another. A student once described freedom as being able to choose each morning what clothes to wear that day. Freedom allows us a large range of personal choices in everyday life from small matters like what to wear to important issues such as one's work, one's intimate partners, one's religion, and one's political affiliations. Freedom is valuable, from this view, for the pleasure it gives us when we can choose what we want. Meeting our needs and fulfilling our desires gives us pleasure; freedom allows us to choose to live as we want and thereby pleases us. Freedom is important because it adds pleasure to our life.

Discussion Question

Freedom allows us many choices. But choosing is often difficult and occasions serious anxiety. Choosing a marriage partner, buying a house, or having children or not—these and many similar decisions are difficult to make. Consider all the painful choices life presents to us. Make a list and then ask yourself again whether being able to choose is an unmixed blessing. Perhaps freedom is not an unmitigated good? Give reasons for your answers.

We know that some things we like are actually bad for us but we are not always able to resist the temptation, however hard we try. Being able to please ourselves in those ways, strictly in the short run, is not good for us; neither is the freedom to do so. Not all freedom is good—only freedom that does not damage us in the long run. Nor is freedom always pleasurable. On the contrary, it often confronts us with decisions that cause us tremendous anxiety. We call on consultants to help us make financial decisions, to tell us how to decorate our house, how to lay out our garden, or to help us shop for clothes. We consult psychologists to help us raise our children; in our marriages we follow the advice of marriage counselors. The tremendous popularity of self-help books testifies to the sense of many people that they cannot run their own life without help. Freedom is a burden and they want help to lighten it. Free choice is often too much, and we, in fact, avoid it where we can. We cannot justify the importance of freedom by the pleasures derived from doing what one wants.

We need a more comprehensive explanation of the importance of freedom.

Freedom Is the Opposite of Slavery

Many persons argue that freedom is important because free men or women are not slaves. The idea of freedom developed over several millennia in opposition to the institution of slavery. Toni Morrison observes that for the new Americans, it was easy to understand what freedom meant and why it was important because they always had the example of slaves before their eyes.[16] Freedom meant, above all, not being a slave.

Many slaves worked hard but never prospered. Their clothes were ragged; the cabins where they lived primitive. Others did much better. Amartya Sen observed that some slaves were more comfortable than many free blacks, but they were not better off than those who were free.[17] They were, after all, still slaves, and the burden of slavery consisted not merely of hard work and physical deprivation. Slaves were not members of society. They were disrespected. They were not allowed any dignity, for instance, when their bodies were inspected as if they were cattle for signs of health or illness in the public slave market. They could not run their own lives; their choices were made for them. Their lives were organized and regulated by others. They were completely powerless:

> Mr. Reed, a former slave interviewed in 1930:
> The most barbarous thing I saw with these eyes . . . I had a sister, my older sister, she was fooling with the clock and broke it, and my old master taken her and tied a rope around her neck . . . just enough to keep it from choking her—and tied her up in the back yard and whipped her I don't know how long. There stood mother, there stood father, and there stood all the children and none could come to her rescue.[18]

The idea of freedom evolved in contrast to the institution of slavery:

> Slavery is the permanent, violent, and personal domination of natally alienated and generally dishonored persons. It is, first, a form of personal domination. One individual is under the direct power of another or his agent. In practice, this usually entails the power of life and death over the slave. Second, the slave is always an excommunicated person. He, more often she, does not belong to the legitimate social or moral community; he has no independent social existence; he exists only through, and for, the master; he is, in other words, natally alienated. As Aristotle observed, 'the slave is not only the slave of his master; he also belongs entirely to him [and has no life or being other than that of so belonging].' Third, the slave is in a perpetual condition of dishonor. What is more, the master and, as we shall see, his group parasitically gain honor in degrading the slave.[19]

Masters have the power of life and death over their slaves. In the ancient world, slaves were usually prisoners of war—enemies one could have killed but instead made into slaves. To be a slave is to be virtually dead. The slave belongs to the master who can do with his property as he pleases. He can use it or misuse it; he can take good care of it or destroy it. You can take excellent care of your new car and clean it and wax it once a week and polish it lovingly in between. Or you can choose to let out your anger and frustration at the world by taking a sledgehammer to it. The slave, as one more item of property, may be used or abused in the same way. In losing freedom, the slave loses the right to life.

Slaves all are completely dependent on others, even for their very existence. They are not persons in their own right. They have lost one of the essential attributes of humanity—their independence, their autonomy, and their self-determination. As a consequence, they have no social standing; they are not members of any human community. That means, in practice, that they are invisible. One can speak about anything one wants in their presence. One can denigrate and insult them in their hearing. One can engage in private acts when they are in the room because they are not really present as human beings. They are more like a piece of furniture or a pet. In the street, one could walk right through them; they, of course, need to yield. Unless one chooses to, one need not think about them or provide for them. Slaves are valued only as economic investments, not as persons. They are things.

They are, for that reason, dishonored. One does not owe them respect. Worse, it makes no more sense to show respect to a slave than it would to show respect to a chair or a hound. We show respect to persons whose competence we admire, who have done great things to gain everyone's admiration. We show respect to the rich for their possessions, to athletes for their skill, to the old for the wisdom they have gathered over the years. We show respect to those who have power over us to placate them, such as the supervisor at work, even though privately we consider him incompetent. We even show respect to those whom we regard as bad human beings. When Saddam Hussein was taunted before his execution, public opinion recoiled. Even a bloody dictator deserves to be treated respectfully in the moment of his death. But not so a slave. Not belonging to the human community, slaves are dishonored. They have no more claim on anyone's respect than does any chattel, any inanimate thing or animal. They may receive good treatment or bad, but they cannot be respected.

To be free, fundamentally, is not to be a slave. As a free person, one has some independence. One has a right to one's life; one belongs to the human community. One is entitled to respect if only for being human, for having the possibilities of human beings, for being capable of pleasure and pain, and for being capable of good and evil, of love and hate. Being free, human beings have rights; they may make claims on others. Conversely, others are entitled to respect from them. From the slave you do not expect respect but at best the loyalty of a dog who has been well taken care of and knows better than to bite the hand that feeds him. Like a domestic animal, the slave lives among humans but does not belong to the human community.

We now see a more powerful reason for valuing freedom. It underlies human dignity, the requirement that one be treated with respect. We expect respect only from other free persons. Only the free have a claim to justice; only they can demand explanations for their treatment. One does not owe an explanation to a slave for one's actions. Only the free have rights. Only they can claim respect from others. Without freedom, persons are unable to use many of the capacities that make us fully human.[20]

Discussion Question

Consider the many ways in which we treat animals differently from human beings: we can call them names or make jokes about them in their presence; we

can train them to perform humiliating tricks in public. We can work them re-
ally hard. We need never ask for their consent for anything we do to them.
Continue this list. What can you learn from this about freedom being essen-
tial to being human? Give reasons for your answer.

In recent years, some liberal political theorists have attempted to clarify the
idea of human freedom by listing some human capabilities, which one must
be able to exercise, to be fully free. Here is a partial list of these capabilities:

> Not dying prematurely; enjoying good health, adequate nutrition, choice in mat-
> ters of sexuality and reproduction; being able to avoid unnecessary pain; being
> able to use one's abilities to perceive and to think; being able to get all the edu-
> cation one can use; being able to form and maintain attachments to other per-
> sons and to things; being able to think about and make choices about one's life;
> being able to live for and with others; being able to laugh . . . being able to live
> one's own life and nobody else's.[21]

Slave owners prevent slaves from exercising any of these human capabilities
whenever that suits them. The eternal struggle of the slave is to maintain
those capabilities and keep them open and available. Freedom consists of being able to exercise these human capabilities; to be a slave is to have no
rights, and certainly no rights to the exercise of these capabilities because one
cannot "live one's own life." The slave's humanity is forever under attack; the
slave is always trying to defend it.

Neither Free Nor Slave

Slaves are exiled from the human community. Many others who are nomi-
nally members of that community lack central freedoms. Their humanity is
also under threat, and they struggle daily to preserve of it what they can.
There are many forms in which humans deny the humanity of other humans.
Some are slaves. There are others who are not free. One such group are inmates of prisons who cannot eat or sleep or work or rest except when told to
do so by a guard; they can be roused from their sleep in the middle of the
night, have their room turned upside down, and their few belongings confis-
cated without reason. Prisoners may be humiliated, insulted, and denigrated
by both the guards, and even worse, other inmates, without any recourse.
Their lives are not their own. They, too, are dishonored.

> What is more prevalent at TCIP [which is a medium security, rural institution]
> is best called 'coercion.' I suppose you have an idea what these engagements en-
> tail. The victim is usually tricked into owing a favor. Here this is usually drugs,
> with the perpetrator seeming to be, to the victim, a really swell fellow and all.

Soon, however, the victim is asked to repay all those joints or licks of dope—
right away. Of course he has no drugs or money, and the only alternative is sexual favors. Once a prisoner is "turned-out," it's pretty much a done deal. I guess
a good many victims just want to do their time and not risk any trouble, so they
submit. . . . The coercion-type abuses continue because of their covert nature.
From the way such attacks manifest, it can seem to others, administrators and
prisoners, that the victims are just homosexual to begin with. Why else would
they allow such a thing to happen, people might ask.[22]

Unfree are also the families of violent alcoholics. They may find themselves
attacked and beaten by a drunken father, husband, mother, or wife for no reason at all; they spend their lives trying to predict when the next attack will
come and doing whatever they can to avoid it. The batterer does not need to
defend his or her violence; his or her victims are not entitled to any justifications; they are brutalized without any reason. They have no rights. They too
lack any possibility of dignity, being liable to vicious attacks without reason
and motivation. They are powerless, living their lives in fear and without recourse to defend themselves.

The conditions of citizens under a dictatorship are often quite similar. No
one is safe from sudden arrest. Thugs, death squads, and secret police may appear at any time to take someone away who will never be seen alive again.
No reasons are given; no accusations leveled. Violent death is an ever present
possibility, and those who cause it need not explain themselves. Their victims
are not even granted the dignity of an accusation. The violence against them
does not need explanation, let alone justification, because the victims do not
deserve that much respect. They not only lose their security but their human
dignity. They are powerless in the face all anonymous persecutors.

All of these—slaves, prisoners, women and children in violent families, and
citizens in a dictatorship—suffer from lack of power—that is, the power to protect themselves and create a zone of safety. They cannot hope for justice. Only
human beings with dignity can demand justice. The truly unfree have no dignity. They cannot claim any privacy; they cannot demand that their punishment
be defended. They cannot demand an indictment before they are judged, im-
prisoned, or killed. No one owes them an explanation or any personal respect.
Their humanity, if not completely lost, has been seriously diminished.

Not unlike slaves, women, men, and children in these and similar oppressive conditions struggle constantly to defend their human capabilities and to
hold open the space for exercising them. Freedom is important because it is
the prerequisite for being fully human.

Discussion Questions

*Are you troubled by the claim that the unfree are less human? Think of the dif-
ferent senses in which we call someone "less than human": those who are*

morally defective such as sociopaths, genetically impaired births that are not viable, victims of extreme deprivation whose world has shrunk to the one issue of staying alive, and those suffering from advanced dementia who remember no one. The humanity of the unfree is not impaired in any of those ways. How does the lack of freedom affect our humanity?

WHAT PRICE FREEDOM?

We all are clearly confused about this question. On the one hand, we applaud with tears in our eyes the young men and women who volunteer to fight and perhaps to die for freedom. Politicians and ordinary citizens alike praise the sacrifice made by soldiers. Some of them have volunteered in the past, or their sons and daughters have done so; others have gone to great length to avoid military service. But all agree that freedom is worth one's life.

But there are, on the other hand, the citizens of Vernon who did not hesitate to give up democracy for the sake of lifetime job security. Nor are they the only ones who do not hold their freedom in high esteem. Think of those who could vote but do not. Think of all the people who kowtow to their employers, who allow themselves to be insulted and disrespected by their supervisors but, for fear of losing their job, refuse to defend their dignity and to assert their liberties and their rights as human beings for respect from others. Think of students who believe that their teacher is treating them unjustly but do not protest for fear of a bad grade. Think of all those who witness others being treated disrespectfully, but who do not say anything in order not to get involved. Standing up for the freedom of others is for them not really worth the inconvenience. Think of neighborhoods protesting plans for a halfway house, where the neighbors are up in arms about poor people or former addicts living close by. Others may well think that even addicts and poor people have a right to a roof over their heads, but they do not say anything for fear of their neighbors' anger. Think of people doing nothing when they see images on television of persons suffering injustice in our country. Think of the television news reports of people in other countries being brutally oppressed by their government, but those who watch are too indolent to even write a letter to their elected representative or too miserly to give money to an organization that tries to help. Many people are unwilling to make even small efforts in defense of freedom.

So we find ourselves both thinking that freedom is worth dying for and thinking that freedom is not worth the inconvenience of going to vote, endangering one's work or one's income, or risking making enemies of one's neighbors for the sake of defending freedom. To be sure, we all have obligations to family members and others; we need to have a job and a roof over our heads before we can begin being politically active. But the political inactivity of many Americans is not merely due to the pressures of earning the bare necessities. Many people believe that paying for their trophy home is more important than defending freedom.

Discussion Questions

What are you willing to do for freedom? What do you believe you ought to be willing to do for freedom? Give reasons for your answers.

JUST WAR

Freedom and Violence

In 2004, there were more than 830,000 policemen in the United States.[23] There were federal and state police, local police, and sheriffs; there were the FBI, Alcohol, Tobacco, and Firearms (ATF), Drug Enforcement Agency (DEA), federal park police, and many other agencies. The task of these many men and women, organized in many different bureaus, is to keep the peace, to deter crime and to investigate, once suspicion arises that a crime has been committed, and to bring the perpetrators to justice. Crimes are inherently coercive, whether violent or not; they violate the freedom of their victims by forcing them or defrauding them. People are forced to give up their money by the threat of force; their homes are violated by forcible entry, their bodies violated if raped. Fraud induces its victims to part with their money by misleading them. In many different forms, crime invades the freedoms of citizens by threatening bodily harm, by doing harm, or by misrepresentation. This massive deployment of police power is intended to abate violence and coercion in the society to preserve the freedoms of all citizens. Its aim is to enhance the security of citizens in their daily life because without security, freedom becomes precarious.

Violence is coercive; it impairs freedom; violence is incompatible with freedom. Freedom is impaired during times of war, in civil unrest, or where crime rates are high and citizens constantly threatened with attacks from armed bands. Commitment to freedom includes the decision to forswear violence, but in wars, nations inflict massive violence on one another. How can a freedom-loving country go to war? Those who value freedom must, sooner or later, confront the question of whether violence can ever be justified because violence is clearly the enemy of freedom.

Questions about violence arise in many different contexts. Police are trained and equipped to suppress violence and defend freedom, through the threat or actual use of violence. Persons convicted of crimes often end up in prison; incarcerating felons involves violence. Most people have no problem with those uses of violence. If employed in the defense of freedom, they think, violence is justified.

But we have no guarantee that the police will always act in the cause of freedom. Some police are corrupt; others fire on unarmed citizens and kill them. Police crowd control is not always on the side of free speech. None of this should be read as impugning the reputation of police forces, but it should remind us that the use of violence for the sake of keeping the peace needs more careful examination. The same is true of the policy of incarceration. In what way does it serve to enhance or protect the freedom of everyone else? Not all prisoners were convicted of crimes affecting the freedoms of other citizens. They may have sold drugs in small quantities or refused to pay their income tax to protest government policies. Remember Charles Schenck, who ended up in prison for opposing the draft in 1917. After considering what sorts of people end up in jail, we also need to ask ourselves what happens to them in prison. Will they emerge reconciled to society and eager to be productive, freedom-loving citizens or will they come out even angrier, more destructive, and dangerous to peace?

Discussion Question

Granting that most violence is a threat to freedom, what sort of violence, if any, serves to enhance freedom? Give reasons for your answer.

There are many important questions here that we cannot take up. We will consider only one aspect of government violence: war.

Just War Theory

War involves violence on a grand scale. If violence can rarely, if ever, be justified, are there any good wars?

In the early years of the Christian era, the answer to that question was negative. The early Christians were pacifists, resting their case on New Testaments texts. When they came to arrest Jesus "one of them which were with Jesus stretched out his hand and drew his sword and struck a servant of the High Priest's and smote off his ear. Then said Jesus unto him: put up again thy sword into his place: for *all they that take the sword, shall perish with the sword.*"[24] This and similar passages persuaded the early Christians to reject war and violence.

The experience of widespread persecution and martyrdom in the early years, as well as the transformation of Christianity from a marginal sect into a politically powerful church, changed Christian thinking about violence and war. By the fifth century of our era, Augustine, one of the great Christian philosophers, had begun to develop what is now known as "just war theory." The basic premise of that theory is that, however repugnant violence and particularly the mass violence of war may be to human sensibilities and to a Christian ethic, we live in a terribly imperfect world where violence threatens constantly; sometimes it can only be deterred by greater violence. We may abhor war, but when an enemy invades our land, it is surely right for us to defend it. Just war theory tries to determine when war is justified. The theory, as usually presented, lists a number of conditions for a just war:

1. The war must have a just cause. That is usually taken to mean either that war is being waged in self-defense or that one goes to war to prevent horrendous injustices threatened to others. When in 1940 German armies invaded France, the French were fully justified in mobilizing their military to fight back. Theirs was a war of self-defense. The United States, although not directly threatened, was equally justified, according to just war theory, in helping defeat the Nazi regime because it had wrought death and destruction all over Europe.
2. The intentions of nations waging a defensive war must be good. When they go to war, governments inevitably claim to be defending themselves, even if they are, in fact, the aggressors. Such protestations do not make it a just war. The war is not just as long as it is motivated by hidden agendas of gaining new territory and power.
3. War must be the last resort. A nation may not begin a war of self-defense until all alternatives have been exhausted. Compromises must have become impossible; negotiations must have collapsed without hope of reviving them.
4. The war must be winnable. Sacrificing one's soldiers in a futile gesture incapable of defending the freedom of the country attacked is not justifiable. War is justified, if at all, only if victory is possible.

These are some of the conditions that the just war theory imposes on wars of defense. They limit the conditions under which a nation may enter such a war. The detailed interpretation of these conditions varies tremendously among theorists. Extended discussions of just war theory have produced many, slightly different versions, of the theory.

A second part of just war theory deals with the actual conduct of the war. It insists that civilian populations must be protected at all costs. Similarly, the theory often insists that the force used must be proportionate to the goal of self-defense. Nations at war may not demand the total surrender of the enemy; the war must end when the attack is repulsed.

Discussion Question

On the Internet find information about the first and the second Gulf wars. Which of these wars is more likely to meet just war criteria? Give reasons for your answer.

Questions about Just War Theory

Morality gives rise to many disagreements, but there is near universal agreement that we have the right, as individuals, to defend ourselves against attacks or threats to our own life or that of loved ones. The analogy between self-defense of individuals and self-defense of nations is also widely accepted as self-evidently true. Nations, most people believe, have a right to defend themselves just as do individuals.

But the details of just war theory and of the individual and national rights to self-defense are unclear. Important questions arise once we reflect more carefully about the theory.

In individual self-defense, one protects one's own life and bodily integrity or that of loved ones. When we speak about the self-defense of nations, what is the "self" that a nation goes to war to defend? There clearly are a number of different answers to that question.

One might say that a nation defends its territorial integrity. If anyone wanted to annex a piece of U.S. territory we would be entitled to go to war against them. But is that really so obvious? Would we not have to weigh the importance of a particular territory to our nation against the cost of human lives—those of our own soldiers and civilian victims of the war, as well as the lives of enemy soldiers and civilians? Places along the border with Mexico are desert and home only to cactus and desert animals. Long stretches along the border with Canada contain only trees and mountains, inhabited by deer and bears and other forest creatures. Suppose our country were to be invaded by Mexico or Canada. How many human lives would we be justified in sacrificing for those uninhabited stretches of land?

Discussion Questions

If you agree to a war conducted by your country in self-defense, you bear some responsibility for the lives of fellow citizens sacrificed in this defense. How much territory must be in danger before you support the sacrifice of the life of one of our citizens? Give reasons for your answer.

But territory, most of the time, comes with people who live on it. If we cede territory to another country we acquiesce in some of our fellow citizens becoming subjects to a different government to share in a different culture. We would allow fellow citizens of our nation to become foreigners. Suppose the Mexican government decided to reconquer the Southwest and California, which the United States took from them after the Mexican War of 1848. Should we fight over the land? Well, the question is more complex. The citizens of California, of Arizona, of New Mexico, and of Texas would now be living in Mexico. Their children would have to go to Spanish-speaking schools; they themselves would have to pay taxes to the Mexican government. National holidays would be different. They would be forced to cease being Americans to become Mexicans just as many Mexicans in the Southwest became Americans after 1848. If we refused to fight the invading Mexican army, we would turn the lives of our fellow citizens upside down.

Discussion Question

This second Mexican war might turn out to be bloody both in U.S. and Mexican casualties. The Mexican Air Force would bomb Houston and Dallas and perhaps Los Angeles. The U.S. Air Force would reduce Mexico City to rubble. Millions of people would die in such a war. Would this carnage be justified to save some of our citizens from becoming members of the Mexican nation? How important would that change be? Give reasons for your answers.

Philosophers tend to say that national self-defense defends "a common life." But that is, of course, terribly vague. It compels us to raise this question about ourselves, and by implication about other countries: do we, as Americans, have a common life? What does it consist of? There are not many things that all Americans believe. We often say that we are a free nation, but half of us do not vote, and most of us cheat on our taxes if we think we can possibly get away with it. Most of our governments have a low approval rating by the time they have been in power for a few years. We tend not to have a great deal of confidence in the governments that we elect and whose power, we say, derives from us. Most Americans do not in fact believe that our system of government works terribly well. They do not have a great deal of confidence in the free system to which they claim to be devoted.

Different Americans grow up and live under different conditions. There are many others with whom they would not want to mix. If your skin is dark, your white neighbor may chat with you over the fence but would not want your son to marry his daughter. If your parents or you are immigrants who, perhaps, have uncertain mastery of the English language, you would not be comfortable with people whose families have been here for many generations. The poor are not comfortable in the company of the rich; and they, in their turn, do not know how to talk to poor people without being patronizing. Some Americans are crazy about sports; others only want to go to the opera. Some go to church daily; others never. The values and practices and traditions that divide us are legion. What do we have in common?

Discussion Questions

If someone talks about protecting the common life of the United States in a defensive war, what would you think they were planning to defend?

Nations go to war to defend their sovereignty, their pride, and their national self-esteem. How many lives are you willing to sacrifice so that you may be able to feel proud to be an American?

Give reasons for your answers.

Criticisms of Just War Theory

The doctrine of just war has seemed extremely plausible for more than a thousand years. But there has been a vocal and eloquent minority that have always resisted it. There was Jesus, and in our times Gandhi and Martin Luther King, Jr. Another of those advocates of pacifism was Ralph Waldo Emerson:

> If you go for no war, then be consistent and give up self-defense in the highway, in your own house. Will you push it thus far? Will you stick to your principle of non-resistance when your strongbox is broken open, when your wife and babes are insulted and slaughtered in your sight? If you say yes, you only invite the robber and assassin; and a few bloody-minded desperadoes would soon butcher the good.

Emerson's essay begins with a very strong restatement of the right to self-defense. As Emerson presents the view, we are not only entitled to defend ourselves but have a duty to do so. If we refuse to defend ourselves against violence, we only encourage the bullies, the "few bloody-minded desperadoes." But Emerson does not accept this argument in favor of using violence in self-defense, even though it appears so plausible. He continues his defense of pacifism:

> In reply to this charge of absurdity of the extreme peace doctrine, as shown in the supposed consequences, I wish to say that such a deduction considers only half of the fact. They look only at the passive side of the friend of peace, only at his passivity; they quite omit to consider his activity . . .
>
> The cause of peace is not the cause of cowardice. . . . If peace is to be maintained, it is by brave men, who . . . will not seek another man's life; men who have . . . attained such a perception of their own intrinsic worth that they do not think property or their own body a sufficient good to be saved by such dereliction of principle as treating a man like a sheep.[25]

Against the vindication of self-defense, Emerson sets the view of the genuine lovers of peace—not to treat humans as sheep. We raise sheep for their wool and as food; we slaughter them when we want meat. Sheep have no right to life; their life is not precious. The advocates of the right to self-defense, Emerson thinks, treat humans as sheep. They are prepared to kill them when that is in their interest. But against that, the consistent pacifist asserts that human life is sacred. One may not kill another under any circumstances.

For that reason this pacifist stance requires exceptional courage. Self-defense is motivated by fear—fear for one's life or property and for those we love. We fight back because we are afraid. To be sure it takes courage to fight back also. But many householders buy guns; they are armed to the teeth but lose heart when thieves appear in the middle of the night, and the gun stays where it was hidden behind the books on the bookshelf. Most of the supporters of the right of self-defense therefore call on others to defend them—the police and the military. These men and women take on the fearful work of defense and will use violence for that purpose. They will try to kill the attacker before they themselves lose their lives or are injured. But the courage of the pacifists is greater than that, Emerson insists, because they are willing to accept death and injury for the sake of maintaining the principle that human life is sacred—without any exception.

We tend to think of the pacifist as passive: when the robbers enter his house the pacifist stands by while they carry off his property. But that, Emerson thinks, is only part of the story; pacifism is not always passive. It is active when the nonviolent resist. When Rosa Parks was arrested for refusing to give her seat a white rider, the black citizens of Montgomery stopped riding the buses and patronizing white merchants. They were not violent but they resisted actively. They took on themselves the burden of walking to work and of not buying in stores they had found convenient before. They braved the hatred and possible violence from white citizens by refusing to cooperate with segregation on the buses. The struggle over segregation had been violent ever since it began after the end of Reconstruction in the early 1870s. Hundreds of blacks had been lynched by whites. Resistance clearly invited more white violence. But the black inhabitants of Montgomery, however fearful, continued their protest. Thus began a new battle in the struggle black Americans had waged literally for centuries. Advocates of the legitimacy of violent self-defense tend, Emerson insists, to overlook this active resistance that is an integral part of pacifism. They tend to forget that such nonviolent resistance requires enormous courage from those who are determined to resist peacefully in the face of threats of violence.

But why are the pacifists on the side of justice? All the great religious and moral traditions urge us to love our neighbor. We are told not just to love the neighbor who is pleasant and lovable, but any neighbor whatsoever—

especially the hostile and violent ones. In the New Testament, Jesus is quoted as saying, "Ye have heard that it hath been said, An eye for an eye and a tooth for a tooth; But I say unto you that you resist not evil: but whoever shall smite thee on thy left cheek, turn to him the other also."[26] All the great religious traditions insist that we not treat our neighbor "like a sheep," as Emerson said. Human life is sacred under all circumstances.

But is the attacker not guilty? Do the aggressors, individuals or nations, not forfeit their right to life? Many persons believe that but the great religions do not. Here is the Christian version of this thought: None of us are perfect; every one of us at one time or another violates the rights and integrity of others. We are in no position to judge those others. Thus Jesus said when asked whether the traditional punishment, stoning to death, should be meted out to a woman caught in adultery: "He that is without sin among you, let him first cast a stone at her."[27] It may be that the attacker is guilty but none of us, saddled with the guilt for our own mistakes and evil acts, are in a position to sit in judgment on the other. Perhaps the murderer or rapist has forfeited the right to life. But are other human beings entitled to judge the one who disturbs the peace? Are they themselves so much above reproach that they can execute the judgment?

Discussion Questions

The right to self-defense does not exist, say the pacifists, because human life is sacred. Punishing the aggressor, they add, is not doing justice. None of us are innocent; none of us are in a position to condemn the other. Consider these two ideas. What can be said in their favor? Give reasons for your answer.

Review Questions

1. *List as many different senses of freedom as you can.*
2. *Why is it important to be free? Is it important to you? Why?*
3. *What is your freedom worth? Is it too much bother to vote? Is it worth engaging in additional political activity? Would you be willing to sacrifice some money for it? Is it worth your life?*
4. *What is the doctrine of just war and how plausible is it?*

QUESTIONS FOR REFLECTION AND DISCUSSION

1. The people of Vernon believed that a regular democratic system was not in their interest. Are there people in your city or town who would be better off if there were no regular elections? Would you?

2. The founders of our country believed that our free institutions could not survive unless we all strove to be highly moral human beings. A population primarily animated by selfish considerations would soon fall apart into special interest groups; the political life of the republic would degenerate into a struggle for the power to benefit oneself and one's friends at the expense of the common good. Were the founders right about that?

3. The founders called for politicians seeking the common good and a population sharing moral values. But most of us believe that "everyone has his or her own moral values." Who is right about that?

   Make two lists in the class, one of the moral judgments on which we all agree and then one of the matters about we disagree. Can you identify the roots of those disagreements (e.g. I believe that the Bible is God's word, and you do not)?

4. Is freedom equally important (or unimportant) to all or is it more important for some people than for others?

5. Law often punishes immorality (e.g. theft or murder, or neglect or abuse of children). There are laws against depriving others of their civil rights.

   Would you advocate punishing people for not voting? Give reasons for your answer.

6. Make a list of the different kinds of freedoms mentioned in this chapter and then arrange them in order of their importance.

7. Everyone agrees that it is important for members of a free society to be tolerant. But what does it mean to be *tolerant*? Are you as tolerant as you would like to be? When is it hard for you to be tolerant? What could you do to be more tolerant? Should one be tolerant of everybody and every action or belief?

8. A recent book about tolerance has argued that tolerance appears a noble virtue, but it is, at the same time, a mechanism for suppressing undesired groups. Before we can be tolerant, there must be groups whose defects we ought to tolerate even though we might have serious objections and aversions to them. The entire discourse of tolerance feeds on the existence of groups who are different from the powerful or the majority. It presupposes groups the majority looks down on. The discourse of tolerance is, often, a means of keeping them "in their place."[28]

   What do you think about that? Give reasons for your answer.

9. Garrett Hardin, in various famous publications, has argued for a view he calls "a lifeboat ethic." Imagine, he says, you and nine other people are in a lifeboat in an ocean where many other survivors of a shipwreck are trying to remain alive by climbing into your boat. You and the other passengers in the lifeboat face this stark choice: you can allow others to climb into your boat until it too will sink and everybody will die or you can prevent others from climbing in by taking very harsh measures against them. It seems clear that in that case the only rational and even compassionate

course of action will be to keep other victims of the shipwreck out of the lifeboat by any means possible.

The imaginary case appears to prove that selfishness is not only the only rational policy, it is also the only compassionate policy. If a false squeamishness prevents the passengers in the lifeboat from keeping everyone else out, by trying to help the person in the water they condemn their fellow passengers to death.

The case Hardin concocts is intended to show how foolish are the arguments, given in this chapter, against a politics of self-interest.

How convincing is Hardin's argument? Try to marshal arguments in support of his position, as well as arguments against it.

NOTES

1. Clinton Rossiter, *The Political Thought of the American Revolution* (New York: Harcourt, Brace and World, 1963), Chapter 13.

2. Alexander Hamilton, James Madison, and John Jay, *The Federalist* (New York: Modern Library, n.d.), 59.

3. Eric Foner, *The Story of American Freedom* (New York: W.W. Norton, 1998), 3–4.

4. Rossiter, *Political Thought*, 208.

5. Derek Bok, *Our Underachieving Colleges* (Princeton: Princeton University Press, 2006), 12–13.

6. Joseph A. Schumpeter, *Capitalism, Socialism and Democracy* (New York: Harper Torchbooks, 1950), 251–52.

7. Adam Smith, *An Inquiry into the Nature and Causes of the Wealth of Nations* (New York: Modern Library, 1985), 16.

8. *Worcester Telegram and Gazette*, May 11, 2006, A15.

9. "Saving the Have-Mores," retrieved January 22, 2007, from Wisconsin Democracy Campaign website: www.wisdc.org/sp031605.php#cap.

10. "Bridge to Nowhere," retrieved May 8, 2006, from Wikipedia website: http://en.wikipedia.org/wiki/Gravina_Island_Bridge; the *Boston Globe* of Sept. 23, 2007, reported the cancellation of this bridge project.

11. Hamilton, Madison, and Jay, *The Federalist*, 54.

12. John Rawls, *Justice as Fairness: A Restatement* (Cambridge: Harvard University, 2001), 167.

13. Gerald Dworkin, *The Theory and Practice of Autonomy* (Cambridge: Cambridge University Press, 1988), 6.

14. George Kateb, "Democratic Individuality and the Meaning of Rights," in *Liberalism and the Moral Life*, edited by Nancy L. Rosenblum (Cambridge: Harvard University Press, 1989), 191.

15. An early, forceful statement of this critique of autonomy may be found in Jean Baker Miller, *Toward a New Psychology of Women* (Boston: Beacon Press, 1979).

16. Tony Morrison, *Playing in the Dark: Whiteness and the Literary Imagination* (Cambridge: Harvard University Press, 1992), 52.

17. Amartya Sen, *Development as Freedom* (New York: Anchor Books, 1999).

18. Orlando Patterson, *Slavery and Social Death* (Cambridge: Harvard University Press, 1982), 8–9.

19. Orlando Patterson, *Freedom: Freedom in the Making of Western Culture* (New York: Basic Books, 1991), 9.

20. It is important not to misunderstand that. Characterizing slaves as not fully human seems to insult persons already condemned to a life of suffering, but that is of course not the intention. There are different perspectives on the existence of the slave. The master regards her as a slave—not fully human. But she knows better and struggles mightily to assert what human rights she can. The actual existence of the slave is an unending struggle about her humanity, a humanity that remains elusive as long as she remains someone's property. It is a struggle which she cannot win as long as she cannot be free.

21. Martha C. Nussbaum, "Human Capabilities; Female Human Beings" in *Women, Culture and Development: A Study of Human Capabilities*, edited by Martha C. Nussbaum and Jonathan Glover (Oxford: Oxford University Press, 1995), 84–85.

22. "No Escape: Male Rape in US Prisons," retrieved January 5, 2007, from Human Rights Watch website: www.hrw.org/reports/2001/prison/voices.html.

23. "Law Enforcement Statistics," retrieved April 14, 2005, from Office of Justice Programs website: www.ojp.usdoj.gov/bjs/lawenf.htm.

24. New International Version, Matthew 26, 51–52.

25. Ralph Waldo Emerson, "Excerpts from 'War'" in *The Power of NonViolence: Writings by Advocates of Peace*, ed. Howard Zinn (Boston: Beacon Press: 2002): 8–14.

26. New International Version, Matthew 5, 38–39.

27. New International Version, John 8, 7.

28. Wendy Brown, *Regulating Aversion: Tolerance in the Age of Identity and Empire* (Princeton: Princeton University Press, 2006).

FURTHER READINGS

Emma Goldman, *Living My Life* (New York: Knopf, 1931). Emma Goldman's autobiography tells her unconventional and often exhilarating story.

Alexander Hamilton, James Madison, and John Jay, *The Federalist* (New York: Modern Library, n.d.). Numbers 9 and 10 explain Hamilton and Madison's project for a republic governed in the public interest, not for private gain.

Clinton Rossiter, *The Political Thought of the American Revolution* (New York: Harcourt, Brace, and World, 1963). It shows the framers of the Constitution in an unaccustomed light as intensely moralistic and deeply religious men.

Virginia Woolf, *To the Lighthouse* (London: Hogarth, 1927). This book paints a chilling portrait of the traditional marriage where husbands take extensive services from their wives in the form of many different kinds of support while asserting their own autonomy.

Orlando Patterson, *Freedom: Freedom in the Making in Western Culture* (New York: Basic Books, 1991). Part I delineates the roots of freedom in the institution of slavery and shows us what makes freedom valuable.

Lawrence Thornton, *Imagining Argentina* (New York: Bantam Books, 1998). This gives a chilling portrait of a country run by a military dictatorship.

Index

About the Author

Born in Nazi Germany, **Richard Schmitt** came to the United States after World War II. He was educated at the University of Chicago and at Yale University. Author of a number of books and many articles about existentialism and political theory, he taught at Brown University and also at Stanford University, the University of California at Santa Barbara and at Miles College in Birmingham, AL.